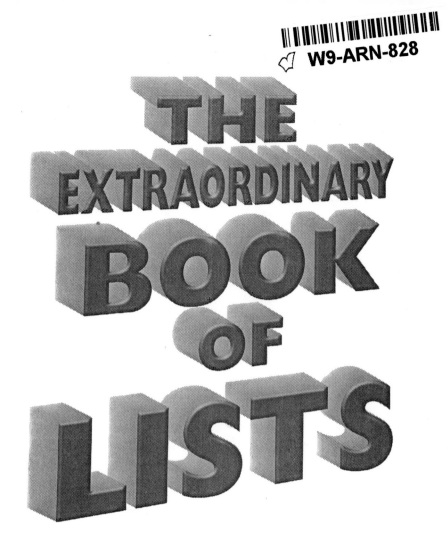

THE EXTRAORDINARY BOOK OF LISTS

A COLOSSAL COLLECTION OF FASCINATING FACTS AND INTRIGUING INFORMATION

WEST
SIDE
PUBLISHING

Contributing writers: Helen Davies, Marjorie Dorfman, Mary Fons, Deborah Hawkins, Martin Hintz, Linnea Lundgren, David Priess, Julie Clark Robinson, Paul Seaburn, Heidi Stevens, and Steve Theunissen

Mary Fons makes her living as a freelance writer, creating snazzy content for clients such as Jellyvision and Content That Works. She also works as a slam poet, actress, and ensemble member of Chicago's longest-running theater show, the Neo-Futurist's *Too Much Light Makes the Baby Go Blind.* Check out www.maryfons.com for more about Mary and to read her juicy blog, PaperGirl.

Julie Clark Robinson is the award-winning author of *Live in the Moment.* She's also the editor of the *General Hospital* and *The Bold and the Beautiful* pages on www.Soaps.com. Her works have been published in *A Cup of Comfort* books and *Family Circle* magazine. Peruse her inspirational tidbits about everyday joy at www.nabbw.com or www.julieclarkrobinson.com.

Paul Seaburn is a comedy writer and teacher. His television credits include *The Tonight Show* and *Comic Strip Live,* and he's also the head writer for *Taylor's Attic,* a family comedy. He is the author of *Jestercises & Gamestorms,* and he teaches "Creative Thinking Through Comedy," a program for gifted students.

Front and back cover: **PhotoDisc Collection**

CONTENTS

✳ ✳ ✳ ✳

✳ ✳ ✳ ✳

Chapter 1—People

✳ ✳ ✳ ✳

Chapter 2—Fun, Games, and Pop Culture

✳ ✳ ✳ ✳

Chapter 3—This Is America

✳ ✳ ✳ ✳

Chapter 4—Movies

❋ ❋ ❋ ❋

Chapter 5—Health, Fitness, and the Human Body

❋ ❋ ❋ ❋

Chapter 6—Religion, Folklore, and the Paranormal

✳ ✳ ✳ ✳

Chapter 7—Food

✳ ✳ ✳ ✳

Chapter 8—Transportation

✳ ✳ ✳ ✳

Chapter 9—Music

✳ ✳ ✳ ✳

Chapter 10—History, Politics, and War

✳ ✳ ✳ ✳

Chapter 11—Death

❊ ❊ ❊ ❊

Chapter 12—Money & Business

❊ ❊ ❊ ❊

Chapter 13—Books

✷ ✷ ✷ ✷

Chapter 14—Television

✷ ✷ ✷ ✷

Chapter 15—Science & Nature

Chapter 16—Travel

❋ ❋ ❋ ❋

Chapter 17—Animals

❋ ❋ ❋ ❋

Chapter 18—This & That

✳ ✳ ✳ ✳

Chapter 19—Law & Disorder

✳ ✳ ✳ ✳

Chapter 20—Words

A LIFELONG LOVE OF LISTS

✳ ✳ ✳ ✳

Endings and beginnings...it's once again time for me to sit down at the end of the process and write the beginning of a book.

As journalist H. Allen Smith once said, "The human animal differs from the lesser primates in his passion for lists." Today, we live in an age of information overload, when the vast quantities of information thrust upon us leave us feeling bemused and bewildered. Lists can help us focus our thoughts, create a sense of order, and consider facts from different perspectives, which may enlighten, challenge, or even amuse us.

I suppose I've been an inadvertent list-maker and fact-collector since childhood, creating lists in my conscious and subconscious, on envelopes, napkins, notepads, or any available writing surface.

You get the picture. I'm a list kind of person.

There are many folks out there who have also been infected with the list bug. I've identified many with similar symptoms—perhaps you know some, too. The other day, as I walked by the office of one of our newest Armchair Reader™ editors, I noticed a poster of Leonard Cohen on her wall. I mentioned how much I like him and she replied, "He is my third-favorite singer of all time." Realizing I'd just met a kindred list-maker, I sat down and we identified her 7 favorite magazines, 12 favorite movies, 5 favorite wines from small European villages, and on and on. I asked her what motivated her to make lists. She summed it up this way: "It's sort of like keeping all your thoughts in a carryall that you can just sling over your shoulder and take with you anywhere."

In a way, that's what we tried to do with this book. For your enjoyment, we've compiled lists of the best, the worst, the peculiar, the banned, the largest, the smallest, and some things we just found too interesting to leave out. And it's all contained in a delightful package that you can indeed take with you anywhere.

We invite you to dive in and discover:

- 9 Medical Myths
- 9 Fictional Bands with Hit Songs
- 8 Famous People Who Died in the Bathroom
- 12 of the World's Greatest Roller Coasters
- 17 Celebrities Who Started on Soap Operas
- 9 Winners of Extreme Eating Contests
- 13 Vintage Businesses on Historic Route 66
- 9 Outrageous Hollywood Publicity Stunts
- 9 Things Invented or Discovered by Accident
- 9 Odd Sporting Events from Around the World

Now the time has come for you to get cozy in your armchair, or any spot you choose to sit, lounge, slouch, recline, loaf, or sprawl. Whatever you do, just sit back and enjoy. We've had a great time putting together this collection of lists for you!

Allen Orso

Allen Orso
The Publisher

P.S. If you have any questions, concerns, or ideas pertaining to this book, or if you would like more information about other West Side Publishing titles, please contact us at: www.armchairreader.com.

Chapter 1
PEOPLE

❋ ❋ ❋ ❋

12 Celebrities and Their Pets

*"Make me the person my dog thinks I am," goes the famous
entreaty. And for those living under the constant scrutiny of the
public eye, that plea is likely invoked with an extra grain of truth.
Dogs—and for that matter cats, pigs, and the occasional
kinkajou—prove loyal companions to the famous and infamous
in a sometimes less-than-friendly world.*

1. Martha Stewart

The woman who twice landed on *Forbes* magazine's list of the
50 Most Powerful Women may be a tough cookie in business, but
she's a softie about her pets. Her brood includes four chow chows:
Zu-Zu, Paw-Paw, Cin-Cin, and Empress Woo; and seven Himalayan cats: Teeny, Weeny, Mozart, Vivaldi, Verdi, Berlioz, and Bartok.

2. Edgar Allan Poe

Edgar Allan Poe wrote essays, short stories, and long
poems, most of them more than a little macabre. Poe's
short story, "The Black Cat," was inspired by his own
tortoiseshell cat, Catarina, who curled up in bed with
the writer's wife to keep her warm while she was dying
of tuberculosis.

3. Bill Clinton

Famous for his foreign diplomacy, former president Bill Clinton
was even able to persuade a cat and dog to peacefully coexist in
the White House. Socks the cat came with Clinton when he moved
into the executive mansion in 1993. Buddy, a chocolate Labrador
retriever, arrived in 1997 as a gift. Socks and Buddy achieved
national fame with the publishing of *Dear Socks, Dear Buddy: Kids'
Letters to the First Pets,* by Hillary Rodham Clinton. Upon leaving

office, Clinton gave Socks to secretary Betty Currie and took Buddy with him to New York. Sadly, Buddy was struck and killed by a car in 2002 near the Clintons' New York home.

4. John Lennon

John Lennon's mother, Julia, had a cat named Elvis (after Elvis Presley), which fostered John's own fascination with felines. Growing up in Liverpool, the Beatle-to-be had three cats: Tich, Tim, and Sam. With wife Cynthia, he had a tabby named Mimi. With May Pang, he had a white cat and a black cat—Major and Minor. John and Yoko Ono shared their New York home with another black and white pair—Salt and Pepper. You can check out his sketches of his cats at play in the books *A Spaniard in the Works* and *Real Love: The Drawings for Sean*.

5. Oprah Winfrey

Named World's Best Celebrity Dog Owner by the readers of *The New York Dog* and *The Hollywood Dog* magazines, Oprah Winfrey plays mommy to cocker spaniels Sophie and Solomon and golden retrievers Luke, Layla, and Gracie. The five canines live with Winfrey in a super-renovated condo (formerly four separate units) in Chicago, where the talk show host has defended her pets against noise complaints and the building's pesky one-pet-per-unit rule. Oprah also gets props from pet lovers for introducing her audience to Cesar Millan, aka "The Dog Whisperer," and his revolutionary dog-training methods.

6. Jessica Simpson

What a difference a year makes. Back in 2004, when Jessica Simpson and Nick Lachey were happily married and starring in the MTV reality series *The Newlyweds,* they acquired Daisy, a Maltipoo (Maltese-poodle). The dog's every scratch, sniff, and wag were dutifully recorded by the ever-present cameras: Daisy being toted around in Jessica's handbag, Daisy on the *Dukes of Hazzard* set, Daisy accompanying Jess to the tanning salon. In 2005, Nick and Jessica split up, but Daisy remains a loyal, yet slightly less photographed, companion to the blonde bombshell.

7. Franklin Delano Roosevelt

Dogs in the White House are nothing out of the ordinary, but a dog at the signing of a war declaration? That would be Fala, Franklin Roosevelt's black Scottish terrier, who was a constant companion to the president—even in December 1941 when the nation entered World War II. In 1944, Fala traveled with the president to the Aleutian Islands, a trip that would live on in presidential infamy. Rumors swirled that Fala was somehow left behind, and Roosevelt sent a destroyer back for him, costing taxpayers millions of dollars. FDR answered critics with the famous "Fala speech" on September 23, 1944, in which he vehemently denied the rumors.

8. Britney Spears

Call her the anti-Oprah: Britney Spears was named World's Worst Celebrity Dog Owner in the same poll by the readers of *The New York Dog* and *The Hollywood Dog* magazines. In 2004, Brit was the proud owner of three Chihuahuas: Lacy, Lucky, and Bit-Bit. But one K-Fed and two kids later, and the pop diva appears to be dogless. Apparently she gave them away to friends.

9. George Clooney

George Clooney may be an eternal bachelor, but the two-time winner of *People* magazine's Sexiest Man Alive had no trouble committing to Max, the beloved potbellied pig he owned for 18 years. The Oscar-winning actor received Max in 1989 as a gift and often brought the 300-pound porker to movie sets with him. When Max died of natural causes in December 2006, Clooney told *USA Today* that he didn't plan to replace his porcine companion.

10. Adam Sandler

The best man at Adam Sandler's 2003 wedding was not a man at all, but an English bulldog named Meatball, dressed appropriately in a tux and yarmulke. Sandler, the comedian known for his goofball roles in films such as *Happy Gilmore* and *Billy Madison,* originally worked with Meatball's dad, Mr. Beefy, in the 2000 film *Little Nicky.* Sandler doted on Meatball, going so far as to film a comedy short with the pooch titled *A Day with the Meatball,* about a typical day in the dog's life. Meatball died of a heart attack at age four, but Sandler and his wife, Jackie, continue to enjoy the company of their other bulldog, Matzoball.

11. Tori Spelling

A pregnant Tori Spelling caused a bit of a tabloid frenzy in December 2006 when she was photographed in Beverly Hills pushing her famous pug, Mimi La Rue, in a baby stroller. But kindness to animals comes naturally to the *Beverly Hills 90210* star and daughter of late TV producer Aaron Spelling. Tori helps run Much Love, an animal rescue foundation that finds families for homeless pets. While Tori purchased Mimi La Rue from a pet store seven years ago, she adopted her other dog, Leah, a wire-haired terrier mix, from Much Love. She also has two cats, Madison and Laurel.

12. Paris Hilton

Paris Hilton's best friends change about as frequently as the weather, but she's held on to her Chihuahua Tinkerbell since 2002. Tinkerbell achieved fame through her costarring role in all four seasons of *The Simple Life* and her memoir entitled *The Tinkerbell Hilton Diaries*. Tinkerbell went missing briefly in 2004 after Paris' apartment was burglarized, but the hotel heiress ponied up a $5,000 reward and the dog was soon returned. For a brief spell, Tinkerbell took a backseat to a pet kinkajou, Baby Luv, until the exotic animal bit Paris on the arm, sending the starlet to the emergency room in August 2006. The kinkajou hasn't been spotted publicly with Paris since.

✳ ✳ ✳

*"Until one has loved an animal,
a part of one's soul remains unawakened."*

—Anatole France

13 Top-Earning Dead Celebrities

✳ ✳ ✳ ✳

*You'd think a person would have to work pretty hard
to make more than $5 million a year. But maybe not.
The people on this list are making more money in one year
than most of us will see in a lifetime—and they're not even alive
to enjoy it! Each year,* Forbes *magazine compiles data on the
top-earning dead celebrities. Altogether, these individuals
earned more than $250 million in 2006.*

1. Kurt Cobain—$50 million

The lead singer of Nirvana took his own life in 1994 but still has
a presence in the music biz. His widow, controversial and drug-
addled Courtney Love, controls his estate and continues to license
his name and song catalog to advertising agencies and television
shows including *Six Feet Under* and *CSI*. In fact, Cobain took over
the number one spot following a huge licensing deal that Love
made in 2006—Elvis usually holds the top position on this list.
Cobain was famously anticommercial, so many fans feel uncomfortable with the money the poster boy of grunge continues to pull in.

2. Elvis Presley—$42 million

Until 2006, Elvis had been the number one money-making dead
celebrity for years. Die-hard fans continue to buy box sets, remastered recordings, biographies, and other Elvis memorabilia by the
millions, even though there's been no new material from the King
since he died in 1977. In addition to merchandising, income comes
from ticket sales at Graceland and the licensing of Elvis's identity to
developers in Las Vegas who are planning a new Elvis attraction.

3. Charles M. Schulz—$35 million

Snoopy, Woodstock, Charlie Brown, Linus, Peppermint Patty, and
Lucy continue to grace the pages of more than 2,400 U.S. newspapers every day. Charles Schulz, the cartoonist behind the *Peanuts*
comic strip, died of cancer in 2000, but annual television specials

and licensing agreements with apparel companies continue to make Schulz a wealthy man.

4. John Lennon—$24 million

In 1980, Beatles member John Lennon was killed by a crazed fan in New York City and mourned by fans around the world. The Beatles still sell more than a million records every year, even though they split up in 1970. Lennon's solo work also moves hundreds of thousands of copies each year. In addition, widow Yoko Ono filed a $10 million lawsuit against record company EMI to obtain back royalties and master recordings, which helped boost Lennon's bank account.

5. Albert Einstein—$20 million

Licensing giant Corbis has image rights to Einstein's wild-haired visage and says that the physics genius is their most requested figure. Disney pays top dollar for the use of Einstein's name in their Baby Einstein line, and T-shirts around the globe feature Einstein's famous face and formula, $E=mc^2$. Einstein died in 1955 at age 76, but every generation since instantly recognizes the great physicist.

6. Andy Warhol—$19 million

Avant-garde pop artist Andy Warhol once said that in the future, everyone will have 15 minutes of fame. He died before he saw how right he was—reality TV appeared only a few years after Warhol's death in 1987. The Andy Warhol Foundation for the Visual Arts continues to sign off on deals with companies such as Levi Strauss and Barney's New York to reproduce Warhol soup cans and portraits for the masses, which keeps the Factory creator cranking out the dough more than two decades after his death.

7. Theodor Geisel, aka Dr. Seuss—$10 million

With movies, apparel, and even Broadway musicals based on Geisel's characters, such as the Cat in the Hat and the Grinch, not to mention dozens of Dr. Seuss titles that continue to fly off the shelves, it's easy to see how Geisel continues to make money even after his death in 1991.

8. Ray Charles—$10 million

Ray, the hit biopic of 2004, clearly had a lot to do with the resurgence of all things Ray Charles. The beloved singer-songwriter died of liver failure in 2004, but his record sales are better than ever. DVD sales of the Oscar-winning film and biographies of the dynamic performer are up, too, and continue to bring money to his estate.

9. Marilyn Monroe—$8 million

No one before or since has embodied Hollywood glamour like iconic sex symbol Marilyn Monroe. Her platinum blonde hair and breathy voice are gold mines for ad campaigns that want to nab the attention of both male and female audiences. General Motors, Absolut, and Dom Perignon have all paid a pretty price for permission to use Monroe in their advertisements. The controversy surrounding Monroe's 1962 death has only served to reinforce her popularity.

10. Johnny Cash—$8 million

Like Ray Charles, the "Man in Black" enjoyed newfound popularity posthumously. The Oscar-winning movie *Walk the Line* greatly increased interest in the country singer-songwriter. In 2006, he sold 3.6 million records, up from 2.8 million the year before. Cash's estate offers a steady stream of compilations, never-before-heard tunes from the song vault, and remastered versions to keep fans coming back for more, even after his passing in 2003.

11. J.R.R. Tolkien—$7 million

If you saw any of the three *Lord of the Rings* movies, you paid Tolkien, even though the fantasy novel genius hasn't been around since 1973. Producer Peter Jackson paid handsomely for rights to make the silver screen version of the trilogy and, financially, it was worth it—the movies are among the highest grossing films of all time. Aside from the novels themselves, which continue to sell well in bookstores around the world, the movie version of the tale brought DVDs, toys, clothes, collectibles, and box sets.

12. George Harrison—$7 million

The "Quiet Beatle" passed in 2001 as a result of cancer, but before he left, he made a lucrative deal with the popular dance/circus/performance troupe Cirque du Soleil. *LOVE* is a production that pays tribute to the Fab Four by showcasing their song catalog and has quickly become one of the company's most popular shows. In addition, Harrison's solo records still sell well, and he collects royalties from Beatles merchandise and lawsuits, too.

13. Bob Marley—$7 million

When people think of reggae music, they think of Bob Marley. This universally recognized Rastafarian still rakes in millions from record sales, largely due to his estate's savvy handlers. Limited edition CDs, digitally remastered copies of classics, and various other Marley-related items are continuously released, even though he died in 1981.

13 Famous People Who Were Adopted

✳ ✳ ✳ ✳

The image of the typical or "normal" American family—with a father, mother, 2.5 kids, and a dog—has become less and less familiar over time. These days, families are "blended" and "progressive" and more than a little creative in terms of structure. Below are a few well-known celebrities that were ahead of the curve. Each famous figure listed below was orphaned, fostered, or adopted at a young age and clearly didn't let that set them back.

1. Babe Ruth

George Herman Ruth, Jr., born in 1895 in Maryland, lost six of his seven siblings in childhood due to disease and poverty. Babe's tavern-owning parents placed him and his sister in orphanages, sending Babe to St. Mary's Industrial School for Boys. It was there that Babe met Brother Matthias, who taught him how to play baseball. The rest is history—Babe Ruth is one of the greatest and most beloved players to ever set foot on a baseball field.

2. Bo Diddley

In 1928, one of America's most influential blues musicians, Ellas Bates—better known as Bo Diddley—was born to a desperately poor couple in rural Mississippi. At a young age, he was adopted, along with three cousins, by his mother's cousin, who moved the family to Chicago in the mid-1930s. Diddley, nicknamed "The Originator," would go on to record nearly 40 records and be inducted into the Rock and Roll Hall of Fame in 1987.

3. Dave Thomas

Dave Thomas, the founder of fast-food restaurant giant Wendy's, was given up for adoption at birth. Sadly, his adoptive mother died when he was five. Thomas left high school in the tenth grade to work full-time at a restaurant. After a stint in the army, Thomas moved to Columbus, Ohio, where he opened his first Wendy's restaurant in 1969. He would later found the Dave Thomas Foundation for Adoption to promote adoption law simplification and reduce adoption costs in the United States.

4. Deborah Harry

Best known as the lead singer of Blondie, the '80s pop sensation who produced hits such as "Call Me" and "Heart of Glass," Deborah Harry was given up at three months and adopted by a couple from New Jersey. Harry led the typical rock-star lifestyle, but she has lived to tell the tale. Blondie was inducted into the Rock and Roll Hall of Fame in 2006, and Harry continues to tour and act.

5. Malcolm X

The childhood of the man who would become "black power" leader Malcolm X was not a happy one. His father, Earl Little, was a Christian minister who was killed in 1931 when Malcolm was a small boy. Following his father's death, his mother had a nervous breakdown and was committed to a mental hospital. Malcolm and his siblings were put into an orphanage and later fostered by various families. Malcolm X would later convert to the Nation of Islam and emerge as one of the most influential civil rights activists of the modern era.

6. Steve Jobs

The eventual cofounder of Apple Computers and the brain behind the iPod, Steven Paul was adopted as an infant by Paul and Clara Jobs in February 1955. Jobs held an internship with Hewlett-Packard and did a stint at Atari, Inc., before he and Stephen Wozniak developed the first Apple computer. These days, the white cord of the iPod is ubiquitous, and Macintosh computers are synonymous with style and technical savvy.

7. Scott Hamilton

Dorothy and Ernest Hamilton adopted Scott in 1958 when he was just six weeks old. In 1984, Hamilton won an Olympic gold medal in men's figure skating, making him the first American male to medal in the sport since 1960. These days, Hamilton produces Stars on Ice, a professional ice show that tours cities around the world.

8. Marilyn Monroe

Born in 1926 to a single mother with a less than stable mental state, legendary screen siren Marilyn Monroe lived in many foster homes as a young girl and spent two years in an orphanage. When she was barely 16, she had the option of another orphanage or marriage. Monroe chose marriage to merchant marine James Dougherty, whom she remained married to for four years. In the years following her rocky beginnings, the blonde bombshell would nab a place in American culture unparalleled before or since.

9. Melissa Gilbert

Best known for her portrayal of Laura Ingalls on *Little House on the Prairie,* Melissa Gilbert was adopted at birth by Ed Gilbert and Barbara Crane, both Hollywood actors. Ed Gilbert died when Melissa was 11, and Michael Landon, who played her father on television, became a surrogate father to her. Melissa's siblings include adopted brother Jonathan Gilbert, who portrayed Willie Oleson on *Little House,* and her sister Sara (who is not adopted) played Darlene on *Roseanne.* Melissa continues to act, mostly in made-for-TV movies, and she served as president of the Screen Actors Guild from 2001 to 2005.

10. Dr. Ruth Westheimer

Everyone's favorite sex therapist was born Karola Ruth Siegel in Frankfurt, Germany, in 1928. Siegel was put on a train when she was ten years old and sent away from home to avoid Hitler's Nazis. Her mother and grandmother told her she was going off to school, but in reality Siegel was sent to an orphanage where she remained for many years. Dr. Ruth would go on to study at the Sorbonne in Paris and reached household name status with her radio program, *Sexually Speaking*, which aired during the 1980s.

11. Harry Caray

During his decades-long career, baseball announcer Harry Caray called the shots for the St. Louis Cardinals, Chicago White Sox, and Chicago Cubs. Harry Christopher Carabina was born in 1914 in one of the poorest sections of St. Louis and was still an infant when his father died. By the time he was ten, his mother had died, too, so an aunt raised him from that point. In 1989, Caray was inducted into the Baseball Hall of Fame as a broadcaster, and, in 1990, he joined the Radio Hall of Fame. A statue of him stands outside legendary Wrigley Field on Chicago's north side.

12. Faith Hill

Adopted when only a few days old, Audrey Faith Perry was raised in Star, Mississippi, by Ted and Edna Perry. The country music superstar was the only adopted kid in the family and formed a good relationship with her biological mother later in life. Faith always knew she was adopted and refers to her childhood as "amazing."

13. Jamie Foxx

Actor and comedian Jamie Foxx was born Eric Bishop in 1967. His parents separated shortly thereafter, and his mother didn't feel capable of raising him on her own, so he was adopted at seven months by his maternal grandmother. Years later, during his Academy Award acceptance speech for his role in the critically-acclaimed biopic *Ray*, Foxx thanked his grandmother for her hard work and unconditional love. He has also hosted holiday specials concerning adoption and often mentions the cause in interviews.

Real Names of 19 Famous People

❋ ❋ ❋ ❋

*"A rose by any other name" is supposed to smell as sweet, but
while that may be true in love, it isn't always so in show business.
Below are the real names of some famous faces—see if you
can match the real name to the alias.*

1. Reginald Kenneth Dwight	a. John Wayne
2. Paul Hewson	b. Cary Grant
3. Mark Vincent	c. Woody Allen
4. David Robert Jones	d. Elton John
5. Caryn Elaine Johnson	e. Mark Twain
6. Nathan Birnbaum	f. Freddie Mercury
7. Archibald Leach	g. Bob Dylan
8. Eleanor Gow	h. George Michael
9. Samuel Langhorne Clemens	i. Whoopi Goldberg
10. Tara Patrick	j. Bono
11. McKinley Morganfield	k. Jason Alexander
12. Farrokh Bulsara	l. Demi Moore
13. Frances Gumm	m. Vin Diesel
14. Robert Allen Zimmerman	n. George Burns
15. Demetria Gene Guynes	o. David Bowie
16. Marion Morrison	p. Muddy Waters
17. Allen Konigsberg	q. Judy Garland
18. Georgios Panayiotou	r. Elle MacPherson
19. Jay Scott Greenspan	s. Carmen Electra

Answers: 1. d; 2. j; 3. m; 4. o; 5. i; 6. n; 7. b; 8. r; 9. e; 10. s; 11. p; 12. f; 13. q; 14. g; 15. l; 16. a; 17. c; 18. h; 19. k

12 Renowned Women of the Wild West

❋ ❋ ❋ ❋

Perhaps no other time in America's history is as steeped in myth, legend, and adventure as the pioneering age of the "Wild West." Outlaws, lawmen, cowboys, American Indians, miners, ranchers, and more than a few "ladies of ill repute" emerged in this era, from 1865 to 1900. Any female settler in the West was a heroine in her own right, but listed here are a few of the more famous (and infamous) women of this intriguing period.

1. Annie Oakley

Probably the best-known woman of the Wild West, Annie Oakley was born Phoebe Ann Oakley Moses in Dark County, Ohio, in 1860, and she was shooting like a pro by age 12. Germany's Kaiser Wilhelm II trusted her with a gun so much that he let her shoot the ash off his cigarette while he smoked it. Oakley is the only woman of the Wild West to have a Broadway musical loosely based on her life (*Annie Get Your Gun*), which depicts her stint in Buffalo Bill's famous traveling show. When she joined the show, Bill touted her as "Champion Markswoman." When she died in 1926, it was discovered that her entire fortune had been spent on various charities, including women's rights and children's services.

2. Belle Starr

Myra Maybelle Shirley Reed Starr was born in Carthage, Missouri, in 1848. Frank and Jesse James's gang hid out at her family's farm when she was a kid, and from then on she was hooked on the outlaw life. Later, when her husband Jim Reed shot a man, the two went on the run, robbing banks and counterfeiting. Starr, who was known to wear feathers in her hair, buckskins, and a pistol on each hip, was shot in the back while riding her horse in 1889. It's still unclear whether her death was an accident—or murder.

3. Charley Parkhurst

Times were rough for ladies in the Wild West, so this crackerjack stagecoach driver decided to live most of her life as a man. Born in 1812, Parkhurst lived well into her sixties, in spite of being a hard-drinking, tobacco-chewing, fearless, one-eyed brute. She drove stages for Wells Fargo and the California Stage Company, not an easy or particularly safe career. Using her secret identity, Parkhurst was a registered voter and may have been the first American woman to cast a ballot. She lived out the rest of her life raising cattle and chickens until her death in 1879. It was then that her true identity was revealed, much to the surprise of her friends.

4. Calamity Jane

Born Martha Jane Canary in Missouri around 1856, Calamity Jane was a sharpshooter by the time she was a young woman. She received her nickname, Calamity Jane, when she rescued an army captain in South Dakota after their camp was attacked by Native Americans. Jane was said to be a whiskey-drinking, "don't-mess-with-me" kind of gal. She is reported to have saved the lives of six stagecoach passengers in 1876 when they were attacked by Native Americans, and she joined Buffalo Bill's show in the mid-1890s. Though she married a man named Burk at age 33, when Jane died in 1903, she asked to be buried next to Wild Bill Hickock. Rumor has it that Hickock was the only man she ever loved.

5. Josephine Sarah Marcus

A smolderingly good-looking actor born in 1861, Marcus came to Tombstone, Arizona, while touring with a theater group performing Gilbert & Sullivan's *HMS Pinafore*. She stuck around to marry sheriff John Behan, but when Wyatt Earp showed up, her marriage went cold, and she and Earp reportedly fell in love. This young lady was supposedly the reason behind the famous gunfight at the OK Corral—a 30-second flurry of gunfire involving Wild West superstars Doc Holliday, the Clayton Brothers, and the Earps. She passed away in 1944 and claimed until her dying day that Wyatt Earp was her one and only true love.

6. Laura Bullion

More commonly referred to as "Rose of the Wild Bunch," this outlaw was born around 1876 in Knickerbocker, Texas, and learned the outlaw trade by observing her bank-robbing father. Eventually hooking up with Butch Cassidy and his Wild Bunch, Bullion fenced money for the group and became romantically involved with several members. Most of those men died by the gun, but "The Thorny Rose" gave up her life of crime after serving time in prison and died a respectable seamstress in Memphis, Tennessee, in 1961.

7. Etta Place

Like many women of the Wild West, Etta Place's life is shrouded in mystery and legend. Was she a schoolteacher who left her quiet life for the drama of the outlaw life? Was she Butch Cassidy's girlfriend? Was she in love with The Sundance Kid or were they just friendly cousins? Evidence seems to indicate that Place was born around 1878 and became a prostitute at Fanny Porter's bordello in San Antonio, Texas. When the Wild Bunch came through, Place went with them to rob banks. She wasn't with the boys when they were killed in South America in 1909, and some believe she became a cattle rustler, but no one really knows for sure.

8. Lillian Smith

Before Britney and Christina, even before Tonya Harding and Nancy Kerrigan, there was the rivalry between this sharpshooter and her nemesis Annie Oakley. Born in 1871, Smith joined Buffalo Bill's show at age 15 and was notorious for bragging about her superior skills, wearing flashy clothes, and cursing like a sailor. When the show went to England in 1887, Smith shot poorly and was ridiculed while Oakley rose to the occasion. This crushing blow put Smith behind Oakley in the history books, and she died in 1930, a relatively obscure relic of the Old West.

9. Pearl de Vere

One of the most famous madams in history, this red-haired siren was born in Indiana around 1860 and made her way to Colorado during the Silver Panic of 1893. De Vere told her family she was a dress designer, but in fact rose to fame as the head of The Old Homestead, a luxurious brothel in Cripple Creek, Colorado. The price of a night's stay could cost patrons more than $200—at a time when most hotels charged around $3 a night! The building was reportedly equipped with an intercom system and boasted fine carpets and chandeliers. De Vere died in 1897 after a huge party at The Old Homestead. An overdose of morphine killed her, but it is unclear whether it was accidental or not.

10. Ellen Liddy Watson

Also known as "Cattle Kate," this lady of the West made a name for herself in the late 1800s when she was in her mid-twenties. Watson worked as a cook in the Rawlins House hotel and there she met her true love, James Averell. The two were hanged in 1889 by vigilantes who claimed Averell and Watson were cattle rustlers, but it is now believed that their murder was unjustified, the result of an abuse of power by land and cattle owners.

11. Pearl Hart

Pearl Hart was born in Canada around 1870, but by the time she was 17, she was married to a gambler and on a train to America. She especially liked life in the West, and, at 22, tried to leave her husband to pursue opportunities there. Her husband followed her and won her back, but Hart was already living it up with cigarettes, liquor, and even morphine. After her husband left to fight in the Spanish-American War, Hart met a man named Joe Boot, and they robbed stagecoaches for awhile before she was caught and jailed. Hart is famous for saying, "I shall not consent to be tried under a law in which my sex had no voice in making." She was eventually released, but the rest of her life is unknown.

12. Rose Dunn

In a family of outlaws, it was only a matter of time before "The Rose of Cimarron" was working in the business, too. Dunn met Doolin Gang member George Newcomb and joined him as he and his crew robbed stagecoaches and banks. During a particularly nasty gunfight, Dunn risked her life to supply Newcomb with a gun and bullets and helped him escape after he was wounded in battle. Dunn died around 1950 in her mid-seventies, a respectable citizen married to a local politician.

15 Notable People Who Dropped Out of School

✳ ✳ ✳ ✳

Everyone knows how important it is to stay in school, get a good education, and graduate with a diploma. But it may be hard to stay focused after reading about the success of these famous dropouts. Hard work, drive, natural talent, and sheer luck helped them overcome their lack of education, but many still returned to school later in life.

1. Thomas Edison

Thomas Edison is probably the most famous and productive inventor of all time, with more than 1,000 patents in his name, including the electric lightbulb, phonograph, and motion picture camera. He became a self-made multimillionaire and won a Congressional Gold Medal. Edison got a late start in his schooling following an illness, and, as a result, his mind often wandered, prompting one of his teachers to call him "addled." He dropped out after only three months of formal education. Luckily, his mother had been a schoolteacher in Canada and home-schooled young Edison.

2. Benjamin Franklin

Benjamin Franklin wore many hats: politician, diplomat, author, printer, publisher, scientist, inventor, founding father, and coauthor  and cosigner of the Declaration of Independence. One thing he was not was a high school graduate. Franklin was the fifteenth child and youngest son in a family of 20. He spent two years at the Boston Latin School before dropping out at age ten and going to work for his father, and then his brother, as a printer.

3. Bill Gates

Bill Gates is a cofounder of the software giant Microsoft and has been ranked the richest person in the world for a number of years. Gates dropped out of Harvard in his junior year after reading an article about the Altair microcomputer in *Popular Electronics* magazine. He and his friend Paul Allen formed Micro Soft (later changed to Microsoft) to write software for the Altair.

4. Albert Einstein

Although he was named *Time* magazine's "Man of the Century," Albert Einstein was not an "Einstein" in school. The Nobel Prize-winning physicist, famous for his theory of relativity and contributions to quantum theory and statistical mechanics, dropped out of high school at age 15. Deciding to continue his education a year later, Einstein took the entrance exam to the prestigious Swiss Federal Institute of Technology, but failed. He returned to high school, got his diploma, and then passed the university's entrance exam on his second attempt.

5. John D. Rockefeller

Two months before his high school graduation, history's first recorded billionaire, John D. Rockefeller, Sr., dropped out to take business courses at Folsom Mercantile College. He founded the Standard Oil Company in 1870, made his billions before the company was broken up by the government for being a monopoly, and spent his last 40 years giving away his riches, primarily to causes related to health and education. Ironically, this high school dropout helped millions get a good education.

6. Walt Disney

In 1918, while still in high school, future Oscar-winning film producer and theme park pioneer Walt Disney began taking night courses at the Academy of Fine Arts in Chicago. Disney dropped out of high school at age 16 to join the army, but because he was too young to enlist, he joined the Red Cross with a forged birth certificate instead. Disney was sent to France where he drove an ambulance that was covered from top to bottom with cartoons that eventually became his film characters. After becoming the multi-millionaire founder of The Walt Disney Company and winning the Presidential Medal of Freedom, Disney received an honorary high school diploma at age 58.

7. Richard Branson

Britain's Sir Richard Branson is a self-made billionaire business-man. He founded Virgin Atlantic Airways, Virgin Records, Virgin Mobile, and most recently, a space tourism company to provide suborbital trips into space for anyone who can afford them. Suffering from dyslexia, Branson was a poor student, so he quit school at age 16 and moved to London, where he began his first successful entrepreneurial activity, publishing *Student* magazine.

8. George Burns

George Burns, born Nathan Birnbaum, was a successful vaudeville, TV, and movie comedian for nearly nine decades. After his father's death, Burns left school in the fourth grade to go to work shining shoes, running errands, and selling newspapers. While employed at a local candy shop, Burns and his young coworkers decided to go into show business as the Peewee Quartet. After the group broke up, Burns continued to work with a partner, usually a girl, and was the funny one in the group until he met Gracie Allen in 1923. Burns and Allen got married, but didn't become stars until George flipped the act and made Gracie the funny one. They continued to work together in vaudeville, radio, television, and movies until Gracie retired in 1958. Burns continued performing almost until the day he died in March 1996.

9. Colonel Sanders

Colonel Harland Sanders overcame his lack of education to become the biggest drumstick in the fried chicken business. His father died when he was six years old, and since his mother worked, he was forced to cook for his family. After dropping out of elementary school, Sanders worked many jobs, including firefighter, steamboat driver, and insurance salesman. He later earned a law degree from a correspondence school. Sanders' cooking and business experience helped him make millions as the founder of Kentucky Fried Chicken (now KFC).

10. Charles Dickens

Charles Dickens, author of numerous classics including *Oliver Twist, A Tale of Two Cities,* and *A Christmas Carol,* attended elementary school until his life took a twist of its own when his father was imprisoned for debt. At age 12, he left school and began working ten-hour days in a boot-blacking factory. Dickens later worked as a law clerk and a court stenographer. At age 22, he became a journalist, reporting parliamentary debate and covering election campaigns for a newspaper. His first collection of stories, *Sketches by Boz* (Boz was his nickname), were published in 1836 and led to his first novel, *The Pickwick Papers,* in March 1836.

11. Elton John

Born Reginald Kenneth Dwight, Rock and Roll Hall of Fame member Sir Elton John has sold more than 250 million records and has more than 50 Top 40 hits, making him one of the most successful musicians of all time. At age 11, Elton entered London's Royal Academy of Music on a piano scholarship. Bored with classical compositions, Elton preferred rock 'n' roll and after five years he quit school to become a weekend pianist at a local pub. At 17, he formed a band called Bluesology, and, by the mid-1960s, they were touring with soul and R&B musicians such as The Isley Brothers and Patti LaBelle and The Bluebelles. The album *Elton John* was released in the spring of 1970 and, after the first single "Your Song" made the U.S. Top Ten, Elton was on his way to superstardom.

12. Ray Kroc

Ray Kroc didn't found McDonald's, but he turned it into the world's largest fast-food chain after purchasing the original location from Dick and Mac McDonald. Kroc amassed a $500 million fortune during his lifetime, and in 2000 was included in *Time* magazine's list of the 100 most influential builders and titans of industry in the 20th century. During World War I, Kroc dropped out of high school at age 15 and lied about his age to become a Red Cross ambulance driver, but the war ended before he was sent overseas.

13. Harry Houdini

The name Houdini is synonymous with magic. Before becoming a world-renowned magician and escape artist named Harry Houdini, Ehrich Weiss dropped out of school at age 12, working several jobs, including locksmith's apprentice. At 17, he teamed up with fellow magic enthusiast Jack Hayman to form the Houdini Brothers, named after Jean Eugène Robert Houdin, the most famous magician of the era. By age 24, Houdini had come up with the Challenge Act, offering to escape from any pair of handcuffs produced by the audience. The Challenge Act was the turning point for Houdini. With its success came the development of the spectacular escapes that would make him a legend.

14. Ringo Starr

Richard Starkey is better known as Ringo Starr, the drummer of The Beatles. Born in Liverpool in 1940, Ringo suffered two serious illnesses at age six. First, his appendix ruptured, leaving him in a coma for ten weeks. After six months in recovery, he fell out of the hospital bed, necessitating an additional six-month hospital stay. After spending a total of three years in a hospital, he was considerably behind in school. He dropped out after his last visit to the hospital at age 15, barely able to read or write. While working at an engineering firm, 17-year-old Starkey joined a band and taught himself to play the drums. His stepfather bought him his first real drum set, and Ringo sat in with a variety of bands, eventually joining Rory Storm and The Hurricanes. He changed his name to Ringo Starr, joined The Beatles in 1962, and is now one of the best-known drummers in history.

15. Princess Diana

The late Diana Spencer, Princess of Wales, attended West Heath Girls' School where she was regarded as an academically below-average student, having failed all of her O-level examinations (exams given to 16-year-old students in the UK to determine their education level). At age 16, she left West Heath and briefly attended a finishing school in Switzerland before dropping out from there as well. Diana was a talented amateur singer and reportedly longed to be a ballerina. Diana went to work as a part-time assistant at the Young England Kindergarten, a day care center and nursery school. Contrary to claims, she was not a kindergarten teacher since she had no educational qualifications to teach, and Young England was not a kindergarten, despite its name. In 1981, at age 19, Diana became engaged to Prince Charles and her working days were over.

COLOSSI OF RHODES
13 Famous Rhodes Scholars

❊ ❊ ❊ ❊

When British businessman Cecil Rhodes died in 1902, his fortune was used to establish the Rhodes scholarship, which brings outstanding students from around the world to study at the University of Oxford in England, generally for two years. Students from any academic discipline are selected on the basis of intellectual distinction, as well as the promise of future leadership and service to the world. Around 90 scholarships are given annually, and some of the most famous scholars are listed below.

1. Edwin Hubble
Famous astronomer Edwin Hubble received his scholarship in 1910. Having studied science and mathematics at the University of Chicago, he used his time at Oxford to study law. Hubble then returned to the States to continue his work in astronomy, most notably discovering the existence of galaxies beyond the Milky Way.

2. Dean Rusk
Dean Rusk, who used his 1931 Rhodes scholarship to study history and political science, served as U.S. Secretary of State from 1961 to 1969 under presidents John F. Kennedy and Lyndon B. Johnson.

3. Lord Howard Florey

Australian pharmacologist Lord Howard Florey was awarded his scholarship in 1921 and studied medicine at Oxford. In 1945, he was awarded the Nobel Prize in Medicine along with Alexander Fleming and Ernst Chain for their work in discovering penicillin.

4. James William Fulbright

James William Fulbright, who used his 1926 Rhodes scholarship to study law, was elected to the House of Representatives in 1943, then served in the Senate from 1945 to 1974. Soon after, he established the Fulbright Program to provide grants for students and professionals to study, teach, and conduct research abroad. To date, more than 250,000 individuals have received Fulbright grants.

5. Bill Bradley

William Warren Bradley already had an Olympic gold medal for basketball when he began his study of politics, philosophy, and economics at Oxford in 1965. He went on to have a Hall of Fame career in basketball before entering the Senate in 1978 and running as a presidential candidate in the 2000 primary.

6. Bill Clinton

Former President Bill Clinton received his Rhodes scholarship in 1968. While at Oxford, he studied law and also played an active part in student life, particularly in protests against the Vietnam War. Fellow Rhodes scholar David E. Kendall later became Clinton's personal lawyer.

7. Strobe Talbott

Strobe Talbott, who also won his scholarship in 1968 and spent his time at Oxford translating Nikita Khrushchev's memoirs into English, was another of Clinton's Oxford friends. He went on to be Deputy Secretary of State from 1994 to 2001. Talbott was also president of the Brookings Institution—a Washington, D.C.-based political research facility that helped negotiate an end to the war in Yugoslavia in 1999.

8. George Stephanopoulos

George Stephanopoulos used his 1984 Rhodes scholarship to earn a master's degree in theology. During the 1992 presidential campaign, Stephanopoulos served as Bill Clinton's senior political adviser, then as communications director during Clinton's presidency. He currently hosts the Sunday morning news show *This Week* and is the chief Washington correspondent for ABC news.

9. Kris Kristofferson

Well-known musician and actor Kris Kristofferson received his Rhodes scholarship in 1958. He studied English literature, and it was while he was at Oxford that he began his performing career. Since then, his hit records have won him several Grammys.

10. Terrence Malik

Best known as director of *The Thin Red Line* and *Badlands,* Terrence Malik won a Rhodes scholarship in 1966. He studied philosophy but had a disagreement with his adviser over his thesis (the concept of the world in the writings of Kierkegaard, Heidegger, and Wittgenstein) and left Oxford without finishing his doctorate.

11. Naomi Wolf

American author and feminist social critic Naomi Wolf used her time at Oxford from 1985 to 1987 to begin the research that eventually became the international best seller *The Beauty Myth,* which condemns the exploitation of women by the fashion and beauty industries.

12. Cory A. Booker

Cory A. Booker began his studies at Oxford in 1992, gaining an honors degree in modern history. He is now a Democratic politician and mayor of racially diverse Newark, New Jersey, the largest city in the state.

13. Randal Pinkett

Randal Pinkett, who earned a masters degree in computer science as a 1994 Rhodes scholar, gained celebrity status when he was hired by Donald Trump after winning season four of *The Apprentice.*

SIBLING RIVALRY
38 Celebrity Siblings

❋ ❋ ❋ ❋

1. Ben and Casey Affleck
2. Kevin and Matt Dillon
3. Sean and Mackenzie Astin
4. Jim and John Belushi
5. River and Joaquin Phoenix
6. Sean and Neil Connery
7. Don and Jim Ameche
8. James Arness and Peter Graves
9. Groucho, Harpo, Chico, Zeppo, and Gummo Marx
10. Ron and Clint Howard
11. Beau and Jeff Bridges
12. Charlie Sheen and Emilio Estevez
13. Moe, Curly, and Shemp Howard (The Three Stooges)
14. Dennis and Randy Quaid
15. Fred and Ben Savage
16. Dean and Guy Stockwell
17. Dick and Jerry Van Dyke
18. Donnie and Mark Wahlberg
19. Keenan Ivory, Damon, Marlon, and Shawn Wayans
20. Pier Angeli and Marisa Pavan
21. David, Rosanna, Patricia, and Alexis Arquette
22. Hilary and Haylie Duff
23. Zsa-Zsa, Eva, and Magda Gabor
24. Joan Fontaine and Olivia de Havilland
25. Margaux and Mariel Hemingway
26. Phylicia Rashad and Debbie Allen
27. Meg and Jennifer Tilly
28. Justine and Jason Bateman
29. Jane and Peter Fonda
30. Jake and Maggie Gyllenhaal
31. Warren Beatty and Shirley MacLaine

32. John and Joan Cusack
33. Michael and Virginia Madsen
34. Julia and Eric Roberts
35. Alec, Daniel, Billy, and Stephen Baldwin
36. Ashley and Wynonna Judd
37. Jessica and Ashlee Simpson
38. Nick and Aaron Carter

10 Countries with the Highest Divorce Rate

❊ ❊ ❊ ❊

Country	*Divorce Rate per 100 Marriages*
1. Belgium	59.8
2. Sweden	53.9
3. Czech Republic	53.7
4. Finland	53.2
5. United Kingdom	52.7
6. United States	50.6
7. Hungary	49.9
8. Austria	49.8
9. Luxembourg	48.0
10. New Zealand	47.1

20 Notable People with a Twin

❊ ❊ ❊ ❊

1. Kofi Annan......................twin sister, Efua
2. Isabella Rossellini............twin sister, Isotta
3. Kiefer Sutherland............twin sister, Rachel
4. Scarlett Johansson ....twin brother, Hunter
5. Alanis Morissette.............twin brother, Wade
6. Mario Andretti................twin brother, Aldo
7. Vin Diesel ....twin brother, Paul

8. Ashton Kutcher ....twin brother, Michael
9. Billy Dee Williams...........twin sister, Loretta
10. José Canseco.....................twin brother, Ozzie
11. Aaron Carter....................twin sister, Angel
12. John Elway.......................twin sister, Jana
13. Jerry Falwell ....twin brother, Gene
14. Deidre Hall......................twin sister, Andrea
15. Pier Angeli ....twin sister, Marisa Pavan
16. Montgomery Clift............twin sister, Roberta
17. Maurice Gibb ....twin brother, Robin
18. Ann Landers ....twin sister, Abigail Van Buren (Dear Abby)
19. Mary-Kate Olsen ....twin sister, Ashley
20. Jim Thorpe......................twin brother, Charlie

10 Famous Native Americans

✳ ✳ ✳ ✳

*Let's face it, America's history is not exactly neat and tidy.
When white settlers arrived in America they realized they had
a big problem: There were people already living there!
These Native Americans tried various tactics to deal with the
European intruders. They tried talking it out, but most of the
settlers were afraid of these seemingly primitive people.
They tried living harmoniously, by signing treaties for shared
land, but the U.S. government had a knack for going back on its
word. They even resorted to fighting and won some victories,
though the war would eventually be lost along with nearly all
of the land they had left. Despite the hardships, some heroes
emerged. The following figures represent the hundreds
of tribal leaders who did everything they could to preserve
the history and culture of their threatened people.*

1. Tatanka Iyotaka, aka Sitting Bull
The principal chief of the Dakota Sioux was fierce, determined,
and less than forgiving of the white miners who tried to take over

the Black Hills in the late 1870s. Sitting Bull was born in 1831 and, while he earned a reputation for being ruthless in the Native American resistance efforts of his younger days, his big moment came in 1876. Trying to protect their land, Sitting Bull and his men defeated Custer's troops at the Battle of Little Bighorn. Sitting Bull then escaped to Canada. In 1881, he returned to America on the promise of a pardon, which he received. The legendary warrior then joined Buffalo Bill's Wild West Show, showcasing his riding skills and hunting prowess. But when he died at 69, Sitting Bull was still advising his people to hold on to their land and their heritage.

2. Tecumseh

While Tecumseh, a Shawnee chief, was no stranger to battle, he is more often recognized for his diplomatic efforts in the Native American plight. Born in Ohio in the late 1760s, Tecumseh was an impressive and charismatic orator. In 1809, when the Treaty of Fort Wayne signed over 2.5 million acres to the United States, Tecumseh was outraged. He tried to get all the Native American nations to join together, claiming that the land belonged to the people who were there first, and no one tribe could buy or sell any part of it. Tecumseh's hopes were to create solidarity among all native peoples, but the idea came too late. Eventually, Tecumseh joined forces with the British and was killed in battle in 1813.

3. Sequoyah, aka George Guess, aka Sogwali

If it weren't for Sequoyah, a huge piece of Native American culture might be missing. Thanks to this Cherokee born around 1766, the Cherokee language is not a mystery. Sequoyah created the syllabary, or syllable alphabet, for his people and taught the Cherokee how to read and write. The ability to communicate via the written word helped make the Cherokee Nation a leader among tribes everywhere. The giant sequoia tree is named after the man who felt that the pen would outlast the sword—and he was right. Sequoyah died in 1843 of natural causes.

4. Pontiac

Not much is known about Pontiac's early life, but it is believed that he was born in the Detroit or Maumee River region to Ottawan parents, and, by age 30, he was a prominent figure within his tribe. After the French and Indian War, Pontiac was none too pleased with the British and their trading policies. He responded with widespread attacks against British forts and settlements in the Ohio region during 1763, which came to be known as Pontiac's Rebellion. However, neighboring tribes and other Native American leaders didn't like the way Pontiac conducted himself. Some felt he used a fake title of "chief" given to him by the white man to exert influence and enjoy undue power. Pontiac was killed by a member of the Peoria tribe in 1769.

5. John Ross

Though only one-eighth Cherokee, John Ross served as a chief in the Cherokee Nation from 1828 until his death in 1866. Over the years, Ross served as a translator for missionaries, a liaison between the Cherokee people and Washington politicians, and owned a farm (and slaves) in North Carolina. By the early 1820s, things did not look good for the Cherokee people. Ross took legal action to try to prevent the forced exile of the tribe. He was president of the Cherokee Constitutional Convention of 1827 and, for the next ten years, worked with the U.S. government and his people to seek assistance and justice for the Cherokee. Even though several court rulings found the Cherokee to be the rightful owners of land, they weren't enforced, and, slowly but surely, Ross's efforts went largely unrewarded. Ross is known for leading the Cherokee to Oklahoma in 1838 on what is commonly referred to as the "Trail of Tears."

6. Geronimo

Historical figures are often described with embellishment, but rarely are they mythologized to Geronimo's levels. Geronimo's wife, children, and mother were killed by Mexicans in 1858. He led many attacks on both Mexican and American settlers and was known for his legendary war skills—some even said he was impervious to bullets. But later in life, this fearless leader of the Chiricahua tribe of the North American Apache was forced to settle on a reservation, his group having dwindled to just a few people. He eventually died a prisoner of war in 1909 and is buried in Oklahoma.

7. Tashunca-uitco, aka Crazy Horse

At the tender age of 13, this legendary warrior was stealing horses from neighboring tribes. By the time he was 20, Crazy Horse was leading his first war party under the instruction of Chief Red Cloud. The Lakota warrior spent his life fighting for the preservation of his people's way of life. He amassed more than 1,200 warriors to help Sitting Bull defeat General Crook in 1876. After that, Sitting Bull and Crazy Horse joined forces, eventually defeating Custer at Little Bighorn. Crazy Horse continued to tirelessly defend his people's rights, but by 1877, there was little fight left in him. When trying to get to his sick wife, Crazy Horse was killed with a bayonet.

8. Hin-mah-too-yah-lat-kekt, aka Joseph the Younger

Born in 1840 in what is now Oregon, Joseph the Younger (also called Chief Joseph) had some big shoes to fill. His father, Joseph the Elder, had converted to Christianity in 1838 in an attempt to make peace with white settlers. His father's efforts seemed to work, for his Nez Percé people were given land in Idaho. But in 1863, the U.S. government took the land back, and Joseph the Younger's father burned his Bible and his flag and refused to sign any new treaties. When Joseph succeeded his father as tribal chief in 1871, he clearly had to deal with a rather delicate situation. He eventually agreed to move his people to the now smaller reservation in Idaho, but never made it. They came under attack by white soldiers, fought back, and then dealt with the wrath of the government. In an impressive battle, 700 Native Americans fought 2,000 U.S. soldiers successfully until Joseph surrendered in 1877. He died in 1904 from what his doctor reported was a broken heart.

9. Makhpiya-Luta, aka Red Cloud

For most of his life, Red Cloud was fighting. At first, it was to defend his Oglala people against the Pawnee and Crow tribes, but by the time he reached his forties, Red Cloud was fighting the white man. His efforts led to the defeat of Fort Phil Kearny in Wyoming in 1867 and kept soldiers at bay (and in fear) for the rest of the winter. In the two years that followed, the government signed the Fort Laramie Treaty and gave the Native Americans land in Wyoming, Montana, and South Dakota. But soon after, the Black Hills were invaded, and Red Cloud and his people lost their land. Until his death in 1909, Red Cloud tried other ways to make peace and preserve the culture of his people, working with government officials and agents to reach a fair agreement.

10. Gall

This Lakota leader played a major role in the Lakotas' long war against the United States. As a Hunkpapa Teton Sioux leader, he also served as commander of the Native American cavalry forces at the Battle of Little Bighorn. Gall was one of the most aggressive Sioux leaders in the final battles for preservation and resistance, though his story is not without controversy. Though he was Sitting Bull's chief military lieutenant during the Little Bighorn battle, he quarreled with Sitting Bull and retreated to Canada shortly thereafter. His talks with settlers did much to improve relations between the groups, but some felt he conceded too much and befriended too many white leaders. Regardless, Gall was integral to the history of the Native American plight.

❋ ❋ ❋

Treat the earth well.
It was not given to you by your parents,
It was loaned to you by your children.
We do not inherit the earth from our ancestors,
We borrow it from our children.
—Native American proverb

A MATCH MADE IN HEAVEN
18 Hopelessly Devoted Couples

✳ ✳ ✳ ✳

Behind every good man is a great woman. Or as Groucho Marx put it: "Behind every successful man is a woman, behind her is his wife." Can you match up the following couples who stayed together till death (or the end of TV syndication) did them part?

1. Robin Hood	a. Betty Bloomer
2. Clark Kent	b. Cleopatra
3. Kermit	c. Dale Evans
4. Romeo	d. Elizabeth Barrett
5. Marc Antony	e. Gracie Allen
6. JFK	f. Harriett Hilliard
7. Ricky Ricardo	g. Jacqueline Bouvier
8. Prince Albert	h. Juliet
9. Robert Browning	i. June Carter
10. Gerald Ford	j. Lauren Bacall
11. Fred Flintstone	k. Lois Lane
12. Ronald Reagan	l. Lucy McGillicuddy
13. Johnny Cash	m. Maid Marian
14. Ozzie Nelson	n. Miss Piggy
15. John Lennon	o. Nancy Davis
16. Humphrey Bogart	p. Queen Victoria
17. Roy Rogers	q. Wilma Slaghoople
18. George Burns	r. Yoko Ono

Answers: 1. m; 2. k; 3. n; 4. h; 5. b; 6. g; 7. l; 8. p; 9. d; 10. a; 11. q; 12. o; 13. i; 14. f; 15. r; 16. j; 17. c; 18. e

ARE YOU GOING TO FINISH THAT?
9 Winners of Extreme Eating Contests

✳ ✳ ✳ ✳

Despite the obesity epidemic in America today, extreme eating contests are more popular than ever. Check out the world-record appetites of these extreme eaters.

1. In October 2006, ESPN2 televised the third annual Krystal Square Off hamburger eating contest in Chattanooga, Tennessee. The winner was Takeru "The Tsunami" Kobayashi, a 160-pound competitive eating champion from Nagano, Japan, who downed 97 square Krystal burgers in just 8 minutes. Kobayashi may have left with a bit of gas, but he also left with a lot of cash—first prize was $10,000. One of the top competitive eaters in the world, Kobayashi held the world record for hot dog eating until 2007, and he won the Nathan's Famous Hot Dog Eating Contest on Coney Island six years in a row (2001–2006).

2. At a mere 105 pounds, Sonya "The Black Widow" Thomas, from Alexandria, Virginia, is the reigning lobster-eating champion, downing 44 Maine lobsters totaling 11.3 pounds of meat in 12 minutes in August 2005, at the second annual World Lobster-Eating Championship in Kennebunkport, Maine. Thomas broke her own lobster record at the event and won $500 and the right to wear "The Claw," the championship belt that goes with the title. Thomas has held more than 40 world titles for competitive eating. She got the nickname "The Black Widow" for outeating male competitors many times her weight.

3. Some like it hot, and Rich "The Locust" LeFevre is no exception. In October 2006, the sixty-something, 132-pound, retired CPA from Henderson, Nevada, set the world record for eating 247 pickled jalapeño peppers in 8 minutes. He also holds world records for eating 1.5 gallons of chili in 10 minutes; 30 Tex-Mex rolls in 12 minutes in March 2005; and 7.75 pounds of huevos rancheros—a spicy Mexican breakfast dish—in 10 minutes in March 2006.

4. Wings are the thing for Joey Chestnut, a 230-pound extreme eater from San Jose, California. He's the world champion chicken wings eater, downing 182 of them in 30 minutes in February 2007, at Wing Bowl 15, an annual event held in Philadelphia on the Friday before the Super Bowl. Chestnut also holds the world record for hot dog eating. In July 2007, he defeated six-time champion Takeru Kobayashi by eating 66 hot dogs (and buns) in 12 minutes at the annual Nathan's Famous Hot Dog Eating Contest.

5. Shoofly pie is a rich Pennsylvania Dutch sponge cake with molasses filling. Patrick Bertoletti, a 190-pounder from Chicago, holds the shoofly pie-eating record, scarfing down 11.1 pounds (37 slices) of pie in 8 minutes in June 2007. Since he emerged on the competitive-eating circuit in 2006, Bertoletti has numerous victories under his belt, including a world record 19 slices of pizza at the Three Brothers Pizza Eating Championship in August 2006.

6. New York City window washer Bill "Crazy Legs" Conti is the world record pancake eater. On July 4, 2002, in his rookie year as  a competitive eater, Conti ate a 3.5 pound stack of pancakes (and bacon) in 12 minutes at the Hibernation Cup in Anchorage, Alaska. A documentary was produced about his life called *Crazy Legs Conti: Zen and the Art of Competitive Eating.*

7. Dale Boone, a 303-pounder from Atlanta, Georgia, holds the world record for eating reindeer sausages, downing 28 of Santa's helpers in 10 minutes in 2002 in Anchorage. He also holds the world record for eating 84 ounces of baked beans in 1 minute, 52 seconds.

8. Oy, vey! Twenty-one matzo balls is a lot of dough for most people, but not for Eric Booker, a 440-pound heavyweight from Copaigue, New York. In January 2004, he ate 21 baseball-sized matzo balls in

5 minutes, 25 seconds, at Ben's deli in Manhattan to set the world record. Booker is also known in hip-hop circles as a rapper with two albums and numerous appearances on *Last Call with Carson Daly,* where he serves as announcer and "Eater in Residence."

9. Erik "The Red" Denmark, a 208-pounder from Seattle, ate a world record 4 pounds, 15 ounces of spot shrimp in 12 minutes in September 2006. He also holds the record for Native American fry bread, eating 9.75 fry breads in 8 minutes in October 2006.

Former Jobs of 12 Celebrities

❄ ❄ ❄ ❄

Most of us aren't born with a silver spoon in our mouths—even celebrities. Just like us, they've had to work their way up the job ladder. Here are a dozen examples that prove the old adage: It's not where you start, it's where you finish that counts.

1. Mick Jagger

Before he began strutting his stuff onstage, Sir Michael Phillip "Mick" Jagger, lead singer of The Rolling Stones, worked as a porter at the Bexley Mental Hospital while he was a student at the London School of Economics. He earned a whopping 4 pounds, 10 shillings per week (about $7.80 US). Perhaps Jagger's gig at the hospital inspired a couple of the Stones' early hits, such as "19th Nervous Breakdown" and "Mother's Little Helper."

2. Jason Lee

Actor Jason Lee, star of *My Name is Earl,* plays a character who never works, but in real life Lee once worked at Taco Bell. Then, in the late 1980s and early 1990s, Lee become a competitive skateboarder, performing flips and other daring maneuvers. After appearing in a promotional skateboarding video shot by Spike Jonze, Lee began getting movie offers and left his skateboarding career in the dust.

3. Paula Abdul

During her freshman year at Cal State University, Paula Abdul tried out for the Los Angeles Lakers cheerleading squad and was selected from more than 700 applicants. Her high-energy, street-funk-inspired dance routines were an instant hit, and it took her all of three weeks to become head choreographer. In 1984, when Abdul's routines got the attention of the Jackson family, they immediately signed her to choreograph their *Torture* video and her career went into overdrive. When Abdul embarked on a singing career in the late 1980s, her debut album, *Forever Your Girl,* went platinum and spawned four number one singles, including "Straight Up" and "Cold Hearted." She has now become popular with a new audience as a judge on *American Idol.*

4. David Letterman

After graduating from Indiana's Ball State University in 1969, future late night talk show host David Letterman landed a job at Indianapolis television station WLWI (now called WTHR) as a local anchor and weatherman. Letterman was eventually let go for his unpredictable on-air behavior, which included erasing state borders from the weather map and predicting hail stones "the size of canned hams." Those canned hams eventually became popular door prizes on *The Late Show with David Letterman.*

5. Dennis Farina

Italian-American actor Dennis Farina often portrays cops, detectives, or mobsters and is best known for his roles in *Law & Order, Crime Story,* and *Get Shorty.* Some may think he's being typecast, but it's no wonder that Farina is so comfortable in his roles—from 1967 to 1985, he actually *was* a police officer with the Chicago Police Department. Farina caught the acting bug after working with director Michael Mann as a police consultant. He started out in community theater and with bit parts on television before landing a starring role in *Crime Story* in 1986.

6. Clint Eastwood

Clint Eastwood has established himself as a Hollywood icon. From Westerns in the 1960s to no-nonsense, rebel cop Dirty Harry in the 1970s to a focus on directing since the 1980s, Eastwood has created a body of work that has garnered respect, box office success, and numerous awards. But before that, Eastwood earned his daily bread digging swimming pools for the rich and famous of Beverly Hills, while at night he'd audition for bit parts. He'd already put in hard time working as a lumberjack, steel mill worker, aircraft factory worker, and gas station attendant. Now, he's the one lounging around the pool.

7. Whoopi Goldberg

With careers as a stand-up comedian, actor, and TV talk show host, Academy Award-winner Whoopi Goldberg has firmly established herself as an outspoken, emancipated, confident star. But Goldberg wasn't always living in the lap of luxury. Growing up in the tough Chelsea projects in New York City, her first job was as a bricklayer. When that position fizzled out, she took on the role of a garbage collector and then a funeral makeup artist—whatever job she could get to make ends meet.

8. Ozzy Osbourne

Singer Ozzy Osbourne, born John Michael Osbourne, is the lead singer of the pioneering heavy metal band Black Sabbath, a popular solo artist, and a reality TV star with his wife Sharon and two children, Kelly and Jack. Growing up in England, Osbourne was once a laborer in a slaughterhouse. This may have influenced some of his famous stunts, like biting off the head of a live dove during a meeting with his newly signed record company and biting the head off a bat thrown onstage during a concert.

9. Sean Connery

Sean Connery is probably best known for portraying James Bond seven times, setting the bar very high for those who would follow.

He also showed his versatility with movies such as *Highlander* and *The Untouchables*, for which he won an Oscar. But Connery's first job was as a milkman in his native Scotland. After a stint in the Royal Navy, he took on numerous jobs in the late 1940s and early 1950s, including lifeguard, ditchdigger, and artist's model. In 1953, he even competed in the Mr. Universe contest, placing third in the tall man's division.

10. Marlon Brando

Nearly a decade before he starred as Stanley Kowalski in *A Streetcar Named Desire,* Marlon Brando worked as a ditchdigger after he was expelled from military school for being "incorrigible." When he grew tired of manual labor, Brando became an elevator operator in New York City. His last non-acting job before his break into film was as a night watchman.

11. Matthew McConaughey

Matthew McConaughey's rugged good looks have won him many fans and seen him cast in a long list of romantic comedies and action films. But after graduating high school in 1988, he spent a year in Australia as an exchange student. During this time, he made some extra cash by shoveling chicken manure and washing dishes. Returning to the United States in 1990, McConaughey considered a career in law but caught the acting bug instead.

12. Madonna

Madonna Louise Veronica Ciccone splashed onto the music scene with an attitude and some catchy pop tunes in the early 1980s. Her *Like a Virgin* album and subsequent tour took the world by storm, and she's never looked back. But the early years in New York City were tough for Madonna, and she found herself working at a number of low-paying jobs, including a stint at a Dunkin' Donuts in Times Square. But, in true Madonna fashion, she was fired for squirting jelly filling all over customers!

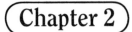

Chapter 2
FUN, GAMES, AND POP CULTURE

✳ ✳ ✳ ✳

MULLETS AND BEEHIVES AND FLIPS, OH MY!
21 Unforgettable Hairstyles

*Some hairstyles stand the test of time while others do not.
No matter what the latest trend happens to be, hairstyles
are a reflection of who we are as individuals and as a culture
on the whole. Below is a selection of hairstyles from
the 1930s and beyond, for better or worse.*

1930s

1. The Finger Wave: Curls and waves were in fashion in the 1930s. Often hailed as the most tasteful decade, the 1930s found women styling themselves after the stars of the burgeoning Hollywood film industry. Think Greta Garbo, Katharine Hepburn, and Carole Lombard, who all kept their hair short to mid-length, wavy, and styled for maximum sex appeal.

1940s

2. The Veronica Lake: The smoky, alluring look of this 1940s screen siren was identifiable by miles of long, wavy blonde hair that covered one eye. This was the hairstyle of a star; everyday women opted for a shorter, shoulder-length version of the wavy style.

3. The Rosie the Riveter: Rosie was a popular icon during the war era when many women pinned their long hair back and covered it with a bandanna while working inside or outside the home.

4. The Cary Grant: The movies struck again, influencing the men's hairstyle of the time. This was a precise cut with a severe side part and a whole lot of styling wax to make it shine. The look was suave and debonair, just like Grant himself.

1950s

5. The Bouffant: When the salon-sized hair dryer was unveiled to the beauty industry, the possibilities seemed endless. Updos and blow-dried styles were literally taken to new heights as the bouffant and the beehive created big, round silhouettes on the head.

6. The Bardot: The bombshell's film performances were only part of the reason women emulated Bardot's hairstyle—a sexy mess of long, strawberry blonde tresses. Bardot was the antithesis of the beehive and other hairstyles of the era that represented the repressed side of women at the time.

7. The Pompadour: This was the era when T-shirts and jeans became the uniform of young men everywhere. And the pompadour, popularized by James Dean and Elvis Presley, was the haircut that went with it. Closely cut in the back, the top and sides were kept a little longer and combed up and back with hair gel for added shine. The look was masculine and instantly iconic.

1960s

8. The Flip: This spunky, youthful style was mega-popular among hordes of modern women throughout the 1960s. Shoulder-length hair was back-combed or teased slightly at the top, then the ends were curled up in a "flip" with rollers or a curling iron. Depending on the age of the woman and her willingness to push the envelope, the flip was combined with the bouffant, which meant that it got bigger and puffier. Mary Tyler Moore sported the classic flip on *The Dick Van Dyke Show,* and Jackie Kennedy had her own more conservative version, too. Later, the style became so ubiquitous it was nicknamed "beauty pageant hair" or "Miss America hair," because for years nearly every contestant sported flip after perfect flip.

9. The Pixie: The pin-up figure went out of style when long, lean supermodel Twiggy came on the scene in the 1960s. Women everywhere tried to emulate her silhouette—and her hair. It took a reported eight hours to create the style on Twiggy the first time, almost as long as it took to put on all those fake eyelashes. The pixie was cut over the ears, with slightly longer hair on the top of the head. The defining feature was the close-cropped layers that framed the face.

10. **The Mop Top:** The influence of The Beatles on popular culture was unlike anything the world had ever seen. Girls and boys alike mimicked the boyish charm of these Liverpool lads, especially when it came to hairstyles. Longer, over the ears, shaggy, and generally floppy on all sides, the mop top was also sported by another mega-band of the time, The Rolling Stones.

1970s

11. **The Farrah Fawcett:** This iconic hairstyle, made famous by *Charlie's Angels* star Farrah Fawcett, came to a soft point at the top of the head, creating a triangular silhouette with long, feathered flips cascading down the sides and the back. This hairdo was revived in the 2000s as part of a retro '70s and '80s fashion trend.

12. **The No-Cut Haircut:** If you were a guy in the 1970s who didn't like getting a haircut, you were in luck. As the decade marched on, men simply stopped cutting their hair. Whether they were influenced by the free-loving culture of the hippies, growing antiwar sentiment, or just plain laziness, men's hair reached new lengths during this era.

1980s

13. **Rock Hair:** Many of the hairstyle changes and fashion trends in the 1980s had to do with the music of the era. "Hair bands" were so named because of their long, voluminous hair, which was often teased or permed. Heavy metal bands such as Mötley Crüe, Poison, and Bon Jovi helped popularize this look for both men and women.

14. **The Mullet:** No one can be totally sure when this notorious hairstyle originated, but its popularity soared in the 1980s. The mullet

was achieved by cutting hair short and spiky or feathered on the top and sides of the head and keeping it shoulder-length or longer in the back.

15. The Rat-Tail: Popular with young men (and some women) of the '80s, this style was characterized by hair cut short all over except for a long strip of hair (usually ½ to 1 inch wide) growing from the nape of the neck and dangling down the back. Rat-tails were typically 4 to 12 inches in length and were often braided.

16. The Mohawk: The Mohawk had its roots in Native American culture but was popular with punk rockers in the '80s. Punk hairstyles in the UK and America reflected the attitude of these antiestablishment youngsters; hair was spiked, sprayed, shaved, and often multi-colored and sent a clear message: We're not like you.

17. The Meg Ryan: Immortalized by the romantic comedy *When Harry Met Sally,* Meg Ryan's tousled, permed locks were all the rage for women everywhere. Hairstylists reportedly did very little else for a period of several years, since women seemed to only want the spiral curls, highlights, and layered cut made famous by elite hairstylist Sally Hershberger.

1990s

18. The Rachel: Unless you lived under a rock in the mid-1990s, you knew about the group of *Friends* that hung out on the NBC sitcom for ten seasons. Jennifer Aniston's character Rachel spawned legions of hair clones. This long to medium length style was cut with many different layers in order to frame the face and give a woman's hair a full, healthy look.

19. The Fade: The early nineties brought hip-hop culture to the masses and the high-top fade haircut came with it. Popularized by rap duo Kid 'N Play, the fade was cut like a flattop but with the sides and back gradually fading from thickness at the top all the way to bare skin. Largely sported by African-American males, men of all ethnic backgrounds gave it a try, often with mixed results.

2000s

20. The Faux-Hawk: Want the edgy look of a Mohawk but don't want to go all the way? Welcome the faux-hawk! By slicking back (or close-shaving) the sides of the hair, a fake or "faux" Mohawk can be achieved. Scores of fashionistas, both male and female, have gotten a lot of mileage out of this look in the early 21st century.

21. The Chelsea: With roots in punk rock culture, this haircut refers to the Chelsea district in London, a popular hangout for punks. But in the UK, this radical cut is called "the feather cut." In the style of many of today's haircuts, this look is one worn by both males and females. This style is achieved by shaving the entire head, except for the bangs and a little on the right and left sides of the head.

10 Classic Amusement Park Rides

✳ ✳ ✳ ✳

Roller coasters get all the attention. But what about the tamer rides with shorter lines and more relaxed height restrictions? Read on to learn about the favorites among the lesser-known rides. Some are unique, some have been copied for decades, but all of them are vital to the atmosphere of the midway.

1. Tilt-A-Whirl

In 1926, Herbert Sellner finished his design for the Tilt-A-Whirl and began building one in his backyard. Sellner's ride involved seven cars attached at various fixed pivot points on a rotating plat-form that raised and lowered itself. The cars themselves were free spinning, but when you added the centrifugal force and the platform's gravitational pull on the cars, they would wildly spin in countless directions at variable speeds. Calculated chaos ensued. Since then, Sellner Manufacturing Company has built more than

1,000 Tilt-A-Whirls and inspired hundreds of knockoffs. Those who look a little green or lose their lunch of hot dogs, cotton candy, and soda pop are probably just coming off a Tilt-A-Whirl.

2. Ferris Wheel

Ah, the mighty Ferris wheel—provider of a million romantic moments and breathtaking views. For the World's Columbian Exposition of 1893 in Chicago, engineer George Ferris presented fair organizers with his idea of a giant rotating wheel that would carry passengers in cars attached around the outer edge. He convinced organizers to allow him to build the structure, which would rival France's Eiffel Tower. Indeed, Ferris's wheel, which cost $380,000 and stood 264 feet tall with a wheel diameter of 250 feet, was a huge success. Each car held 60 people, and, at 50 cents a ride, the wheel was one of the most popular attractions at the World's Fair. The Ferris wheel is a must-have for any carnival, and thousands of replications continue to delight passengers of all ages.

3. Insanity

Built in 2005 at the top of the Stratosphere Hotel Tower in Las Vegas, this ride isn't kidding around. The second-highest thrill ride in the world at 906 feet above terra firma (second to its nearby Stratosphere brother, "Big Shot"), the Insanity arm extends 64 feet over the edge of the hotel tower, spinning passengers at top speeds. If that's not insane enough for you, hang on. Soon, the spinning gets even faster, and riders are propelled upwards at a 70-degree angle. Insanity creators claim that "riders will experience the thrill of being flung over the edge of the tower" as they look down for a couple of breathless seconds at a glittering Las Vegas far below.

4. Scrambler

There are many names for this ride and its variations, but Americans usually call it the Scrambler. Whatever name is emblazoned on its side, this ride is fast—really fast. Picture this: the ride has three arms. On the ends of each of those arms are clusters of individual cars, each on a smaller arm of its own. When the Scrambler starts, the main arm and the little arms all rotate. The outermost arms are slowed and the inner arms are accelerated, creating an illusion of frighteningly close collisions between the cars and their passengers. The Scrambler proves that you don't have to go on a roller coaster to lose your lunch or have the wits scared out of you.

5. Bumper Cars

If you've ever wanted to recreate the excitement and thrill of a fender bender, this is your ride! Bumper cars (or "dodgem cars"), which were introduced in the 1920s, feature a large ring or pen with a graphite floor designed to decrease friction. Riders climb into miniature electric cars that draw power from an overhead grid and proceed to slam into the other cars in the pen. Wide rubber bumpers keep things safe—as safe as you can get with no brakes! Still, bumper cars are so popular you'll find them in just about every theme park, county fair, or carnival you visit—just follow the crashing noises and laughter.

6. "It's a Small World"

The theme song to "It's a Small World" is woven into American (and international) pop culture—even if you've never been to a Disney theme park, you probably know the chorus. In 1964, the World's Fair came to New York, and Walt Disney and team created animatronic children of the world that featured anthems from various countries around the globe. In order to streamline the ride, which takes guests on boats through the animated panoramas, composers Robert and Richard Sherman came up with the now famous tune. Many find the "small world" experience to be a little naive and simplistic, but that's what they were going for—people everywhere getting along so well they sing songs and hold hands. All day. For hours. The same song...over and over again.

7. Log Rides

If you were a lumberjack in America in the late 1800s, a "log ride" wasn't something you'd line up to do. Log flumes were handmade channels created by loggers to transport felled trees to the sawmill.

Stories of lumberjacks riding logs down the flume inspired the many versions of the log rides we know today. The first one, called El Aserradero ("the sawmill" in Spanish), was located at Six Flags Over Texas back in 1963. Passengers boarded a hollowed out "log" and rushed down the flume, getting soaked in the process. The ride was so popular that the park added another log ride a few years later. Famous log rides include Disney's Splash Mountain and Perilous Plunge at Knott's Berry Farm in California, the tallest and steepest log ride with a 115-foot drop.

8. The Haunted Mansion

The "Happiest Place on Earth" gets a bit scary with the Haunted Mansion, another juggernaut of an amusement park attraction created by the fine folks at Disney. The ride opened in August 1969 in Disneyland and featured ghosts, murderous brides, blood-spilling families, and a host of other specters designed to scare park-goers silly as they ride through in a "doom buggy." The Haunted Mansion is among the most popular Disney rides in history, and it even inspired a movie—*The Haunted Mansion,* starring Eddie Murphy, was released in 2003.

9. The Rotor

Quick! Get up and twirl around as fast as you can for three straight minutes, then jump as high as you can into the air! Feel that free-falling, vertigo sensation? If not, why not go on a rotor ride? Designed in the 1940s by engineer Ernst Hoffmeister, the Rotor has many versions in theme parks all over the world. The premise is pretty much a simple lesson in centrifugal force: Take a large barrel and revolve the walls of said barrel really fast. When it's going super fast, drop the bottom out of the barrel, and watch as all the people inside stick to the walls. Other names for this simple but popular ride include Gravitron and Vortex.

10. Carousel

The most elegant of all amusement park rides, the carousel dates back to around A.D. 500. Drawings from this time period show riders in baskets circling a post. The carousel, or merry-go-round, remains a carnival staple worldwide. The ride consists of a rotating platform with seats that move up and down. The seats are the really special part, made of wood, fiberglass, or plastic and shaped to look like decorated animals, such as deer, cats, fish, rabbits, giraffes, and, of course, horses. Old carousels and carousel pieces can be worth lots of money these days depending on the level of artistry that went into their manufacture. Fun for young and old alike, even when the Triple-Threat-Xtreme-Screamer roller coaster is phased out, the carousel will still be turning round.

GEE, THAT ROCK 'N' ROLL MUSIC SURE IS SWELL!
5 Fabulous Fads from the 1950s

❊ ❊ ❊ ❊

If you were around in the 1950s, you probably remember the Korean War and McCarthyism. But that's not the fun stuff to visit on Memory Lane. It's much more fun to remember the fads, the crazes, and the pop culture sensations that emerged in an age when moms still made dinner every night and a car with fins could get you a date. The following is a list of some of the most decade-defining fads and trends of the 1950s. Don't get too excited, though—nice boys and girls never do.

1. Poodle Skirts

Undoubtedly, the poodle skirt was one of the most iconic fashion trends of the 1950s. The long, swingy, often pastel-hued skirts had a motif appliquéd below the knee. Some common images were musical notes, flowers, and, of course, poodles. Dancing to the new rock 'n' roll music was popular, but it required dancers to wear clothes that allowed them to move. Since women rarely wore pants at the time, A-line poodle skirts were a nice alternative.

2. Sock Hops

Those 1950s teens were so thoughtful! Informal high school dances were named "sock hops" because students would remove their shoes so as to not scuff the floor while they danced. And they really liked to dance! Elvis made his famous appearance on *The Ed Sullivan Show* in 1956, and youngsters across the country were moving to the beat of the neat, new sound of rock 'n' roll. The always chaperoned sock hops were hugely popular—where else could you show off your hand-jive, bop, stroll, or box step?

3. 3-D Movies

Just as the proliferation of downloadable music sent the record industry scrambling at the turn of this century, the advent of television spooked movie executives. Would anyone go to the movies when they could be entertained at home? In an attempt to offer something unique, studios like Warner Brothers released movies in "3-D." This meant that the movies were projected simultaneously from two different angles in two different colors, red and blue or green, and viewed with special glasses. The colored filters in the funky, paper-framed glasses separated the two different images so each image only entered one eye, creating a three-dimensional effect. Early 1950s titles included *Bwana Devil* and *House of Wax*. In 1953, there were more than 5,000 theaters in the United States equipped to show 3-D movies.

4. The Conical Bra

Though it was invented in 1943, the cantilevered brassiere really came into the spotlight in the 1950s. Jane Russell sported one of the bras in *The Outlaw,* and her lifted and separated bosom caused quite a sensation. The new silhouette was invented by none other than director, eccentric, and ladies' man Howard Hughes, who directed Russell in the movie. The look became popular and heavy-duty brassieres stuck around—at least until women started burning them a decade later.

5. Beatniks

Every generation has a rebellion and the "beats" emerged from the 1950s underground. While good girls and boys were heading to sock hops, these writers, artists, and musicians were pushing cultural expectations and embracing taboo subject matter. Writers Jack Kerouac and Allen Ginsberg were admired by this group of largely New York City-based artists. Today, the beatnik has been reduced to an image of a guy with a goatee wearing sunglasses and a beret and beating bongo drums. That's not exactly what the beats had in mind, but many were intrigued by their acts of "spontaneous creativity" that blended words and music, and they continue to influence poetry and music today.

Origins of 12 Modern Icons

❋ ❋ ❋ ❋

Who knows what makes some images endure while others slip through our consciousness quicker than 50 bucks in the gas tank. In any case, you'll be surprised to learn how some of our most endearing "friends" made their way into our lives.

1. The Aflac Duck

A duck pitching insurance? Art director Eric David stumbled upon the idea to use a web-footed mascot one day when he continuously uttered, "Aflac...Aflac...Aflac." It didn't take him long to realize how much the company's name sounded like a duck's quack. There are many fans of the campaign, but actor Ben Affleck is not one of them. Not surprisingly, he fields many comments that associate his name with the duck and is reportedly none too pleased.

2. Alfred E. Newman, the face of *Mad* magazine

Chances are you're picturing a freckle-faced, jug-eared kid, right? The character's likeness, created by portrait artist Norman Mingo, was first adopted by *Mad* in 1954 as a border on the cover. Two years later, the humor magazine used a full-size version of the image as a write-in candidate for the 1956 presidential election. Since then, several *real* people have been said to be "separated at birth" from Mr. Newman, namely Ted Koppel, Jimmy Carter, and George W. Bush.

3. Betty Crocker

Thousands of letters were sent to General Mills in the 1920s, all asking for answers to baking questions. Managers created a fictional character to give the responses a personal touch. The surname Crocker was chosen to honor a retired executive, and Betty was selected because it seemed "warm and friendly." In 1936, artist Neysa McMein blended the faces of several female employees to create a likeness. Crocker's face has changed many times over the years. She's been made to look younger, more professional, and now has a more multicultural look. At one point, a public opinion poll rating famous women placed Betty second to Eleanor Roosevelt.

4. Duke the Bush's Baked Beans Dog

Who else to trust with a secret recipe than the faithful family pooch? Bush Brothers & Company was founded by A. J. Bush and his two sons in 1908. A few generations later, the company is currently headed by A. J.'s grandson, Condon. In 1995, the advertising agency working for Bush's Baked Beans decided that Jay Bush (Condon's son) and his golden retriever, Duke, were the perfect team to represent the brand. The only problem was that the real Duke is camera shy, so a stunt double was hired to portray him and handle all the gigs on the road with Jay. In any case, both dogs have been sworn to secrecy.

5. The California Raisins

Sometimes advertising concepts can lead to marketing delirium. In 1987, a frustrated copywriter at Foote, Cone & Belding was working on the California Raisin Advisory Board campaign and said, "We have tried everything but dancing raisins singing 'I Heard it Through the Grapevine.'" With vocals by Buddy Miles and design by Michael Brunsfeld, the idea was pitched to the client. The characters plumped up the sales of raisins by 20 percent, and the rest is Claymation history!

6. Joe Camel

Looking for a way to revamp Camel's image from an "old-man's cigarette" in the late 1980s, the R.J. Reynolds marketing team uncovered illustrations of Old Joe in their archives. (He was originally conceived for an ad campaign in France in the 1950s.) In 1991, the new Joe Camel angered children's advocacy groups when a study revealed that more kids under the age of eight recognized Joe than Mickey Mouse or Fred Flintstone.

7. The Coppertone Girl

It was 1959 when an ad for Coppertone first showed a suntanned little girl's white buttocks being exposed by a puppy. "Don't be a paleface!" was the slogan, and it reflected the common belief of the time that a suntan was healthy. Artist Joyce Ballantyne Brand created the pig-tailed little girl in the image of her three-year-old daughter Cheri. When the campaign leapt off the printed page and into the world of television, it became Jodie Foster's acting debut. As the 21st century beckoned, and along with it changing views on sun exposure and nudity, Coppertone revised the drawing to reveal only the girl's lower back.

8. Juan Valdez

This coffee lover and his trusty donkey have been ensuring the quality of coffee beans since 1959. Back then, the National Federation of Coffee Growers of Columbia wanted to put a face on the thousands of coffee growers in the industry. The Doyle Dane Bernback ad agency found one alright! By 1981, Valdez's image was so well known that it was incorporated into the Federation's logo. Originally played by Jose Duval, the role was taken over by Carlos Sanchez from 1969 to 2006. In his spare time, Sanchez manages his very own small coffee farm in Columbia.

9. The Gerber Baby

Contrary to some popular beliefs, it's not Humphrey Bogart, Elizabeth Taylor, or Bob Dole who so sweetly looks up from the label of Gerber products. In fact, the face that appears on all Gerber baby packaging belongs to mystery novelist Ann Turner Cook. In 1928, when Gerber began their search for a baby face to help promote their new brand of baby food, Dorothy Hope Smith submitted a simple charcoal sketch of the tot—promising to complete it if chosen. As it turned out, that wasn't necessary because the powers that be at Gerber liked it just the way it was. In 1996, Gerber updated its look, but the new label design still incorporates Cook's baby face.

10. Mr. Whipple

The expression "Do as I say, not as I do" took on a persona in the mid-1960s—Mr. Whipple, to be specific. This fussy supermarket manager (played by actor Dick Wilson) was famous for admonishing his shoppers by saying, "Ladies, *please* don't squeeze the Charmin!" The people at Benton & Bowles Advertising figured that if, on camera, Mr. Whipple was a habitual offender of his own rule, Charmin toilet paper would be considered the cushiest on the market. The campaign included a total of 504 ads and ran from 1965 until 1989, landing it a coveted spot in the *Guinness Book of World Records*. A 1979 poll listed Mr. Whipple as the third most recognized American behind Richard Nixon and Billy Graham.

11. The Pillsbury Doughboy

Who can resist poking the chubby belly of this giggling icon? This cheery little kitchen dweller was "born" in 1965 when the Leo Burnett advertising agency dreamt him up to help Pillsbury sell its refrigerated dinner rolls. The original vision was for an animated character, but, instead, agency producers borrowed a unique stop-action technique used on *The Dinah Shore Show.* After beating out more than 50 other actors, Paul Frees lent his voice to the Doughboy. So, if you ever craved Pillsbury rolls while watching *The Adventures of Bullwinkle and Rocky*, it's no wonder... Frees was also the voice for Boris Badenov and Dudley Do-Right.

12. Ronald McDonald

Perhaps the most recognizable advertising icon in the world, this beloved clown made his television debut in 1963, played by future *Today* weatherman Willard Scott. Nicknamed the "hamburger-happy clown," Ronald's look was a bit different back then: He had

He had curly blond hair, a fast-food tray for a hat, a magic belt, and a paper cup for a nose. Ronald's makeover must have been a hit because today McDonald's serves more than 52 million customers a day around the globe.

8 Groovy Fads of the 1960s

✳ ✳ ✳ ✳

With so many straight-laced teens in the 1950s,
it was only natural that there would be a backlash.
Welcome to the 1960s! Free love, flower power, hippies,
psychedelic drugs, and political mayhem—these were the
trends of a decade that saw upheaval of social mores and
cultural behaviors. As The Beatles rocked and Bob Dylan
rolled, the world saw changes in the political climate (Vietnam
War protests, the sexual revolution, civil rights), the fashion
world ("It's called a 'mini-skirt,' Mom"), and even in the realm
of food (the mighty processed cheese slice). Read on to learn
about some of the most iconic fads of the decade
that just wanted everyone to get along.

1. Hippies

U.S. troops were sent to Vietnam in 1954 and, by the 1960s, thousands of soldiers had died fighting a war that was growing more and more unpopular by the day. The cry "Make Love, Not War" was a mantra among the hippies—the antiestablishment, counterculture of America. Hippies were easily spotted: both men and women grew their hair long, wore ethnic-inspired clothes accessorized with puka shells, dabbled in Eastern religions, used words like *groovy*, and referred to "the Man" when talking about the flawed government. They were known to experiment with mind-altering drugs (marijuana, mushrooms, LSD) and hang out in places such as Greenwich Village in New York City and the Haight-Ashbury section of San Francisco. The hippie movement sparked music, art, and cultural dialogue that continues well into the 21st century.

2. Go-go Boots and Minidresses

The postwar baby boom had produced 70 million teenagers by the time the 1960s came along. All of those hormones dictated some changes in the world of fashion. Long gone was the poodle skirt. Skirts in the '60s got shorter—much, much shorter. Skirts and minidresses often came up four to five inches above the knee in the United States and an eye-popping seven to eight inches above the knee in the UK. While skirts got shorter, boots got taller. The most popular boot was the go-go boot, which was often white patent leather and went almost to the knee. Singer Nancy Sinatra and TV's *The Avengers* helped popularize the look.

3. Fallout Shelters

With the Cold War in full force, the Cuban Missile Crisis exposed, and the constant threat of nuclear attack, many people in the early 1960s decided that building a fallout shelter wasn't such a paranoid notion. Kits began at around $100 (flashlight, shortwave radio, can opener), but a family could spend thousands on special basements equipped with board games, gas masks, and escape hatches.

4. Surfing

What better place than a sunny beach to spread peace, goodwill, and free love? Polynesians had been surfing for centuries, but when lightweight surfboards became affordable in the late 1950s, every-one could grab a board and hang ten. By the early 1960s, the fad had really caught a wave, and movies like *Beach Party* and *Beach Blanket Bingo* helped popularize surfing and beach culture.

5. Peace Symbol

Thanks to British graphic designer Gerald Holtom, no hippie had to go without a peace symbol talisman. Holtom, who was hired to create an image for the Campaign for Nuclear Disarmament, claimed his inspiration for the symbol came from the shape of the letters *N* and *D* in the semaphore alphabet. The icon was adopted by the hippies and remains as popular today as it was when protests and antiwar marches were daily events.

6. The Twist

This dance craze of the early 1960s came as the result of Chubby Checker's number one song of the same name. The Twist was the first modern dance style that did not require a partner, and couples did not have to touch each other while dancing. Checker said, "It's like putting out a cigarette with both feet, [or] coming out of a shower and wiping your bottom with a towel to the beat of the music." It seemed like everyone was jumping on the bandwagon with a Twist record. Checker also recorded "Let's Twist Again," and Joey Dee and The Starliters reached number one with "The Peppermint Twist," while Sam Cooke was "Twistin' the Night Away."

7. Tie-Dye

The ancient fabric dyeing method of *shibori* began in Japan centuries ago, but it became a fashion trend symbolic of the 1960s. By wrapping fabric around sticks or gathering and securing it with rubber bands, then submerging it in a bucket of dye, a funky, almost hallucinogenic pattern emerges when the sticks or rubber bands are removed. This homemade method became popular with hippies, providing living color to the ethnic look that so many embraced during the era of free love and liberation. Tie-dyed clothing is still pretty much the standard uniform for peaceniks today.

8. Lava Lamp

Invented by Edward Craven Walker, this novelty lighting instrument featured a glass bottle full of wax and oil with a coil in the metal base. When the lamp was turned on, the coil would heat up and globs of wax would bubble around in the oil, producing a "lava" effect. Some claimed the lava lamp was meant to simulate the hallucinogenic visuals from the drugs that were becoming so popular.

❋ ❋ ❋

"Turn on, tune in, drop out."

—Timothy Leary

23 Must-Have Toys from 1950 and Beyond

✳ ✳ ✳ ✳

Times have changed since the days when an imaginative kid was happy to play with an empty cardboard box. Today, about 2.6 billion toys are sold every year, creating a $20.3 billion industry. It seems that every decade manufacturers create a toy that launches a buying craze. Some just flash past on their way to a rummage sale table; others are timeless treasures. So without further ado, here are some of the best toy fads of the 20th century.

1950s

1. Silly Putty was developed in 1943 when James Wright, a General Electric researcher, was seeking a synthetic rubber substitute. His silicone-based polymer was elastic, could bounce, be easily molded, and always held its shape. Parents liked the fact that the putty was nontoxic and nonirritating. Since its debut as a toy in 1950, more than 300 million eggs of Silly Putty have been sold.

2. In 1943, naval engineer Richard James stumbled across an invention that would become a beloved toy worldwide. Made of 87 feet of flat wire coiled into a three-inch-diameter circle, the Slinky could  "walk" down stairs when one end was placed on one step and the other on the step below. The classic slinky really took off in the 1950s, and today more than 300 million of the simple-yet-clever toys have sold worldwide.

3. Mr. Potato Head, with his interchangeable facial features, was patented in 1952 and was the first toy to be advertised on television. But for the first eight years, parents had to supply children with a real potato until a plastic potato body was included in 1960.

4. Intending to create a wallpaper cleaner, Joseph and Noah McVicker invented Play-Doh in 1955. Initially available in only one color (off-

white) and in a 1.5-pound can, Play-Doh now comes in a rainbow of colors. The recipe remains a secret, but more than 700 million pounds of this nontoxic goop have sold since its introduction.

5. The concept of the hula hoop had been around for centuries. Then, in the late 1950s, Wham-O, a maverick California toy company, rolled out a plastic hoop for swivel-hipped kids. The concept caught on and 25 million sold in the first six months. They cost $1.98 each, and, by 1958, 100 million of them had been sold around the world—except in Japan and the Soviet Union where they were said to represent the "emptiness of American culture." Ouch.

6. Barbie vamped onto the toy scene in 1959, the creation of Ruth Handler and her husband Elliot, who along with Harold Matson founded the Mattel toy company. Handler noticed that her daughter Barbara (Barbie) and her friends played with an adult female doll from Switzerland more than their baby dolls. So, Handler came up with her "Barbie" concept, and the rest is toy history.

7. Chatty Cathy, also released by the Mattel Corporation in 1959, was the era's second most popular doll. Yakking her way onto store shelves, Cathy could speak 11 phrases when a string in her back was pulled. "I love you" or "Please take me with you" could be disconcerting at first, but Chatty Cathy was a '50s classic.

8. Betsy Wetsy also made a splash with 1950s-era children. Created by the Ideal Toy Company, Betsy's already-open mouth would accept a liquid-filled bottle. The premise was simple and straightforward: Whatever goes in quickly comes out the other end, helping youngsters gain valuable diaper-changing experience.

1960s

9. Since 1963, when they were first introduced, more than 16 million Easy Bake Ovens have been sold. A lightbulb provided the heat source for baking mini-cakes in America's first working toy oven. The original color was a trendy turquoise, and the stoves also

sported a carrying handle and fake range top. As children, several celebrity chefs, including Bobby Flay, owned an Easy Bake Oven, which perhaps provided inspiration for their future careers.

10. Toy lovers have to salute manufacturer Hasbro for its G.I. Joe action figure, which first marched out in 1964. The 11½-inch-tall doll for boys had 21 moving parts and was the world's first action figure. Hasbro's 40th Anniversary G.I. Joe collection in 2004 included a re-creation of the original doll, his clothes, accessories, and even the packaging. Nostalgic Joe pals snapped up thousands of these new recruits.

11. Hot Wheels screeched into the toy world in 1968, screaming out of Mattel's concept garage with 16 miniature autos. The glamorous Python, Custom Cougar, and Hot Heap immediately attracted attention and plenty of buyers. Track sets were also released in the same year so that children could simulate a real auto race. Today, more than 15 million people collect Hot Wheels cars.

1970s

12. "Weebles wobble but they don't fall down...." This was the unforgettable advertising slogan for these egg-shaped playthings first released by Hasbro in 1971. Each weeble had a sticker mounted on its short, fat "body" so it resembled a human or an animal. At the height of their popularity, the Weeble family had its own tree house and cottage, and a host of other characters and accessories were also produced, including a firefighter and fire truck, a playground, and a circus complete with a ringmaster, clown, and trapeze artist.

13. Also extremely popular in the '70s, the Big Wheel was the chosen mode of transportation for most young boys, and many girls, too. With its 16-inch front wheel and fat rear tires, this low-riding, spiffed up tricycle was even a hit with parents, who considered it safer than a standard trike.

1980s

14. Strawberry Shortcake was the sweetest-smelling doll of the 1980s. Created in 1977 by Muriel Fahrion for American Greetings, the company expanded the toy line in the 1980s to include Strawberry's friends and their pets. Each doll had a fruit- or dessert-scented theme complete with scented hair. Accessories, clothes, bedding, stickers, movies, and games followed, but by 1985 the fad had waned. The characters were revived in the 2000s with DVDs, video games, an animated TV series, and even a full-length animated film.

15. Xavier Roberts was a teenager when he launched his Babyland General Hospital during the 1970s in Cleveland, Georgia, allowing children to adopt a "baby." In 1983, the Coleco toy company started mass-producing these dolls as Cabbage Patch Kids. Each "kid" came with a unique name and a set of adoption papers, and stores couldn't keep them on the shelves, selling more than three million of the dolls in the first year.

16. Teenage Mutant Ninja Turtles were created by Kevin Eastman and Peter Laird, who had both studied art history. As such, they named their characters Leonardo, Raphael, Donatello, and Michelangelo. In 1984, with a mere $1,200, the Turtle creators launched the swashbuckling terrapins in a black-and-white comic book. More comics, as well as an animated television series, clothing, toys, and several full-length feature films followed, proving that the Green Team could earn some green, as well.

17. One of the biggest toy crazes of the 1980s was the brain-teasing Rubik's Cube. Created by Hungarian architect Erno Rubik, this perplexing puzzle was first introduced in 1977, and from 1980 to 1982 more than 100 million of the cubes sold. It sparked a trend and similar puzzles were created in various shapes, such as a pyramid and a sphere. The Rubik's Cube has seen a recent resurgence in popularity and retains a place of honor on many desktops.

1990s

18. From 1996 until around 1999, you couldn't escape the Beanie Baby. Like Cabbage Patch Kids and troll dolls of decades past, Ty Warner's Beanie Babies became a nationwide toy-collecting craze. The little plush-bodied, bean-filled animals came in dozens of different styles and colors and had special tags that included a poetic description of the character and its name. To feed the frenzy, Ty limited the release of certain Beanies and therefore sent the price of characters such as the "Blue Elephant" into the thousands. The fad died out before the millennium, but Beanie Babies still grace cubicles around the world.

19. Based on a Japanese toy called "Poketto Monstaa," Pokémon were tiny "pocket monsters" that battled each other when ordered by their "trainer." In 1996, Nintendo adapted the Japanese characters to promote its portable video game system, Game Boy. Pokémon trading cards and a television series were also wildly popular.

20. Undoubtedly the must-have toy of 1996, the immensely popular Tickle Me Elmo doll was based on the furry, red *Sesame Street* character. He'd giggle, saying, "Oh boy, that tickles," when he was tickled or squeezed. Manufacturer Tyco sold more than a million of the creatures that year, and when stores ran out of the dolls, some parents resorted to online auctions to secure one for their child.

21. Another plush gizmo, animatronic Furbies spoke their own "language" and became wildly successful in late 1998. Although they retailed for $30, they often fetched $100 or more online from desperate parents. More than 27 million Furbies sold in the first year, and a new, revamped Furby was introduced in 2005 with new features, including advanced voice recognition, so Furby can respond to questions based on its "mood."

2000s

22. The big fad toy of 2000 was the scooter, with approximately five million sold that year. These foot-propelled devices, a spin-off of the 1950s models, were made of lightweight aluminum and used tiny, low friction wheels similar to those on in-line skates. Weighing about ten pounds, they could be folded up and easily stored. Yet the scooters were relatively dangerous until operators became skilled at riding them. From January through October 2000, more than 27,000 people (mostly young males under the age of 15) were treated for scooter-related injuries.

23. Popular with kids of the new millennium (and adults, too), Heelys are a brand of sneakers with one or more wheels embedded in the soles. Somewhat similar to in-line skates, Heelys enable the wearer to roll from place to place, rather than mundanely walking. As of March 2006, manufacturer Heelys, Inc. has sold more than two million of these specialty sneaks, which are available in a wide variety of styles and colors for the whole family. And for added convenience and safety, they also sell helmets!

10 Notable Beauty Pageant Moments

✳ ✳ ✳ ✳

In 1921, Atlantic City businessmen created a two-day beauty contest to keep tourists in town past Labor Day. This wasn't the first beauty pageant the world had seen, but it was the one that spawned the Miss America contest. Hundreds of beauty contests have followed, but it hasn't been all roses and tiaras. Here are a few highlights (and lowlights) in the history of beauty pageants.

1. Sideshow/Freak Show

The first American beauty pageant was staged in 1854 by circus magnate P. T. Barnum. But even before women's suffrage changed the role of women in modern society, no one was terribly excited about their wives and sisters being part of a circus sideshow, and the competition didn't last long.

2. You're Never Too Young for Drama

Marian Bergeron won the Miss America crown in 1932. Trouble was, she was only 15 years old at the time. Pageant officials were duly upset, but another scandal kept them from setting things straight: Before they could reclaim the crown, someone stole it from Bergeron's dressing room.

3. Like Beauty Queens to the Slaughter

In 1935, beauty pageants needed a little boost. Enter Lenora Slaughter, a woman who would forever shape the world's concept of the beauty pageant. Slaughter was a savvy businesswoman who pandered to the nation's Hollywood fever, offering screen tests to Miss America winners—Dorothy Lamour was "discovered" this way. Slaughter was also the brain behind adding the talent competition in 1938 and offering college scholarships to winners beginning in 1945. She ruled the pageant for more than 30 years.

4. Mazel Tov, Miss America!

In 1945, America crowned its first Jewish Miss America when New York's Bess Myerson won the title, even after being told that unless she changed her name to something "less Jewish," she would never win the competition. Myerson refused and won anyway, though her reign was not without controversy. Catalina swimsuits, the Miss America swimsuit supplier, did not ask Myerson to be a spokeswoman for their product, even though every queen before her had inked a deal. Myerson wasn't fazed and went on to serve in politics and won numerous awards for her philanthropic work.

5. Miss Black America Fights Back

Not until 1983 did an African-American woman win the Miss America crown. However, African-Americans didn't wait around to be recognized in the beauty pageant circuit; instead, they organized the first Miss Black America contest in 1968. The pageant started as a local contest in Philadelphia but went national a year later. In the 1969 contest, The Jackson 5 made their first television appearance, and an ambitious young woman named Oprah Winfrey competed as Miss Black Tennessee in 1971.

6. So Long, Bert

The opening line of the Miss America theme song—"There she is, Miss America"—sparked thousands of girlhood dreams. The man who sang it was Bert Parks, host of the pageant from 1954 to 1980. Pageant producers thought a host change would boost ratings, but many Parks loyalists emerged, including Johnny Carson, who launched a letter-writing campaign to reinstate Parks. Despite their efforts, the "Bring Back Bert" campaign failed and Parks was replaced by various hosts over the years, including Regis Philbin and Kathie Lee Gifford in the early 1990s.

7. Say It Ain't So, Vanessa

Statuesque and articulate with a voice like an angel, Vanessa Williams was the darling of the 1983 competition and won the crown with ease, becoming the first black Miss America. But by July 1984, controversy had erupted. *Penthouse* magazine planned to publish nude photos of the beloved beauty queen without her consent, so she resigned. Williams was then replaced by runner-up Suzette Charles, also an African-American. The scandal didn't faze Williams for long; she went on to record several R&B albums and had a number one song in 1992 with "Save the Best for Last."

8. Heather Makes History

Although a childhood illness left Heather Whitestone profoundly deaf, the strikingly pretty girl excelled in a school for the hearing impaired and began competing in local beauty pageants during college. In 1994, she danced a ballet routine to music she couldn't hear and aced the interview with Regis Philbin by reading his lips. Whitestone was crowned the first Miss America with a disability.

9. Platforms: Not Just Shoes Anymore

In 1989, the Miss America organization officially required each contestant to choose a cause or charity to support. The idea was to not only give airtime to myriad issues affecting the nation, but to also have Miss America use her stature to "address community service organizations, business and civic leaders, the media and others about [her] platform issues." Since then, the role of Miss America has been strictly philanthropic. The beauty queen travels, speaking to community leaders, politicians, and school organizations about her cause, which might be STD prevention, homelessness, domestic violence, voter registration, or literacy.

10. Mike Tyson: Miss Black America Special Guest/Defendant

Heavyweight boxing champ Mike Tyson was asked to be a special guest at the Miss Black America pageant in 1991. As it turned out, this was not the best move on the part of pageant producers. Contestant Desiree Washington claimed that Tyson had raped her in the days before the contest, and numerous other contestants came forth to say that they too were groped and harassed by Tyson. The boxing star was convicted and sentenced to six years in prison.

8 Funky Fads of the 1970s

✵ ✵ ✵ ✵

In the wake of the political upheaval and social reform of the 1960s, the 1970s may seem fairly frivolous. Sure, there were discos, polyester suits, and gold chains, but there was much cultural and political change happening as well. The second wave of feminism, the end of the Vietnam War, Roe v. Wade—many ideas that are de rigueur today were introduced in the 1970s. Read on to learn about the crazes that made this decade so far-out.

1. Disco

In the 1970s, disco arrived armed with keyboards, drum machines, sugary lyrics, and extended dance breaks. Artists such as the Bee-Gees, ABBA, and Donna Summer crooned their way into the hearts of people in America, Europe, and beyond. Bell-bottom pants, feathered hair, and big sunglasses were all disco accessories. Most people knew the lyrics to "Stayin' Alive" whether they liked it or not, thanks to disco movies like *Saturday Night Fever.* Disco music, disco dancing, and disco culture usually get a bad rap for being frivolous and over the top, but today's pop, techno, and club music all have their roots in disco.

2. Afros

The Black Power movement of the late '60s and early '70s claimed the mantra "Black is Beautiful," and the Afro was one way to show solidarity among black people. Rather than continue to straighten their hair, African-Americans let their textured, kinky manes grow unhindered. The effect was a kind of halo or ball shape around the head resembling a dandelion puff and sometimes growing disproportionately large. Anyone with curly hair could achieve this style, made popular by '70s stars such as Angela Davis and the Jackson 5, but it was generally reserved for the "Black is Beautiful" set.

3. Roller Skates

Way back in the 18th century, people were hip to the idea of attaching wheels to their feet to get around faster. But not until the 1970s did roller-skating become enmeshed in American culture. As mate-rials and technology advanced, wheels and skates became slicker and faster, and roller-skating became more fun. By the mid-1970s, thousands of roller rinks had opened across the United States. Most rinks combined disco with skating, so patrons could skate under the mirror ball and groove to the music of K. C. and The Sunshine Band while they strutted their stuff.

4. Pet Rock

California entrepreneur Gary Dahl was joking around with friends one night in 1975 about the perfect pet. It wouldn't eat, make noise, or need to be potty trained. Dahl joked that a rock would fit the bill. Everyone laughed, but within two weeks, he had written *The Pet Rock Training Manual* and marketed the idea at a trade show. A story in *Newsweek* and an appearance on *The Tonight Show* followed, and, within a few months, a million pet rocks had sold for $3.95 a piece. Dahl made a dollar for each rock sold, making him an instant millionaire.

5. Leisure Suits

If you were a with-it kind of guy in the '70s, you had at least one leisure suit. Made popular via television shows such as *Charlie's Angels* and movies like *Saturday Night Fever* (yes, that one again), suits made of polyester were marked by flamboyant colors, wide pockets on the legs, and winged collars. Bands like the Bay City Rollers used satiny fabric in their suits, too, a trend that trickled down into the mainstream—for better or worse.

6. Mood Rings

Who knew a thermochromic liquid crystal could foretell the mood of humans? Joshua Reynolds didn't really believe it could, but he did figure that he could sell the idea to the general public as a novelty. That's exactly what he did in 1975 with the mood ring, which was invented in the late 1960s by Marvin Wernick. Heat from the wearer's hand would cause crystals in the ring to warm up, making the face of the ring change from black to green to blue to purple. Reynolds sold more than a million dollars worth of mood rings within three months of their debut, and everyone checked in with their mood rings with nearly religious fervor.

7. CB Radio

Before chat rooms, there were CB radios. Citizens' Band radios were (and still are) largely used by truckers on the road to communicate with other drivers in their range. However, in the 1970s and into the early 1980s, people across the United States, the UK, and Australia took back the meaning of "citizens' radio" and began to use the low-frequency radio waves to chat with other CB users. They had their own special slang terms and nicknames, and First Lady Betty Ford even got into the action. She was known by the CB handle "First Mama" when she crackled over the airwaves. That's a big 10–4... over and out.

8. Punk Rock

Not everyone in the '70s was feeling the love. Across the pond, disillusioned youth in the UK were forgoing the Hustle for the fast, hard, raw power of what they called "punk." Bands such as the

Sex Pistols, The Ramones, and The Clash showcased their anger, frustration, and disregard for authority in songs such as "God Save the Queen," "I Wanna Be Sedated," and "London Calling." Just as disco laid the groundwork for later dance genres like techno and house, grunge and heavy metal are rooted in the riotous sounds of punk rock.

ARE THOSE PANTS MADE OUT OF A PARACHUTE?
8 Awesome Fads of the 1980s

❊ ❊ ❊ ❊

In the 1980s, the hair was big, the clothes were big (nice shoulder pads), the music was big, and the political climate was grandiose, too (Reaganomics, Star Wars). With the introduction of the cellular phone and cable television, this decade triggered much of the tech boom that would really get cooking in subsequent decades. With the ever-increasing range and scope of the media, music- and electronics-based fads got bigger and faster in the '80s. Here are a few fads that took the country by storm and helped define the generation that just wanted its MTV.

1. "Valspeak"

Did you, like, realize that in the '80s, like, everyone totally got pulled into this thing called Valspeak? Seriously! The old way of talking with, like, specificity and declarative statements was, like, super lame-o! Like, whatever! So, like, the San Fernando Valley in California was, like, the place where it started. But soon it was a nationwide, like, trend. Can you even stand it? And it's totally still, like, a thing? You know, like, a totally awesome way of speaking. And, like, you thought Valley Girls were a passing fad. Whatever!

2. The Walkman

Though the technology looks ancient to us today, we wouldn't have the beloved iPod if it wasn't for the Walkman. In 1979, Sony introduced their first portable music player in Japan. By 1980, America had jumped on the bandwagon, and there were dozens of portable cassette players on the market. They were heavy, didn't deliver great sound quality, and initially cost upwards of $150, but it didn't matter—they were delivering tunes to the masses, one tape at a time.

3. Atari

The name of the gaming system that started them all loosely translates from Japanese to mean "prepare to be attacked." Thus, it's fitting that the first video games were simple UFO shooting games or games such as Frogger, which required players to move a frog across a busy road without getting squished. Atari, Inc., was formed in 1972, and five years later one of the most successful gaming consoles of all time—the Atari 2600—was released. Millions of consumers bought the devices and spent hours (and days) glued to the TV set, playing Q*Bert, Pac-Man, and Space Invaders. The Atari company consolidated a few years ago but still has a hand in shaping today's much more advanced gaming world.

4. Break Dancing

When DJ Kool Herc took the dance break sections off vinyl records and remixed them into one another to create a longer, funkier song, break dancing was born. These extended breaks gave NYC street dancers all the time in the world to showcase their gravity-defying moves, including the pop and lock, the windmill, the freeze, the moonwalk, the worm, and the closing "suicide." It's believed that the first break-dancing trend occurred among rival gang members who used the dance style to settle disputes. As the media attention grew for this competitive, visually exhilarating dance style, so did its popularity. The fashion, the music, and the dance moves themselves became hallmarks of '80s youth culture.

5. Parachute Pants

If you're thinking about break dancing, you'd be wise to consider your outfit—not only do you need to look "fresh" and "fly," you need to be able to slide, slip, and spin on a dance floor and regular pants just won't do. Baggy in the thigh and narrow at the ankle, parachute pants increased mobility for dancers who needed more flexible clothing. The pants were often made of synthetic materials (you can backspin way better in a poly-blend than you can in cotton) and usually came in bright colors. As break dancing became cooler, the clothes of these street dancers became the "in" fashion trend and even kids in the suburbs were donning parachute pants.

6. Swatch Watches

In 1983, the Swatch Group, Ltd., of Switzerland had an idea. They thought that watches could be less of a financial investment for the stuffy and time-conscious and more of a disposable, funky accessory. Their idea was a big hit. Swatch watches came in hundreds of different colors and styles, and some were even scented! Many people chose to wear several styles at once, loading up two, three, even six Swatches on their wrists at the same time. If you wanted to know what time it was in the 1980s, you probably got your information from a Swatch watch. Swatch Group is still the largest watch company in the world, although it is hard to find someone using a Swatch as a ponytail holder these days.

7. Hair Bands

The heavy-metal music of the 1980s was typified by a heavy, guitar-and-drums-centered sound with highly amplified distortion, fairly raunchy lyrics (for the time), and plenty of dramatic builds. The heavy-metal lifestyle was typified by beer, girls, leather, and really big hair. As the music got louder and bolder from groups like Warrant, Mötley Crüe, and Poison, the hair got bigger and fluffier—and we're not just talking about the girls. These "hair bands" were so named because of the impossible-to-ignore hair swung around by the guitar-playing men onstage.

8. Preppies

While some kids were break-dancing, and others were coiffing their hair sky-high with hair spray and mousse, preppies were busy wearing chinos and loafers, talking about sailboat races, and working with their financial advisors. *Preppie* was a word used to describe the clean-cut teens, twenty- and thirtysomethings of the '80s who could usually be spotted wearing pink and playing tennis. With the release of the tongue-in-cheek (but frighteningly accurate) *Official Preppy Handbook* in 1980, it was easy to spot a preppie—or a preppie wannabe—anywhere.

THERE SHE IS, MISS...*WHAT*?
6 Unusual Beauty Pageants

✳ ✳ ✳ ✳

Beauty may only be skin deep, but beauty pageants go a lot deeper, right to the heart of what makes us Americans. We don't just love the Miss America pageant, we love everything leading up to it, from Miss Ohio all the way down to Miss Drumsticks. Check out some of America's more unusual beauty pageants.

1. Miss Drumsticks

Every October, Yellville, Arkansas, gets ready for Thanksgiving with two days worth of turkey-related fun and games, culminating with the selection of Miss Drumsticks. Contestants are judged on their legs only, with their faces and bodies hidden behind a picture of a turkey, so as not to influence the judges. The prize is nothing to shake a tail feather at—past winners have received trips to Los Angeles to compete on game shows and to New York for appearances on the *Late Show with David Letterman.*

2. Miss Klingon Empire

Beam me down, Scotty, there's a Miss Klingon Empire beauty pageant held every year in September at the Star Trek Convention at Dragon*Con in Atlanta. Contestants assume the persona of a female Klingon character from any *Star Trek* TV series or movie. The Klingon babes are judged on beauty, personality, and talent, which includes singing and dancing but no planetary destruction allowed. Winners receive a trophy, a tiara, and a satin sash outlined in blue and green—the official colors of the Klingon Empire.

3. Mr. or Ms. Mosquito Legs

To become Miss America, contestants need good-looking legs, but to win the title of Mr. or Ms. Mosquito Legs, guys and gals need skinny legs. Clute, Texas, hosts the pageant as part of the Great Texas Mosquito Festival, held each July. Anyone attending the festival is eligible to strut their skinny legs in short shorts for the honor of being named Mr. or Ms. Mosquito Legs.

4. Miss Sweet Corn Queen

It's tough buttering up judges who are buttering their sweet corn, but that's the task of competitors in the Miss Sweet Corn Queen pageant held each August in Mendota, Illinois. Local high-school girls compete for the coveted title and a place of honor in the parade held at one of the largest harvest festivals in the Midwest.

5. Miss Exotic World

True practitioners of the dance form known as the striptease flock to the Exotic World Burlesque Museum and Striptease Hall of Fame in Las Vegas every Memorial Day weekend for the annual Miss Exotic World Pageant. Ranging in age from 18 to 80, these burlesque beauties flirt with the judges with smiles, winks, and teases. The winner of the Miss Exotic World pageant gets a trophy and the right to be called the Miss America of Burlesque.

6. The Armpit Queen

In Battle Mountain, Nevada, nobody raises a stink about the Armpit Beauty Pageant. After humorist Gene Weingarten of *The Washington Post* dubbed Battle Mountain "the armpit of America" for its "lack of character and charm," the small town's residents turned the joke into an annual celebration of all things smelly every August. Sweaty T-shirt contests, deodorant throws, and a "quick-draw" antiperspirant contest lead up to the selection of the Armpit Queen. The pageant and festival are sponsored by Old Spice deodorant and draw an estimated 3,500 visitors with signs along the highway proclaiming: "Make Battle Mountain Your Next Pit Stop."

7 Fantastic Fads of the 1990s

✳ ✳ ✳ ✳

*In the 1990s, the World Wide Web was born, grunge reigned over
the music scene, and O. J. took off in his Bronco. For many,
the 1990s were a golden era. The tech boom made many people
rich, the fashion scene was much less ridiculous, and hip-hop
hit the mainstream. Despite the slacker attitude, the last decade
of the 20th century had its fair share of fads, too.
Here are a few that stand out.*

1. Grunge

After the glitz and glamour of disco and the excess and pomp of
hair bands, it was inevitable that the music pendulum would swing.
That shift created grunge—a genre of music categorized by disso-
nant harmony, lots of guitars, and cynical lyrics. Grunge was initially
delivered by young men and women from the Pacific Northwest
who dressed in flannel shirts and ripped jeans. Groups like Nirvana
and Pearl Jam were the first to emerge on the scene around 1991,
but when the indie scene exploded into the mainstream, groups like
Soundgarden, Alice in Chains, and Stone Temple Pilots became
household names.

2. Hypercolor T-shirts

Clothing manufacturer Generra created these fad-ready T-shirts in
the late '80s, but they really caught on in the '90s. The shirts were
dipped in temperature-sensitive pigment, which meant that when
heat was applied to the fabric, the color would change. Shirts would
turn vague shades of blue, yellow, pink, and gray depending on the
level of heat they received, working much like the body-heat acti-
vated fad of a previous decade—the mood ring.

3. The Macarena

"Macarena," a catchy tune from Spanish group Los del Rio, became
a worldwide phenomenon in 1996, smashing records by staying
at number one on *Billboard*'s Hot 100 chart for an astonishing

14 weeks. The jovial, bouncy tune (that repeats itself over and over and over again) had its own dance, making it two fads in one. The group remains popular in their home country, but once the Macarena had played itself out a year later, the song and the two men behind it were only a distant memory in America.

4. The Waif Look

While they weren't exactly "full-figured," 1980s supermodels like Cindy Crawford were zaftig compared to the half-starved, heroin-chic look embodied by models like Kate Moss, who weighed in at barely 100 pounds. The super-skinny look was a worldwide trend in fashion and came with some serious backlash. Girls everywhere were literally starving to look like the women in the fashion magazines. The waif look garnered much criticism and controversy, but it only fueled the fire. Not until the 2000s did the pendulum begin to swing to the "real women are beautiful" direction—in the 1990s, thin was definitely "in."

5. Tattoos and Piercing

Human beings have many pierceable body parts: ears, noses, lips, tongues, eyebrows, and bellybuttons, just to name a few. In the last decade of the 20th century, no cartilage was safe from the needle of a piercing gun. If you had your fill of metal rings and studs, you could move on to some ink and round out your counterculture look. Both tattooing and piercing were all the rage in the 1990s and many people today have the tats and scars to prove it.

6. Hip-Hop Fashion

When hip-hop music became more mainstream in the early '90s, its fashion style became a trend as well. Rappers such as The Fresh Prince, Kid 'N Play, and Left Eye of TLC sparked a trend in wearing brightly colored, baggy clothing and baseball caps. Often the jeans were so baggy that they hung down several inches below the waist, making the question, "Boxers or briefs?" irrelevant. An offshoot of the hip-hop fashion was the fad of wearing clothes backwards, which was popularized by teen rappers Kris Kross.

7. Tags

As hip-hop music gained major ground in the '90s, the luxury life-style of rap artists and hit makers was emulated by the masses. Rather than assume that everyone knew how much you spent on your hat, jeans, or shoes, teens took a more obvious route—they just left the price tag on the clothes.

FOR THRILLS 'N' CHILLS

12 of the World's Greatest Roller Coasters

❈ ❈ ❈ ❈

On Coney Island—a spit of Brooklyn beachfront—the first American roller coasters were created in the late 1880s. One of the pioneer coasters, the Flip-Flap Railway, had the unfortunate problem of snapping riders' necks due to the extreme g-forces experienced when accelerating through its circular loop. Engineering innovations and steel construction have made coasters safer, and now the sky's the limit. Here are some of today's biggest thrillers.

1. The Matterhorn Bobsleds

While not necessarily the tallest, fastest, or scariest ride in the world, the Matter-horn deserves a nod as the grandfather of modern coasters. Still thrilling riders at Disneyland, this ride was the world's first major steel coaster when it opened in 1959. Inspired by the Matterhorn, a 14,692-foot mountain in the Swiss Alps, the structure is made up of two linking steel roller coasters with loops and corkscrews. Top speed is 18 miles per hour.

2. Kingda Ka

Kingda Ka, at Six Flags Great Adventure in Jackson, New Jersey, is the ultimate ride on several fronts. As of 2007, it was the tallest and fastest roller coaster on the planet. Reaching 128 miles per hour in 3.5 seconds, the train rockets straight up to the 456-foot apex.

Crossing over the pinnacle, the train plummets straight down into a vertical, hair-raising descent through a spiral twist at speeds of more than 100 miles per hour. Riders then face a 129-foot tall hill that bounces them out of their seats for a few seconds.

3. Apollo's Chariot

Opened in 1999, Apollo's Chariot is an award-winning steel coaster at Busch Gardens in Williamsburg, Virginia. Holding the world record for a gulping 825 feet of drops on a coaster, Apollo's Chariot starts with a 170-foot lift hill, then hits a maximum speed of 73 miles per hour. At the peak, riders drop down a few teasing feet before the cars swoop down 210 feet to graze a water-filled gully at a 65 degree angle. Riders then soar up a second hill and back down a 131-foot drop. Then, the coaster screams through a short tunnel and then takes off up a third incline, before screeching around a curved 144-foot plunge. Riders slow down with a series of bunny bumps before the train brakes and returns safely to the station.

4. Steel Dragon 2000

Steel Dragon 2000, located at Nagashima Spa Land Amusement Park in Japan, represents "The Year of the Dragon." As of 2006, it had the longest track of any coaster in the world, hurtling its riders along at speeds up to 95 miles per hour for 8,133.17 feet. With a peak at 318.25 feet, it is also the world's tallest coaster to use a chain lift: Two chains are utilized, one for the bottom half and one for the top half because a single chain would be too long and heavy. For earthquake protection, more steel was used in this $50 million machine than in any other coaster in the world.

5. Dodonpa

When it first opened in 2001 at Fuji-Q Highland in Japan, Dodonpa was the world's fastest steel coaster, but by 2006, it had slipped to third place. However, it retains the title for the fastest acceleration in the world, reaching a top speed of 106.8 miles per hour in a mere 1.8 seconds! At speeds like that, ride time is only 55 seconds, but that seems like an eternity when rushing down 170 feet at a 90-degree angle.

6. Son of Beast

Son of Beast, built in 2000 at Paramount's Kings Island in Cincinnati, Ohio, is touted as the world's tallest and fastest wooden coaster, with a 218-foot apex and speeds up to 78 miles per hour. At the time of its construction, Son of Beast was also the world's only looping wooden roller coaster, although in 2007, the loop was removed. Son of Beast's daddy, The Beast, was constructed at King's Island in 1979 and holds the title as the longest wooden roller coaster, at 7,400 feet.

7. Rock 'n' Roller Coaster

Located at Disney parks in Florida and France, the Rock 'n' Roller Coaster is an indoor experience, called a "dark ride." Accelerating to 57 miles per hour in 2.8 seconds, windblown hair is guaranteed. But the highlight of this coaster is that rides are accompanied by music by Aerosmith, including songs such as "Back in the Saddle," "Sweet Emotion," and "Love in an Elevator."

8. Dueling Dragons

Located at Islands of Adventure in Orlando, Florida, Dueling Dragons is the world's first high-speed, dueling inverted roller coaster; inverted means that the cars travel under the track rather than on top of it. Dueling Dragons is actually two roller coasters, one representing fire and the other ice. Each has several throat-gulping inversions, including corkscrews, vertical loops, and a cobra roll. Top speed is 55 miles per hour with a maximum height of 125 feet. Riders on each track zoom within inches of each other in three near-miss experiences that elicit plenty of screaming.

9. Magnum XL-200

Opened in 1989 at Cedar Point in Sandusky, Ohio, Magnum XL-200 is a steel roller coaster that was the first constructed circuit roller coaster to break the 200-foot barrier, with its 205-foot peak and 194.67-foot drop. The view of Lake Erie from the pinnacle is breathtaking, with plenty of opportunity to see the countryside along the nearly mile-long track. That is, if passengers can keep their eyes open while speeding along at 72 miles per hour. Expert riders prefer the third row of seats in the first car because of numerous, intense airtime moments.

10. Superman—Ultimate Flight

If you've ever wanted to fly like a superhero, this is the ride for you! Located at Six Flags theme parks in Illinois, New Jersey, and Georgia, this ride's specially-designed cars tilt passengers facedown into a flying position, so that they're suspended horizontally from the track above. Riders get a bird's-eye view at the top of a 109-foot hill, before sailing through the air at 60 miles per hour in a series of loops, spirals, turns, and rolls. And with the first-of-its-kind pretzel-shaped loop, this truly is a unique thrill ride.

11. The Raptor

The Raptor is a steel inverted coaster at Cedar Point, America's roller coaster capital, in Sandusky, Ohio. When it opened in 1994, this sweet ride was the largest of its type ever built. Passengers soar up 137 feet before gliding down 119 feet. Reaching a maximum speed of 57 miles per hour, there are six inversions, including a cobra roll and two corkscrews that are great for shaking up the digestive system. Rides last an enjoyable 2 minutes, 16 seconds—an adventure enjoyed by nearly two million thrill seekers every year.

12. Top Thrill Dragster

Top Thrill Dragster also located at Cedar Point in Ohio, is labeled an "accelerator coaster" with trains shaped like rip-roaring dragsters. But the ride feels more like a jaw-tightening space launch. Reaching a speed of 120 miles per hour in just four seconds, passengers are thrust to the top of a 420-foot peak before plunging straight down 400 feet, while at the same time twisting and turning through 270-degree spirals.

✳ ✳ ✳

"If a man . . . never allowed himself a bit of fun and relaxation, he would go mad or become unstable without knowing it."
—Herodotus, ancient Greek historian

OMG, THIS LIST IS GR8! LOL!
5 Cyber-Chic Fads of the 2000s

❊ ❊ ❊ ❊

The fads of the 2000s can be described as technologically-driven and convenience-based. Everyone seems to be looking for the fastest, easiest ways to communicate, advertise, entertain themselves, eat, and even fall in love. Soon these fads will be a thing of the past, but don't move too fast—this decade still has a few years left!

1. Reality TV

The craze that continues to keep us glued to the TV started in the 1990s with a little MTV show called *The Real World,* where seven strangers were picked to live together in a cool apartment in Manhattan. The show was a huge hit—people everywhere tuned in to see real people interacting in real life. But it wasn't until 2000 that reality television really exploded, spawning shows like *Survivor, Amazing Race, American Idol,* and *Dancing with the Stars.* By the mid-2000s, the industry was saturated with reality TV shows for every imaginable subject.

2. Text Messaging

These usually abbreviated, often truncated, and sometimes cryptic messages are sent via cell phones. The United States was actually behind the times when this trend initially hit in the late '90s. Asia and Europe had been using the Short Message System (or SMS) for several years, but we only got hip to "txt msgs" in the mid-2000s. We're making up for lost time apparently; in 2006, cellular provider Cingular reported 12 billion text messages sent in the fourth quarter alone, an increase of 20 percent from the previous quarter.

3. Sudoku

In Japanese, *su do ku* means "one number." A sudoku puzzle is a grid to fill with numbers so that the numerals one through nine occur only once in each row, column, and box. Each puzzle has some numbers filled in—you just need to work out the rest using your powers of deduction. It may not sound like it, but it's really fun. In 2005, British newspaper *The Times* published a sudoku puzzle by Wayne Gould and the game's popularity boomed. Soon, U.S. newspapers were printing the puzzles and everyone had their heads down, crunching the numbers.

4. YouTube and MySpace

Sharing videos, songs, e-mail messages, pictures, favorites lists, and profiles is becoming de rigueur in the 21st century. With online sites like YouTube, you can search for, watch, and share video clips of just about everything—no TV required. If you find a really great video clip on YouTube, you can post a link to it on your MySpace page. MySpace is one of the most popular Web sites in existence, operating as a networking tool for anyone who can type their name and think of a password. Members have profiles, links to other people's profiles, primary and extended networks, and can use their MySpace pages for fun, personal use, or to promote themselves in business and artistic endeavors.

5. Speed Dating

With so many MySpace profiles to update, text messages to type, and sudoku puzzles to solve, who has time to meet that special someone? Thanks to speed-dating services, busy people of the new millennium can meet dozens of singles—while a timer keeps the whole thing moving along at a steady pace. A couple will chat for three to eight minutes or so, figuring out if there's any point in continuing their discussion later. A bell rings or a glass clinks and it's bye-bye to person number one and on to person number two. Fans of speed dating say it's a great way to meet a lot of people and, since first impressions are telling, you won't waste your time on someone who doesn't tickle your fancy right away. Critics say it's not fair to judge someone on a three-minute conversation, but with the pace we've set in the 2000s, three minutes may be all anyone has!

Chapter 3
THIS IS AMERICA
✳ ✳ ✳ ✳
THE MOTHER LODE ON THE MOTHER ROAD
13 Vintage Businesses on Historic Route 66

This 2,400-mile stretch of Americana, dubbed "The Mother Road" by John Steinbeck, is dotted with iconic saloons, motels, and kitschy pit stops. In the early 1920s, when the national highway system was in its infancy, Oklahoma highway commissioner Cyrus Stevens Avery envisioned a superhighway linking Chicago and Los Angeles by way of small, rural towns. Route 66 opened in 1927, although the entire road wasn't paved until 1938. But the Federal Highway Act of 1956 led to its demise with the creation of several new interstates, and, by 1985, Route 66 had been formally decommissioned, although most of the winding route through Illinois, Missouri, Kansas, Oklahoma, Texas, New Mexico, Arizona, and California can still be traveled today. Ready for a road trip? Here are some places you may want to stop.

1. Buckingham Fountain (Chicago, Illinois)
Located in Chicago's Grant Park, Buckingham Fountain is where Route 66 began. The fountain, which represents Lake Michigan, is adorned with sculptures of four sea horses that symbolize the states bordering the lake—Illinois, Indiana, Michigan, and Wisconsin. The fountain's 134 jets shoot 14,000 gallons of water (per minute) 150 feet into the air for a magnificent display, which incorporates music and a light show in the evening.

2. The Cozy Dog Drive-In (Springfield, Illinois)
Anyone who's ever been to a county fair has probably had a corn dog—a breaded hot dog on a stick. While working at an army base in the early 1940s, Illinois native Ed Waldmire was toying with the idea of wrapping hot dogs in corn bread. Following the advice of

a friend that the key was frying the meat in the batter, Waldmire started experimenting at the USO in Amarillo, Texas. Originally called crusty curs, Waldmire changed the name to cozy dogs and opened up his first stand in Springfield in 1946, after being discharged from the army. The Cozy Dog Drive-In continues to be a popular family-run business.

3. Ted Drewe's Frozen Custard (St. Louis, Missouri)

Ted Drewe started selling frozen custard (his own concoction) in Florida in 1929. The ever-busy entrepreneur split his time between midwestern carnivals during the summer and Florida beaches in the winter, finally opening a permanent stand in St. Louis in 1931. In 1941, he opened another store in St. Louis along Route 66. Despite offers to franchise, the business has remained family-owned and operated. During the winter season—a less appealing time to down a cup of frozen custard—they sell Christmas trees.

4. 66 Drive-In Theater (Carthage, Missouri)

In 1949, when drive-in movies were as hot as buttered popcorn, the 66 Drive-In Theater was a new attraction. Along with most drive-in theaters across the country, it fell into disrepair until the Goodman family bought it and set out to return it to its former glory. They started work in 1996 and finished renovations in 1998. During the summer months, feature films are still shown under the stars. Today there are only around 800 drive-in theaters still operating in the United States out of about 5,000 that existed in the '50s and '60s.

5. Ed Galloway's Totem Pole Park (Foyil, Oklahoma)

What better place to stretch your legs on a road trip than at the park that boasts the world's largest totem pole? It's 90 feet tall, made of 200 carved pictures, and was sculpted by Ed Galloway between 1937 and 1948. He used 28 tons of cement, 6 tons of steel, and 100 tons of sand and rock to pay tribute to Native American culture. Galloway's creation was added to the National Register of Historic Places in 1999.

6. Lucille's (Hydro, Oklahoma)

Lucille's is currently one of only two porch-style gas stations still operating on Oklahoma's portion of Route 66. Lucille Hamons and her husband bought the structure (originally built in 1927 and called the Provine Station) in 1941, and she operated it herself until she died in 2000. Lucille was known as "the Mother of the Mother Road" because of her many stories of the people who stopped by for a tank of gas or a snack.

7. Cadillac Ranch (Amarillo, Texas)

Artists and auto enthusiasts alike will appreciate the beauty of ten Cadillacs, buried halfway into the ground, nose first. Passersby are encouraged to add a personal touch by wildly decorating the vehicles, which span the model years 1949 to 1963. In fact, the cars are frequently painted over to create a fresh canvas for road-weary artists. Created in 1974 by the Ant Farm, a San Francisco art collective, Cadillac Ranch has become part of the nation's kitschy culture. The unusual attraction was the subject of a Bruce Springsteen song and was even depicted in the 2006 animated film *Cars*.

8. Haunted Natatorium (Amarillo, Texas)

This indoor swimming pool opened in 1922, but by 1926 it had been purchased by J. D. Tucker, who converted it to a dance hall. Tucker covered the pool with a wooden dance floor and hosted flappers during the Roaring Twenties. Musical legends such as Tommy Dorsey, Louis Armstrong, Buddy Holly, and Roy Orbison came to play, and, at one time, it took a staff of 52 to serve the crowds. It is said that several apparitions, including a ghostly couple, can be spotted dancing among today's dancers. In 1996, the Nat conducted an all-night "ghost-busting" of sorts. The cameras mysteriously turned themselves off, but a solo drummer and a female vocalist were recorded on audio. The Natatorium has been meticulously restored to reflect the whimsical roadway architecture of Route 66. It still hosts musical acts and is a popular entertainment venue, attracting artists such as the Dixie Chicks.

9. Tee Pee Curios Trading Post (Tucumcari, New Mexico)

Tucumcari has a five-mile stretch of pure Route 66 nostalgia in the form of motels, diners, and curiosity shops. One neon sign after another tempts motorists to put on the brakes and kick around for a while. One of the famed shops is Tee Pee Curios Trading Post, which was built in the early 1940s as a gas station that sold groceries and novelty items. When the road was widened in the 1950s Tee Pee got rid of its gas pumps and focused solely on the fun stuff.

10. The Wigwam Village Motels (Holbrook, Arizona, and Rialto, California)

Frank Redford built the first of several Wigwam Village motels in 1934 near popular tourist spot Mammoth Cave in Kentucky. Two more opened out west by the mid-1950s—one in Holbrook, Arizona, and one in Rialto, California. Each wigwam featured a guest room that was naturally suited to the southwestern stretch of Route 66. The Arizona, California, and Kentucky locations are still in business, with the marquee in front of the Holbrook location posing the question: "Have you slept in a wigwam lately?"

11. Jackrabbit Trading Post (Joseph City, Arizona)

In 1949, James Taylor (not the folksinger) converted a simple shack into one of the most popular souvenir shops along the Mother Road. To attract the growing throngs of tourists passing through town, Taylor painted dancing American Indians on the facade and lined the rooftop with 30 jackrabbits that appear to hop along the top of the building. Inside, he sold turquoise jewelry and southwestern souvenirs. And to ensure that the road weary noticed his shop among the many, he and another local retailer traveled from Arizona to Springfield, Missouri, and dotted more than 1,000 miles of roadside with billboards of jackrabbits and dancing cowgirls!

12. Roy's (Amboy, California)

During the 1930s, Roy and Velma Crowl owned the café, motel, and service station that comprised most of Amboy, a tiny town on a desolate stretch of Route 66. Years later, Roy's daughter Betty and her husband, Buster Burris, took over the business and continued the tradition of caring for road-weary travelers. In fact, Buster was still changing tires for folks when he retired in 1995, well into his eighties. Today, the entire 690-acre town and all of its contents are owned by the Route 66 Museum in San Bernardino, California. The owners plan to restore the famous gas station, convenience store, diner, motel, and cottages to their 1950s-era charm.

13. Georgian Hotel (Santa Monica, California)

The Santa Monica Pier is literally the end of the road, not only for Route 66, but for the contiguous United States as well. Within walking distance is the Georgian Hotel, a luxurious art deco hotel steeped in history since opening its doors in 1933. The hotel, which served as a speakeasy during Prohibition, has also been a hideaway for the famous and infamous. Clark Gable and Carole Lombard hid from the press at the Georgian, and you might find today's Hollywood royalty doing the same.

11 Fastest-Growing U.S. Cities*

✳ ✳ ✳ ✳

1. Bakersfield, California
2. Raleigh, North Carolina
3. Fort Worth, Texas
4. Phoenix, Arizona
5. Stockton, California
6. Albuquerque, New Mexico
7. Charlotte, North Carolina
8. Miami, Florida
9. Aurora, Colorado (tie)
10. Las Vegas, Nevada (tie)
11. Plano, Texas

* *Populations over 250,000, from 7/1/04–7/1/05*
Source: U.S. Census Bureau

10 U.S. Cities with the Highest Cost of Living

❋ ❋ ❋ ❋

1. New York City, New York
2. Los Angeles, California
3. San Francisco, California
4. Chicago, Illinois
5. Miami, Florida
6. Honolulu, Hawaii
7. Houston, Texas
8. Washington, D.C.
9. Boston, Massachusetts
10. Atlanta, Georgia

14 of the New Deal's Alphabet Agencies

❋ ❋ ❋ ❋

When Franklin Delano Roosevelt took office in 1933, America was in the darkest depths of the Great Depression. But Roosevelt promised a "New Deal"—an America free from economic deprivation—and he kept his word, launching major legislation in his effort to revitalize the American spirit and its fading dream. Between 1933 and 1939 dozens of federal programs, often referred to as the Alphabet Agencies, were created as part of the New Deal. With FDR's focus on "relief, recovery and reform," the legacy of the New Deal is with us to this day. The following are 14 of the most notable Alphabet Agencies.

1. CCC (Civilian Conservation Corps)

The CCC was created in 1933 and lasted for ten years. Its function was the conservation of resources, which it achieved by hiring more than 2.5 million young men to work on environmental projects such as planting trees, building roads and parks, and fighting soil erosion on federal lands. These men earned $30 per month and contributed to many of the outdoor recreation areas that exist today, including the Blue Ridge Highway. Between 1934 and 1937, this program also funded similar programs for 8,500 women.

2. CWA (Civil Works Administration)

This agency, created in 1933, lasted only one year, but it provided construction jobs for more than four million people who were paid $15 per week to work on schools, roads, and sewers. Some of these jobs were considered frivolous, such as raking leaves. But this program contributed to the morale and self-esteem of millions of displaced people by providing them with steady employment.

3. FDIC (Federal Deposit Insurance Corporation)

During the summer of 1933, the Glass-Steagall Act was passed, setting forth stringent regulations for banks and providing depositors with insurance of up to $5,000 through the newly formed FDIC. The FDIC successfully restored confidence in the nation's banks and encouraged savings because people no longer feared that all their money would be lost in a bank failure.

4. FERA (Federal Emergency Relief Administration)

Established in 1933 by Harry Hopkins, a close advisor to Franklin Roosevelt, this agency was the first of the New Deal's major relief operations. It provided assistance for the unemployed, supporting nearly five million households each month by funding work projects for more than 20 million people. It also provided vaccinations and literacy classes for millions who could not afford them. Both Hopkins and Roosevelt believed in a work ethic based on payment for services and that "earning one's keep" was an important aspect in building the morale and self-esteem of the dole recipients.

5. TVA (Tennessee Valley Authority)

Of all of the reform programs initiated by the Roosevelt administration, the TVA was by far the most ambitious. Created in 1933 for the purpose of developing the Tennessee River watershed, this comprehensive federal agency revitalized the region by building 16 dams to control flooding, generate hydraulic power, and increase agricultural production. This agency also provided jobs, low-cost housing, reforestation, and many other conservation-related services to the region.

6. FCC (Federal Communications Commission)

The Communications Act of 1934 established the FCC as the successor to the Federal Radio Commission. Its function was to merge the administrative responsibilities for regulating broadcasting and wire communications into one centralized agency. Today, this independent, quasi-judicial agency is charged with the regulation of all nonfederal governmental use of radio and television broadcasting and all interstate telecommunications (wire, satellite, and cable), as well as all international communications that originate or terminate in the United States. It is much more powerful today than in the days of its inception, given the incredible growth of the communications industry over the last 70 years.

7. FHA (Federal Housing Administration)

Established in 1934 as part of Roosevelt's recovery campaign, this program focused on stimulating the growth of the building industry. A similar agency, the Home Owners' Loan Corporation (HOLC) was also established. The FHA promised a stable future by providing the funds necessary to construct low-income housing. Today, percentage-wise, more Americans own homes than people in any other country in the world. More than 70 years since its inception, the FHA is the largest insurer of home mortgages in the world.

8. SEC (Securities Exchange Commission)

Established by Congress in 1934 as an independent, nonpartisan regulatory agency, the SEC was created primarily to restore the stability of the stock market after the crash of October 1929 and to prevent corporate abuses relating to the offering and sale of securities. Today, the SEC is responsible for the enforcement and administration of the laws that govern the securities industry. It also serves as a federal watchdog against stock market fraud and insider manipulation on Wall Street and offers publications on investment-related topics for public education.

9. NLRA (National Labor Relations Act)

Also known as the Wagner Act of 1935, this reform legislation created the National Labor Relations Board, whose purpose was to protect the rights of organized labor by legalizing practices such as "closed shops" in which only union members could work and collectively bargain.

10. REA (Rural Electrification Administration)

The purpose of this legislation was to supply electricity to rural communities. Before the onset of the New Deal, only 10 percent of areas outside cities had electricity. Established in 1935, the REA granted low-cost loans to farm cooperatives to bring electric power into their communities. The program was so successful that 98 percent of American farms were equipped with electric power under this initiative.

11. SSA (Social Security Administration)

The original purpose of the SSA, which was established in August 1935 under the Social Security Act, was to administer a national pension fund for retired persons, an unemployment insurance system, and a public assistance program for dependent mothers, children, and the physically disabled. Today, it is the nation's most important and expensive domestic program, covering nearly 49 million Americans and accounting for about 20 percent of the federal budget. However, as the population ages, more and more funds will be needed to keep recipients above the ever-shifting poverty line. Many claim that if nothing is done to adjust social security benefits and taxes, the system will be unable to meet its financial obligations after the year 2040.

12. WPA (Works Progress Administration)

The WPA, which lasted from 1935 to 1943, was the largest and most comprehensive New Deal agency, affecting every American locality. It employed more than eight million people to build roads and highways, bridges, schools, airports, parks, and other public projects. In total, the WPA built 650,000 miles of roads, 78,000 bridges, 125,000 buildings, and 700 miles of airport runways. Under the arts program, many artists, photographers, writers, and actors became government employees, working on a myriad of public projects ranging from painting murals to writing national park guidebooks.

13. FSA (Farm Security Administration)

This relief organization was originally called the Resettlement Administration Act of 1935. Its purpose was to improve the lot of the poor farmers so poignantly depicted in John Steinbeck's novel *The Grapes of Wrath*. The FSA established temporary housing for Dust Bowl refugees from Oklahoma and Arkansas who had migrated to California in hopes of finding employment. In total, the FSA loaned more than a billion dollars to farmers and set up many camps for destitute migrant workers.

14. FLSA (Fair Labor Standard Act)

This labor law, enacted in 1938, was the last major piece of New Deal legislation intended to reform the economy, and it is still with us today. This law established the minimum wage, which at the time was twenty-five cents an hour. It also set the standard for the 40-hour work week and banned the use of child labor.

20 Facts About the Statue of Liberty

❊ ❊ ❊ ❊

1. The statue's real name is "Liberty Enlightening the World."

2. Construction of the statue began in France in 1875.

3. Lady Liberty was sculpted by Frédéric Auguste Bartholdi; Alexandre Gustave Eiffel was the structural engineer.

4. The statue was completed in Paris in June 1884, given to the American people on July 4, 1884, and reassembled and dedicated in the United States on October 28, 1886.

5. The model for the face of the statue is reputed to be the sculptor's mother, Charlotte Bartholdi.

6. A quarter-scale bronze replica of Lady Liberty was erected in Paris in 1889 as a gift from Americans living in the city. The statue stands about 35 feet high and is located on a small island in the River Seine, about a mile south of the Eiffel Tower.

7. There are 25 windows and 7 spikes in Lady Liberty's crown. The spikes are said to symbolize the seven seas.

8. The inscription on the statue's tablet reads: July 4, 1776 (in Roman numerals).

9. More than four million people visit the Statue of Liberty each year.

10. Symbolizing freedom and the opportunity for a better life, the Statue of Liberty greeted millions of immigrants as they sailed through New York Harbor on their way to nearby Ellis Island.

11. Lady Liberty is 152 feet 2 inches tall from base to torch and 305 feet 1 inch tall from the ground to the tip of her torch.

12. The statue's hand is 16 feet 5 inches long and her index finger is 8 feet long. Her fingernails are 13 inches long by 10 inches wide and weigh approximately 3.5 pounds each.

13. Lady Liberty's eyes are each 2 feet 6 inches across, she has a 35-foot waistline, and she weighs about 450,000 pounds (225 tons).

14. Lady Liberty's sandals are 25 feet long, making her shoe size 879.

15. There are 192 steps from the ground to the top of the pedestal and 354 steps from the pedestal to the crown.

16. The statue functioned as an actual lighthouse from 1886 to 1902. There was an electric plant on the island to generate power for the light, which could be seen 24 miles away.

17. The Statue of Liberty underwent a multimillion dollar renovation in the mid-1980s before being rededicated on July 4, 1986. During the renovation, Lady Liberty received a new torch because the old one was corroded beyond repair.

18. The Statue of Liberty's original torch is now on display at the monument's museum.

19. Until September 11, 2001, the Statue of Liberty was open to the public and visitors were able to climb the winding staircase inside the statue to the top of her crown for a spectacular view of New York Harbor.

20. Although the pedestal and the museum are once again open to the public, the interior of the Statue remains closed. Legislation has been proposed to reopen the inside of the statue to the public, but until then visitors can view the interior framework through the pedestal's glass ceiling.

CELEBRATE THE OFFBEAT!
8 Quirky Festivals in North America

✳ ✳ ✳ ✳

Looking for somewhere wacky to have a good time?
Festivals, no matter how kooky, bring out the best in creativity.
A festivalgoer can celebrate animals, insects, foods,
historical events, and just about any other topic under
the sun. It's easy to fill your calendar with events,
just check out these examples.

1. Frozen Dead Guy Days (Nederland, Colorado)
The fun at the annual Frozen Dead Guy Days festival heats up Nederland during Colorado's typically frosty March. The fest commemorates a cryogenically-preserved Norwegian who has been kept in a shed by his grandson since 1994. Visitors are encouraged to come dressed as a frozen or dead character to a dance tagged

"Grandpa's Blue Ball." Coffin races and a parade featuring antique hearses are among the liveliest attractions, along with salmon tossing and a frozen beach volleyball tournament. The event started in 2002 and annually attracts about 7,000 visitors.

2. Secret City Festival (Oak Ridge, Tennessee)

The annual Secret City Festival highlights the important role Oak Ridge played in World War II. In the 1940s, researchers there developed the top secret atomic bomb—hence the city's nickname—and today visitors can tour Manhattan Project sites to see where the bomb was devised. One of the country's largest World War II reenactments is also a popular draw, with roaring tanks, motorcycles, and other vintage military gear. Each June, the event draws about 20,000 people to Oak Ridge, which is nestled between the picturesque Cumberland and Great Smoky Mountains.

3. Nanaimo Marine Festival (Nanaimo, British Columbia)

At the Nanaimo Marine Festival held in mid-July, up to 200 "tubbers" compete in the Great International World Championship Bathtub Race across a 36-mile course. Using just about any conceivable watercraft, most of which at least vaguely resemble a bathtub, contestants must make it to Vancouver's Fisherman's Cove across the Straits of Georgia. The first race was held in 1967 and activities have expanded since to include a food fair, craft show, Kiddies' Karnival, and waiters' race.

4. BugFest (Raleigh, North Carolina)

Billed as the nation's largest single-day festival featuring insects, BugFest attracts around 25,000 people to Raleigh each September. The event started in 1997 and now covers beekeeping demonstrations, a flea circus, and roach races. The festival features many exhibits on insects, from live spiders and centipedes, to displays on how bugs see. At Café Insecta, festivalgoers can sample Buggy Bean Dip with Crackers, Quivering Wax Worm Quiche, Stir-fried Cantonese Crickets over rice, and Three Bug Salad, among other aptly named goodies that actually include worms, ants, and related critters raised for cooking.

5. Rattlesnake Roundup (Freer, Texas)

Billed as the biggest party in Texas, the Freer Rattlesnake Roundup held each May features nationally known country and Tejano artists... and loads and loads of snakes. In addition to daredevil snake shows, snake twirling displays, a carnival, arts and crafts, and fried rattlesnake to chaw, prizes are given out for the longest and smallest rattlesnakes, and for the most nonvenomous snakes brought to the fest by one person.

6. Barnesville Potato Days (Barnesville, Minnesota)

Up to 14,000 visitors head to west-central Minnesota for Barnesville Potato Days in late August when this small town celebrates the lowly spud with a great menu of activities. The Potato Salad Cook-off attracts onlookers eager to compare the year's winning recipe with how Grandma used to make this popular picnic dish. Things can get messy during mashed potato wrestling, but the Miss Tator Tot pageant is much more refined. Of course, there is plenty of food to sample, including Norwegian lefse, potato pancakes, potato sausage, potato soup, and traditional German potato dumplings. On Friday, there's even a free French Fry Feed. Barnesville, tucked away in the fertile Red River Valley, has been honoring the crop of choice of many nearby farmers with this festival since 1938.

7. Faux Film Festival (Portland, Oregon)

For anyone who loves fake commercials or movie trailers, Portland's Faux Film Festival is the ticket to a surreal filmic never-never land. Mockumentaries and other celluloid spoofs are among the dozens of goofy entries shown in the historic 460-seat Hollywood Theatre. Past viewings have included the silly classic, *It Came from the Lint Trap* and the quirky *The Lady from Sockholm,* a film noir featuring sock puppets. The fest is usually staged at the end of March, with a packed house at each screening.

8. Contraband Days Pirate Festival (Lake Charles, Louisiana)

Legend has it that buccaneer Jean Lafitte buried an enormous treasure somewhere along Lake Charles's sandy shoreline. Since

1958, Contraband Days Pirate Festival, which attracts more than 100,000 people, has been honoring the legend each May. Perhaps one of the funniest sights of the festival is when the mayor is made to walk the plank after pirates take over the town. The plucky civic chief is naturally rescued quickly, then is free to enjoy the rest of the fest with its carnival, arm wrestling competition, sailboat regatta, and bed races. With an eclectic selection of nearly 100 different events, Contraband Days is frequently chosen by the American Bus Association as a Top 100 Event in North America.

HIP, HIP, HOORAY FOR THE WPA!
12 WPA Projects that Still Exist

❈ ❈ ❈ ❈

In the darkest days of the Great Depression,
the U.S. government stepped in to assist the needy and get
the economy started again. Perhaps the widest-ranging and
most productive New Deal measure was the Works Progress
Administration. This group provided more than $10 billion
in federal funds from 1935 through the early 1940s,
employing millions of people in hundreds of thousands of jobs.
Here are some of the most notable projects.

1. Doubleday Field in Cooperstown, New York
This minor league stadium—which has hosted the annual major league Hall of Fame game every active baseball season since 1939—sits on the lot where Abner Doubleday supposedly invented baseball in 1839. A century later, the WPA refurbished the site's existing field, adding a grandstand, drainage system, wooden bleachers, and new fencing.

2. Camp David, Maryland
In 1936, the WPA began work on a recreational area in western Maryland's Catoctin Mountains, completing Camp Hi-Catoctin by 1939. For three years, it was used as a family camp for federal

employees until President Franklin Delano Roosevelt visited in April 1942 and selected it as the location for presidential retreats. In the early 1950s, President Eisenhower renamed the camp for his grandson. Camp David has hosted dozens of visiting foreign dignitaries for casual meetings with U.S. presidents, but it remains closed to the general public.

3. Dealey Plaza, Texas

In 1940, WPA workers completed this park in the heart of Dallas. Named for an early publisher of the *Dallas Morning News,* the plaza lives in infamy as the location of President John F. Kennedy's assassination on November 22, 1963. There may be other "grassy knolls" in American parks, but none have gone down in history like the one in Dealey Plaza.

4. LaGuardia Airport, New York

The Big Apple's desire for a city airport was only a dream until September 1937, when the WPA  joined with the city to build one. Soon after opening in 1939, it was named New York Municipal Airport–LaGuardia Field to honor mayor Fiorello LaGuardia. The name was shortened to LaGuardia Airport in 1947.

5. John Augustus Walker's Murals, Mobile, Alabama

The WPA commissioned John Augustus Walker—a native of Mobile, Alabama—to create a series of oil on canvas murals in the city's Old City Hall/Southern Market complex. They memorialize a range of Mobile's historic events, from the ship that brought the last payload of African slaves into the United States in 1859 to the importance of education and science to the city. Hurricane Katrina, which slammed into the city in August 2005, damaged the Museum of Mobile, where the murals are now located. The murals were not harmed, and the museum reopened in March 2006.

6. The *American Guide* Series

The Federal Writers Project was a WPA program that employed authors, playwrights, and poets between 1935 and 1943. The project used more than 6,000 writers—including future award-winning authors like Saul Bellow and Ralph Ellison—to produce travel guides for each of the (then) 48 states as well as the District of Columbia. Each book in the series described the state's geography, history, and culture and was filled with maps, drawings, and pictures. Today, collectors seek many of the original volumes, which can fetch hundreds of dollars. Not bad for a series that supposedly started after a casual conversation between the WPA administrator and a writer at a cocktail party!

7. Jackson Pollock, *Male and Female*, Pennsylvania

Before he developed his famous drip method of painting—a technique in which the canvas is placed on the floor and splashed with paint—Pollock worked for the WPA's Federal Art Project from 1938 to 1942. He created *Male and Female,* one of his earliest paintings, in 1942. Now in the Philadelphia Museum of Art, the painting is an excellent example of Pollock's early abstract expressionism, characterized by vibrant color and texture.

8. The Mathematical Tables Project

Before the advent of computers, *people* created mathematical tables to compute complex calculations and formulas. The WPA's groundbreaking Mathematical Tables Project, which began in 1938 in New York City, employed hundreds of workers to mass-calculate the tables. Twenty-eight volumes of mathematical information were published, including navigation tables used by the Navy in World War II. The work was so valuable that the program was absorbed into the National Bureau of Standards in 1948.

9. Donal Hord, *Aztec* Statue, California

In 1936, San Diego sculptor Donal Hord was commissioned to carve a statue for the campus of San Diego State University. He completed the work, which he named *Aztec,* in 1937, and it soon became the inspiration for the school's mascot. Nicknamed "Montezuma," the statue makes its home in the university's Prospective Student Center. The funding for the project was twofold—student groups raised $130 to purchase the one-ton chunk of black diorite for Hord to work with and the WPA Federal Arts Project supplied $6,000 to Hord and his assistants for their labor.

10. Outer Bridge Drive, Illinois

In the heart of the Windy City, this bridge, which crosses the Chicago River near Lake Michigan, was started in 1929, but the Great Depression prevented its completion until the WPA delivered funds in the mid-1930s. When completed in 1937, the bridge was 356 feet long and 100 feet wide, making it the world's longest and widest bascule bridge. Also known as the Lake Shore Drive Bridge, it still stands today, forming part of the scenic Chicago waterfront.

11. Alton Tobey, *The Founders of Hartford,* Connecticut

By age nine, Alton Tobey was a well-regarded artist who had won a scholarship to a class at New York's Metropolitan Museum of Art. In 1940, while studying at Yale's University School of Fine Arts, he accepted a commission from the WPA for a mural to adorn the East Hartford post office. Thus, *The Founders of Hartford* was born. His full-color preparatory painting for the mural is in the Smithsonian American Art Museum's collection in Washington, D.C.

12. George Stanley's Muse Statues, California

One of the world's largest and most famous natural amphitheaters—with a capacity of nearly 18,000—has a WPA link as well. The Hollywood Bowl's entrance, a massive fountain structure designed by sculptor George Stanley, contains three granite art deco statues representing the muses of music, dance, and drama. From 1938 to 1940, the statue project cost the WPA $100,000 and was the largest of hundreds of WPA sculpture projects in southern California. Stanley is also known for designing the "Oscar" statuette that goes to Academy Award winners.

✳ ✳ ✳

"Whatever America hopes to bring to pass in the world must first come to pass in the heart of America."
—Dwight Eisenhower

10 Largest U.S. Universities by Enrollment

Enrollment	*University*	*City*
1. 51,818	Ohio State University	Columbus
2. 51,234	Arizona State University	Tempe
3. 50,785	University of Florida	Gainesville
4. 50,402	University of Minnesota	Minneapolis
5. 49,738	University of Texas at Austin	Austin
6. 46,719	University of Central Florida	Orlando
7. 45,487	Texas A&M University	College Station
8. 45,166	Michigan State University	East Lansing
9. 44,038	University of South Florida	Tampa
10. 42,914	Pennsylvania State University	University Park

11 Structures that Define America

The United States has a penchant for building. As such, there are numerous buildings and other structures that represent the freedom and opportunity expressed in the American dream. Here are a few of those defining monuments.

1. Statue of Liberty

The Statue of Liberty is perhaps the most enduring symbol of America and has become a universal symbol of freedom and democracy. Located on a 12-acre island in New York Harbor, the Statue of Liberty was a friendly gesture from the people of France to the people of the United States. The statue, designed by French sculptor Frédéric Auguste Bartholdi, was dedicated on October 28, 1886, designated a national monument in 1924, and underwent a face-lift for its centennial in 1986. Lady Liberty stands 305 feet 1 inch high, from the ground to the tip of her torch.

2. Empire State Building

The Empire State Building is the crown jewel of the New York City skyline. Designed by William Lamb, the art deco structure was the world's tallest building when it opened in 1931, soaring 1,454 feet from the ground to the top of its lightning rod. More than 3,000 workers took less than 14 months to build the structure, with the framework erected at a pace of 4.5 stories per week. Today, visitors still marvel at the breathtaking views visible from the observatory, which on a clear day offers glimpses of the five surrounding states.

3. Brooklyn Bridge

Every day, thousands of commuters cross the East River via the Brooklyn Bridge. And they have John A. Roebling and his son, Washington, to thank. In 1867, the elder Roebling was hired as chief engineer to build "the greatest bridge in existence." But he died in 1869 before construction began. His son, Washington, stepped in and construction finally began on the 5,989-foot-long structure in January 1870. The 85-foot-wide bridge was the first steel wire suspension bridge and the largest suspension bridge in the world at the time. On May 24, 1883, the bridge opened to the public, carrying pedestrians, livestock, horse-drawn vehicles, and trolley cars between Manhattan and Brooklyn. The pedestrian toll that day was a penny but was raised to three cents the next morning. Today, the bridge carries upwards of 144,000 vehicles a day in six lanes of traffic. About 2,000 pedestrians and hundreds of bicyclists also cross the bridge's 1.14 miles each workday.

4. St. Louis Arch

The St. Louis Arch on the bank of the Mississippi River marks the city as the "Gateway to the West." Thomas Jefferson's vision of freedom and democracy spreading from "sea to shining sea" inspired architect Eero Saarinen's contemporary design for a 630-foot stainless steel memorial. Construction began in 1963 and was completed on October 28, 1965. The Arch's foundation is set 60 feet into the ground and is built to withstand earthquakes and high winds. A 40-passenger train takes sightseers from the lobby to the observation platform, where on a clear day the view stretches for 30 miles.

5. Sears Tower

In 1969, retail giant Sears, Roebuck and Company wanted to consolidate its employees working in offices around the Chicago area. Designed by chief architect Bruce Graham and structural engineer Fazlur Khan of Skidmore, Owings and Merrill architects, construction on Chicago's Sears Tower began in 1970. The colossal structure opened in 1973, making it the world's tallest building. In 1998, it was surpassed by the Petronas Towers in Malaysia, but it is still the tallest building in the United States. With 110 stories, the distance to the roof is 1,450 feet 7 inches. However, in 1982, two television antennas were added, increasing its total height to 1,707 feet. To improve broadcast reception, the western antenna was extended in 2000, bringing the total height to 1,725 feet. The Skydeck observatory on the 103rd floor can be reached in 45 seconds by an express elevator. At 1,353 feet, sightseers can see Illinois, Indiana, Michigan, and Wisconsin on a clear day.

6. Golden Gate Bridge

San Francisco's Golden Gate Bridge, named for the Golden Gate Strait, which it spans, was the vision of chief engineer Joseph B. Strauss, who was told by contemporaries that such a bridge could not be built. Nevertheless, construction began on January 5, 1933. Nearly four and a half years, $35 million, and 11 worker fatalities later, the bridge was finally opened to an estimated 200,000 pedestrians on May 27, 1937, and to vehicles the next day. The bridge is 1.7 miles long and 90 feet wide. The suspension span was the longest in the world until New York City's Verrazano Narrows Bridge opened in 1964. The bridge has two principal cables passing over the tops of the two main towers. If laid end to end, the total length

of wire in both main cables would total 80,000 miles. The Golden Gate Bridge is painted "International Orange," making it more visible to ships and the 38 million vehicles that cross it annually in the lingering and persistent fog.

7. Washington Monument

The Washington Monument, a 555-foot-high white obelisk situated at the west end of the National Mall in Washington, D.C., honors George Washington as the first president of the United States and a Revolutionary War hero. Comprised of 36,491 marble, granite, and sandstone blocks, the structure was designed by Robert Mills, a prominent American architect. Construction began in 1848, but due to the outbreak of the Civil War and lack of funding, it took nearly 40 years to complete. It is clearly visible where work resumed in 1876 by the difference in the marble's shading, about 150 feet up the obelisk. The monument was dedicated in 1885, on Washington's birthday, February 22, but did not officially open to the public until October 9, 1888, after the internal construction was complete. At the time it was the world's tallest structure, a title it held only until 1889, when the Eiffel Tower was completed in Paris.

8. Vietnam Veterans Memorial

The Vietnam Veterans Memorial in Washington, D.C., honors the men and women who served in the Vietnam conflict, one of America's most divisive wars. The memorial was intended to heal the nation's emotional wounds and was designed to be neutral about the war itself. Three components comprise the memorial: the Wall of Names, the Three Servicemen Statue and Flagpole, and the Vietnam Women's Memorial. The Wall was built in 1982 and designed by 21-year-old Maya Lin, who submitted the winning sketch. Visitors descend a path along two walls of black granite with one wing pointing at the Washington Monument a mile away and the other at the Lincoln Memorial about 600 feet away. When viewed closely, the names of the more than 59,000 soldiers killed or missing in action dominate the structure.

9. White House

The history of the White House began when President George Washington and city planner Pierre L'Enfant chose the site for the presidential residence, now listed at 1600 Pennsylvania Avenue. Irish-born architect James Hoban's design was chosen in a competition to find a builder of the "President's House."

Construction began in October 1792. Although Washington oversaw the building of the house, he never lived in it. When the White House was completed in 1800, President John Adams and his wife, Abigail, moved in as the first residents. Since then, each president has made his own changes and additions. It survived a fire at the hands of the British in 1814 during the War of 1812 and another blaze in the West Wing in 1929 when Herbert Hoover was president. President Harry Truman gutted and renovated the building during his time there. Encompassing approximately 55,000 square feet, the White House has 132 rooms, including 35 bathrooms and 16 family and guest rooms. It is the world's only private residence of a head of state that is open to the public.

10. Lincoln Memorial

"In this temple, as in the hearts of the people for whom he saved the Union, the memory of Abraham Lincoln is enshrined forever." Beneath these words rests the Lincoln Memorial on the National Mall in Washington, D.C. Designed by architect Henry Bacon, sculptor Daniel Chester French, and artist Jules Guerin, the monument was completed in 1922 to honor the sixteenth president of the United States. The structure resembles a Greek Doric temple ringed by 36 columns, each representing a state in the Union at the time of Lincoln's death. Seated within the monument is a sculpture of Lincoln, and inscriptions from both the Gettysburg Address and his second inaugural address adorn the south and north walls, respectively. The Lincoln Memorial served as the site of Martin Luther King, Jr.'s famous, "I Have a Dream" speech on August 28, 1963.

11. World Trade Center

A list of some of the nation's iconic structures would be incomplete without mentioning the 110-story Twin Towers and five smaller buildings of the World Trade Center in New York City, which were destroyed by a terrorist attack on September 11, 2001. The Twin Towers, which were located in lower Manhattan, opened in 1973. Tower One was 1,368 feet tall, and Tower Two was 1,362 feet tall. Of the approximately 50,000 people who worked in the 13.4 million square foot complex, 3,000 died when hijackers slammed two passenger jets into the buildings' upper floors on that fateful day. Construction is underway to rebuild the World Trade Center complex, with an expected completion date in 2012.

11 Slowest-Growing U.S. Cities*

✳ ✳ ✳ ✳

1. St. Louis, Missouri
2. Cincinnati, Ohio
3. Boston, Massachusetts
4. Detroit, Michigan
5. New Orleans, Louisiana
6. Cleveland, Ohio (tie)
7. Pittsburgh, Pennsylvania (tie)
8. Toledo, Ohio
9. Buffalo, New York
10. Baltimore, Maryland
11. Milwaukee, Wisconsin

* *Populations over 250,000, from 7/1/04–7/1/05*
Source: U.S. Census Bureau

✳ ✳ ✳

"I predict future happiness for Americans if they can prevent the government from wasting the labors of the people under the pretense of taking care of them."
—Thomas Jefferson

(Chapter 4)
MOVIES
✳ ✳ ✳ ✳
10 Movie Stars and Their Early Roles

The hair is big, and the script is bad, but everyone has to start somewhere. In show biz, a job is a job and young actors take what they can get. These stars might be famous today, but they weren't born on the A-list. They worked their way up through bit parts and the strange, often painfully mediocre jungle of Hollywood. Here are some of the early films of today's red-carpet royalty.

1. Nicole Kidman in *BMX Bandits* (1983)

Before the Chanel campaign, even before Tom, there was *BMX Bandits.* Nicole Kidman filmed several movies in 1983, but this one stands out. Hilarity ensues when two BMX bikers and their friend (Kidman) become entangled with a group of bank robbers. The Aussie has said this is one of her favorite films from the early days, and while it's no *Moulin Rouge,* the reviews weren't that bad.

2. Alec Baldwin in *Forever, Lulu* (1987)

Forever, Lulu tried to score Deborah Harry, lead singer of Blondie, the success Madonna enjoyed when she starred in *Desperately Seeking Susan.* The story follows an aspiring novelist as she gets tangled up in a real-life mystery involving Harry's character, Lulu. The critics hated it, but took time to mention that Alec Baldwin, who played a cop, gave a "decent performance."

3. Madonna in *A Certain Sacrifice* (1985)

In 1985, when it was clear the world had a pop icon on its hands, the creators of *A Certain Sacrifice* released this low-budget movie, much to Madonna's chagrin. The movie, filmed in New York in the late '70s, offers Madonna as a streetwise teen who gets in over her head with some unsavory characters.

Madonna may not be known as a great actor, but *A Certain Sacrifice* shows she had star appeal long before she ruled MTV.

4. Courtney Cox in *Masters of the Universe* (1987)

Life was pretty sweet while playing Monica in NBC's megahit sitcom, *Friends*, but in 1987 Courtney Cox was running for her life from characters named Gildor and Karg. Cox had done a Bruce Springsteen video and television work before this He-Man movie, and she completed other film projects in 1987, but this role made her a favorite among the sci-fi set and possibly foretold her future work in kitschy movies such as the 1996 thriller *Scream*.

5. Jack Nicholson in *The Cry Baby Killer* (1958)

One of the better-known and most-respected screen actors of our time, Jack Nicholson has won three Oscars and has been nominated for many more. But before that he had to pay the rent. At age 21, Nicholson got a part in *The Cry Baby Killer*, a super low-budget, not-yet-ready-for-prime-time movie about an unstable young man who finds himself in dire circumstances. Nicholson plays Jimmy, the "cry baby killer," and does a good job with a weak script. But if you want to see Jack at his best, check out *One Flew Over the Cuckoo's Nest*, *The Shining*, or *The Departed*.

6. Tom Cruise in *Endless Love* (1981)

The only people to benefit commercially from this story of two star-crossed lovers (played by Brooke Shields and Martin Hewitt) were Diana Ross and Lionel Richie, who sang the hit song of the same name. The movie itself, directed by Franco Zefferelli, was pretty much a disaster. Tom Cruise makes a quick appearance as Billy— he auditioned for the lead but was beat out by Hewitt. Not only did Cruise, the future *Top Gun* hunk/Oscar nominee/media magnet, make his big-screen debut in this sappy teen flick, James Spader, Jamie Gertz, and Ian Ziering were also rookies in *Endless Love*.

7. Julia Roberts in *Firehouse* (1987)

Julia Roberts got super famous relatively early in her career, so there wasn't too much time for clunkers. But there were a few.

Firehouse is a raunchy comedy à la *Police Academy* that used the tagline, "When the fire's out…the heat is on!" Roberts plays a character named Babs, but doesn't do enough in the film to even get a screen credit. Roberts filmed another movie entitled *Blood Red* before *Firehouse,* but it wasn't released until 1989, making this lowbrow farce her big-screen debut.

8. Keanu Reeves in *One Step Away* (1985)

The man who cracked *The Matrix* and was one half of the cultural phenomenon known as *Bill and Ted's Excellent Adventure* (he was Ted), Reeves did some TV work before his role in this troubled-teen flick produced by the National Film Board of Canada. He plays a kid with tough choices to make in a world that has stacked the odds against him. *One Step Away* is a couple steps away from being a good movie, but the future *Speed* star showed promise.

9. Tom Hanks in *He Knows You're Alone* (1980)

Long before he made us laugh in *Big,* before he made us cry in *Forrest Gump,* and way before he made mega-blockbusters like *The Da Vinci Code,* Tom Hanks was in a simple teen horror flick called *He Knows You're Alone.* The tagline of the movie was: "Every girl is frightened the night before her wedding, but this time…there's good reason!" A young bride-to-be is being stalked while her future husband is out of town. Hanks plays the grieving boyfriend of another victim. Maybe the promise of a shelf full of Oscars would have cheered him up.

10. Chris Rock in *Beverly Hills Cop II* (1987)

Surely no one on the set of *Beverly Hills Cop II* looked at the young actor playing "Playboy Mansion valet" and thought, "That kid's going to be hosting the Academy Awards someday!" Chris Rock has made a name for himself as one of the most brilliant voices in stand-up comedy, but before his own original material opened doors at HBO and network television, Rock was opening car doors for Eddie Murphy in this '80s comedy classic.

YOU WOULD HAVE BEEN PERFECT IN THAT MOVIE!
9 Stars Who Turned Down Memorable Roles

❊ ❊ ❊ ❊

It seems that the actors cast in our favorite movies are perfect for the part, but they're often not the director's first choice. Most celebs have turned down more roles than they've taken, some with regrets but many with thanks to their lucky stars.

1. Will Smith

Actor Will Smith started as the MC of the hip-hop duo DJ Jazzy Jeff & the Fresh Prince, winning the first ever Grammy in the Rap category in 1988. Smith was nearing bankruptcy in 1990 when he was hired to star in the sitcom *The Fresh Prince of Bel-Air,* which became a huge success. His movies include *Independence Day* (1996), *Men in Black* (1997), and *Ali* (2001). He was also offered the lead role in *The Matrix* (1999). Despite the film's phenomenal success, Smith later said that he didn't regret turning down the role because Keanu Reeves "was brilliant as Neo." Smith also originally passed on *Men in Black,* but his wife convinced him to reconsider.

2. Gwyneth Paltrow

Gwyneth Paltrow is one of those actors who seems to know which roles to take and which ones to turn down. She's received praise for her roles in *Emma* (1996) and *The Royal Tenenbaums* (2001), and she won a Best Actress Oscar for *Shakespeare in Love* (1998). But she's turned down her fair share, including Rollergirl in *Boogie Nights* (1997), which went to Heather Graham; Emma Peel in *The Avengers* (1998), which went to Uma Thurman; and Rachel in *The Ring* (2002), which went to Naomi Watts. Paltrow may have inherited her good eye for roles from her late father, film director Bruce Paltrow, and her mother, actor Blythe Danner.

3. Sean Connery

A star with a career as long as Sean Connery's is bound to make both good and bad decisions. The good ones include roles in *Indi-*

ana Jones and the Last Crusade (1989), *The Hunt for Red October* (1990), seven James Bond movies, and his Academy Award-winning role in *The Untouchables* (1987). But one questionable decision was turning down the 007 role in *Live and Let Die* (1973), which became a great career move for his replacement, Roger Moore. Connery later turned down the role of Gandalf in the *Lord of the Rings* trilogy, which went to Ian McKellen, and the role of Morpheus in *The Matrix* films, which went to Laurence Fishburne—two decisions that he later admitted regretting.

4. Mel Gibson

Mel Gibson has had a blockbuster career as an actor, starring in both the *Mad Max* and *Lethal Weapon* series, and as a director, winning an Academy Award for *Braveheart* (1995), in which he also starred. Gibson turned down the lead role in *The Terminator* (1984), which went to Arnold Schwarzenegger instead. Gibson was also offered the lead in the first *Batman* movie (1989) (which went to Michael Keaton), but he was already committed to *Lethal Weapon 2* (1989). Later, he turned down the part of villain Two Face in *Batman Forever* (1995), which went to Tommy Lee Jones.

5. Bill Murray

Bill Murray got his start on *Saturday Night Live,* which led to juicy roles in comedies such as *Caddyshack* (1980) and *Ghostbusters* (1984), and later to serious roles in films such as *Lost in Translation* (2003), for which he received an Oscar nomination. Murray was chosen for the role of Donald "Boon" Schoenstein in *Animal House* (1978), but passed to honor a previous commitment. Murray probably made a wise decision when he turned down the lead in *Bad Santa* (2003) (which went to Billy Bob Thornton) because of a scheduling conflict with *Lost in Translation.*

6. Al Pacino

Al Pacino rose to fame playing Michael Corleone in *The Godfather* movies and has since starred in many great movies, including *Scarface* (1983), *Donnie Brasco* (1997), and *Scent of a Woman* (1992), for which he won an Oscar. But can you imagine Big Al as Han Solo in *Star Wars* (1977), the role that started the career of Harrison Ford? Pacino also turned down the lead role in *Close Encounters of the Third Kind* (1977), which, instead, went to Richard Dreyfuss. But the actor Pacino has had the most close encounters with is Dustin Hoffman. Pacino turned down starring roles in *Midnight Cowboy* (1969), *Marathon Man* (1976), and *Kramer vs. Kramer* (1979), all of which went to Hoffman.

7. Marilyn Monroe

Marilyn Monroe starred in many great movies in her short career, including *Gentlemen Prefer Blondes* (1953), *How to Marry a Millionaire* (1953), and *The Seven Year Itch* (1955). But the blonde bombshell passed on the lead in *Goodbye Charlie* (1964), a comedy directed by Vincente Minnelli, in which a gangster dies and gets reincarnated as a woman. Debbie Reynolds took the part instead. Monroe also refused a starring role in the Western *Heller in Pink Tights* (1960) because she believed the role was weak. Sophia Loren took the part, wearing a blonde wig.

8. Rock Hudson

Rock Hudson, a favorite leading man of the 1950s and 1960s, starred in films such as *Come September* (1961), *Send Me No Flowers* (1964), and *Pillow Talk* (1959), the first of several films with Doris Day. He signed on to play the lead in *Ben Hur* (1959), but when contract negotiations broke down, the part went to Charlton Heston, a move that would prove to be Hudson's only career regret.

9. Brad Pitt

Brad Pitt has had hunky roles in many films including *Ocean's Eleven* (2001), *Legends of the Fall* (1994), and *Thelma & Louise* (1991). But he turned down a role in *Apollo 13* (1995) to make the movie *Se7en* (1995), which won an MTV Movie Award for Best Movie, beating out *Apollo 13*. But *Apollo 13* received nine Academy Award nominations and won two Oscars, leaving *Se7en* in the dust.

9 Outrageous Hollywood Publicity Stunts

The movie industry isn't exactly shy about self-promotion. After all, the Academy Awards began in 1928 simply to generate press coverage for the movies and stars of the day. Well-orchestrated PR campaigns designed to get people into theaters have helped many films' box office success. Here are some of the wildest feats in the long history of movie publicity.

1. *The Prisoner of Zenda* (1937)

Legendary Hollywood publicist Russell Birdwell created a buzz for this David O. Selznick-directed swashbuckling movie by arranging for an airplane to bring a dozen residents from Zenda, Ontario, to the world premiere in New York City. The publicity apparently worked because the film received two Oscar nominations.

2. *Gone With the Wind* (1939)

Birdwell was also involved in one of the industry's most famous PR efforts: The search for the actress to play Scarlett O'Hara in the screen version of Margaret Mitchell's novel created much hoopla as the casting director traveled the country holding open auditions. After three years of interviews and auditions with stars such as Katherine Hepburn, Paulette Goddard, and Lana Turner, the role went to Vivien Leigh, who had appeared in a few films, but remained largely unknown outside of Great Britain. Frankly, the public didn't seem to give a damn, because they made *Gone With the Wind* the highest grossing film in movie history (adjusted for inflation). Its original release and seven rereleases over the years have raked in nearly $2.7 billion in today's figures.

3. *Down Missouri Way* (1946)

This musical features an agriculture professor who secures a movie role for her trained mule, Shirley. To promote the film, a studio publicity man led Shirley, with an ad for the movie on her back, down Fifth Avenue and into the restaurant overlooking Rockefeller Plaza's ice rink. Managers naturally refused to seat the animal. The press showed up to record the event, so it accomplished the publicist's mission...but it didn't appear to do much for the movie, which was not a box office smash.

4. *Teacher's Pet* (1958)

Clark Gable and Doris Day star in this comedy about a newspaper editor. For publicity purposes, Paramount filmed 50 Hollywood newsmen sitting at desks and gave a few of them lines in the film. What better way to get reporters to focus on your movie than to put them in it? The buzz may have worked; the *New York Times* placed *Teacher's Pet* in its top ten of 1958, and the movie received two Oscar nominations.

5. *Mr. Sardonicus* (1961)

Colombia Pictures executives told director William Castle to film an alternate, happy ending for this dark movie. Castle turned the episode into a publicity opportunity, giving audience members cards with thumbs-up and thumbs-down to "vote" for the main character's fate. Castle apparently understood human nature well— there are no accounts of audiences wanting a happy ending. But he may not have known their movie desires quite as well because they gave their thumbs-down to the movie.

6. *The Blair Witch Project* (1999)

Producers intimated that this thriller's documentary style was authentic and implied that the footage making up the entire movie had been discovered after three student filmmakers searching for the so-called "Blair Witch" disappeared in the woods of rural Maryland. They even listed the film's lead actors (the supposed filmmakers) as "missing, presumed dead" on the Internet Movie Database before the movie's release. The stunt seemed to work: The movie made the *Guinness Book of World Records* for the highest box-office-proceeds-to-budget ratio in film history. It cost only around $35,000 to make but pulled in more than $140 million in the United States and more than $248 million worldwide.

7. Office Space (1999)

The corporate "cube farm" is the target of both this cult classic—which follows three company workers who rebel against their less-than-rewarding work environment—as well as its publicity stunt. For a week, the studio had a man sit inside a Plexiglas work cubicle on top of an office building overlooking Times Square. Everyone from Howard Stern to nearby office workers expressed sympathy. The publicity seemed to help the film, which ranked number 65 on Bravo's 2006 list of the 100 funniest movies of all time.

8. House of Wax (2005)

Producers often use a celebrity's star power to draw audiences to their films. But Joel Silver took things in a darker direction for this horror flick by advertising the death of Paris Hilton's character in the movie. Turning her notoriety to his advantage, he sold shirts reading "See Paris Die May 6." The publicity may have been for naught. *House of Wax* was almost universally panned, and U.S. ticket sales came a few million dollars short of covering the movie's $35 million production costs. But it made up for its weak domestic performance overseas, grossing more than $70 million worldwide.

9. Borat (2006)

As the title character, British actor Sacha Baron Cohen played a misspeaking journalist from Kazakhstan. In September 2006, Secret Service officers prevented Cohen (dressed fully in character, as he often does for his stunts) from entering the White House where he hoped to invite "Premier George Walter Bush" to a screening of the film. His antics even prompted the Kazakh government to remind audiences that the obnoxious character does *not* properly represent the country's values. Whether due to Cohen's antics, generally positive reviews, or word-of-mouth, the film made more than $248 million worldwide.

✳ ✳ ✳

"Many a small thing has been made large
by the right kind of advertising."
—Mark Twain, *A Connecticut Yankee in King Arthur's Court*

19 Hollywood Hunks

❋ ❋ ❋ ❋

Match the Hollywood hunk to one of his most memorable roles.

1. John Travolta	a. Jim Stark (*Rebel Without a Cause*)
2. Patrick Swayze	b. Michael Green (*When a Man Loves a Woman*)
3. Kevin Bacon	c. Crash Davis (*Bull Durham*)
4. Tom Cruise	d. Dirk Diggler (*Boogie Nights*)
5. Keanu Reeves	e. Danny Zuko (*Grease*)
6. Mel Gibson	f. Jim Braddock (*Cinderella Man*)
7. Denzel Washington	g. Johnny Castle (*Dirty Dancing*)
8. Al Pacino	h. Han Solo (*Star Wars*)
9. Robert De Niro	i. Jack Sparrow (*Pirates of the Caribbean*)
10. Brad Pitt	j. Sgt. Martin Riggs (*Lethal Weapon*)
11. James Dean	k. Michael Corleone (*The Godfather*)
12. George Clooney	l. Officer Jack Traven (*Speed*)
13. Kevin Costner	m. Jake LaMotta (*Raging Bull*)
14. Johnny Depp	n. Zack Mayo (*An Officer and a Gentleman*)
15. Andy Garcia	o. Ren McCormack (*Footloose*)
16. Mark Wahlberg	p. Tristan Ludlow (*Legends of the Fall*)
17. Russell Crowe	q. Lincoln Rhyme (*The Bone Collector*)
18. Harrison Ford	r. Maverick (*Top Gun*)
19. Richard Gere	s. Dr. Doug Ross (*ER*)

Answers: 1. e; 2. g; 3. o; 4. r; 5. l; 6. j; 7. q; 8. k; 9. m; 10. p; 11. a; 12. s; 13. c; 14. i; 15. b; 16. d; 17. f; 18. h; 19. n

126

THE MOTHER OF ALL CHICK FLICKS
11 Movies Written by Nora Ephron

✳ ✳ ✳ ✳

Nora Ephron, likely the most successful female screenwriter in film history, has garnered the respect and admiration of the industry and the worship of fans around the world who love her "love conquers all" happy endings. Grab a box of tissues and check out this list of her best.

1. *Silkwood* (1983)

Ephron was at the top of her game with this script based on the true story of Karen Silkwood, a whistle-blower on safety violations at an Oklahoma plutonium plant. Meryl Streep stars as Silkwood, and Kurt Russell and Cher round out the cast. The movie won Oscar nominations for Streep, Cher, Ephron (for screenwriting), and director Mike Nichols and grossed more than $35 million.

2. *Heartburn* (1986)

The all-star cast of *Heartburn* included Meryl Streep, Jack Nicholson, and Jeff Daniels in a story based on Ephron's best-selling novel, which captured her real-life transition between marriages. The movie was in good hands with frequent collaborator Mike Nichols directing and brought in more than $25 million.

3. *When Harry Met Sally* (1989)

Probably the most popular and iconic Ephron film to date, *When Harry Met Sally* is widely understood to be the romantic comedy by which all others are measured. Directed by Rob Reiner, the film stars comedian Billy Crystal and Ephron favorite Meg Ryan as Harry and Sally try to answer the question: Can men and women be just friends? A bona fide blockbuster, this favorite raked in $93 million at the box office.

4. *My Blue Heaven* (1990)

This light comedy stars Steve Martin, Rick Moranis, Joan Cusack, and Carol Kane as FBI agents, mobsters, and other suburbanites.

The script was written by Ephron and did okay in theaters, pulling in around $25 million, but it wasn't the follow-up to *When Harry Met Sally* that Ephron had hoped it would be.

5. *This Is My Life* (1992)

In this typically quirky-with-a-message Ephron film (she directed this one, too), a single mom chucks her sales job to trailblaze a career as a stand-up comedian in New York City. That's a tough road, especially for a mom whose family has to make its own transitions. The film wasn't one of Ephron's biggest hits, but it grossed nearly $3 million at the box office and was received warmly by critics who were ready to find fault with the first-time director.

6. *Sleepless in Seattle* (1993)

Tom Hanks and Meg Ryan make this Ephron-original sparkle all the more under her precise direction. Hanks plays a recent widower who finds new possibilities for love when his son puts him on national radio. A long-distance relationship sparks, and challenges present themselves as the couple tries to meet. *Sleepless* was anything but a sleeper, bringing in more than $125 million at the box office and garnering positive reviews from critics.

7. *Mixed Nuts* (1994)

Steve Martin, one of Ephron's favorite actors, stars in this madcap comedy about a crisis hotline business during the busy holiday season. Late comedy great Madeline Kahn also stars, along with Anthony LaPaglia. Ephron served as writer and director for *Mixed Nuts,* so when the critics universally panned it, she was doubly to blame, though the film still took in around $6 million.

8. *Michael* (1996)

The lives of two tabloid reporters (Andie MacDowell and William Hurt) are changed forever when they find themselves investigating a claim that the archangel Michael is living in Iowa. The movie that reignited John Travolta's career was also a huge hit for Ephron, who wrote and directed *Michael.* This time the formula worked, and the movie took in $95 million at the box office.

9. *You've Got Mail* (1998)

Ephron reunited *Sleepless in Seattle* stars Meg Ryan and Tom Hanks for this romantic comedy about an indie-bookstore owner and a bookstore chain bigwig. The two are business rivals but fall for each other over the Internet, not realizing the true identity of the other until they're hooked. A whopping $115 million in box office receipts later, Ephron showed that she was still the master of the romantic comedy genre.

10. *Hanging Up* (2000)

Ephron and her sister Delia teamed up for the first Ephron film of the 21st century, about a trio of sisters who bond over the death of their father. Stereotypical "hysterical-female" breakdowns and makeups occur, played out by A-list actors Meg Ryan, Diane Keaton (who also directed), and Lisa Kudrow. The film was panned by critics and only brought in $36 million—about half as much as it cost to make. The movie was based on a book written by Delia Ephron, but it simply didn't translate to the screen as well as the sisters would've liked.

11. *Bewitched* (2005)

With megastar Nicole Kidman and popular funnyman Will Ferrell, the film version of the 1960s TV series should've brought bigger box office returns than it did. Ephron wrote and directed this much-hyped film, but it didn't do as well as expected. Still, the movie pulled in $62 million at the box office, even though critics didn't find much "bewitching" about it.

THE QUEEN OF SCREAM
17 Films of Linnea Quigley

❋ ❋ ❋ ❋

Curvy, blonde, and petite (5' 2", 98 pounds), Linnea Quigley has made 90 feature films since she moved to Hollywood in 1975. She landed her first acting gig while still in her teens, and quickly became a "scream queen"—a beauty active mainly in R-rated horror thrillers. It's not much of a living, though—in 1987, Quigley was paid just $400 for her starring role in Nightmare Sisters. *Here are some of her most piquantly titled films.*

1. *Psycho from Texas* (1975)
A drifter is hired to kidnap and kill a Texas oil millionaire; Quigley plays a barmaid in this, her first feature film.

2. *The Return of the Living Dead* (1985)
Flesh-eating zombies assault teens trapped in a warehouse. This was Quigley's breakthrough movie. She plays Trash, a punk rocker who performs an exotic dance atop a tombstone.

3. *Creepozoids* (1987)
Ragged survivors of World War III straggle into an abandoned laboratory that is crawling with cannibalistic humanoids created following a botched government experiment in food research. Quigley fights monsters and takes a shower.

4. *Nightmare Sisters* (1987)
Three geeky college girls are possessed by an evil spirit and become ravenous sex bombs. Can the boy geeks save them? Top-billed Quigley is joined by fellow scream queens Brinke Stevens and Michelle Bauer.

5. *Sorority Babes in the Slimeball Bowl-O-Rama* (1988)
Skimpily attired sorority gals are trapped in a bowling alley with an evil imp who has been released from a shattered bowling trophy. Quigley battles the imp and bowls.

6. *Hollywood Chainsaw Hookers* (1988)

A private detective runs up against prostitutes who carve up their johns in cultish blood rites. The movie's tagline: "They charge an arm and a leg!"

7. *Blood Nasty* (1989)

An ordinary fellow dies and is reanimated with the soul of a serial killer. Problem: The innocent guy's mom would rather he stay dead (life insurance, you see). Meanwhile, the serial killer is determined to continue his mischief.

8. *Assault of the Party Nerds* (1989)

A four-member fraternity tries to enlist more members in the days before graduation. Quigley plays Bambi, a cutie enlisted to help swell the rolls.

9. *Robot Ninja* (1990)

A lonely comic book artist transforms himself into Robot Ninja, a violent crime fighter. Besides Linnea, this one features Burt Ward, who enjoyed fame in the '60s as Robin on TV's *Batman*.

10. *Beach Babes from Beyond* (1993)

Interstellar beach girls land on Earth and enter a bikini contest to help an old fella hang on to his beach house. Burt Ward makes an appearance as do Jackie Stallone (Sly's mom) and Joey Travolta (John's brother).

11. *Sick-o-Pathics* (1996)

Art imitates life in this horror-comedy: Quigley plays a scream queen in a segment called "Commercial: Dr. Riker's Hair Lotion."

12. *Mari-Cookie and the Killer Tarantula* (1998)

Spider queen Mari-Cookie (played by vintage cult actress Lina Romay) kidnaps men and strings them up in gigantic gooey webs. Quigley, in a costarring role, wears a teeny bikini.

13. *Kannibal* (2001)

Quigley plays crime boss Georgina Thereshkova, who finds herself in the crosshairs of the police *and* a male mob chief.

14. *Corpses Are Forever* (2003)

When the gates of hell open, the world is overrun with zombies. Humankind's only hope is an amnesiac spy and his odd assortment of allies. Third-billed Quigley takes a back seat to scream queens Brinke Stevens and Debbie Rochon.

15. *Zombiegeddon* (2003)

It's a zombie apocalypse as the walking dead take over the world. At age 45, Quigley plays a school principal.

16. *Hoodoo for Voodoo* (2006)

College students at Mardi Gras pick up a dose of real voodoo and drop dead. Quigley plays a more mature character, Queen Marie.

17. *Spring Break Massacre* (2007)

Six sorority girls on a sleepover are stalked by an escaped serial killer. No bikini for Quigley in this one; she's the deputy sheriff.

AN OSCAR FOR OPIE
13 Notable Movies Directed by Ron Howard

❋ ❋ ❋ ❋

At the tender age of four, a freckle-faced boy with a toothy grin began a film career that would last several decades. America would soon come to recognize Ron Howard as a lovable little kid on The Andy Griffith Show *and later as a lovable teen on* Happy Days, *two of the most popular shows in the history of television. But Howard wasn't content to be an actor; he had dreams of directing. With a penchant for telling a good story, Howard has been criticized for sometimes being too sentimental, but you can't fault him for having a heart—and legions of movie fans prove that, sappy or not, Howard's heart is in the right place.*

1. *Splash* (1984)

Tom Hanks and Darryl Hannah star in this film about a young man in love with a mermaid. *Splash* made a bundle for Disney's new

Touchstone division and was the studio's most successful live-action feature up to that time. Burgeoning star Hanks took the role of Allen (after it was turned down by John Travolta and Bill Murray), then watched as it launched him as one of Hollywood's most popular stars. With *Splash,* Howard proved his ability to warm audience's hearts while keeping them laughing.

2. *Cocoon* (1985)

Hot on the heels of the mermaid love story, Howard took on another seemingly too-bizarre-to-work plot and made a hit out of it. In 1985, audiences watched a bunch of elderly people discover the fountain of youth in a swimming pool occupied by aliens. Not only did the uplifting movie go over well with audiences of all ages, the Academy saw an inspired performance by lead Don Ameche and gave him the Best Supporting Actor Oscar in 1986. Another Oscar went to the special effects team that worked on *Cocoon*—incredibly enough, those misty, glowing aliens from the mid-1980s still hold up in today's world of computer-generated imaging.

3. *Willow* (1988)

If you were a kid in the 1980s, chances are good you saw *Willow* at least once. This sci-fi/fantasy story, penned by George Lucas, follows the adventures of a diminutive farmer and amateur magician named Willow as he attempts to save a baby princess from death at the hands of evil queen Bavmorda. With the help of a swordsman named Madmartigan (played by Val Kilmer), Willow executes his quest with courage, will, and more than a few lucky breaks. The movie did pretty well at the box office, but not well enough for a sequel. *Willow* was a big break for Howard, who, until the movie's release, had been pigeonholed as a director of light comedy.

4. *Parenthood* (1989)

Producer Brian Grazer, along with writers Babaloo Mandel and Lowell Ganz, teamed up with Howard to develop this story, loosely based on their own experiences as parents. Steve Martin stars as a hapless dad with a wildly extended middle-class family, including Dianne Wiest as a frazzled mother of two, Rick Moranis as a type-A father, Jason Robards as Grandpa, and a host of other quirky characters. *Parenthood* was a hit, grossing more than $100 million, a coup for a character-driven, non-action film at the time.

5. *Backdraft* (1991)

Howard established himself as a bona fide blockbuster director with *Backdraft* in 1991. The story follows a pair of fire-fighting brothers as they work and toil in the Chicago Fire Department. Kurt Russell and William Baldwin star as the brothers who play cat and mouse with a mysterious arsonist. Robert De Niro stars as the cut-the-crap arson investigator and Donald Sutherland shines as his creepy nemesis. While some of the lines in *Backdraft* are a little heavy-handed, the filming of the fire is proof of Howard's directorial prowess. The fire itself was often cited by critics as being the most interesting character in the film.

6. *Far and Away* (1992)

Years before he was lambasted for his frenetic behavior, Tom Cruise and then-wife Nicole Kidman made a respectable movie with Howard about two young Irish immigrants in the Oklahoma Territory in the late 19th century. Life is hard for the young couple, but with love on their side, anything is possible. Well, except for good reviews and a big box office draw. Though *Far and Away* had many fans, the studio was disappointed with the box office returns and confused about why it wasn't a bigger hit. After all, Cruise and Kidman were huge stars at the time, and Howard had more than established his reputation.

7. *Apollo 13* (1995)

Not much attention was paid to the many moon missions in the years following the first lunar landing—until something went wrong. *Apollo 13* is based on the true story of NASA astronauts Lovell, Haise, and Swigert, who encountered massive technical difficulty when returning to Earth. The phrase "Houston, we have a problem" originated on this mission and is delivered by Tom Hanks's Lovell in this edge-of-your-seat movie. The rest of the cast includes Bill Paxton, Kevin Bacon, Gary Sinise, Ed Harris, and

Kathleen Quinlan. *Apollo 13* was a summer blockbuster, raking in more than $175 million at the box office and scoring two Oscars.

8. *Ransom* (1996)

Mel Gibson stars in this modern remake of a 1956 film of the same name. Gibson plays Tom Mullen, the wealthy father of a recently kidnapped boy. When the FBI's plan goes awry, Mullen takes matters into his own hands by going on national television to offer a deal to anyone who can bring his son safely home. It's a risky proposal and the film takes audiences through a multitude of twists and turns before the resolution. *Ransom* wasn't an Oscar contender, but it pleased audiences nonetheless, drawing in almost $140 million.

9. *EdTV* (1999)

In the early days of reality TV, even Howard jumped on the bandwagon. *EdTV* is the story of television producer Cynthia (played by Ellen DeGeneres), who believes that the way to save her station's ratings is to broadcast a person's life, 24 hours a day, 7 days a week. Matthew McConaughey plays the feckless Ed Pekurny, whose life starts out fairly normal but doesn't stay that way for long. It's a mix of love story, morality play, and social commentary, but it didn't make a huge impression at the box office.

10. *How the Grinch Stole Christmas* (2000)

Theodor Geisel, better known as Dr. Seuss, wrote the children's book *How the Grinch Stole Christmas* in 1957. After countless attempts to create a live-action film version were denied by Geisel, Howard won the chance to direct an adaptation of this silly but charming story of redemption and the magic of Christmas. Jim Carrey plays the Grinch, a large, green monster who steals the presents of the defenseless Whos of Whoville. Carrey's makeup and costume were notoriously awful, requiring three hours in the makeup chair each day. But it paid off for the makeup artists—they won an Oscar for their efforts and the costume department was also nominated for their work. The movie did fairly well at the box office, grossing $260 million, but critics didn't find much to like— it's tough to improve on Seuss, even if your name is Ron Howard.

11. *A Beautiful Mind* (2001)

Howard showcased his love of a good underdog story in this biopic about mathematician John Nash. The film follows the genius Nash as he falls deeper and deeper into paranoia after the U.S. government asks him to help break Soviet codes—it doesn't help that Nash is a diagnosed schizophrenic. Only his wife, Alicia, played by Jennifer Connelly (in the role that garnered her an Oscar), can help bring him back to reality. *A Beautiful Mind* swept the box office and the Oscars, earned Howard his first Best Director and Best Picture awards, and nabbed an award for Best Screenplay. You've come a long way, Opie.

12. *Cinderella Man* (2005)

In 2005, Howard brought Depression-era prizefighter Jim Braddock's life story to the big screen. The film received international accolades for its nuanced performances and what many felt was flawless execution. The tale is dramatic: As an impoverished ex-boxer working odd jobs, Braddock was unable to support his family during the bleak days of the Great Depression. In a true-grit change of heart, the fighter steps into the ring again and goes on to become a true underdog legend. Russell Crowe stars as Braddock, Renée Zellwegger plays his wife, and Paul Giamatti earned an Oscar nod as Braddock's manager, Joe Gould.

13. *The Da Vinci Code* (2006)

If you want to cause controversy, question the whole foundation of Christianity via numerology, secret societies, and the *Mona Lisa.* Dan Brown's novel came first, selling around 60 million copies before Howard released his film version of *The Da Vinci Code* in 2006. Tom Hanks stars as Robert Langdon, a symbologist caught up in the middle of a murder mystery with ancient implications. He is assisted/thwarted by French actors Audrey Tatou and Jean Reno and British star Ian McKellen. *The Da Vinci Code* scored serious hype before its release and claims the highest-grossing foreign start in history, raking in $152.6 million in its first days in theaters around the world. The film captures rarely seen images of Paris's Louvre museum and the story, which is full of twists, turns, and intrigue, is captivating even if you don't buy into the premise.

FROM COMIC BOOK TO THE BIG SCREEN
26 Comic Books that Were Made into Movies

✳ ✳ ✳ ✳

1. *Spider-Man*
2. *Batman*
3. *Superman*
4. *X-Men*
5. *Teenage Mutant Ninja Turtles*
6. *Richie Rich*
7. *Popeye*
8. *Men in Black*
9. *Josie and the Pussycats*
10. *The Incredible Hulk*
11. *Howard the Duck*
12. *Road to Perdition*
13. *The Fantastic Four*
14. *Dick Tracy*
15. *Casper*
16. *The Mask*
17. *Sabrina the Teenage Witch*
18. *The Rocketeer*
19. *Spawn*
20. *Judge Dredd*
21. *Sin City*
22. *The Crow*
23. *Swamp Thing*
24. *Timecop*
25. *Blade*
26. *Daredevil*

14 Films Directed by Steven Spielberg

✳ ✳ ✳ ✳

As a child, Cecil B. DeMille's production of The Greatest Show
on Earth *was the first movie Steven Spielberg ever saw, marking
the beginning of his love affair with the world of film.
Spielberg began making home movies at an early age, and, at 14,
he won an award for a 40-minute war movie he called* Escape
to Nowhere. *Spielberg attended Long Beach University,
but dropped out to pursue his dream of a career in film.
Television assignments followed, but it wasn't until 1971 with
his direction of a Richard Matheson television adaptation
called* Duel *that Spielberg's burgeoning reputation as
a superb filmmaker was cemented.*

1. Sugarland Express (1974)

Sugarland Express marked the big-screen directorial debut of
Steven Spielberg. Starring Goldie Hawn, Ben Johnson, and William
Atherton, this movie, based on a true story, revolves around a young
woman who helps her husband escape from prison so they can
kidnap their child who's been placed in foster care. Along the way,
they take a policeman hostage, and the movie becomes a madcap
escape caper. The film grossed more than $12 million and won Best
Screenplay at the Cannes Film Festival. Incidentally, *Sugarland
Express* was the first movie to feature a 360-degree pan with dialogue from within a car by utilizing a tracking shot from the front
seat to the back.

2. Jaws (1975)

Based on the Peter Benchley novel, this horror film was
released just in time for beach season. The villain was a
carnivorous and very homicidal great white shark that
attacked people in a quiet coastal town. But
the film, which Spielberg calls the most
difficult he's made, often played on the

power of suggestion, proving that what the mind conjures in the imagination can sometimes be more powerful than an actual image. *Jaws* made the most of that, earning more than $260 million in the United States and setting a record at the time for box office gross. The film also won Oscars for editing, sound, and original score.

3. *Close Encounters of the Third Kind* (1977)

This unique UFO story tells the tale of an electrician (Richard Dreyfuss) who is drawn to an isolated area in the wilderness where an alien spaceship has landed. It is not a terror-filled tale of alien conflict or hostility, and therein lies its remarkable difference from other films of this ilk. Instead, it is a compelling story of contact and communication, foreshadowing the power of *E.T.* a few years later. The special effects were dazzling, and the movie gleaned many Oscar nods, including a win for Best Cinematography.

4. *Raiders of the Lost Ark* (1981)

Spielberg struck pure gold in 1981 with the release of this movie, which was written by George Lucas and Philip Kaufman. Set in the 1930s, the film stars Harrison Ford as archaeologist and adventurer Indiana Jones and follows his breathtaking journey in search of the Ark of the Covenant, which is said to hold the Ten Commandments. He must find it before the Nazis do, because, according to the story, Hitler has plans to use the Ark as a weapon. The film received glowing reviews and grossed more than $242 million.

5. *E.T. (The Extra Terrestrial)* (1982)

If Spielberg struck gold with *Raiders of the Lost Ark*, he struck platinum with *E.T.* A classic film that appeals to all age groups, the story centers around a cute but very odd alien who gets marooned on Earth. He chances upon a boy named Elliot (Henry Thomas), and the two form a powerful bond. The film captivates and enthralls with its message of friendship, love, and generosity. *E.T.* was critically acclaimed and became one of the biggest money-makers in box office history, grossing more than $435 million in the United States alone, followed by a marketing frenzy that ensued from the sale of *E.T.* memorabilia.

6. *The Color Purple* (1985)

Based on Alice Walker's Pulitzer Prize-winning novel, this 1985 production chronicles the life of a young African-American woman named Celie (Whoopi Goldberg), who lives in the South at the turn of the 20th century. She is a poor mother of two with an abusive husband (Danny Glover) whom she fears so greatly that she calls him "Mister." Often criticized as being compelling but too careful and slick, *The Color Purple* still grossed more than $98 million at the box office and was nominated for 11 Oscars, although it did not win any.

7. *Hook* (1991)

This adaptation of J. M. Barrie's classic story is a film of élan and rambunctious spirit, but it is also a bit messy and undisciplined. According to the story line, an adult Peter Pan (Robin Williams) must regain his youthful spirit and confront his old enemy Captain Hook (Dustin Hoffman), who has kidnapped Peter's children. Julia Roberts as Tinkerbell accompanies Peter on his return to Neverland and helps him become "Peter Pan" again. Although Spielberg himself admitted that he was disappointed with the final version of the movie, it still grossed more than $119 million and garnered five Oscar nominations.

8. *Jurassic Park* (1993)

Written by Michael Crichton, *Jurassic Park*—the book and subsequent movie—generated so much interest in dinosaurs that the study of paleontology increased dramatically and has been at an all-time high ever since. The setting is a remote island where a wealthy businessman has secretly created a theme park featuring live dinosaurs cloned from prehistoric DNA found encased in amber. As preposterous as this may sound, it works, and there is genuine suspense, especially when the prehistoric creatures break free. The special effects are dazzling and eye-popping, earning the film three Oscars—Best Effects (Sound Effects), Best Effects (Visual),

and Best Sound. *Jurassic Park* held the box office record gross of $357,067,947 before it was beaten by *Titanic* in 1997.

9. *Schindler's List* (1993)

This masterpiece, based on the true horrors of the Holocaust, is quite possibly Spielberg's finest achievement. The plot concerns a greedy Czech-born businessman, Oskar Schindler (Liam Neeson), who is determined to make his fortune in Nazi Germany by exploiting cheap Jewish labor. Despite his fervent affiliation with the Third Reich, Schindler turns his factory into a refuge for Jews—working in a factory guaranteed longer life to those slated for extermination in the barbaric concentration camps. Although Schindler ended up penniless, he single-handedly saved about 1,100 Jews from certain death. *Schindler's List* won seven Academy Awards including Best Picture and Best Director, and the film grossed more than $321 million worldwide.

10. *Amistad* (1997)

This film relates the true story of mutiny aboard the slave ship *Amistad,* which was destined for America in 1839. The slaves revolted, murdered the crew, and remained adrift for weeks. After discovery by some American marine officers, the slaves were tried for murder. A few noble people stood to defend them—no matter what the cost—to end the dehumanizing institution of slavery in the New World. Those few are the strength of *Amistad,* which means "friendship" in Spanish. Starring Morgan Freeman, Anthony Hopkins, Nigel Hawthorne, and newcomer Djimon Hounsou, *Amistad* was nominated for four Academy Awards and grossed more than $44 million.

11. *Saving Private Ryan* (1998)

Based on a true story, this war drama centers around a group of U.S. soldiers trying to rescue paratrooper Ryan, a comrade who is stationed behind enemy lines during World War II. Spielberg's camera is graphic and wild, deliberately evoking the reality of war. The opening scene is mayhem and chaos mingled with blood, vomit, and tears. In one memorable moment a soldier has his arm blown off, then he bends over and picks it up as if it were a fallen handkerchief. Starring Tom Hanks and Matt Damon, the film grossed more than $481 million worldwide, raking in $30 million in its opening weekend. *Saving Private Ryan* also took home five Oscars, including Best Director and Best Cinematography.

12. *Catch Me If You Can* (2002)

Based on a true story, this movie stars Leonardo DiCaprio as Frank Abagnale, Jr., a con artist who, in the 1960s, passed more than $2.5 million in fake checks in 26 countries and also posed as a pilot, pediatrician, and attorney, all by age 21. Tom Hanks plays FBI agent Carl Hanratty, who pursued Abagnale for years. The film earned two Oscar nods and grossed more than $164 million at the box office. Incidentally, Abagnale is now a multimillionaire who advises businesses on fraud detection and prevention.

13. *War of the Worlds* (2005)

Based on the original story by H. G. Wells, *War of the Worlds* depicts the frenzy that ensues when aliens invade Earth. The 2005 production is a remake of the 1953 sci-fi thriller of the same name. Two members of the original cast, Gene Barry and Ann Robinson, have cameos in this new production, which also stars Tom Cruise, Dakota Fanning, and Tim Robbins. Although not well received by critics, the film was nominated for three Academy Awards and grossed more than $591 million worldwide.

14. *Munich* (2005)

Nominated for five Oscars, including Best Picture, this film, based on a book by George Jonas, is one of courage and conscience. It relates the true story of 11 Israeli athletes who were murdered during the 1972 Olympics by the Palestinian terrorist group Black September, and the retaliation that followed. One of the actors, Guri Weinberg, plays his own father, Moshe Weinberg, who was one of the athletes killed in the massacre. *Munich* grossed more than $47 million in the United States and $127 million worldwide.

ROLES OF A REBEL
6 Movie Roles of James Dean

✳ ✳ ✳ ✳

This Indiana boy lived only 24 years, but his legend as an American icon continues to thrive. He started in show biz in a Pepsi commercial, standing around a jukebox with a group of teens singing "Pepsi-Cola hits the spot." Within a decade, Dean had two Oscar nominations. Sadly, both were posthumous. In 1955, Dean bought a Porsche Spyder, bragging that it could reach speeds of 150 miles per hour. Upon hearing this, actor Alec Guinness told him not to set foot inside the car because he would be dead before the week was out. Six days later, Dean's body was pulled from the twisted wreckage of his new car on a stretch of California highway. Dean's career was cut short, but his legacy lives on in the movies he left behind.

1. *Fixed Bayonets* (1951)

James Dean's first movie role was far from "cushy." This Korean War film was the first to depict the violence of combat. Director Samuel Fuller was given free reign to portray the grisly "kill or be killed" premise of the film, and he took it! Actors and camera crews were pushed to their physical limits, including lead actors Richard Basehart, Gene Evans, and Michael O'Shea. Twenty-year-old Dean was uncredited in the film and had only one line, which was cut in the final production.

2. *Sailor Beware* (1952)

Dean's next film was a pleasant departure from Korean combat. With Dean Martin and Jerry Lewis at the helm, production must have been more pleasant. This Paramount film took only five weeks to film, and even though it technically deals with the military, the plot centers around a good-natured bet between sailors that involves kissing girls. Dean went uncredited again, playing a guy in the locker room, but at least his line wasn't cut this time.

3. *Has Anybody Seen My Gal?* (1952)

Rock Hudson carried this film about a wealthy older man trying to decide if the family of his former love is worthy of inheriting his estate. James Dean remained one of many guys with a bit part. Specifically, he's on a bar stool at a soda fountain without any lines. He's listed as "youth at soda fountain" in the credits.

4. *East of Eden* (1955)

Dean's first major film role gave him top billing along with Julie Harris, Raymond Massey, and Burl Ives. Dean played Cal Trask, who competes with his brother for their father's love. This was the only major film released while Dean was alive. The role landed him an Oscar nomination for Best Actor, although it came posthumously. However, Ernest Borgnine won for his role in *Marty*.

5. *Rebel Without a Cause* (1955)

This is the film for which James Dean is best remembered. It came out just a month after his tragic death, and costarred a young Natalie Wood and Sal Mineo. Dean played the new kid in town, Jim Stark, who finds trouble when searching to replace the love that is lacking in his family life. A daring commentary on tough teenage existence, this movie pitted boys against each other in knife fights that used real switchblades. The actors wore chest protectors under their shirts, but Dean still ended up with a cut on his ear.

6. *Giant* (1956)

Rock Hudson worked one last time with James Dean, and this time legendary star Elizabeth Taylor rounded out the top billing. Dean played Jett Rink, a ranch hand who became a Texas oil tycoon. The actor finished shooting his scenes just days before he died, but a few voice-over lines still needed to be recorded, so actor Nick Adams stepped to the microphone to read the part of Jett Rink. Dean received a second posthumous Oscar nomination for Best Actor for this role. Rock Hudson was also nominated, but the award went to Yul Brynner for his role in *The King and I*.

16 Unexpectedly Influential Film Directors of the 20th Century

✳ ✳ ✳ ✳

Many celebrated film directors have influenced their peers and artistic descendants, and even casual film fans know their names: Alfred Hitchcock, George Lucas, Orson Welles, Steven Spielberg, and D. W. Griffith, just to name a few. The following is a list of some noteworthy directors who are considerably less well known, yet played a significant role in inspiring future directors.

1. Oscar Micheaux

Before Oscar Micheaux, African-Americans had only a marginal presence in American movies, and only then as figures of menace or derision. In 1919, Micheaux made a film of his book *The Homesteader,* and followed it with *Within Our Gates* in 1920, a tough-minded drama designed to expose the ugliness of racism. For the next 30 years, Micheaux wrote, produced, and directed nearly 40 films that portrayed the difficulties of black Americans. Hollywood regarded his productions as unimportant "race films" that were played only in segregated theaters. But to African-American audiences and the black actors he employed, Micheaux was a trailblazer who addressed contemporary concerns. Today's black cinema—and the mainstream stardom of Denzel Washington, Forest Whitaker, and others—has roots in the work of Oscar Micheaux.

2. David Hand

For years, Walt Disney allowed the general public to believe that he alone was the creator of his cartoons and live-action movies, and even the originator of such stories as *Robin Hood, Cinderella,* and *Alice's Adventures in Wonderland.* But Disney's landmark 1937 release, *Snow White and the Seven Dwarfs*, was directed by a longtime animator and animation supervisor named David Hand. *Snow White* was the first feature-length cartoon, and its visual beauty and mammoth commercial success inspired generations of future animators, including those who work today with computer-generated images instead of pen and ink. Hand also directed *Bambi* (1942) and remained active until 1980's *Mickey Mouse Disco*.

3. Anthony Mann

Anthony Mann was a highly skilled Hollywood studio director who pushed the limits of film noir in the late 1940s with *T-Men* (1947) and *Raw Deal* (1948) and later reinvigorated the Western via driven, neurotically vengeful antiheroes. Many of these Mann productions star James Stewart, including *Winchester '73* (1950), *Bend of the River* (1952), and *The Naked Spur* (1953). From this new approach came the concept of the "adult Western," which carried through Clint Eastwood's *Unforgiven* (1992) and beyond.

4. Robert Aldrich

Though highly influential in the development of the contemporary Gothic thriller (*What Ever Happened to Baby Jane?*, 1962) and the war film (*The Dirty Dozen,* 1967), Aldrich's most penetrating influence comes from his 1955 adaptation of Mickey Spillane's crime novel *Kiss Me Deadly*. With disorienting camera angles, grotesque violence, and a bleak portrayal of a world out of control, it knocked audiences back in their seats and made a tremendous impression on Jean-Luc Godard, François Truffaut, and other important young directors of the French "New Wave" of the late 1950s.

5. Roger Corman

Roger Corman, the legendary "King of the Bs," directed scores of films in just over 15 years (sometimes six or seven a year), and became not just a busy director, but Hollywood's most successful and prolific independent producer. From Westerns to Gothic horror, science fiction, crime, juvenile delinquent, and hot rod flicks—Corman made them all with a sense of fun, and continues to sponsor and inspire low- and no-budget filmmakers today.

6. Russ Meyer

When he was unable to crack the Hollywood unions, this robust, perpetually grinning cameraman and glamour photographer became an independent filmmaker. Meyer's first feature, *The*

Immoral Mr. Teas (1959) brought humor, color film stock, and even a shred of plot to the "peekaboo" genre. *Teas* was a boisterous financial success and led to other Meyer films including *Lorna* (1964), *Mudhoney* (1965), *Vixen!* (1968), and the highly regarded *Faster, Pussycat! Kill! Kill!* (1965). In 1970, 20th Century Fox financed and released Meyer's most elaborate production, *Beyond the Valley of the Dolls* (with a script by film critic Roger Ebert). Adult movies became drearily explicit in the late 1970s, and Meyer lost interest in pursuing his career, but before that happened, he inspired hundreds of films by other, lesser directors.

7. Herschell Gordon Lewis

This Chicago ad exec and direct-mail marketer partnered with financier Dave Friedman to invent the "gore" genre in 1963 with the ineptly made *Blood Feast*. Lewis elaborated on his no-holds-barred approach to violence with *Two Thousand Maniacs!* (1964), *Color Me Blood Red* (1965), and many others. He earned the dubious title "Godfather of Gore" and helped create the climate that made possible latter-day gore fests such as *Saw* (2004).

8. Richard Lester

British director Richard Lester's freewheeling approach to The Beatles' first two films, *A Hard Day's Night* (1964) and *Help!* (1965), gave swingin' London a visual style marked by handheld cameras, flip humor, and breakneck pacing. Every other director who worked with a Brit pop group followed Lester's lead, including the talented John Boorman, who guided the Dave Clark 5 through *Having a Wild Weekend* in 1965. On a broader level, Lester's influence was felt in a variety of British films that were made in the mid- to late 1960s, such as John Schlesinger's *Darling* (1965).

9. Mike Nichols

An iconoclastic American director, Mike Nichols came to movies after a successful live comedy career with partner Elaine May. Nichols's first splash was *Who's Afraid of Virginia Woolf?* (1966), which came along at a time when America was on the verge of a great liberalization of thought and cultural mores. With *The Gradu-*

ate in 1967, Nichols wittily examined youthful angst with the story of a freshly minted college grad who desires the daughter but beds the mother. Hollywood grew up in the mid-1960s, and Nichols was at the forefront.

10. Frederick Wiseman

Documentary filmmaker Frederick Wiseman made a controversial splash with his first picture, 1967's *Titicut Follies*, a harrowing look at a Massachusetts institution for the mentally ill. The movie became the template for Wiseman's subsequent work—a keen interest in the everyday but frequently hidden aspects of American life. *Titicut Follies* was followed by a score of poignant documentaries, and Wiseman's work is a direct link to latter-day socially conscious documentaries, such as *Hoop Dreams* (1994), *Stevie* (2002), *The Thin Blue Line* (1988), and even *Fahrenheit 9/11* (2004).

11. Gordon Parks

Brilliantly talented African-American photographer and filmmaker Gordon Parks revolutionized black cinema with *Shaft* in 1971. For the first time, audiences saw a black man—here, a private detective named John Shaft—pursue his own agenda in the white world and control his own life, establishment be damned. The movie launched the so-called "blaxploitation" genre that brought stardom to Jim Brown, Fred Williamson, Pam Grier, Ron O'Neal, and *Shaft's* Richard Roundtree. Blaxploitation flourished throughout the 1970s and has lately been honored—and gently parodied—by nonconformist directors Quentin Tarantino and Larry Cohen.

12. Tobe Hooper

In 1974, Tobe Hooper was a young indie filmmaker in Texas. Hooper and his partner, writer Kim Henkel, wanted to do something more commercial, so they decided to make a horror thriller, which they called *The Texas Chainsaw Massacre*. This tale of college kids victimized by a family of demented cannibals shocked audiences who thought they saw gore where there was none (blood appears only once, when a man purposely cuts his thumb). *Texas Chainsaw Massacre* exploited extreme psychological unease as audiences witnessed the helplessness of innocent victims. Other filmmakers followed with similar films that were heavy with gore but lacking Hooper's flair for bilious suspense and sick humor.

13. Robert Altman

With his peerless skill at guiding ensemble casts through a rich tapestry of interwoven stories (*Nashville,* 1975), Robert Altman made films that were short on explosions and shootouts, and long on thoughtful characterization, rueful wit, and the complexities of emotion and desire that nudge (or sometimes propel) us through life. Altman inspired some equally intelligent later filmmakers, including Paul Thomas Anderson (*Magnolia,* 1999).

14. John Carpenter

A lifelong fan of horror movies, John Carpenter reinvented the genre in 1978 with *Halloween,* and unwittingly inspired a flood of "holiday" horror films: *Mother's Day, My Bloody Valentine, Friday the 13th,* and many more. Carpenter laid the ground rules with a young woman in peril inside a weirdly shadowed house, an indestructible maniac on the loose, dark rooms that the heroine has an inexplicable urge to enter, and fiendishly effective shock moments. *Halloween* is a perennial favorite, and still a high point of blunt, low-budget moviemaking.

15. Andy and Larry Wachowski

Usually credited as The Wachowski Brothers, American writers and directors Andy and Larry Wachowski brought a fresh spin to blackmail and murder with *Bound* (1996), and became highly influential with *The Matrix* (1999) and its sequels. These science-fiction thrillers brought a fresh approach to special effects, notions of space and time, and virtual reality. Widely imitated and frequently parodied, *The Matrix* films may have outstayed their welcome, but their reverberations will be felt for many years.

16. Steven Soderbergh

Steven Soderbergh is a versatile American director who moves easily between smart action films (*Ocean's Eleven,* 2001), social commentary (*Erin Brockovich*, 2000), and crime epics (*Traffic*, 2000). Soderbergh's eclectic career is noteworthy, but his greatest influence may come from *Bubble* (2005), a low-budget drama about three underachieving employees at a doll factory and the circumstances that lead to jealousy and murder. Unassuming but extraordinarily powerful, *Bubble* shook up the film industry because Soderbergh elected to release it in theaters, on DVD, and to pay-per-view TV all on the same day, which may be the wave of the future for movie distribution.

20 Audrey Hepburn Films

✳ ✳ ✳ ✳

Movie	Character
1. *Roman Holiday* (1953)	Princess Ann
2. *Sabrina* (1954)	Sabrina Fairchild
3. *War and Peace* (1956)	Natasha Rostov
4. *Funny Face* (1957)	Jo Stockton
5. *Love in the Afternoon* (1957)	Ariane Chavasse
6. *Green Mansions* (1959)	Rima
7. *The Nun's Story* (1959)	Sister Luke
8. *The Unforgiven* (1960)	Rachel Zachary
9. *Breakfast at Tiffany's* (1961)	Holly Golightly
10. *The Children's Hour* (1961)	Karen Wright
11. *Charade* (1963)	Reggie Lampert
12. *Paris—When It Sizzles* (1964)	Gabrielle Simpson
13. *My Fair Lady* (1964)	Eliza Doolittle
14. *How to Steal a Million* (1966)	Nicole Bonnet
15. *Two for the Road* (1967)	Joanna Wallace
16. *Wait Until Dark* (1967)	Susy Hendrix
17. *Robin and Marian* (1976)	Lady Marian
18. *Bloodline* (1979)	Elizabeth Roffe
19. *They All Laughed* (1981)	Angela Niotes
20. *Always* (1989)	Hap

15 Stephen King Stories Made into Films

✳ ✳ ✳ ✳

Stephen King sold numerous short stories to magazines before Doubleday published his full-length novel Carrie *in 1973, launching a career that has spanned decades. As King churned out hit books like* Christine *and* The Green Mile, *Hollywood clamored for the opportunity to turn his prose into box office gold. More than 50 King stories have been filmed for the big screen or TV so far, and there's no sign of stopping.*

1. *Carrie* (1976)

This story about a young girl named Carrie (Sissy Spacek) has a spot in the hallowed halls of classic horror movies. Carrie's over-protective mother shelters her so much that when she gets taunted mercilessly by her classmates, they learn that teasing Carrie is a bad idea—the girl's got a few nasty tricks up her sleeve. The movie, which also stars Piper Laurie and John Travolta, grossed more than $33 million. This was the first film adaptation of a King story and years later, the first Broadway adaptation, too. *Carrie*, the musical, was one of the biggest theater flops ever, closing after just five performances and losing around $7 million.

2. *The Shining* (1980)

The term *cult classic* doesn't really cover what *The Shining* is to American pop culture. Starring Jack Nicholson and Shelley Duvall and directed by Stanley Kubrick, *The Shining* is essentially a story about cabin fever—really, really, bad cabin fever in a haunted cabin where tidal waves of blood occur from time to time and a force called "the shining" possesses little kids. There is an element of camp that can't be denied about this particular adaptation (there have been others, including a 1997 TV version), but King intensely disliked what Kubrick did with the story. Nevertheless, the movie spawned a dozen catchphrases, including, "Heeeeere's Johnny?" and "Redrum! Redrum!"

3. *Christine* (1983)

Stephen King was so popular in the early 1980s that *Christine* wasn't even published before preproduction began on the movie version. Producers took a chance on his latest story about a boy and his car. That's right—Christine is a car, not a girl. Arnie Cunningham, who might have been played by Kevin Bacon if he hadn't chosen *Footloose* instead, is a high-school nerd who falls in love with a 1958 Plymouth Fury. The car is possessed and threatens to kill anyone who tries to get in its way. The story and the film are well known but not regarded as King's best. The author has the uncanny ability to tap into people's basic fears (rejection, clowns, ghosts...), but his portrayal of a fearsome car didn't terrorize audiences as much as some of his other menaces.

4. *Cujo* (1983)

Here, doggie-doggie! Here, doggie—AAAAGGGGH! That pretty much sums up the plot behind this King adaptation. Dee Wallace plays Donna Trenton, a mom with marital problems, and a young Danny Pintauro (of *Who's the Boss?* fame) stars as her son Tad. The two find themselves in big trouble when their car breaks down miles from town and the family dog appears to be very, very ill. Cujo, a Saint Bernard, has been bitten by a rat and is none too friendly for most of the film. It took five different dogs, one mechanical head, and one guy in a dog suit to get the shots of Cujo's raging, and perhaps that's why this film has a slight cheese factor. The movie might not have nabbed any nominations or awards, but it remains a horrifying tale.

5. *The Dead Zone* (1983)

A talented cast including Christopher Walken, Tom Skerritt, and Martin Sheen plays out this story of a schoolteacher involved in an auto accident that puts him in a coma for five years. When he awakens, he's got a knack for seeing the future. This is not as fun as it sounds and scary stuff ensues. The story is loosely based on the life of Peter Hurkos, a famous psychic. While this film hasn't reached the cult status of some other King adaptations, it's regarded as a pretty decent movie. The Academy of Science Fiction, Fantasy & Horror named the film Best Picture.

6. *Children of the Corn* (1984)

This tale of terror came from a book of short stories entitled *Night Shift*, which also included future adaptations such as *The Lawnmower Man* and *Graveyard Shift*. The children of Gatlin, a little town in Nebraska, are called to murder by a preacher-boy named Isaac. A young couple gets in the way of their plans and creepy shots of wigged-out kids follow. Peter Horton and Linda Hamilton star as the doomed couple Burt and Vicky. In one scene, a copy of *Night Shift* can be seen on the dashboard of their car. This movie was universally panned, but that didn't stop it from spawning seven sequels. Most of them are as weak as the original, but the seventh film, released in 2001, is reportedly the best (and scariest) of the bunch.

7. *Firestarter* (1984)

College students beware: Those medical tests you participate in to earn money for rent could result in serious trouble later in life. So it goes with Andy and Vicky McGee, who were given doses of a nasty chemical in college that would adversely affect their future daughter, played by a cute but dangerous Drew Barrymore. A TV miniseries entitled *Firestarter: Rekindled* was produced in 2002, possibly because King is rumored to have hated the original, something filmmakers have to be wary of when working with him.

8. *Stand By Me* (1986)

A King collection entitled *Different Seasons* included a story called "Fall from Innocence: The Body." *Stand By Me,* one of King's greatest movie successes, was based on this story. A group of preteens go on an adventure to find the body of a classmate who is missing and presumed dead. They are tailed by bullies and must make very grown-up decisions throughout the course of the film, which garnered an Oscar nod for Best Adapted Screenplay. A critical and box office success, *Stand By Me* starred teen heartthrobs River Phoenix, Wil Wheaton, and Corey Feldman and is one of the most widely enjoyed King films to date, perhaps due to the focus on tension among humans rather than killer clowns or deadly cars.

9. *The Running Man* (1987)

What other Stephen King screen adaptation can boast a cast that included not one but two future U.S. governors? Only *The Running Man*, which stars Arnold Schwarzenegger as the lead and Jesse Ventura in a smaller role. The story, based on the novel of the same name written under King's nom de plume Richard Bachman, is set in the year 2017. America is a police state where criminals have the opportunity to run for their freedom on a weirdly ahead-of-its-time reality show. The movie did well when it was released, earning almost $40 million, and reviews were decent, especially for a story that King reportedly penned in less than three days.

10. *Pet Sematary* (1989)

When the Creed family's cat gets smooshed on the highway, an elderly neighbor instructs Mr. Creed to bury the cat in the "pet sematary" and watch what happens. The cat comes back, but he's a little different this time around. When Mr. Creed's son dies, guess what bright idea daddy has? Watch for a King cameo in the funeral scene. This campy, but intensely creepy, movie did well at the box office and got decent reviews for a horror movie. It also generated a sequel three years later, but it didn't do as well as the original.

11. *Misery* (1990)

King often centers his stories on a protagonist who bears a striking resemblance to himself. *Misery* is one of these. Novelist Paul Sheldon finds himself being nursed back to health by Annie Wilkes after crashing his car in the Colorado mountains. Annie is Paul's self-proclaimed number one fan and relishes the opportunity to help her favorite author. Kathy Bates won an Oscar for her role as Annie—she's terrifyingly good as the obsessed, isolated woman. If you're paying attention, you'll catch a reference to another King adaptation, *The Shining*. At one point, the odd couple discusses the "guy who went mad in a hotel nearby."

12. *Needful Things* (1993)

This adaptation was a bit of a clunker, collecting more negative reviews than ticket sales. The movie didn't make much more than $15 million at the box office, which isn't too hot in terms of movie sales. The Faustian story, however, based on the King novel of the same name, is a strong one. Satan has a shop in a small New England town and gladly sells his customers whatever they need—for a price. The best-known actor in the movie is Ed Harris, who plays doomed Sheriff Alan Pangborn.

13. *The Shawshank Redemption* (1994)

The Shawshank Redemption may be King's most critically-acclaimed adaptation, garnering seven Oscar nods and grossing nearly $30 million at the box office. The story came from King's *Different Seasons* short story collection. Morgan Freeman and Tim Robbins star as Red and Andy, two inmates in prison beginning in the 1940s who strive to reconcile their fates in different ways. This story is effectively frightening not because of supernatural events but because of the terror of watching one's life pass by.

14. *Dolores Claiborne* (1995)

This psychological thriller tells the story of Dolores, a maid who works for a wealthy woman in Maine, the setting for many of King's stories. When the rich woman is murdered, Dolores's daughter comes in from New York to sort out all the details. Lots of flashbacks about the family's domestic problems ensue and a cast that includes Kathy Bates and Jennifer Jason Leigh play out the vivid drama with engaging results and a suspenseful ending with a twist. The movie received excellent reviews, especially for the performances by the leading ladies. It did well at the box office, too, pulling in almost $25 million.

15. *The Green Mile* (1999)

The Green Mile was based on King's series of six short books of the same name. In one of King's most successful movie adaptations, Tom Hanks stars as Paul Edgecomb, a cynical death row prison guard. Michael Clarke Duncan, Oscar-nominated for his role in the film, plays John Coffey, a prisoner accused of murdering two children. The movie grossed $136 million at the box office and DVD sales are still strong. King reportedly came to the set and asked to sit in the electric chair being used in the film. He didn't like how "Old Sparky" felt and asked to be released right away.

A BRIEF HISTORY OF THE MASTER OF SUSPENSE
20 Films Directed by Alfred Hitchcock

✳ ✳ ✳ ✳

Perhaps no other director in the history of film has had a greater impact on the industry or on popular culture than Alfred Hitchcock. "Hitch" made more than 65 full-length movies that have defined cinema for generations. Nicknamed "the Master of Suspense," the round, gravelly-voiced man (who never won a Best Director Oscar) made films that put viewers on the edge of their seats time and time again. Strong characterization, symbolism, surprise endings, and extended chase scenes were a few of Hitch's trademarks. Here are 20 of his most memorable movies.

1. *Rebecca* (1940)

This early Hitchcock film tells the spooky tale of Rebecca (played by Joan Fontaine), the naive second wife of a rich widower portrayed by Sir Laurence Olivier. It becomes abundantly clear that Rebecca's husband and the servants in his mansion aren't totally over the death of his first wife, and Rebecca is driven mad. Winner of the Academy Award for Best Picture, this movie was tied up in legal trouble over the rights to the script for several years before and after its release.

2. *Mr. & Mrs. Smith* (1941)

Leave it to Hitchcock to surprise everyone by making a movie with no murder and no mystery at all. Lighthearted and purely entertaining, *Mr. & Mrs. Smith* stars Carole Lombard and Robert

Montgomery as a couple with a rather odd relationship. When the two find out that they might not be married at all, their strained commitment is given new life. It was Lombard who is said to have convinced Hitch to do this beloved departure movie. Sadly, she wouldn't live to see its long-standing success: Lombard died in a plane crash outside of Las Vegas in 1942. Another movie of the same title was made in 2005 with Brad Pitt and Angelina Jolie, but it bears little resemblance to the original.

3. *Saboteur* (1942)
This Hitchcock film tells the tale of Barry Kane, a factory worker who sees a Nazi agent blow up his plant. Robert Cummings plays the leading man-on-the-run (though it's rumored that Hitch wanted Cary Grant in the role), and lots of classic Hitchcock moments ensue—cross-country chases, a lovely blonde, a slimy antagonist, and a big finish. Although it's not one of Hitchcock's top ten, it's definitely a thrilling film.

4. *Shadow of a Doubt* (1943)
Who knew Thornton Wilder, the playwright who penned *Our Town,* had it in him to write such a murderous tale? Hitchcock, ever the innovator, teamed up with Wilder to create this tale starring Joseph Cotten as Uncle Charlie and Teresa Wright as his niece. Uncle Charlie seems to be a mild-mannered guy, but his loving niece finds out something sinister about him and has to make some tough, dangerous decisions about how to handle the sticky situation. Hitch often said that *Shadow* was his favorite of all his films.

5. *Lifeboat* (1944)
Long before *Survivor* and *Lost,* there was *Lifeboat.* Two World War II ships crash at sea and a group of survivors have to figure out how to stay afloat and reach safety with limited options. The group in the cramped boat includes a journalist, a radio operator, a businessman, and a nurse, among others. Many in the cast suffered from pneumonia during filming, but the set's chilly conditions created tension and incredible atmosphere for this fan favorite.

6. *Rope* (1948)

The first picture Hitch made with his own production company, Transatlantic Pictures, was also his first film in color. Two young men murder for fun and play cat and mouse with a former teacher, played by Jimmy Stewart. This movie, which was based on a true story, is noted for its incredibly long takes—the film often goes seven or eight minutes without an edit.

7. *Dial "M" for Murder* (1954)

The first of Hitch's so-called "blonde films," this double-crossing plot is among the filmmaker's best. Grace Kelly is a woman torn between her husband (a handsome but murderous Ray Milland) and her new love (a dashing but philandering Robert Cummings). When Milland learns of the affair, he decides to blackmail an old acquaintance into murdering his wife. Things go a bit haywire, so Milland switches plans and attempts to frame his wife for the murder of the would-be assassin. Everything seems to be going according to Plan B, until an inspector starts snooping around. This film was originally done in 3-D, but switched to 2-D soon after. The 3-D version of this thriller is now available as a reissue.

8. *Rear Window* (1954)

One of the most acclaimed suspense films of all time features Hitch favorites Grace Kelly and Jimmy Stewart. Stewart stars as Jeff, a snoop who sees a murder take place in his neighbor's house while looking out his window. Jeff's apartment was the set for the movie and except for one or two exterior shots, all shooting was done within the set—at the time, the largest set Paramount had ever constructed. The suspenseful ending is one of the more gripping finales ever committed to celluloid.

9. *To Catch a Thief* (1955)

Hitch was among the first to film the engaging story of the reformed thug. Cary Grant plays John Robie, a retired cat burglar who lives a quiet life in the plush Riviera. Naturally, when a fresh set of burglaries explodes in the area, Robie is suspected. In order to clear his name, he sets out to catch the thief himself. He is aided by Grace Kelly, an American heiress initially convinced that Robie is guilty. Look for a long Hitch cameo in this film—he's an unassuming bus passenger for about ten minutes.

10. *The Trouble with Harry* (1955)

Fans either love or hate *The Trouble with Harry*, a suspenseful satire made in 1955. Jerry Mathers, Academy Award-winner Edmund Gwenn, John Forsythe, and Shirley MacLaine (in her first film role) all try to solve the problem—Harry is dead and no one knows what to do with the body—with mixed results. This comedy revealed the range that the director was capable of, even though many wondered where the dark, foreboding Hitch had gone.

11. *The Man Who Knew Too Much* (1956)

Jimmy Stewart is back again, this time opposite Doris Day as a naive American couple vacationing in Morocco. When a French spy dies in Stewart's arms and the couple's son is kidnapped, a tense international espionage story plays out. Stewart is chased by the bad guys, since he knows too much about an assassination set to be carried out in London. The scene known as "The Albert Hall Scene" is about 12 minutes long and contains no dialogue whatsoever, delighting film students and cinephiles the world over—it's a risky filmmaking move and a Hitchcock masterstroke.

12. *Vertigo* (1958)

Based on a French novel, Jimmy Stewart and Kim Novak star in this megahit movie—filmed in "VistaVision" color. The dark story is set in San Francisco and features Stewart as an obsessive man who falls for a girl who kills herself. Novak plays two roles in the film. This is said to be Hitch's most "confessional" movie, dealing directly with how he feared women and tried to control them. Stewart is essentially playing Hitchcock himself.

13. *North by Northwest* (1959)

This movie sold itself as "A 3,000 mile chase scene!" with a star-studded cast that included Cary Grant, Eva Marie Saint, and James

Mason. The chase reaches its climax on Mount Rushmore. Naturally, Hitch wanted to go big and film on location, but the powers that be didn't want an attempted murder taking place on a national monument. The entire set was constructed on a soundstage instead. The film was nominated for three Oscars and is often touted by critics as one of the best movies of all time.

14. *Psycho* (1960)

Hitchcock didn't use his usual, expensive production unit for this cultural juggernaut, opting instead to use his TV crew because he wanted *Psycho* to look like "a cheap exploitation film." Anthony Perkins stars as Norman Bates, a creepy mama's-boy innkeeper who offers Marion Crane (Janet Leigh) a place to stay for the night. Hitchcock chose to shoot in black and white to resemble the newsreels of the time—and also because the gory nature of the film would be too much in living color. *Psycho* is truly Hitchcock's masterpiece, a must-see for anyone who has ever wanted to be entertained—or scared out of their mind.

15. *The Birds* (1963)

Alfred Hitchcock will forever be known as "the Master of Suspense" because of his ability to take the everyday and make it terrifying. Hotels, heights, neighbors, women, and birds were benign until Hitch got ahold of them. *The Birds* is the ultimate example of this—any shred of avian cuteness is obliterated when swarms of birds attack a northern California town. Tippi Hedren plays the doomed blonde alongside handsome Rod Taylor. Hitch said the characters in *The Birds* "are the victims of Judgment Day," making the film an acceptably horrifying follow-up to *Psycho*.

16. *Marnie* (1964)

Tippi Hedren is back, playing a compulsive thief in this rock-solid psychological thriller. Sean Connery is the dashing leading man who tries to get Marnie to confront her schizophrenia. Long scenes and heavy dialogue kept this picture from having the mass appeal of *Psycho* or *The Birds*, but the suspense is every bit as potent. Hitch originally wanted Grace Kelly to play Marnie but she had just married the Prince of Monaco and his people weren't thrilled about their new princess portraying such an unstable character.

17. *Torn Curtain* (1966)

Nothing is what it appears to be in this "trust no one" thriller set during the Cold War. Paul Newman and Julie Andrews star as a young couple caught up in an international mystery in which everyone is a suspect. This would be the last picture that Hitch and composer and longtime collaborator Bernard Herrmann would work on together. Universal Pictures convinced Hitch that the score Herrmann penned wasn't upbeat enough, so the director cut the score and a brilliant, 11-year relationship was officially over.

18. *Topaz* (1969)

Another tense Cold War adventure, *Topaz* is based on a Leon Uris novel about the Cuban Missile Crisis. John Forsythe is a CIA agent who hires a French operative to investigate rumors of missiles in Cuba and a shady NATO spy known as "Topaz." True to Hitchcock form, much intrigue, double-crossing, and death transpire. Hitch admitted that *Topaz* was one of his more experimental films and had elements that didn't totally work, but true fans still appreciate the film as a risky but important fixture in the Hitchcock arsenal.

19. *Frenzy* (1972)

Stop the presses! *Frenzy* was the first Hitch film to earn an R rating with the new ratings system that took effect in 1968. This ultra-dark comedy about an innocent man on the run was filmed in England, putting Hitch back home for the first time in nearly 20 years. Jon Finch, Alec McCowen, and Barry Foster make up the strong cast in this gallows-humor story that incorporates many trademark Hitchcock touches—bathrooms, continuous camera shots, and criminals around every corner.

20. *Family Plot* (1976)

Hitch's final film uses both humor and suspense to tell a tongue-in-cheek tale of a rich lady's eccentric foibles and the trouble they cause. Stars abound in this film, including Bruce Dern and William

Devane, but Hitch had originally wanted the likes of Liza Minnelli and Al Pacino in the picture. If you look closely, there is a street sign in *Family Plot* that reads "Bates Ave.," a nod to *Psycho,* one of the many films that made this director one of the most influential men of the 20th century.

Real Names of 26 Vintage Film Stars

✳ ✳ ✳ ✳

1. Frederic Austerlitz . . . . Fred Astaire
2. Benjamin Kubelsky. . . . . Jack Benny
3. Edward Israel "Izzy" Iskowitz . . . . Eddie Cantor
4. Lucille Fay LeSueur. . . . . Joan Crawford
5. Harry Lillis Crosby. . . . . Bing Crosby
6. Frank James Cooper. . . . . Gary Cooper
7. Ruth Elizabeth Davis . . . . Bette Davis
8. Milton Berlinger. . . . . Milton Berle
9. Nathan Birnbaum. . . . . George Burns
10. Doris Kappelhoff . . . . Doris Day
11. Frances Smith. . . . . Dale Evans
12. Leonard Slye. Roy Rogers
13. Norma Jean Baker . . . . Marilyn Monroe
14. Frances Gumm. . . . . Judy Garland
15. Archibald Leach . . . . Cary Grant
16. Margarita Cansino . . . . Rita Hayworth
17. Joseph Levitch . . . . Jerry Lewis
18. Dino Crocetti . . . . Dean Martin
19. Ruby Stevens . . . . Barbara Stanwyck
20. Julia Jean Turner. . . . . Lana Turner
21. Marion Morrison . . . . John Wayne
22. Bernard Schwartz. . . . . Tony Curtis
23. William Beedle. . . . . William Holden
24. William Henry Pratt. . . . . Boris Karloff
25. Béla Blaskó . . . . Bela Lugosi
26. Asa Yoelson . . . . Al Jolson

THAT'S ALL FOLKS!
Last Movies of 9 Noteworthy Stars

✳ ✳ ✳ ✳

There's something eerily gripping about watching a late movie star in his or her final role. Whether it's a comedy or a drama, a flop or a smash, that last glimpse is always worth savoring. Below are the last movies of nine notable stars.

1. James Dean

Rising star James Dean was just 24 years old, with a mere three starring roles under his belt, when he was killed in a car accident in 1955. The astonishingly talented actor became an enduring cult icon with his roles in *East of Eden* and *Rebel Without a Cause.* But *Giant,* released in 1956, was Dean's farewell picture. In the movie, Dean plays Jett Rink, a nonconforming ranch hand who becomes a rich oil tycoon. Dean's character ages about 30 years in the film, so his hair was dyed gray. When Dean was killed on September 30, 1955, while driving his Porsche Spyder to an auto race in Salinas, California, he eerily appeared much older, due to his hairstyle. Dean received Oscar nominations for Best Actor for his roles in *Giant* and *East of Eden,* the first person ever to receive a posthumous nod from the Academy.

2. Katharine Hepburn

On the American Film Institute's list of Top 100 U.S. Love Stories, six of the movies star Katharine Hepburn, more than any other actress on the list. So it's fitting that her final movie, 1994's *Love Affair,* tells the tale of a budding romance, and stars famous lovebirds Warren Beatty and Annette Bening. It's also fitting that in addition to her immense talent, Hepburn was known for a razor-sharp wit, a willingness to speak her mind freely, and a decades-long love affair with costar Spencer Tracy. The actress, who earned four Oscars (a record for any actress), starred on the big screen for more than 60 years before retiring in the mid-1990s. *Love Affair,* in fact, was the only big-screen project she embarked on in the '90s. Hepburn died at home in 2003, at age 96.

3. Jayne Mansfield

Jayne Mansfield's career had taken a nosedive by the time she died at age 34. Her notoriety reached its peak in 1963 when she starred in *Promises! Promises!,* in which she appeared nude. The film was banned in some areas, but enjoyed box office success where it was shown. Once a highly sought-after actor, by the early 1960s the blonde bombshell had resorted to tacky roles that traded heavily on her sex appeal. But she gave an honest, clear-eyed performance in what would prove to be her last movie, *Single Room Furnished,* released in 1968 after her death. In the film, she portrays a woman who turns to prostitution after her husband and later her fiancé both desert her. Mansfield was killed on June 29, 1967, when the car she and three of her children were riding in crashed into a tractor-trailer. The children survived with minor injuries.

4. Christopher Reeve

Christopher Reeve is best remembered as Superman, both on screen and off, after portraying Clark Kent in the 1978 box office smash *Superman.* After he was paralyzed during a horse-riding accident in 1995, his grace, courage, and devotion to furthering the cause of paralysis victims earned him worldwide respect and adoration. Reeve devoted the majority of his time after the accident to advocacy work, but he continued to focus on his acting career and dabbled in directing, as well. He appeared on several TV shows, including *The Practice* and *Smallville,* and directed a number of made-for-TV movies, including 1997's *In the Gloaming,* which was nominated for five Emmys. His final role was in *Rear Window* (1998), a remake of the Alfred Hitchcock classic, in which he portrayed a paralyzed architect who thinks he witnessed a murder from his apartment window. Reeve won a Screen Actors Guild Award for his performance. The courageous actor died in 2004 from cardiac arrest brought on by a reaction to antibiotics he had taken for an infection. He was 52 years old.

5. John Belushi

You'd think John Belushi's last role would be as some wild-eyed, ranting lunatic who scared the neighbors, or at least sent them on a frenetic car chase. Instead Belushi played the *victim* of a crazy neighbor in 1981's *Neighbors,* his third film with *Saturday Night Live* partner Dan Aykroyd. Belushi portrayed straight-laced Earl to Aykroyd's wacky Vic in the dark comedy about suburban life. Belushi's fame came on *SNL* and with *Animal House* in 1978. And when he left *SNL* in 1979, he quickly churned out *1941* and *The Blues Brothers.* Three months after *Neighbors* was released, he died of a cocaine and heroin overdose on March 5, 1982, at age 33.

6. Chris Farley

As a child, Chris Farley idolized comedian John Belushi. In his own career, Farley was known for playing portly misfits who'd stop at nothing for a laugh, and his last role was no exception. In 1998's *Almost Heroes,* Farley and Matthew Perry starred as two early American explorers who set out to beat Lewis and Clark. Offscreen, Farley, who got his start at Chicago's Second City and broke into Hollywood via *Saturday Night Live,* had battled drug and alcohol addiction and chronic obesity for years. Still, he completed a string of successful comedies, including *Tommy Boy* in 1995. But by the time he began work on *Almost Heroes,* his addictions were out of control, and filming reportedly had to be stopped several times while he was in rehab. Shortly after completing the movie, Farley died on December 18, 1997, ironically, of a cocaine and heroin overdose at age 33, just as his idol John Belushi had.

7. Henry Fonda

You know you've had a stellar acting career when your greatest film is a toss-up between *The Grapes of Wrath* and *12 Angry Men.* Or was it *The Ox-Bow Incident* or *Mister Roberts*? Some critics pass over those classics altogether and declare Henry Fonda's best film to be his last, *On Golden Pond.* The actor received numerous Oscar nods during a career that spanned five decades, but by the 1980s, he had limited most of his work to television, with the exception of

1981's *On Golden Pond*. The film, which also starred his daughter Jane and Katharine Hepburn, tells the story of an aging couple who spend a life-changing summer at their vacation home. It earned 11 Academy Award nominations and a Best Actor win for Fonda, his first and only Oscar. He died of heart disease at age 77, just eight months after the film was released.

8. Audrey Hepburn

As a child, Audrey Hepburn grew up in Nazi-occupied Amsterdam and carried secret messages to the Resistance. After World War II ended, Audrey trained as a ballerina and worked as a model before embarking on an award-winning acting career. The graceful and elegant brunette was an instant success, winning a Best Actress Oscar for her first major film role as Princess Ann in *Roman Holiday* (1953). But she is best remembered for her roles in *Breakfast at Tiffany's* and *My Fair Lady*, two roles that garnered her nods from the Academy, but no Oscars. One of only a handful of performers to win a Tony, an Emmy, an Oscar, and a Grammy Award, Hepburn portrayed an angel in her final film role in Steven Spielberg's *Always* (1989). She died of cancer in January 1993 at age 63.

9. Marilyn Monroe

Marilyn Monroe packed a number of memorable roles into her tragically short career, but her final completed film, *The Misfits*, is remembered for its offscreen turmoil as much as its big-screen success. Written by Monroe's third husband, playwright Arthur Miller, the 1961 movie was filmed in the Nevada desert and was plagued by Monroe's chronic tardiness. Ironically, costar Clark Gable suffered a massive heart attack the day after filming wrapped and died 11 days later. Meanwhile, Monroe's marriage to Miller was about to end in divorce, and she was battling substance abuse. She died at age 36 from acute barbiturate poisoning on August 5, 1962.

✳ ✳ ✳

"Hollywood is a place where they'll pay you a thousand dollars for a kiss and fifty cents for your soul."
—Marilyn Monroe

Chapter 5

HEALTH, FITNESS, AND THE HUMAN BODY

✳ ✳ ✳ ✳

9 Medical Myths

If you trust the source, you're most likely going to trust the information. That's what makes the following medical myths so hard to discredit—you usually hear them first from Mom, Dad, or someone else you trust—but it is nice to know the truth.

1. Chocolate and fried foods give you acne. Some speculate that this myth dates back to the baby boom generation, who had worse acne than their parents and also more access to chocolate and fried foods. Wherever this idea came from, it's wrong. Pimples form when oil glands under the skin produce too much of a waxy oil called sebum, which the body uses to keep skin lubricated. But when excess sebum and dead skin cells block pores, that area of the skin gets irritated, swollen, and turns red—the telltale signs of a pimple. It is unknown why sebaceous glands produce excess sebum, but hormones are the prime suspects, which explains why teenagers are affected more than others. Stress and heredity may also be factors, but chocolate bars and onion rings are off the hook.

2. Coffee will sober you up. If you've had too much to drink, no amount of coffee, soda, water, or anything else is going to sober you up. The only thing that will do the trick is time. The liver can metabolize only about one standard drink (12 ounces of beer, 6 ounces of wine, or 1.5 ounces of hard liquor) per hour, so if you're drinking more than that every 60 minutes, you'll have alcohol in your system for some time. The idea of coffee's sobering effect may have started because caffeine acts as a stimulant, counteracting the sedative effect of alcohol to a small degree. However, it has no effect on the amount of alcohol in the blood. So if you've been drinking, spend your money on a cab rather than a cappuccino.

3. Cold weather can give you a cold. "Put your jacket on or you'll catch a cold!" How times have you heard that? You may not want to tell her this, but dear old Mom was wrong. Viruses (more than 200 different kinds) cause colds, not cold weather. In order for you to catch a cold, the virus must travel from a sick person's body to yours. This usually happens via airborne droplets you inhale when an infected person coughs or sneezes. You can also get a cold virus by shaking hands with an infected person or by using something where the virus has found a temporary home, such as a phone or door handle. Colds are more prevalent during the colder months because people tend to spend more time inside, making it much easier for viruses to jump from person to person.

4. Cracking your knuckles causes arthritis. The knuckles are the joints between the fingers and hand, and these joints contain a lubricant called synovial fluid. When you crack your knuckles, you are pulling apart two bones at the joint, which means the synovial fluid has to fill more space. This decreases the pressure of the fluid, and dissolved gases that are present, such as nitrogen, float out of the area in tiny bubbles. The bursting of these bubbles is the familiar sound we hear when someone "cracks" his or her knuckles. This bubble-bursting is not the same as arthritis, which is when the body's immune system attacks joints. However, constant knuckle-cracking can injure joints and weaken fingers.

5. Too much sugar makes kids hyperactive. Many parents limit sugary foods, thinking they cause hyperactivity. It's right to restrict these treats, but the reasoning is wrong. These high-calorie foods offer little nutrition and can lead to obesity and other problems, but no scientific evidence says sugar causes hyperactivity. Sugar can provide a short-term energy boost, but that isn't the same as hyperactivity. The children at a birthday party acting like little tornadoes probably has more to do with the excitement of being around other kids, rather than the cake. And that unruly child in the grocery store throwing a fit with a sucker in his mouth and candy clutched in each fist? His parents probably haven't set appropriate behavior limits, and they most likely give him what he wants—which is more candy.

6. Don't swallow gum—it takes seven years to digest. Some misconceptions are hard to swallow, but people have been chewing on this one for years. This myth has probably been around since chewing gum became popular in the late 19th century and most likely originated thanks to a single word: *indigestible.* Gum is comprised of flavor, sweeteners, softeners, and gum base. The body is able to break down the first three ingredients, but gum base is indigestible. That simply means your body can't dissolve it and extract nutrients. In the end, gum base works its way through your digestive system much like fiber—in two or three days it goes out in basically the same shape it went in.

7. Feed a cold and starve a fever. This bit of folk wisdom has been bouncing around for centuries. This advice may have evolved from the idea that illnesses could be classified as either low temperature (those that give chills, such as a cold) or high temperature (those with fever). With chills, it sounds reasonable to feed a person's internal fireplace with food. The logic follows that when an illness raises the body's temperature, cutting back on the "fuel" should help. However, scientific evidence does not endorse this advice—many illnesses must simply run their course. Nevertheless, if you are stuck in bed with a cold and a loved one brings over your favorite healthful foods, it is still okay to chow down. Alternatively, you may lose your appetite while fighting a fever-based sickness. When you're sick, it's okay to miss a meal or two as long as you are keeping up with fluid intake.

8. Wait 30 minutes after eating before swimming. For a kid, nothing ruins the fun of a carefree summer day like a worried parent banning swimming right after the big cookout, fearing that the child will get cramps and drown. There is a slight chance of minor abdominal cramping, but for the vast majority of people, this isn't dangerous. The body does divert blood flow from the muscles to the gastrointestinal system to spur digestion, but not in amounts that diminish muscle function. Listen to your body and swim when you're comfortable—just like you probably don't run a marathon right after Thanksgiving dinner, you don't want to start swimming laps right after a seven-course picnic. It is perfectly safe, though, to eat a light meal and then get wet. After all, athletes commonly eat right before competing.

9. **You can get the flu from a flu shot.** Vaccinations are misunderstood because they are created from the offending viruses themselves. But when you get a flu shot, you're not being injected with a whole virus—you're receiving an inactivated, or dead, virus. That means the part of the virus that can infect you and make you sick is turned off, but the part of the virus that stimulates your body to create antibodies is still on. The body's antibodies will kill the flu virus should you come into contact with it later. Even pregnant women are advised to get flu vaccinations, so you know they're safe. The only people who should avoid them are those who have severe allergies to eggs, because eggs are used to create the vaccines. No vaccine is 100 percent effective, so there is still a chance you can get the flu after receiving the shot, but that doesn't mean the vaccination gave it to you.

WHAT ARE YOU AFRAID OF?
28 Phobias and Their Definitions

❋ ❋ ❋ ❋

1. Ablutophobia ....Fear of washing or bathing
2. Acrophobia ....Fear of heights
3. Agoraphobia...................................Fear of open spaces, crowds, or leaving a safe place
4. Ailurophobia..................................Fear of cats
5. Alektorophobia...............................Fear of chickens
6. Anthropophobia.............................Fear of people
7. Anuptaphobia ....Fear of staying single

8. Arachnophobia .... Fear of spiders
9. Atychiphobia.................................... Fear of failure
10. Autophobia .... Fear of oneself or of being alone
11. Aviophobia .... Fear of flying
12. Caligynephobia................................ Fear of beautiful women
13. Coulrophobia.................................... Fear of clowns
14. Cynophobia...................................... Fear of dogs
15. Gamophobia .... Fear of marriage
16. Ichthyophobia.................................. Fear of fish
17. Melanophobia................................... Fear of the color black
18. Mysophobia .... Fear of germs or dirt
19. Nyctophobia .... Fear of the dark or of night
20. Ophidiophobia/Herpetophobia ...... Fear of snakes
21. Ornithophobia .... Fear of birds
22. Phasmophobia/Spectrophobia .... Fear of ghosts
23. Philophobia...................................... Fear of being in love
24. Photophobia..................................... Fear of light
25. Pupaphobia...................................... Fear of puppets
26. Pyrophobia...................................... Fear of fire
27. Thanatophobia or Thantophobia .... Fear of death or dying
28. Xanthophobia .... Fear of the color yellow

20 Everyday Activities and the Calories They Burn

❄ ❄ ❄ ❄

*The simple truth of weight loss, no matter what the latest trendy diet says, is that you have to use more calories than you consume. The good news is that you don't have to spend all your waking hours at the gym attached to some complicated, beeping hunk of metal because everything you do burns calories. Check out the following activities and the number of calories they burn.**

1. Shop 'til you drop. Pushing a cart up and down the supermarket aisles for an hour will burn 243 calories and you'll get acquainted with all kinds of nutritious, healthful foods. Bag your own groceries, take them out to the car yourself, and return the cart to the corral, and you'll burn even more.

2. Open up. Most dentists recommend that you brush your teeth for at least two minutes. In that time, you'll burn a whopping 5.7 calories, but then again, not everything is about weight loss.

3. Make it shine. Do your tables, shelves, and knickknacks fail the white-glove test? Burn 80 calories by dusting the surfaces in your home for 30 minutes and you'll be ready the next time a drill sergeant stops by for an inspection.

4. Pucker power. It may not burn as many calories as dusting, but 30 minutes of kissing is a lot more fun. You'll burn 36 calories and probably miss a bad sitcom.

5. Wrinkle-free weight loss. Burn 76.5 calories with 30 minutes of ironing; just be careful that you don't burn the clothes.

6. Paint thinner. You know you need to paint the house, but you're lacking the motivation. Does it help to know that three hours of house painting will burn 1,026 calories? And by putting on that second coat, you might drop a whole pants size.

7. Sock it to me. You can now look forward to laundry day because 30 minutes of folding clothes will burn 72 calories. Fold enough clothes and you may soon be putting away smaller sizes.

8. Pick up trash and drop pounds. Pick up some waste and reduce your waist by spending an afternoon cleaning up the neighborhood. In four hard-worked hours, you'll burn 1,800 calories and improve your community.

9. Swab the deck. Don't cry over spilled milk or anything else, especially when 30 minutes of mopping the floor will burn 153 calories.

10. Fire the lawn boy. One hour of pushing the lawn mower around the yard burns 324 calories. Sorry, sitting on a riding mower doesn't count. Lose the bag attachment and spend another 30 minutes raking up the clippings and you'll burn another 171 calories.

11. **How about Texas Lose 'Em?** Three hours of playing cards burns 351 calories. Ante up and go all in, but don't load up on high-calorie chips and dip.

12. **Work up an appetite.** You'll burn 74 calories during the 30 minutes you spend preparing dinner. Of course, that work will be voided by high-calorie, fat-filled meals. Instead, choose healthful meals that contain plenty of fruits and vegetables.

13. **Get moving.** Offer to help your pals move. What's in it for you? Every hour of moving furniture burns 504 calories.

14. **Flake out.** Those of you who live in warm climates have no idea what a great workout you're missing. Thirty minutes of shoveling snow burns 202.5 calories.

15. **A lean sweep.** Moving a broom back and forth for ten minutes will burn 28 calories and you'll have a prop that can be anything from a microphone stand to a dance partner.

16. **Suck it up.** You know the rug needs it, but you may not know that 20 minutes of vacuuming will burn 56 calories.

17. **Suds it up.** Break out the bucket and hose—a mere 20 minutes of washing the car will burn 102 calories.

18. **Count calories instead of sheep.** Even when you're sleeping you're burning calories. Eight hours of good shut-eye will erase 360 calories.

19. **Dig the benefits.** Two hours of gardening will burn 648 calories, and you'll grow some nice healthful veggies at the same time.

20. **Click to fit?** Even watching TV is worth something. One hour spent in front of the tube burns 72 calories. Of course, if you dusted at the same time....

Calories based on a 150-pound person. (A heavier person will burn more calories.)

10 Heaviest States

❋ ❋ ❋ ❋

Why are some states heavier than others? Some speculate that there is a correlation between poverty level and obesity. That's because high-calorie, less healthful foods are usually cheaper. As you can see below, eight of the ten states with the greatest percentage of obese and overweight adults are in the South.

State	Percentage of Overweight/ Obese Adults	Poverty Rank
1. Mississippi	65.9	1
2. Alabama	64.1	7
3. Kentucky	63.8	8
4. West Virginia	63.7	4
5. North Dakota	63.3	33
6. Arkansas	63.1	6
7. Texas	62.9	5
8. Alaska (tied)	62.7	33
9. Louisiana (tied)	62.7	2
10. Tennessee	62.3	11

Sources: Centers for Disease Control and Prevention, Behavioral Risk Factor Surveillance System, 2003–2005; U.S. Census Bureau, 2005

BODY ODDITIES
16 Unusual Facts About the Human Body

❋ ❋ ❋ ❋

1. Don't stick out your tongue if you want to hide your identity. Similar to fingerprints, everyone also has a unique tongue print!

2. Your pet isn't the only one in the house with a shedding problem. Humans shed about 600,000 particles of skin every hour. That works out to about 1.5 pounds each year, so the average person will lose around 105 pounds of skin by age 70.

3. An adult has fewer bones than a baby. We start off life with 350 bones, but because bones fuse together during growth, we end up with only 206 as adults.

4. Did you know that you get a new stomach lining every three to four days? If you didn't, the strong acids your stomach uses to digest food would also digest your stomach.

5. Your nose is not as sensitive as a dog's, but it can remember 50,000 different scents.

6. The small intestine is about four times as long as the average adult is tall. If it weren't looped back and forth upon itself, its length of 18 to 23 feet wouldn't fit into the abdominal cavity, making things rather messy.

7. This will really make your skin crawl: Every square inch of skin on the human body has about 32 million bacteria on it, but fortunately, the vast majority of them are harmless.

8. The source of smelly feet, like smelly armpits, is sweat. And people sweat buckets from their feet. A pair of feet have 500,000 sweat glands and can produce more than a pint of sweat a day.

9. The air from a human sneeze can travel at speeds of 100 miles per hour or more—another good reason to cover your nose and mouth when you sneeze—or duck when you hear one coming your way.

10. Blood has a long road to travel: Laid end to end, there are about 60,000 miles of blood vessels in the human body. And the hard-working heart pumps about 2,000 gallons of blood through those vessels every day.

11. You may not want to swim in your spit, but if you saved it all up, you could. In a lifetime, the average person produces about 25,000 quarts of saliva—enough to fill two swimming pools!

12. By 60 years of age, 60 percent of men and 40 percent of women will snore. But the sound of a snore can seem deafening. While snores average around 60 decibels, the noise level of normal speech, they can reach more than 80 decibels. Eighty decibels is as loud as the sound of a pneumatic drill breaking up concrete. Noise levels over 85 decibels are considered hazardous to the human ear.

13. Blondes may or may not have more fun, but they definitely have more hair. Hair color helps determine how dense the hair on your head is, and blondes (only natural ones, of course), top the list. The average human head has 100,000 hair follicles, each of which is capable of producing 20 individual hairs during a person's lifetime. Blondes average 146,000 follicles. People with black hair tend to have about 110,000 follicles, while those with brown hair are right on target with 100,000 follicles. Redheads have the least dense hair, averaging about 86,000 follicles.

14. If you're clipping your fingernails more often than your toenails, that's only natural. The nails that get the most exposure and are used most frequently grow the fastest. Fingernails grow fastest on the hand that you write with and on the longest fingers. On average, nails grow about one-tenth of an inch each month.

15. No wonder babies have such a hard time holding up their heads: The human head is one-quarter of our total length at birth but only one-eighth of our total length by the time we reach adulthood.

16. If you say that you're dying to get a good night's sleep, you could mean that literally. You can go without eating for weeks without succumbing, but ten days is tops for going without sleep. After ten days, you'll be asleep—forever!

❋ ❋ ❋

"[The body is] a marvelous machine… a chemical laboratory,
a power-house. Every movement, voluntary or involuntary,
full of secrets and marvels!"
—Theodor Herzl

25 Steps to a Healthier You

❉ ❉ ❉ ❉

In the late 20th century, along came aerobics, isometrics, Richard Simmons, Dr. Atkins, and a nonstop barrage of exercise gadgets, all of which have left the average person dazed, confused, and in worse shape then ever! So what really works? Here are some helpful tips for getting in shape.

1. **Follow a balanced exercise program.** A brisk 30-minute walk while enjoying the sunset will burn 1,500 calories per week—that's 78,000 calories a year! Cardio is great for your heart and lungs, but add a couple sessions of weight training to tone or build muscle.

2. **Schedule family fitness time.** Play basketball, chase a Frisbee, or hike the hills together. You'll be getting closer to each other as you shape up.

3. **Invest in a jump rope.** It's a great workout anytime. Set a goal of skipping rope for ten minutes per day and watch those love handles melt away.

4. **Get a training partner.** Knowing that someone is waiting is great motivation to get on with it. You'll also have a ready-made spotter.

5. **Exercise in water to relieve stress on the joints and back.** Check out the aerobics programs at your local pool and go aqua—the wave of the future.

6. **Get active at work.** Walk around outside on your breaks. When in front of a computer, sit up and pull in your abs.

7. **Eat more frequent, smaller meals.** It is better to eat six small meals a day than three large meals. The smaller the meal, the less your stomach will stretch.

8. **Hydrate with water.** Drink at least eight glasses of water every day. This does not include coffee, soda, or fruit-flavored drinks, which have extra calories.

9. **Don't pollute your body.** Avoid tobacco, excess alcohol, and illegal drugs. These are bad for health and can also inhibit weight loss.

10. **Always eat a good breakfast.** Skipping breakfast is a method of dieting for many people. But studies have found that people who eat breakfast are actually less likely to be obese.

11. **Start cooking healthy.** Stop frying your food and opt for roasting or grilling instead. Frying only adds unnecessary calories to food.

12. **Enjoy every morsel of food.** When eating, chew food slowly. Relish it and pay attention to flavors and taste. The longer you chew, the fuller you'll feel!

13. **Be an early riser.** Start your day early. Rising with the sun helps reset your body's clock. This builds better sleep patterns so you're energized all day.

14. **Be sun smart.** Skin cancer is the most common type of cancer. Sun exposure increases your risk, so when you're in the heat of it, either cover up or slip, slap, slop on a high SPF sunscreen!

15. **Stay emotionally in shape.** Poor emotional health can weaken your body's immune system. Don't ignore what's going on in your heart and mind. It is healthy to acknowledge your emotions.

16. **Keep your teeth healthy.** A common cause of tooth loss after age 35 is gum disease. Keep your teeth and gums healthy and free of plaque by brushing and flossing every day.

17. **Eat five or more servings of fruits and veggies per day.** Keep fruits and vegetables on the front shelves of your refrigerator so they are easy to get to when you reach for a snack!

18. **De-stress your life.** Stress can cause or aggravate many health conditions. So, don't sweat the small stuff!

19. **Know thyself.** Knowing your family's health history can help you stay healthy. Many diseases are hereditary and preventable with early screening.

20. Look after your mental health. Depression is a serious illness that needs to be treated. It's not your fault, so you shouldn't be afraid to talk to a doctor for help.

21. Get a good night's sleep. Lack of sleep causes stress on the body. It increases cortisol and insulin, promoting fat storage and making weight loss difficult.

22. Ladies, perform regular breast examinations. The best time to perform a breast self-examination is the week after your menstrual period, when breast tissue is less tender and swollen.

23. Take a nap. Many have commended the benefits of a good 30- to 45-minute nap a day to keep refreshed and lower stress. Try it—it doesn't mean you've passed your use-by date!

24. Open your lungs. Sing your heart out! It doesn't matter what you sound like! In the shower, in the car, or wherever you are, sing out loud. It's a great stress reliever.

25. Take time to enjoy your life. While it's important to do a good job and take care of responsibilities, life is also meant to be enjoyed. Loosen up! Laugh at yourself, and play as hard as you work!

18 Cures for the Hiccups

❊ ❊ ❊ ❊

When you have the hiccups, something has triggered involuntary contractions in your diaphragm. You may have swallowed air while you were eating, and irritating foods can cause hiccups, too. It's hard to tell why they strike and when, so next time you get them, see if the following suggestions help.

1. The Drinking Cure

Swallowing water interrupts the hiccupping cycle, which can quiet the nerves. Gargling with water may also have the same effect, but swallowing is probably the fastest way to cure hiccups.

2. The Pineapple Juice Cure

Some say that the acid in pineapple juice obliterates hiccups, but it's probably just the swallowing action that comes from drinking.

3. The Gulp Cure

Whatever you want to gulp down, go for it. Just like drinking water, swallowing any food or drink is a good way to dispel the dreaded hiccups. If water or juice bores you, why not have a snack? Chips, crackers—okay, carrots and broccoli—will work, too.

4. The Little Brother Cure

If you stick out your tongue, you'll stimulate your glottis, the opening of the airway to your lungs. Since a closed glottis is what causes hiccups in the first place, this usually works pretty well.

5. The Drink Upside Down Cure

If gulping down water is good, drinking it upside down must be, too. As with many home remedies, this one is a bit unusual, but it's not totally illogical. In addition to swallowing the water, it's pretty hard to figure out how to drink upside down. The concentration needed might equalize the breathing and cure the hiccups.

6. The Cotton Swab Cure

This cure works just like the Little Brother Cure. Take a cotton swab and tickle the roof of your mouth. People will wonder what you're doing, but it's better than drinking upside down, isn't it?

7. The Scaredy-Cat Cure

The effectiveness of this cure is dubious at best, since once you ask someone to scare you, you're not going to be really, truly surprised. However, if you have a friend with ESP, he or she might be able to help. Losing your breath or gasping might just reset your glottis automatically. Boo!

8. The Sugar Cure

Especially popular among the six-year-old set, a lump of sugar not only tickles the glottis, it gets the hiccupping person swallowing—a double threat to the hiccups.

9. The Squeeze Cure

Can't stop hiccupping? Squeeze those suckers outta there! Sit in a chair and compress your chest by pulling your knees up to your chin. Lean forward and feel those hiccups magically disappear.

10. The Sternum Cure

Some hiccup experts claim that by massaging the sternum, hiccups will melt away. There's not a lot of science to substantiate this claim, but we've never met a massage we didn't like.

11. The Hear No Evil Cure

This cure was reported in the medical journal *Lancet,* so it has to work, right? The article claims that if you plug your ears, you will, in effect, short-circuit your vagus nerve, which controls hiccups.

12. The Brown Bag Cure

It might be that breathing into a brown paper bag cures hiccups because the hiccupping person is taking in more carbon dioxide when inhaling. Or, it might be that the person is concentrating more on breathing, slowing it down and smoothing it out.

13. The Hold Your Breath Cure

This is one of the oldest hiccup remedies, and it usually works pretty well. What is the science behind it? It probably works the same way a paper bag does—it forces a little more control over your breathing.

14. The Earlobe Cure

Earlobes aren't just good for nibbling or wearing earrings. If you rub them, you can cure your hiccups! This silly cure has no basis in logic or fact, but try it, what do you have to lose?

15. The Headstand Cure

Not everyone can stand on their head, but if you can, you might have a good hiccup cure. By standing on your head, you're probably using a fair amount of concentration and messing with your breathing. This should lead to a cessation of the hiccups.

16. The Sound of Music Cure

If you sing or yell as loudly as you can for at least two minutes or longer, you might notice your hiccups leave the building. But your friends might leave the building, too.

17. The Sleeper Cure

Give your glottis, throat, and diaphragm a break—lie down on your back. This is a gentler way to get rid of those obnoxious hiccups.

18. The Run for It Cure

Run. Fast. For ten minutes. See?

DRUG MONEY

10 Most Profitable Prescription Drugs

❋ ❋ ❋ ❋

With all the lustful TV commercials, you might think it's the drugs for erectile dysfunction that make the hearts of drug company execs go pitter-patter. But it's medications that treat heart disease and high blood pressure that most excite them. The following were the top ten best-selling prescription drugs in 2005.

1. Lipitor (Pfizer)

Consistently ranking number one, Lipitor holds the title by a wide margin. Its annual sales of $12.9 billion were more than twice those of the next drug on the list. Lipitor treats high cholesterol, which is a major risk factor for heart disease.

2. Plavix (Bristol-Myers Squibb/Sanofi-Aventis)

This medication is used to prevent heart attacks and strokes. Although it has risen to the second spot on the list, its sales were a mere $5.9 billion, less than half those of Lipitor. However, Plavix had 2.5 times the annual growth of Lipitor.

3. Nexium (AstraZeneca)

You probably know this drug by its color: Advertisements call Nexium "the purple pill," and its sales numbers certainly merit the royal hue. Nexium, prescribed for heartburn and acid reflux, had sales of $5.7 billion, with an annual growth of 16.7 percent.

4. Seretide/Advair (GlaxoSmithKline)

Although it's ranked number four, this asthma inhaler is in the number one spot when it comes to annual growth. GlaxoSmith-Kline must have been breathless with its 19 percent annual growth rate. Sales for Seretide/Advair were just slightly lower than those for Nexium, coming in at $5.6 billion.

5. Zocor (Merck)

This is another medication used to treat high cholesterol and prevent heart disease. In 2005, Zocor had global sales of $5.3 billion, and its annual growth wasn't shabby either, at 10.7 percent.

6. Norvasc (Pfizer)

The second biggest seller for manufacturer Pfizer, Norvasc is used to treat high blood pressure. It had global sales of $5 billion in 2005 and an annual growth rate of 2.5 percent.

7. Zyprexa (Eli Lilly)

Used to treat schizophrenia and bipolar disorder, Zyprexa is Eli Lilly's top-selling drug. In 2005, it had global sales of $4.7 billion. However, unlike other drugs on the list, Zyprexa experienced a significant decrease in annual growth—a dismal −6.8 percent.

8. Risperdal (Janssen)

This is the world's most commonly prescribed atypical antipsychotic medication. At $4 billion, its sales were lower than Zyprexa's, but it had a much larger annual growth rate at 12.6 percent.

9. Prevacid (Abbott Labs/Takeda Pharmaceutical)

Another popular drug to treat heartburn, Prevacid had global sales of $4 billion in 2005 and an annual growth rate of 0.9 percent.

10. Effexor (Wyeth)

An antidepressant, Effexor had $3.8 billion in sales in 2005 and an annual growth rate of 1.2 percent.

8 Most Common Blood Types

✳ ✳ ✳ ✳

In love, they say that opposites attract. But when it comes to blood types, opposites can be deadly. Scientists have discovered eight major blood types; some are compatible, but others are not. See which types you're compatible with.

1. O+: 38 percent

O+ blood is needed more often than any other blood type because it's the most common. O+ blood can be given to a person with A+, B+, AB+, or O+ blood. A person with O+ blood can receive blood from O+ or O− donors.

2. A+: 34 percent

A person with A+ blood can receive A+, A−, O+, or O− blood. However, A+ blood can be given only to a person with the A+ or AB+ blood types.

3. B+: 9 percent

B+ blood can be given only to those with either AB+ or B+ blood. This blood type can receive blood from B+, B−, O+, or O− donors.

4. O−: 7 percent

O− is considered the universal donor because it can be given to anyone, regardless of blood type. However, a person with the O− blood type can receive blood only from other O− donors.

5. A−: 6 percent

A− blood can be given to a person with AB−, A−, AB+, or A+. This blood type can only receive blood from O− or A− donors.

6. AB+: 3 percent

AB+ is considered a universal receiver because people with this blood type can receive blood of any type. But AB+ blood can only be given to a person who also has AB+ blood.

7. B−: 2 percent

B− blood can be given to those with B−, AB−, B+, or AB+ blood. A person with B− blood can receive blood from O− or B− blood types.

8. AB−: 1 percent

AB− is the least common blood type. A person with this type can give blood to AB+ or AB− blood types, but must receive blood from O−, A−, B−, and AB− blood types.

10 Leanest States

❋ ❋ ❋ ❋

The following list examines the ten slimmest states, based on the percentage of obese and overweight adults and poverty rank.

State	Percentage of Overweight/ Obese Adults	Poverty Rank
1. Hawaii	51.6	44
2. Colorado	53.0	35
3. Massachusetts	54.5	40
4. Vermont	55.2	32
5. Utah	55.8	41
6. Arizona (tied)	56.4	15
7. Connecticut (tied)	56.4	48
8. Montana	57.1	13
9. Rhode Island	57.4	26
10. New York	57.9	18

Sources: Centers for Disease Control and Prevention, Behavioral Risk Factor Surveillance System, 2003–2005; U.S. Census Bureau, 2005

MODERN MALADIES
7 Health Problems for the Modern Age

✳ ✳ ✳ ✳

Modern life, with its emphasis on information, automation, computerization, and globalization, has made work easier and given us more leisure options, but we now have a whole host of new health problems. Only time will tell if these modern health problems disappear like 8-track tapes and rotary phones. Until then, here are some of the new maladies we have in store for us.

1. Computer vision syndrome. If you spend all day staring at a computer screen, you may be at risk for computer vision syndrome (CVS), also called occupational asthenopia. CVS encompasses all eye or vision-related problems suffered by people who spend a lot of time on computers. According to the American Optometric Association, symptoms of CVS include headaches; dry, red, or burning eyes; blurred or double vision; trouble focusing; difficulty distinguishing colors; sensitivity to light; and even pain in the neck or back. As many as 75 percent of computer users have symptoms of CVS due to glare, poor lighting, and improper workstation setup. To overcome CVS, keep your monitor about two feet away from you and six inches below eye level, and be sure it's directly in front of you to minimize eye movement. Adjust lighting to remove any glare or reflections. You can also adjust the brightness on your monitor to ease eyestrain. Even simple steps can help, like looking away from your monitor every 20 or 30 minutes and focusing on something farther away. And you can always use eyedrops to perk up your peepers!

2. Earbud-related hearing loss. Earbuds are the headphones used with many digital music players. They fit inside the ear but don't cancel out background noise, requiring users to turn up the volume, often to 110 to 120 decibels—loud enough to cause hearing loss after only an hour and 15 minutes. And today, people spend much more time listening to their portable players, exposing themselves to damaging noise for longer periods of time. As a result, young people are developing the type of hearing loss normally seen in much older adults. Experts recommend turning down the volume and limiting the amount of time spent listening to music players to about an hour a day. Headphones that fit outside the ear canal also help, as can noise-canceling headphones that reduce background noise so listeners don't have to crank up the volume.

3. E-thrombosis. This condition is related to deep vein thrombosis, where blood clots form in deep veins, such as those in the legs. These clots can be fatal if they migrate to the lungs and cause a pulmonary embolism. Clots can form when blood supply slows or stops, such as in a period of prolonged immobility. Similarly, e-thrombosis is the development of clots in the deep veins of someone who spends long amounts of time in front of a computer without moving. Although only a handful of e-thrombosis cases have been reported, millions of people who spend most of their time in front of a computer are at risk. Avoiding e-thrombosis is simple: stand up and move around every hour, tap your toes while you work, put equipment and supplies in different parts of your work area so you have to move to get them, don't cross your legs while sitting at your desk, don't spend your lunch break at your desk (go for a quick walk instead), and don't get too comfortable— if your workspace is ultra-cozy, you won't want to get up.

4. Generalized anxiety disorder. We all have worries, uncertainties, and fears, but generalized anxiety disorder (GAD) is excessive or unrealistic unease or concern about life's problems. Although the disorder often manifests without any specific cause, large issues of modern life (such as terrorism, the economy, and crime) can bring it about, as can individual circumstances like dealing with an illness. GAD affects about 6.8 million people in the United States, and symptoms include restlessness, fatigue, irritability, impatience, difficulty concentrating, headaches, upset stomach, and shortness of breath. Anxiety disorders like GAD are treated with antianxiety drugs, antidepressants, psychotherapy, or a combination of these.

5. Orthorexia nervosa. It seems like every day there's a new report about something you shouldn't eat. The constant bombardment of information about food and health can confuse anyone, but for people who have the eating disorder orthorexia nervosa, it can be downright dangerous. People with this condition are obsessed with eating healthful food and have constructed strict diets that they follow religiously. Although many people who have orthorexia nervosa become underweight, thinness is not their goal—nutritional purity is. Among the signs of orthorexia nervosa are: spending more than three hours a day thinking about healthful food; planning meals days in advance; feeling virtuous from following a strict healthful diet, but not enjoying eating; feeling socially isolated (such strict diets make it hard to eat anywhere but at home); and feeling highly critical of those who do not follow a similar diet. Although the psychiatric community does not officially recognize orthorexia nervosa as a disorder, those with the condition benefit from psychological treatment and sessions with eating-disorder specialists.

6. Sick building syndrome. Rising energy costs aren't just harmful to your wallet; if you work in an office building, they could be making you physically ill. Businesses have found that by packing buildings with insulation, then adding caulking and weather stripping, they can seal buildings tight, keep indoor temperatures constant, and cut energy costs in the process. Such measures require the heating, ventilating, and air conditioning (HVAC) systems to work harder to recycle air. After all, when the building is sealed, you can't open a window to let fresh air circulate. The result is sick building syndrome, which the Environmental Protection Agency (EPA) classifies as a situation where building occupants experience discomforting health effects even though no specific cause can be found. Symptoms include headache; eye, nose, or throat irritation; dry cough; dry or itchy skin; dizziness; nausea; fatigue; and sensitivity to odors. The EPA estimates that 30 percent of all U.S. office buildings could be "sick," so they recommend routine maintenance of HVAC systems, including cleaning or replacing filters; replacing water-stained ceiling tiles and carpeting; restricting smoking in and around buildings; and ventilating areas where paints, adhesives, or solvents are used.

7. Social anxiety disorder. Despite all the ways to interact with others in our technologically savvy world, those with social anxiety disorder feel boxed in by the shrinking globe. According to the National Institutes of Health (NIH), people with social anxiety disorder have an "intense, persistent, and chronic fear of being watched and judged by others and of doing things that will embarrass them," and that fear can be so intense that it interferes with work, school, and other ordinary activities and can make it hard to make and keep friends. But the condition has physical manifestations, too, including trembling, upset stomach, heart palpitations, confusion, and diarrhea. The cause hasn't been nailed down, but social anxiety disorder is probably due to a combination of environmental and hereditary factors. About 15 million people in the United States are affected by social anxiety disorder, which usually begins during childhood. Like other anxiety disorders, treatment often involves medication and psychotherapy.

LIVE LONG AND PROSPER
10 Countries with the Highest Life Expectancy

�֍ �֍ �֍ �֍

Want to live to a ripe old age? By far the most important factor in life expectancy is wealth; richer people tend to eat healthfully, smoke and drink less, and have access to the best health care. Affluent countries also tend to have low rates of violent crime and civil unrest. The following countries have the highest average life expectancies in the world. In case you're wondering, the United States, with an average life expectancy of 77.85, ranks 48th.

1. Andorra: 83.51

Located between France and Spain, Andorra was one of Europe's poorest countries until it became a popular tourist destination after

World War II. Its 71,000 inhabitants now enjoy all the benefits of a thriving economy, which include excellent nutrition and public health-care facilities.

2. Macau: 82.19

Like Andorra, this island in the South China Sea is reaping the rewards of a booming economy. The money has come from visitors, particularly from the Chinese mainland, coming to take advantage of a recently liberalized gaming industry. Gambling profits now provide about 70 percent of the country's income, and the government uses the money to invest heavily in public health care.

3. San Marino: 81.71 (tied)

This enclave in central Italy is the third smallest state in Europe (after Vatican City and Monaco), as well as the world's oldest republic. Here, the long life expectancy is due to prosperity and the fact that the majority of the population is involved in office-based work rather than heavy industry and labor, which shorten life spans.

4. Singapore: 81.71 (tied)

Aside from prosperity, one factor in Singapore's long average life expectancy is that in the early 1980s, the government recognized that it had an aging population, with the average age of its citizens increasing all the time. The government planned accordingly, and now Singapore has excellent health-care facilities for the elderly.

5. Hong Kong: 81.59

People in Hong Kong generally eat a healthful and balanced diet, based around rice, vegetables, and tofu, with only small amounts of meat. This means that obesity rates are low, as are the rates for most dietary-based cancers and heart disease.

6. Japan: 81.25

Japan has one of the lowest adult obesity rates in the industrialized world, at only 3 percent. As in Hong Kong, this is mainly due to a healthful diet based around vegetables, fish, rice, and noodles. Many Japanese people also stop eating when they feel about 80 percent full, rather than continuing until they can't manage another mouthful. The Japanese are also much less reliant on cars than people in Western countries, preferring to walk whenever possible, and therefore get plenty of exercise.

7. Sweden: 80.51 (tied)

Although an economic downturn in the late 1990s did some damage to Sweden's world-renowned welfare and public health systems, they are still among the best in the world. Also, Sweden has the lowest rate of smokers in the developed world—about 17 percent—so tobacco-related deaths are half the European average.

8. Switzerland: 80.51 (tied)

Aside from a stable economy with all of the usual factors that increase longevity, such as a healthful diet and high standard of health care, Switzerland's much-vaunted neutrality means that its inhabitants are highly unlikely to die in an armed conflict.

9. Australia: 80.50

All the usual factors relating to prosperity apply here, but the life expectancy of indigenous Australians is about 20 years less than that of white Aussies, due to higher rates of just about every factor that shortens life, including smoking, obesity, and poverty. Incidentally, research suggests that Australia's life expectancy may start falling as obesity reaches epidemic proportions in the land down under.

10. Guernsey: 80.42

The island of Guernsey, located in the English Channel, is a British Crown dependency, but it is not part of the UK. The reason for its high life expectancy is simple: it's extremely wealthy. Very low taxes make Guernsey a popular destination for tax exiles who can afford the very best in nutrition and medical care. More than half of the island's income comes from financial services—which means well-paid desk jobs—with very few people working in heavy industry.

✳ ✳ ✳

"Seek not, my soul, the life of the immortals; but enjoy to the full the resources that are within thy reach."
—Pindar, ancient Greek poet

12 Deadly Diseases Cured in the 20th Century

✳ ✳ ✳ ✳

*According to the U.S. Census Bureau, the average life expectancy
at the beginning of the 20th century was 47.3 years. A century
later, that number had increased to 77.85 years, due largely to
the development of vaccinations and other treatments for deadly
diseases. Of course, vaccines and treatments only work if they're
given, which is why many of these diseases still persist in poorer,
developing countries. Despite the success of vaccines, only one of
these diseases—smallpox—has been erased from the globe.
Here are 12 diseases that could be completely eradicated from the
world if vaccines were made available to all.*

1. Chicken Pox. Before 1995, a case of the chicken pox was a rite of
passage for kids. The disease, caused by the *varicella-zoster* virus,
creates an itchy rash of small red bumps on the skin. The virus
spreads when someone who has the disease coughs or sneezes, and
a nonimmune person inhales the viral particles. The virus can also
be passed through contact with the fluid of chicken pox blisters.
Most cases are minor but in more serious instances, chicken pox
can trigger bacterial infections, viral pneumonia, and encephalitis
(inflammation of the brain). According to the Centers for Disease
Control and Prevention (CDC), before the chicken pox vaccine
was approved for use in the United States in 1995, there were
11,000 hospitalizations and 100 deaths from the disease every year.
Many countries do not require the vaccination because chicken pox
doesn't cause that many deaths. They'd rather focus on vaccinating
against the really serious diseases, so the disease is still common.

2. Diphtheria. Diphtheria is an infection of the bacteria *Corynebac-
terium diphtheriae* and mainly affects the nose and throat. The
bacteria spreads through airborne droplets and shared personal
items. *C. diphtheriae* creates a toxin in the body that produces a
thick, gray or black coating in the nose, throat, or airway, which can

also affect the heart and nervous system. Even with proper antibiotic treatment, diphtheria kills about 10 percent of the people who contract it. The first diphtheria vaccine was unveiled in 1913, and although vaccination has made a major dent in mortality rates, the disease still exists in developing countries and other areas where people are not regularly vaccinated. The World Health Organization (WHO) estimates that worldwide there are about 5,000 deaths from diphtheria annually, but the disease is quite rare in the United States, with fewer than five cases reported each year.

3. Invasive H. Flu. Invasive H. flu, or Hib disease, is an infection caused by the *Haemophilus influenzae* type b (Hib) bacteria, which spreads when an infected person coughs, sneezes, or speaks. Invasive H. flu is a bit of a misnomer because it is not related to any form of the influenza virus. However, it can lead to bacterial meningitis (a potentially fatal brain infection), pneumonia, epiglottitis (severe swelling above the voice box that makes breathing difficult), and infections of the blood, joints, bones, and pericardium (the covering of the heart). Children younger than five years old are particularly susceptible to the Hib bacteria because they have not had the chance to develop immunity to it. The first Hib vaccine was licensed in 1985, but despite its success in the developed world, the disease is still prevalent in the developing world. WHO estimates that each year Hib disease causes two to three million cases of serious illness worldwide, mostly pneumonia and meningitis, and 450,000 deaths of young children.

4. Malaria. This disease is a parasitic infection of the liver and red blood cells. In its mildest forms it can produce flu-like symptoms and nausea, and in its severest forms it can cause seizures, coma, fluid buildup in the lungs, kidney failure, and death. The disease is transmitted by female mosquitoes of the genus *Anopheles*. When the mosquito bites, the parasites enter a person's body, invading red blood cells and causing the cells to rupture. As the cells burst, they release chemicals that cause malaria's symptoms. About 350 million to 500 million cases of malaria occur worldwide every year. About

one million are fatal, with children in sub-Saharan Africa accounting for most of the deaths. Other high-risk areas include Central
and South America, India, and the Middle East. Malaria is treated
with a variety of drugs, some of which kill the parasites once they're
in the blood and others that prevent infection in the first place. Of
course, if you can avoid the parasite-carrying mosquitoes, you can
avoid malaria, so the disease is often controlled using mosquito
repellent and bed netting, especially in poor countries that cannot
afford medications.

5. Measles. Measles is a highly contagious viral illness of the respiratory system that spreads through airborne droplets when an
infected person coughs or sneezes. Although the first symptoms
of measles mimic a simple cold, with a cough, runny nose, and red
watery eyes, this disease is more serious. As measles progresses, the
infected person develops a fever and a red or brownish-red skin
rash. Complications can include diarrhea, pneumonia, brain infection, and even death, although these are seen more commonly in
malnourished or immunodeficient people. Measles has historically
been a devastating disease, but WHO reported in 2006 that measles
mortality rates dropped from 871,000 to 454,000 between 1999 and
2004, thanks to a global immunization drive. Until 1963, when
the first measles vaccine was used in the United States, almost
everyone got the measles by age 20. There has been a 99 percent
reduction in measles since then, but outbreaks have occurred when
the disease is brought over from other countries or when children
don't get the vaccine or all the required doses. Most children today
receive the measles vaccine as part of the MMR vaccination, which
protects against measles, mumps, and rubella (German measles).

6. Pertussis. Whoop, there it is—and if you suspect someone has it,
move away. Pertussis, or whooping cough, is a highly contagious
respiratory infection caused by the *Bordetella pertussis* bacteria.
The descriptive nickname comes from the "whooping" sounds that
infected children make after one of the disease's coughing spells.
The coughing fits spread the bacteria and can last a minute or

longer, causing a child to turn purple or red and sometimes vomit. Severe episodes can cause a lack of oxygen to the brain. Adults who contract pertussis usually have a hacking cough rather than a whooping one. Although the disease can strike anyone, it is most prevalent in infants under age one because they haven't received the entire course of pertussis vaccinations. The pertussis vaccine was first used in 1933, but adolescents and adults become susceptible when the immunity from childhood vaccinations wanes and they don't get booster shots. According to the CDC, pertussis causes 10–20 deaths each year in the United States, and there were 25,000 cases reported in 2004. Worldwide, the disease causes far more damage—about 50 million people around the world are infected annually, and WHO estimates around 294,000 deaths each year. However, 78 percent of the world's infants received three doses of the vaccine in 2004.

7. Pneumococcal Disease. Pneumococcal disease is the collective name for the infections caused by *Streptococcus pneumoniae* bacteria, also known as *pneumococcus.* This bacteria finds a home all over the body. The most common types of infections caused by S. *pneumoniae* are middle ear infections, pneumonia, bacteremia (blood stream infections), sinus infections, and bacterial meningitis. There are more than 90 types of *pneumococcus,* with the ten most common types responsible for 62 percent of the world's invasive diseases. Those infected carry the bacteria in their throats and expel it when they cough or sneeze. Like any other germ, S. *pneumoniae* can infect anyone, but certain population groups are more at risk, such as the elderly, people with cancer or AIDS, and people with a chronic illness such as diabetes. The CDC blames pneumococcal disease for the deaths of 200 children under the age of five each year in the United States. WHO estimates that annually pneumococcal disease is responsible for one million fatal cases of respiratory illness alone; most of these cases occur in developing countries. There are two types of vaccines available to prevent pneumococcal disease, which the CDC recommends that children and adults older than age 65 receive.

8. Polio. Of the deadly infectious diseases for which science has developed vaccines and treatments, people are most familiar with the victory over polio. The disease is caused by a virus that enters the body through the mouth, usually from hands contaminated with the stool of an infected person. In about 95 percent of cases, polio produces no symptoms at all (asymptomatic polio), but in the remaining cases of polio, the disease can take three forms. Abortive polio creates flu-like symptoms, such as upper respiratory infection, fever, sore throat, and general malaise. Nonparalytic polio is more severe and produces symptoms similar to mild meningitis, including sensitivity to light and neck stiffness. Finally, paralytic polio produces the symptoms with which most people associate the disease, even though paralytic polio accounts for less than 1 percent of all cases. Paralytic polio causes loss of control and paralysis of limbs, reflexes, and the muscles that control breathing. Today, polio is under control in the developed world, and world health authorities are close to controlling the disease in developing countries, as well. Dr. Jonas Salk's inactivated polio vaccine (IPV) first appeared in 1955, and Dr. Albert Sabin's oral polio vaccine (OPV) first appeared in 1961. Children in the United States receive IPV, but most children in developing areas of the world receive OPV, which is cheaper and doesn't have to be administered by a health-care professional; however, in rare instances, OPV can cause polio.

9. Tetanus. Reproductive cells (spores) of *Clostridium tetani* are found in the soil and enter the body through a skin wound. Once the spores develop into mature bacteria, the bacteria produce tetanospasmin, a neurotoxin (a protein that poisons the body's nervous system) that causes muscle spasms. In fact, tetanus gets its nickname—lockjaw—because the toxin often attacks the muscles that control the jaw. Lockjaw is accompanied by difficulty swallowing and painful stiffness in the neck, shoulders, and back. The spasms can then spread to the muscles of the abdomen, upper arms, and thighs. According to the CDC, tetanus is fatal in about 11 percent of cases, but fortunately, it can't be spread from person to person—you need direct contact with *C. tetani* to contract the disease.

Today, tetanus immunization is standard in the United States, but if you are injured in a way that increases tetanus risk (i.e. stepping on a rusty nail, cutting your hand with a knife, or getting bitten by a dog), a booster shot may be necessary if it's been several years since your last tetanus shot. According to the CDC, since the 1970s, only about 50 to 100 cases of tetanus are reported in the United States each year, mostly among people who have never been vaccinated or who did not get a booster shot. And WHO says that globally there were about 15,500 cases of tetanus in 2005.

10. Typhoid Fever. Typhoid is usually spread when food or water has been infected with *Salmonella typhi,* most often through contact with the feces of an infected person. Once the typhoid bacteria enter the bloodstream, the body mounts a defense that causes a high fever, headache, stomach pains, weakness, and decreased appetite. Occasionally, people who have typhoid get a rash of flat red spots. Because sewage treatment in the United States is quite good, the disease is very rare, and the CDC reports only about 400 cases of it annually. However, people who live in developing countries where there is little water and sewage treatment, or where hand washing is not a common practice, are at high risk. Prime typhoid fever areas are in Africa, Asia, the Caribbean, India, and Central and South America. WHO estimates 17 million cases occur globally with 600,000 deaths each year. Despite these daunting statistics, typhoid fever vaccination is available for people who travel to high-risk areas, and the disease can be effectively treated with antibiotics. Without treatment, the fever can continue for weeks or months, and the infection can lead to death.

11. Yellow Fever. Yellow fever is spread by mosquitoes infected with the yellow fever virus. Jaundice, or yellowing of the skin and eyes, is the hallmark of the infection and gives it its name. Most cases of yellow fever are mild and require only three or four days to recover, but severe cases can cause bleeding, heart problems, liver or kidney failure, brain dysfunction, or death. People with the disease can ease their symptoms, but there is no specific treatment, so prevention via the yellow fever vaccine is key. The vaccine provides immunity from the disease for ten years or more and is generally safe for everyone older than nine months. Yellow fever occurs only in Africa, South America, and some areas of the Caribbean, so only travelers who are destined for these regions need to be concerned about it. WHO estimates that there are 200,000 cases of yellow fever every year, and 30,000 of them are fatal. The elderly are at highest risk of developing the most severe symptoms. Although vaccination and mosquito-eradication efforts have made a great difference, WHO says yellow fever cases are on the rise again.

12. Smallpox. Unlike other diseases on this list, which can still appear in outbreaks when vaccination vigilance weakens, smallpox has been wiped off the face of the earth, except for samples of the virus held in labs in the United States and Russia for research purposes. Symptoms of smallpox included a high fever, head and body aches, malaise, vomiting, and a rash of small red bumps that progressed into sores that could break open and spread the virus (the virus could also be spread via contact with shared items, clothing, and bedding). Smallpox was an entirely human disease—it did not infect any other animal or insect on the planet. Thus, once vaccination eliminated the chances of the virus spreading among the human population, the disease disappeared; in fact, the United States has not vaccinated for smallpox since 1972. Although smallpox was one of the most devastating illnesses in human history, killing more than 300 million people worldwide during the 20th century alone, scientists declared the world free of smallpox in 1979. The naturally occurring disease has been eradicated, but fears remain about the smallpox samples being used as bioweapons.

✳ ✳ ✳

"The art of medicine consists in amusing the patient while nature cures the disease."
—Voltaire

MIRROR, MIRROR, ON THE WALL,
DON'T LIKE WHAT YOU SEE AT ALL?
20 Most Common Plastic Surgeries

❋ ❋ ❋ ❋

If you're not happy with the body you see in the mirror, you're not alone. According to the American Society of Plastic Surgeons (ASPS), there were more than 1.8 million cosmetic surgeries and 8.4 million minimally invasive cosmetic procedures (i.e. Botox injections, laser hair removal) performed in the United States in 2005. Here are the top 20 cosmetic surgeries.

1. Liposuction: Liposuction is the removal of fat deposits using a tube inserted beneath the skin; fat is then sucked out using a vacuum-like device. The procedure is often performed on the abdomen, buttocks, hips, thighs, and upper arms. Of the 323,605 liposuctions performed in 2005, 89 percent of the patients were women. Recovery times range from one to four weeks, but it may take up to six months for all the swelling to go down. This procedure will suck about $2,300 out of your wallet.

2. Rhinoplasty: Commonly called a nose job, rhinoplasty is the reshaping of the nose to make it bigger or smaller, to narrow the span of the nostrils, or to change the angle between the nose and upper lip. Rhinoplasty is popular with men and women—of the 298,413 rhinoplasty procedures done in 2005, 67 percent were performed on women. People typically need one to three weeks to recover, but they are advised to avoid bumping their noses or getting them sunburned for eight weeks. Rhinoplasty will run about $3,500 for physician's fees.

3. Breast augmentation: Breast augmentation, or augmentation mammaplasty, is the enlarging of a woman's breasts using saline- or silicone-filled implants. There were 291,350 breast augmentation procedures performed in 2005, making this the top cosmetic surgery procedure among women. The surgery requires only a few days of recovery time, although the ASPS recommends there be no physical contact with the breasts for three to four weeks. Physician's fees for breast augmentation average $3,400.

4. Eyelid surgery: In eyelid surgery, or blepharoplasty, drooping upper eyelids and bags below the eyes are corrected by removing extra fat, muscle, and skin. Women improve their peepers far more often than men—of the 230,697 blepharoplasty procedures performed in 2005, 86 percent of patients were women. Patients need a week to ten days to recover, but those who wear contacts need two weeks or more before they wear their corrective lenses. Although the procedure doesn't improve your sight, your eyes will look better as you write the $2,500 check for physician's fees.

5. Tummy tuck: Beer guts may be more associated with men, but women by far get more abdominoplasty procedures. The abdomen is flattened during the surgery when extra fat and skin are removed and abdominal muscles are tightened. In 2005, plastic surgeons performed 134,746 tummy tucks—96 percent of them on women. Patients need two to six weeks of recovery time, but the wallet will probably need longer to replenish the $4,400 in physician's fees.

6. Face-lift: Is anything actually being raised? Not really, but excess fat is removed and muscles are tightened before the skin is redraped. Besides, *face-lift* is easier to say than *rhytidectomy,* the medical name of the procedure. No matter what you call it, a face-lift results in tighter skin on the face and neck. Of the 108,955 face-lifts performed in 2005, women received 90 percent of them. It takes ten days to three weeks to recover, but sun exposure must be limited for several months. Your face will be tighter, but you won't smile when you see the average bill of $4,500 for physician's fees.

7. Breast lift: A breast lift, or mastopexy, is performed on women who want to raise and reshape their sagging breasts. The procedure removes extra skin and repositions the remaining tissue and nipples. In 2005, surgeons performed 92,740 breast lifts at an average cost of $3,600. Recovery can take a week to a month.

8. Dermabrasion: Although it sounds like a medieval torture tactic, 69,359 people received dermabrasion in 2005. With dermabrasion, wrinkles and facial blemishes are literally rubbed out as a surgeon uses a high-speed, rotating tool to scrape away the top layers of skin, leaving softer, newer layers. Women make up 88 percent of dermabrasion patients. Recovery time is typically two to six weeks, but the face may have a red tint for three months. The actual procedure will leave you a little red in the face, but the cost won't. Physician's fees average $875.

9. Forehead lift: This procedure straightens out lines and droops by removing tissue and tightening the skin and forehead muscles. Getting over this procedure will take you one to three weeks or more, but you will have to stay out of the sun for several months. Women received 87 percent of the 55,518 forehead lifts in 2005. Physician's fees will set you back about $2,400.

10. Hair transplantation: Finally, men have an insecurity they can own! If things are a little too bare on top, a surgeon can reduce the amount of scalp you have or insert clusters of hair (plugs) right into the noggin. Depending on the technique used, several visits to the surgeon over 18 months may be required to restore your mane to its former glory. Men were the recipients of 83 percent of the 47,462 hair transplants in 2005. You'll have more hair, but you may not have much money left for hair gel or mousse after shelling out $4,750 in physician's fees.

11. Ear surgery: Large ears or ears that prominently stick out from the head can cause a lot of grief, especially for children. That's why kids make up most of the patients who undergo ear surgery (otoplasty), where the ear's skin or cartilage is removed or bent back to bring the ears closer to the head. Of the 27,993 otoplasty procedures performed in 2005, 59 percent were done on females. The head is usually bandaged for a few days and stitches are removed in about a week. Any activity that might bend the ear should be avoided for about a month. Physician's fees cost about $2,400.

12. Lip augmentation: If your puckers aren't as prominent as you like, you can pump them up with lip augmentation, where a surgeon will hollow out a portion of your lip and insert an implant to give your lips more body. It usually takes two or three weeks for the swelling from this procedure to subside. Full lips are more valuable to women than they are to men—of the 25,878 lip augmentation procedures performed in 2005, 95 percent were done on women. How many smackers will this surgery set you back? Physician's fees average about $1,200.

13. Breast implant removal: Some women who have their breasts surgically enlarged later decide to have the implants removed. This, of course, requires another surgery and another couple weeks of recovery. In 2005, 24,694 women had their breast implants removed. Breast implant removal is a cheaper proposition than having them inserted, with physician's fees averaging $2,300.

14. Breast reduction (men): A condition called gynecomastia causes some men to develop breasts that resemble women's. There are many possible causes of gynecomastia, including hormonal changes during puberty, drug use, tumors, genetic disorders, liver disease, and some medications. The larger breasts are often due to excess fat or glandular tissue; in a breast reduction surgery, this extra matter is removed. Gynecomastia is fairly common; in fact, according to the ASPS, the condition affects 40 to 60 percent of men. In 2005, 16,275 breast reduction surgeries were performed on men at an average cost of $3,000. Recovery usually takes two to three weeks.

15. Chin augmentation: Those who feel their face lacks a certain amount of proportion often have their chin altered to enhance their profile. Chin augmentation, or mentoplasty, usually involves either inserting an implant into the chin or changing the shape of the bone. This is often done to improve facial symmetry after another cosmetic procedure. Most patients can return to normal living a week after surgery, but numbness or discomfort may continue for three months. Men received 58 percent of the 15,161 chin augmentation surgeries in 2005. You won't take it on the chin when paying for this operation because physician's fees average $1,600.

16. Upper arm lift: One of the hardest places to tone is the upper arm, especially in women. The skin in this area becomes loose and fat deposits lead to a jellylike movement when waving. One solution is an upper arm lift, or brachioplasty, where a surgeon removes the excess fat (often using liposuction) and tightens the skin. Most people bounce back from the surgery in a week or less and can resume exercise in two weeks. Women received 96 percent of the 11,873 upper arm lifts done in 2005. Physician's fees average $3,260.

17. Thigh lift: Cottage cheese is a tasty source of protein, but it's not a good look on the thighs. Cellulite causes that dimpled look, but a thigh lift can remove extra skin and fat to make legs look better. Women are much more likely to get a thigh lift than men; of the 9,533 thigh lifts performed in 2005, women received 95 percent of them. Be sure you use your shapely new legs to lift the bill—physician's fees average $4,200.

18. Cheek implant: As a child you may have cringed when old Aunt Gertrude would grab your plump cheeks and give them a good squeeze, but these days, people are paying good money for those pinch-inspiring cheeks. A cheek implant, or malar augmentation, is a procedure in which an implant is inserted below the cheekbone to give the face a fuller look. Of the 9,326 cheek implants performed in 2005, women received 62 percent of them. It might take a month or two to fully recover from the swelling caused by this surgery. Those high cheekbones don't come with a high price tag; average physician's fees are $1,760.

19. Lower body lift: If you're going to get plastic surgery, why not get more than one part worked on at the same time? A lower body lift corrects sagging areas of the hips, thighs, and buttocks by removing excess fat and tissue and tightening the skin. Women underwent 86 percent of the 8,696 lower body lifts in 2005. This major procedure requires a month or two of recovery time, and it will be even longer before exercising and heavy lifting can be resumed. If you're going in for that much tightening, you better not have a tight grip on your wallet. This surgery costs about $6,400.

20. **Buttock lift:** Maybe your hips and thighs are okay, but your rump could use a bump up. If so, a buttock lift is in order to remove excess skin and tissue and raise the buttocks. In some cases, implants are used to give the area more shape. Of the 5,193 buttock lifts performed in 2005, women were the recipients of 92 percent of them. Recovery takes about two weeks, but swelling may remain for several months. Improving your derriere will set your financial bottom line back about $3,790.

Decoding 28 Medical Slang Terms

❊ ❊ ❊ ❊

Doctors, nurses, and other health-care professionals need to communicate with each other quickly and effectively. They also have a sense of humor, as you'll notice in the following list of slang terms used in hospitals.

1. **Appy:** a person's appendix or a patient with appendicitis

2. **Baby Catcher:** an obstetrician

3. **Bagging:** manually helping a patient breathe using a squeeze bag attached to a mask that covers the face

4. **Banana:** a person with jaundice (yellowing of the skin and eyes)

5. **Blood Suckers/Leeches:** those who take blood samples, such as laboratory technicians

6. **Bounceback:** a patient who returns to the emergency department with the same complaints shortly after being released

7. **Bury the Hatchet:** accidentally leaving a surgical instrument inside a patient

8. CBC: complete blood count; an all-purpose blood test used to diagnose different illnesses and conditions

9. Code Brown: a patient who has lost control of his or her bowels

10. Code Yellow: a patient who has lost control of his or her bladder

11. Crook-U: similar to the ICU or PICU, but referring to a prison ward in the hospital

12. DNR: do not resuscitate; a written request made by terminally ill or elderly patients who do not want extraordinary efforts made if they go into cardiac arrest, a coma, etc.

13. Doc in a Box: a small health-care center, usually with high staff turnover

14. FLK: funny-looking kid

15. Foley: a catheter used to drain the bladder of urine

16. Freud Squad: the psychiatry department

17. Gas Passer: an anesthesiologist

18. GSW: gunshot wound

19. MI: myocardial infarction; a heart attack

20. M & Ms: mortality and morbidity conferences where doctors and other health-care professionals discuss mistakes and patient deaths

21. MVA: motor vehicle accident

22. O Sign: an unconscious patient whose mouth is open

23. Q Sign: an unconscious patient whose mouth is open and tongue is hanging out

24. Rear Admiral: a proctologist

25. Shotgunning: ordering a wide variety of tests in the hope that one will show what's wrong with a patient

26. Stat: from the Latin *statinum,* meaning immediately

27. Tox Screen: testing the blood for the level and type of drugs in a patient's system

28. UBI: unexplained beer injury; a patient who appears in the ER with an injury sustained while intoxicated that he or she can't explain

BURN, BABY, BURN
12 Sports and Recreational Activities and the Calories They Burn

※ ※ ※ ※

*Everybody wants to burn the most calories in the least amount of time. So it would be helpful to know which sports and recreational activities burn the most calories. Here are 12 activities and the approximate number of calories they burn. Before launching into any of these activities, be sure to consult your doctor. And always remember to properly warm up and stretch.**

1. Running: Burning about 450 calories every 30 minutes (based on an 8-minute mile), running also gives a fantastic cardiorespiratory workout. Leg strength and endurance are maximized, but few benefits accrue to the upper body. Warm up thoroughly, wear the proper shoes, and keep a moderate pace to avoid injury.

2. Rock Climbing: Rock climbing relies on quick bursts of energy to get from one rock to the next. It won't do a lot for your heart, but your strength, endurance, and flexibility will greatly benefit, and you'll burn about 371 calories every half hour.

3. Swimming: Swimming provides an excellent overall body workout, burning up to 360 calories in a half hour depending on the stroke used. However, most people have difficulty maintaining proper form for that long. The best swim workout is based on interval training; swim two lengths, catch your breath, and then repeat.

4. Cycling: Cycling is an excellent non-weight-bearing (your weight is not being supported by your body) exercise, and depending on your speed, burns around 300 or 400 calories in a half hour. It provides a great cardio workout and builds up those thighs and calves. However, it doesn't provide much in the way of an upper body workout.

5. Boxing: If you're game enough to step into the ring, you'll be rewarded with a 324-calorie deficit for every half hour of slugging it out. In addition, your cardiorespiratory fitness and muscular endurance will go through the roof. Make sure you're match fit, though, or it may be all over before you build up a sweat!

6. Racquetball: Churning through about 300 calories in 30 minutes, racquetball gives you a fantastic cardiorespiratory workout, builds lower body strength and endurance, and with all that twisting and pivoting, develops great flexibility around the core (back and abs). Just warm up first to avoid twisting an ankle.

7. Basketball: The nonstop action of b-ball will see you dropping around 288 calories every half hour, while at the same time developing flexibility, endurance, and cardiorespiratory health. But warm up properly because the sudden twists and turns can be high risk for the unprepared.

8. Rowing: Burning about 280 calories per half hour, rowing is a very effective way to rid yourself of extra energy. It also builds up endurance, strength, and muscle in your shoulders, thighs, and biceps. The key to rowing is in the technique—coordinate the legs, back, and arms to work as one. Kayaking and canoeing each burn around 170 calories in a half hour.

9. Tennis: Here's a fun game that demands speed, agility, strength, and reaction time. It consumes about 250–300 calories in a half hour session, providing a great opportunity to burn excess calories while developing cardiorespiratory fitness. Wear proper footwear to avoid ankle injuries.

10. Cross-Country Skiing: The very fact that you're out in the snow has already fired up your metabolism. As soon as you start mushing through it, you'll be churning through those calories at the rate of 270 every half hour. The varied terrain will provide a great interval training workout, too!

11. Ice Skating: Ice skating gives you all the benefits of running without the joint stress. A half hour on the ice consumes about 252 calories. Skating provides an excellent workout for your thighs, calves, hamstrings, and buttocks. The twists and turns also tighten and tone your abs. Holding out your arms helps you balance and also works the deltoids, biceps, and triceps.

12. Swing Dancing: Yes, you can dance your way to fitness! Swing dancing burns about 180 calories in a half hour and gives you a moderately intense aerobic workout. You'll be developing flexibility, core strength, and endurance—and you won't even feel like you're exercising. So, get out there and celebrate the joy of movement!

Calories based on a 150-pound person. (A heavier person will burn more calories.)

EXTRA! EXTRA!
13 People with Extra Body Parts

✳ ✳ ✳ ✳

Doctors call them supernumerary body parts, but here are a few people who always had a spare hand (or finger, or head . . .).

1. Anne Boleyn, second wife to Henry VIII of England, is commonly believed to have had 11 fingers and possibly a third breast. Historians believe that she did have an extra finger or at least some sort of growth on her hand that resembled an extra finger, but it is unlikely that she had an extra breast. This rumor may have been started by her enemies because in Tudor times an extra breast was believed to be the sign of a witch.

2. Major league baseball pitcher Antonio Alfonseca has six fingers on each hand, but he claims the extra fingers do not affect his pitching, as they do not usually touch the ball. In most cases of polydactylism (extra fingers or toes), the extra digit has only limited mobility, or cannot be moved at all, and is often surgically removed shortly after birth. The condition is reported in about one child in every 500.

3. Actor Mark Wahlberg has a third nipple on the left side of his chest. Early in his career, he considered having it removed, but he later came to accept it. Around 2 percent of women and slightly fewer men have a supernumerary nipple, although they are often mistaken for moles. They can be found anywhere between the armpit and groin, and range from a tiny lump (like Wahlberg's) to a small extra breast, sometimes even capable of lactation.

4. In 2006, a 24-year-old man from India checked himself into a New Delhi hospital and asked doctors to remove his extra penis so that he could marry and lead a normal sex life. To protect his privacy, doctors would not disclose his identity or that of the hospital but did confirm that the operation took place. The condition, known as diphallia or penile duplication, is extremely rare, with only around 100 cases ever documented.

5. Craniopagus parasiticus is a medical condition in which a baby is born with a parasitic twin head. The extra head does not have a functioning brain, which is what differentiates this condition from that of conjoined twins. In effect, the baby is born with the head of its dead twin attached to its body. There have only ever been eight documented cases, and, of these, only three have survived birth. One of these was Rebeca Martínez, born in the Dominican Republic in December 2003, the first baby to undergo an operation to remove the second head. She died on February 7, 2004, after an 11-hour operation.

6. A similar condition is polycephaly, the condition of having more than one functioning head. There are many documented occurrences of this in the animal kingdom, although in most human cases we refer to the condition as conjoined twins. One recent case was that of Syafitri, born in Indonesia in 2006. These conjoined twins were given just one name by their parents who insisted that they were, in fact, one baby girl since they had only one heart and shared a body. It would have been impossible for doctors to separate the conjoined twins, and Syafitri died of unknown causes just two weeks after she was born.

7. Hermaphroditism—the condition of being born with both male and female reproductive organs—is more common than you might think, existing in some degree in around 1 percent of the population. In 1843, when Levi Suydam, a 23-year-old resident of Salisbury, Connecticut, wanted to vote for the Whig candidate in a local election, the opposition party objected, saying Suydam was really a woman and therefore did not have the right to vote. A doctor examined Suydam and declared that he had a penis and was therefore a man. He voted and the Whig candidate won by a single vote.

8. In 2006, a boy named Jie-Jie was born in China with two left arms. Although all three of his arms looked normal, neither left arm was fully functional, and, when he was two months old, doctors in Shanghai removed the one closest to his chest after tests revealed it was less developed.

9. While advances in medical technology mean that Jie-Jie will go on to lead a relatively normal life, Francesco Lentini, who was born in Sicily in 1889, had a life that was anything but. He was born with three legs, two sets of genitals, and an extra foot growing from the knee of his third leg—the remains of a conjoined twin that had died in the womb. Rejected by his parents, he was raised by an aunt, then in a home for disabled children before moving to America when he was eight. He became "The Great Lentini" and toured with major circus and sideshow acts, including the Ringling Brothers' Circus and Barnum and Bailey. Part of his act included using his third leg to kick a soccer ball across the stage. He married, raised four children, and lived longer than any other three-legged person, dying in Florida in 1966 at age 78.

10. Josephene Myrtle Corbin, born in 1868, could see Lentini his three legs and raise him one. She was a dipygus, meaning that she had two separate pelvises and four legs. As with Lentini, these were the residual parts of a conjoined twin. She could move all of the legs, but they were too weak to walk on. Like Lentini, she was a great success in sideshows with the stage name "The Four-Legged Girl from Texas." She married a doctor with whom she had five children. Legend has it that three of her children were born from one pelvis, and two from the other.

11. Born in 1932 to a poor farming family in Georgia, Betty Lou Williams was the youngest of 12 children. Doctors claimed she was a healthy child . . . except for the two extra arms and legs emerging from the side of her body. From the age of two, Williams worked for Ripley's Believe It Or Not and earned quite a living on the sideshow circuit—she put her siblings through college and bought her parents a large farm. She grew up to be a lovely and generous young lady, but when she was jilted by her fiancé at age 23, she died from an asthma attack exacerbated by the head of the parasitic twin lodged in her abdomen.

12. Another sideshow star of the early 20th century was Jean Libbera, "The Man with Two Bodies," who was born in Rome in 1884. Libbera was born with a parasitic conjoined twin attached to his front. Photos of Libbera show a shrunken body, about 18 inches long, emerging from his abdomen with its head apparently embedded inside. He died in 1934, at age 50.

13. It might seem unusual for a woman to have two uteruses, but the condition known as uterine didelphys occurs in about one in 1,000 women. In fact, Hannah Kersey, her mother, and her sister all have two wombs. But Hannah made history in 2006 when she gave birth to triplets—a set of identical twin girls from one womb and a third, fraternal sister from the other womb. There have been about 70 known pregnancies in separate wombs in the past 100 years, but the case of triplets is the first of its kind and doctors estimate the likelihood is about one in 25 million.

Chapter 6

RELIGION, FOLKLORE, AND THE PARANORMAL

✳ ✳ ✳ ✳

"SHIP TO SHORE! SHIP TO SHORE! OH S—T!"

7 Disappearances in the Bermuda Triangle

The Bermuda Triangle, also known as the Devil's Triangle, is an infamous stretch of the Atlantic Ocean bordered by Florida, Bermuda, and Puerto Rico that has been the location of strange disappearances throughout history. The Coast Guard does not recognize the Bermuda Triangle or the supernatural explanations for the mysterious disappearances in its midst. There are some probable explanations for the missing vessels, including hurricanes, undersea earthquakes, and magnetic fields that interfere with compasses and other positioning devices. But it's much more interesting to think the following vessels got sucked into another dimension, abducted by aliens, or simply vanished into thin air.

1. Flight 19

On the afternoon of December 5, 1945, five Avenger torpedo bombers left the Naval Air Station at Fort Lauderdale, Florida, with Lt. Charles Taylor in command of a crew of 13 student pilots. About an hour and a half into the flight, Taylor radioed the base to say that his compasses weren't working, but he figured he was somewhere over the Florida Keys. The lieutenant who received the signal told Taylor to fly north toward Miami, as long as he was sure he was actually over the Keys. Although he was an experienced pilot, Taylor got horribly turned around, and the more he tried to get out of the Keys, the further out to sea he and his crew traveled. As night fell, radio signals worsened, until, finally, there was nothing at all from Flight 19. A U.S. Navy investigation reported that Taylor's confusion caused the disaster, but his mother convinced them to change the official report to read that the planes went down for "causes unknown." The planes have never been recovered.

2. Flight 201

This Cessna left Fort Lauderdale on March 31, 1984, en route for Bimini Island in the Bahamas, but it never made it. Not quite midway to its destination, the plane slowed its airspeed significantly, but no radio signals were made from the plane to indicate distress. Suddenly, the plane dropped from the air into the water, completely vanishing from the radar. A woman on Bimini Island swore she saw a plane plunge into the sea about a mile offshore, but no wreckage has ever been found.

3. USS *Cyclops*

As World War I heated up, America went to battle. The *Cyclops*, commanded by Lt. G. W. Worley, stayed mostly on the East Coast of the United States until 1918 when it was sent to Brazil to refuel Allied ships. With 309 people onboard, the ship left Rio de Janeiro in February and reached Barbados in March. After that, the *Cyclops* was never heard from again. The Navy says in its official statement, "The disappearance of this ship has been one of the most baffling mysteries in the annals of the Navy, all attempts to locate her having proved unsuccessful. There were no enemy submarines in the western Atlantic at that time, and in December 1918 every effort was made to obtain from German sources information regarding the disappearance of the vessel."

4. *Star Tiger*

The *Star Tiger,* commanded by Capt. B. W. McMillan, was flying from England to Bermuda in January 1948. On January 30, McMillan said he expected to arrive in Bermuda at 5:00 A.M., but neither he nor any of the 31 people onboard the *Star Tiger* were ever heard from again. When the Civil Air Ministry launched a search and investigation, they learned that the S.S. *Troubadour* had reported seeing a low-flying aircraft halfway between Bermuda and the entrance to Delaware Bay. If that aircraft was the *Star Tiger*, it was drastically off course. According to the Civil Air Ministry, the fate of the *Star Tiger* remains an unsolved mystery.

5. *Star Ariel*

A Tudor IV aircraft like the *Star Tiger* left Bermuda on January 17, 1949, with 7 crew members and 13 passengers en route to Jamaica. That morning, Capt. J. C. McPhee reported that the flight was going smoothly. Shortly afterward, another more cryptic message came from the captain, when he reported that he was changing his frequency, and then nothing more was heard, ever. More than 60 aircraft and 13,000 men were deployed to look for the *Star Ariel*, but not even a hint of debris or wreckage was ever found. After the *Ariel* disappeared, Tudor IVs were no longer produced.

6. The *Spray*

Joshua Slocum, the first man to sail solo around the world, never should have been lost at sea, but it appears that's exactly what happened. In 1909, the *Spray* left the East Coast of the United States for Venezuela via the Caribbean Sea. Slocum was never heard from or seen again and was declared dead in 1924. The ship was solid and Slocum was a pro, so nobody knows what happened. Perhaps he was felled by a larger ship or maybe he was taken down by pirates. No one knows for sure that Slocum disappeared within Triangle waters, but Bermuda buffs claim Slocum's story as part of the legacy of the Devil's Triangle.

7. *Teignmouth Electron*

Who said that the Bermuda Triangle only swallows up ships and planes? Who's to say it can't make a man go mad, too? Perhaps that's what happened on the *Teignmouth Electron* in 1969. The *Sunday Times* Golden Globe Race of 1968 left England on October 31 and required each contestant to sail his ship solo. Donald Crowhurst was one of the entrants, but he never made it to the finish line. The *Electron* was found abandoned in the middle of the Bermuda Triangle in July 1969. Logbooks recovered from the ship reveal that Crowhurst was deceiving organizers about his position in the race and going a little nutty out there in the big blue ocean. The last entry of his log was dated June 29—it is believed that Crowhurst jumped overboard and drowned himself in the Triangle.

14 Greek and Roman Gods

❋ ❋ ❋ ❋

Greek	Job Title	Roman
1. Aphrodite	Goddess of love and beauty	Venus
2. Apollo	God of beauty, poetry, music	Apollo
3. Ares	God of war	Mars
4. Artemis	Goddess of the hunt and moon	Diana
5. Athena	Goddess of war and wisdom	Minerva
6. Demeter	Goddess of agriculture	Ceres
7. Dionysus	God of wine	Bacchus
8. Hades	God of the dead and the Underworld	Pluto
9. Hephaestus	God of fire and crafts	Vulcan
10. Hera	Goddess of marriage (Queen of the gods)	Juno
11. Hermes	Messenger of the gods	Mercury
12. Hestia	Goddess of the hearth	Vesta
13. Poseidon	God of the sea, earthquakes, and horses	Neptune
14. Zeus	Supreme god (King of the gods)	Jupiter

❋ ❋ ❋

"The gods, likening themselves to all kinds of strangers, go in various disguises from city to city, observing the wrongdoing and the righteousness of men."
—Homer, *The Odyssey*

10 Little-Known Patron Saints

✳ ✳ ✳ ✳

*To qualify for sainthood, one must live a life worthy of being
rewarded with the Kingdom of God. Even then, it's not a beeline
to the top. The first rung on the ladder is "Servant of God,"
then "Venerable," then "Blessed." After that, the holy person is
considered a "Friend of God," otherwise known as a saint.
Here are ten lesser-known saints and the people they watch over.*

1. Geneviève—Patron Saint of Disasters and Paris
Feast day: January 3

By age 15, Geneviève was a nun. When her hometown of Paris was
under siege by Childeric, King of the Franks, she risked her own
safety to go into the city to find food and supplies for the suffering. Years later, she faced another dangerous conqueror—Attila the
Hun. As Parisians prepared to leave their homes rather than face
the wrath of the barbarians, Geneviève convinced them to stay in
their homes and pray instead. Today, it is still unknown why Attila
the Hun didn't attack Paris. Geneviève died in A.D. 500.

2. Blaise—Patron Saint of Throat Ailments, Veterinarians,
and Wild Animals
Feast day: February 3

As a bishop, Blaise was arrested for praying and went into hiding to
avoid martyrdom. He shared a cave with wild animals that he cared
for. He was eventually found and ordered to stand trial, but on his
way to the trial, he convinced a wolf to return a woman's stolen
pig. When he was sentenced to a slow, painful death by starvation,
the grateful owner of the pig secretly slipped him food so that he
wouldn't die. During this time, a woman came to Blaise in need
of help. Her son was choking on a fish bone, but Blaise was able
to save his life. When the governor learned that Blaise hadn't yet
starved to death, he ordered him skinned alive and then beheaded.
He died in A.D. 316.

3. Casimir of Poland—Patron Saint of Bachelors
Feast day: March 4

Born a prince in Poland, this exceptional young man rose through the ranks of the Catholic church and was ultimately put in charge of his native country. His father tried to arrange a marriage with the daughter of the emperor of Germany, but Casimir wanted to stay single. He died soon afterward in 1484. Stories of his great charm, sense of justice, and belief in chastity abound.

4. Denis—Patron Saint of Headaches
Feast day: October 9

In A.D. 258, during the persecution of Emperor Decius, Denis, the first bishop of Paris, was imprisoned, tortured, and beheaded. But wait... there's more. His headless body is said to have carried his severed head away from his own execution. In any case, his body was dumped into the River Seine, but his followers pulled it out.

5. Edward the Confessor—Patron Saint of Difficult Marriages
Feast day: October 13

Edward became the King of England in 1042. He was a very peaceful leader, only going into battle when necessary to defend his allies. He was concerned with the fair treatment of all people and wanted to do away with unjust taxation. He built churches, the most famous being Westminster Abbey. Early in life, he took a vow of chastity, but he took a wife, Editha, to please the people of his kingdom. He remained celibate throughout his life and died in 1066.

6. Felicity—Patron Saint of Barren Women and Parents Who Have Had a Child Die
Feast day: March 7

Felicity rose from slave to sainthood, but the road wasn't easy. The legend of Felicity varies: One version says that her seven sons were killed in front of her for choosing Christianity, then she was beheaded. Another version says that Felicity was eight months pregnant when she and five others were sentenced to die a martyr's death. They were baptized and led away to suffer greatly in prison.

Felicity was upset because she didn't think she would be able to suffer martyrdom at the same time as the others—the law forbade the execution of pregnant women. As luck would have it, in A.D. 203 she delivered a baby girl just two days before the "games" and was able to die in the amphitheater along with the others. Their killers? A wild boar, a bear, and a leopard ripped the men apart; a wild cow slaughtered the women.

7. Lydwina—Patron Saint of Ice Skaters
Feast day: April 14

Lydwina was from a poor family in Holland. She was a very religious girl and prayed often. In 1395, she broke several ribs in an ice-skating accident and gangrene spread throughout her body, causing her severe pain for the rest of her life. Lydwina experienced visions throughout her life, including one of a rosebush with the inscription, "When this shall be in bloom, your suffering will be at an end." In 1433, she saw the rosebush and died soon after.

8. Columba—Patron Saint of Bookbinders, Poets, and Ireland
Feast day: June 9

Columba was born in Ireland in 521. Legend has it that around 560, he became involved in a battle with St. Finnian, which resulted in the deaths of many people. As penance, Columba went to Scotland to work as a missionary to convert as many people as had been killed in the battle.

Columba reputedly wrote several hymns and more than 300 books in his lifetime, so it is not surprising that he is the patron saint of bookbinders and poets. Columba died in 597, and although he spent much of his life in Scotland, he is one of the patron saints of Ireland, along with St. Patrick and St. Brigid.

9. Alexis of Rome—Patron Saint of Beggars
Feast day: July 17

Alexis, the son of a distinguished Roman, fled his father's house on his wedding night and sustained a frugal and religious existence for 17 years. As his fame as a holy man grew, he returned to Rome and lived as a beggar beneath the stairs of his father's palace for the remaining 17 years of his life. When he died in A.D. 417, he was found with a document on his body that declared his identity.

10. Apollonia—Patron Saint of Dentists
Feast day: February 9

Apollonia was an elderly woman who, in A.D. 248, was persecuted for being a Christian. She found herself in the midst of an angry anti-Christian mob. They smashed out all of her teeth and then dragged her to a huge fire. They offered to spare her life if she would renounce her faith. She paused as if to curse God, then flung herself into the fire instead. St. Apollonia is often depicted wearing a necklace of her own teeth.

The 10 Commandments

❋ ❋ ❋ ❋

1. Thou shalt have no other gods before me.
2. Thou shalt not make unto thee any graven image, or any likeness of any thing that is in heaven above, or that is in the earth beneath, or that is in the water under the earth.
3. Thou shalt not take the name of the Lord thy God in vain.
4. Remember the sabbath day, to keep it holy.
5. Honor thy father and thy mother.
6. Thou shalt not kill.
7. Thou shalt not commit adultery.
8. Thou shalt not steal.
9. Thou shalt not bear false witness against thy neighbor.
10. Thou shalt not covet thy neighbor's wife.

WHO YOU GONNA CALL?
5 Ways to Get Rid of a Ghost

✳ ✳ ✳ ✳

Something strange in your neighborhood? Something weird and it don't look good? Here's a do-it-yourself guide to ghost-busting. But please note: in the world of ghost-busting, there are no guarantees, so proceed at your own risk.

1. **Give it a good talking-to.** The first tactic is simply to ask your ghost, politely but firmly, to leave. If you think the ghost is hanging around the physical world because of fear of punishment in the spirit world, tell it that it will be treated with love and  forgiveness. Try not to show anger (which may give a negative spirit more power) or fear (since it's unlikely that a spirit will be able to harm you, especially in your own home).

2. **Clean and serene.** If tough talking doesn't work, the next step is a spiritual cleansing or "smudging." Open a window in each room of your home, then light a bundle of dry sage and walk around with it (have something handy to catch the ashes), allowing the smoke to circulate while you intone the words: "This sage is cleansing out all negative energies and spirits. All negative energies and spirits must leave now through the windows and not return." Do this until you sense that the negative energy has left the building (and before you set fire to the house), and then say, "In the name of God, this room is now cleansed."

3. **Bless this house.** If smudging doesn't do the trick, it may be time to call in the professionals. Ask a local priest or minister to come to your home and bless it. There is usually no charge for this service, but you might be expected to make a small donation to the church.

4. **The Exorcist.** Exorcism is usually carried out by clergy using prayers and religious items to invoke a supernatural power that will

cast out the spirit. Roman Catholic exorcism involves a priest reciting prayers and invocations, often in Latin. The priest displays a crucifix and sprinkles holy water over the place, person, or object believed to be possessed. Exorcism has been sensationally depicted in movies but it's no laughing matter—in the past, people who would now be diagnosed as physically or mentally ill have undergone exorcism, sometimes dying in the process.

5. What not to do. Don't be tempted to use Ouija boards, tarot cards, or séances, as these may "open the door" to let in other unwanted spirits. Also be very suspicious of anyone offering a commercial ghost-busting service, including any medium or spiritual adviser who offers to rid your home of a spirit in return for payment. They're almost certain to be charlatans, and you're unlikely to get your money back if their services don't work.

HEY THERE... WHAT'S YOUR SIGN?
12 Signs of the Zodiac

✳ ✳ ✳ ✳

The ancient Greek term zodiac *means "circle of little animals." The stargazing Greeks used the zodiac symbols to make sense of the connection between time, space, and humans. Astrologers swear we can all find insight into our personalities by studying the zodiac sign that corresponds to our birthday.*

1. Aries: The Ram (March 21–April 19)

Aries personalities are Minotaur-like, meaning that they are headstrong folks who seek excitement. They are often innovative, assertive, quick-tempered, and self-assured. If you find yourself playing golf with Aries Russell Crowe, watch out: He'll either bop you on the head or leave you hanging, since Aries are notoriously bad at finishing what they start.

2. Taurus: The Bull (April 20–May 20)

 These folks are stubborn, cautious, persistent, conservative, materialistic, and dependable. But Tauruses are most noted for their determination. Case in point: Cher, who is on comeback number 4,628.

3. Gemini: The Twins (May 21–June 21)

 Named after the twin brothers of Helen of Troy, Geminis can like something and its opposite at the same time. They are known to be flexible, lively, quick-witted conversationalists that embody the yin and the yang. Watch out for duplicity in a Gemini (a trait some would say business tycoon Donald Trump possesses), and enjoy the fruits of a Gemini's boundless curiosity (as with award-winning journalist Bill Moyers).

4. Cancer: The Crab (June 22–July 22)

 Cancers are emotional, sensitive, security-conscious, moody, maternal, and can be quite traditional. The word *cancer* literally means "the crab," and modern slang has produced the misconception that Cancers are grouchy. Famous Cancer the Dalai Lama proves that simply isn't true.

5. Leo: The Lion (July 23–August 22)

The lion symbol has origins in Hebrew culture, but is also connected to the Greek myth of Apollo. Apollo was an impressive god, representing order and intellectual pursuits while serving as the leader of the Muses—the spirits that bring inspiration to artists. Leos are notoriously egocentric and love the limelight. They are also optimistic, honorable, dignified, confident, flamboyant, charismatic, competitive, and have strong leadership skills. All this *and* a desperate need for approval? Just ask Leos Madonna and Martha Stewart.

6. Virgo: The Virgin (August 23–September 22)

 Modesty is one of the main traits of a Virgo, as exhibited in Virgo Mother Teresa. That doesn't mean Virgos are prudish, however—considering that Pee Wee Herman was also born under this sign. Other traits Virgos possess include practicality, responsibility, discriminating taste, and a critical eye. Virgos are as loyal as Leos but can become obsessed with perfection.

7. Libra: The Scale (September 23–October 23)

 The judicial system adopted the Libra image of the scales to represent the balance of justice. This makes sense, considering Libras are idealistic peacemakers, diplomatic, poised, kind, courteous, and fair-minded. Unfortunately for the judicial system, the scales represent people who can be painfully indecisive. Famous level-headed Libras include Barbara Walters, Sting, and Jimmy Carter.

8. Scorpio: The Scorpion (October 24–November 21)

 These stingers are intense and powerful, courageous, resourceful, mysterious, and self-reliant. Aside from the scorpion, the phoenix is another symbol for this sign. Some believe that within one year before or after the death of a Scorpio, there will be a birth within the same family. Wonder if that was true when Scorpios Bill Gates or Hillary Clinton were born?

9. Sagittarius: The Centaur (November 22–December 21)

 The centaur is a character from Greek mythology that was half man, half horse. People born under this sign follow their big hearts but can become bulls in china shops if they're not careful. Famous Sag Jon Stewart is a good example of someone using their strong Sagittarius opinions to their advantage. These generally friendly people are often idealistic, optimistic, freedom-loving, casual, gregarious, enthusiastic, and philosophical. Woody Allen and Britney Spears are well-known Sagittarians.

10. Capricorn: The Goat (December 22–January 19)

 According to Greek mythology, Zeus was weaned on goat's milk and that was enough to include the animal in the pantheon of astrological signs. Capricorns are ambitious, self-disciplined, conservative, practical, persistent, and methodical.

Famous Capricorn Mel Gibson has lost his footing a few times, but he's good at dusting himself off and starting again, a classic Capricorn maneuver.

11. Aquarius: The Water Bearer (January 20–February 18)

 Symbolized by the water bearer—a young man or woman with water barrels hoisted over the shoulder, who brings together the community of humankind—these folks hold on to the concept of friendship stronger than anyone. Always individualistic, progressive, independent, and altruistic, they can sink into detachment. They seem to "march to the beat of a different drummer." Think of Oprah Winfrey, a textbook Aquarius, who is famous for her generous and independent nature.

12. Pisces: The Fish (February 19–March 20)

The symbol of two fish pointing in different directions tends to throw people off, making them think Pisces people can't make up their minds. On the contrary, this group is focused and choosy, going for the big time or the quiet time with little in between. Think Liza Minnelli blazing her public career path or Bobby Fischer (no pun intended) checkmating cloistered monks in Madagascar. These fishy folks are compassionate, artistic, dedicated, and can be more than a little reclusive.

The 7 Holy Virtues

✳ ✳ ✳ ✳

1. Faith.....................................Complete trust
2. Hope ....To expect with confidence
3. Charity ....Goodwill and the love of humanity
4. Prudence...........................Control and discipline
5. Justice ....Being impartial and fair
6. Temperance.......................Moderation in action
7. Fortitude...........................Strength

The 9 Muses

✳ ✳ ✳ ✳

The nine muses were Greek goddesses (the daughters of Zeus and Mnemosyne) who ruled over the arts and sciences and offered help and inspiration to mortals.

1. Calliope.................................... Muse of epic poetry
2. Clio... Muse of history
3. Erato .... Muse of love poetry
4. Euterpe................................... Muse of music
5. Melpomene .... Muse of tragedy
6. Polyhymnia .... Muse of sacred poetry or mime
7. Terpsichore........................... Muse of dance
8. Thalia .... Muse of comedy
9. Urania .... Muse of astronomy

9 Legends of American Folklore

✳ ✳ ✳ ✳

The grit and determination of the American pioneers was truly impressive. Those who crossed the country to settle the West, slogged through the muggy South, and fished the seas and wild rivers all had to face formidable obstacles including famine, predators, and what must have been extended periods of sheer boredom. Without television and movies, entertainment in late 18th- and early 19th-century America was limited to campfire stories and tales told around the fireplace. You can't blame story-tellers for embellishing here and there to raise interest levels and inspire tired and weary listeners. The following folk legends helped pioneers cope with uncertainty during hard times and inspired the blind ambition needed to explore the American frontier.

1. Paul Bunyan

If it weren't for Paul Bunyan, America just wouldn't be as interesting geographically. French-Canadian lumber camp legends about

Bunyan, which were later adapted by Americans, claimed that he was delivered to Earth by five giant storks, since he was already dozens of feet tall as a baby. Wherever he went as he got older, he created major landmarks. His footprints created Minnesota's 10,000 lakes; his shovel created the Grand Canyon as it dragged behind him; his use of rocks to extinguish a campfire created Mount Hood. Bunyan was accompanied by his blue ox, Babe, who was almost as big as he was. Statues of Bunyan and Babe have been erected all across the country as a testament to America's love of a tall tale.

2. John Henry

Unlike a lot of the tall tales from America's formative years, the story of John Henry is somewhat based in fact. There probably really was a John Henry who was born a slave in the South in the mid-1800s. Legend has it that he was around six feet tall and weighed more than 200 pounds. In those days, that was big enough to guarantee you'd be given exceptionally tough work—like building railroads or tunnels. If Henry did exist, he likely worked on the Big Bend Tunnel that went through the mountains of West Virginia. From there, the legend has thousands of variations. Some say Henry challenged the tunnel-making machinery to a duel to see who could drive stakes and blast rock faster. Most stories claim that he won, but that he died from exhaustion after the contest. Some say he won and went on swingin' his hammer from coast to coast.

3. Sally Ann Thunder Ann Whirlwind Crockett

Women in tall tales were few and far between, but there are some who made it into folklore as hard as nails, larger-than-life folks. Sally Ann Thunder is one that emerges, however infrequently, as the wife of Davy Crockett. In reality, Crockett married several times and none of the record books have him married to anyone with *Thunder* in her name. But stories do exist of a gun-totin', fast-talking lady who helped get Davy out of sticky situations and wouldn't miss a trick. She reportedly wore a real beehive as a hat and enjoyed wrestling alligators in her spare time.

4. Johnny Appleseed

If you dig too deep into the origins of American folk heroes, you might be disappointed—the man known as Johnny Appleseed wasn't a magical scatterer of apple seeds from sea to shining sea, he was just a regular guy named John Chapman who worked as a nurseryman in the late 1700s. While that's not as exciting as the legend, Chapman's real life was interesting enough—he owned land from Ohio to Indiana, worked as a Christian missionary, and helped make peace between Native Americans and white settlers.

5. Mike Fink

Tales of Mike Fink originated in the 19th century and were based on a real man born near Pittsburgh around 1780. The real Fink sailed keelboats on the Ohio and Mississippi rivers and fought against various tribes of Native Americans. Fink was noted as being an exceptional marksman, though he was reportedly a rather hard-drinking and hard-living character. By many accounts it was Fink who started spreading tall tales about himself, which may explain his low standing among more noble legends like Paul Bunyan and John Henry. Still, tales of Fink being "half-man, half-alligator" and being totally impervious to pain keep him in the canon.

6. Pecos Bill

Pecos Bill, one of the most popular American tall tales, was lost while crossing the Pecos River with his parents. He was found by a pack of coyotes and lived among them until he met a cowboy and realized his true calling. No one was better at ranching than Pecos Bill because he had an uncanny ability to convince animals to work for him. Bill married a nice girl named Slue Foot Sue and lived a long life of ranching, herding, and singing by the campfire.

7. Geronimo

Geronimo, an Apache leader from the Arizona area, was captured and forced onto a reservation by the U.S. Army in 1876. The persecuted Apache leader fled to Mexico, but after that, things get murky and exaggerated. The story goes that Geronimo's wrath toward the white man was such that he killed thousands over the years, using magical powers and ESP to seek them out. It's said that it took many thousands of soldiers and scouts to track the warrior down. By the time Geronimo finally surrendered in 1886, his group consisted of only 16 warriors, 12 women, and 6 children. Geronimo and his people were shipped to Florida, then relocated to Alabama and Oklahoma where they were placed in prisons and reservations. Geronimo died a prisoner of war in 1909.

8. Old Stormalong

Though stories about Stormalong vary, most place him in Cape Cod as a big baby—a baby more than 18 feet tall! Stormalong, a gifted sailor, joined the crew of a ship. When the ship had an encounter with a kraken—a beast from Norse mythology—Stormalong fought back but didn't kill the sea giant. Eventually, he wound up back on the high seas in search of the kraken that had escaped him. The ship he used was said to have slammed into the coast of Panama, forming the Panama Canal. According to legend, the same boat supposedly got stuck in the English Channel, requiring the crew to slick it up with soap in order to get it out. The soap and the scraping action turned the White Cliffs of Dover white.

9. Davy Crockett

Born in 1796, Davy Crockett was nearly a legend without fictitious additions to his story, but they came nonetheless. By Crockett's own account, he killed a bear when he was only three years old. True? Maybe not, but Crockett swore it happened. More stories emerged of Crockett's rough and tough childhood with lots of bear, bully, and snake encounters that all ended with him as the victor—whether or not these stories are true is unclear. What is true is that Crockett represented Tennessee in Congress, but when he was defeated for reelection, he went off to explore Texas. His travels led him into battle at the Alamo, where he was shot and killed. Tales of Davy Crockett show him wearing a coonskin cap and carrying his rifle, which he lovingly called "Old Betsy."

NOT A HALO IN THE BUNCH
9 Types of Angels

✳ ✳ ✳ ✳

We may be able to speak directly to God through prayer, but according to the Bible, he reaches us through a variety of angels, each with distinct duties. There are nine types of angels within three major groups known as choirs. Regardless of where they are on the hierarchy, like us, they are individuals. Unlike us, because they are able to see far beyond a mortal timeline, they are extremely patient and forgiving. They are aware of our personal life goals and are assigned to assist us, but never interfere with our free will.

The first choir, in its celestial form, is represented by wavelengths of light and force fields and frequencies of sound. These entities emanate vibrations, or waves, of devotional love into the universe.

1. Seraphim

These are the angels who are closest to God. They encircle his throne and emit an intense fiery light representing his love. Seraphim are considered "fiery serpents" and not even the other divine beings may look at them. There are only four of them and each has four faces and six wings. When they come to Earth, they leave their serpent appearance behind, preferring tall, thin, clean-cut human embodiments.

2. Cherubim (Plural of Cherub)

These angels are the keepers of celestial records and hold the knowledge of God. They are sent to Earth with great tasks, such as expelling humankind from the Garden of Eden. Ancient art depicts cherubim as sphinx-like, winged creatures with human faces, not the fat babies with wings that now grace greeting cards and book covers. Ophaniel, Rikbiel, and Zophiel are cherubim, as was Satan before his fall to evil.

3. Thrones

Thrones' appearance is perhaps the most bizarre of the first grouping. They are said to look like great glowing wheels covered with many eyes. They serve as God's chariot and dispense his judgment in order to carry out his desires for us.

The angels in the second choir can exist in a state of transition between the celestial and human worlds. They are considered heavenly governors, attempting to strike a balance between matter and spirit, good and bad.

4. Dominions or Dominations

Think of dominions as middle management. They receive orders from seraphim and cherubim, then dish out duties to the "worker bee" angels of the lower orders. Their main purpose is to make sure that the cosmos remains in order by sending down power to heads of government and other authority figures. Zadkiel (sometimes called Hashmal) is the chief of this order.

5. Virtues

Shaped like sparks of light, virtues are in charge of maintaining the natural world, and they inspire living things in areas such as science. They also take orders from the angels above and convert them into miracles for the deserving. When they make themselves known to us in their earthly form, they are musicians, artists, healers, and scientists who work with the power of love, as well as physics. The two angels at the ascension of Jesus are believed to have been virtues.

6. Powers

In their celestial form, powers appear like brightly colored, hazy fumes. Powers are border patrol agents between heaven and Earth. They are the angels of birth and death. Some believe that they also preside over demons who wish to overthrow the world, while others, namely St. Paul, thought the powers themselves were the evil ones. In any case, powers are a group of experts who serve as advisers in terms of religion, theology, and ideology.

The third choir is best known to us because they are most like us with their vulnerability to the act of sinning.

7. Principalities

These angelic beings are shaped like rays of light. Just like a principal in school, it's the principalities who oversee everything. They guide our entire world—nations, cities, and towns. What's more, they are in charge of religion and politics. As if their plate isn't full enough, they are also in charge of managing the earthly duties of the angels below them.

8. Archangels

They, along with the angels, are guardians of people and all things physical. But don't call on them to help you personally; archangels respond best when dealing with matters involving all humankind. They are the first order of angels that appear only in human form. As such, they function among us as pioneers for change in the form of explorers, philosophers, and human rights leaders. This order is most commonly known because they are mentioned by name in the Bible—Michael, Gabriel, and Raphael.

9. Angels

Angels are the true intermediaries between God and individual people. Angels don't watch over nations; they safeguard households and individuals who believe in God and keep them safe from demons. They nurture, counsel, and heal. We all have a "personal angel," better known as our guardian angel, with us daily.

✳ ✳ ✳

*"An angel doesn't have to speak to be heard,
be visible to be seen, or be present to be felt.
Believe in angels, and they will always be near."*
—Kelly Womer

14 Mythical Creatures

❈ ❈ ❈ ❈

1. Basilisk .... a serpent, lizard, or dragon said to kill by breathing on or looking at its victims
2. Centaur .... half human, half horse
3. Cerberus .... a dog with many heads that guards the entrance to the underworld
4. Chimera .... part serpent, lion, and goat
5. Faun .... half man, half goat
6. Gorgons .... winged and snake-haired sisters
7. Griffin .... half eagle, half lion
8. Harpy .... a creature with the head of a woman and the body, wings, and claws of a bird
9. Hippocampus .... a creature with the tail of a dolphin and the head and forequarters of a horse
10. Hippogriff .... a creature with the wings, head, and claws of a griffin but the hindquarters of a horse
11. Pegasus .... a winged horse with the ability to fly
12. Siren .... half bird, half woman
13. Unicorn .... a horse with a horn
14. Wyvern .... a winged dragon with a serpent's tail

The 7 Deadly Sins

❈ ❈ ❈ ❈

1. Pride .... Excessive belief in one's own abilities
2. Envy .... Having an excessive desire for possession of another's traits or abilities
3. Gluttony .... Wanting to consume more than one needs
4. Lust .... Excessive thoughts and actions of a carnal nature
5. Anger .... Uncontrolled feelings of hatred and rage
6. Greed .... Excessive desire for material wealth or gain
7. Sloth .... Avoidance of physical and spiritual work

Chapter 7
FOOD
* * * *
7 Disgusting Things Found in Food Products

You've probably heard about the woman who claimed she found a human finger in a bowl of Wendy's chili. It turned out to be a hoax, but many such claims turn out to be true. The following is a sampling of some of the most disgusting items found in food products. Bon appétit!

1. In 2002, a woman was enjoying a bowl of clam chowder at McCormick & Schmick's Seafood in Irvine, California, when she bit down on something rubbery. Assuming it was calamari, she spit it into her napkin, only to find that it was actually a condom. The woman won an undisclosed amount in a lawsuit, but the restaurant unsuccessfully sued a supplier.

2. In Baltimore, Maryland, in 2003, a man was eating a three-piece combo meal at Popeyes Chicken & Biscuits when he bit down and found a little surprise wedged between the skin and the meat of his chicken—a deep-fried mouse! Sadly, the restaurant had other rodent infestation citations on its record.

3. During the summer of 2004, David Scheiding was enjoying an Arby's chicken sandwich, but it came with an unexpected topping— sliced human flesh. Turns out that the store manager sliced his thumb while shredding lettuce. Of course, he thoroughly sanitized the area, but the lettuce was still used! Scheiding refused to accept a settlement from Arby's and filed a lawsuit in 2005.

4. It's not a body part or a rodent, but *E. coli*—the bacteria that thrive in the lower intestines of mammals and are excreted through feces—definitely qualifies as disgusting. In 1993, more than 600 hungry Jack in the Box customers, mostly children, became very ill from ingesting the little buggers. Sadly, four customers died. Several multimillion-dollar lawsuits later, it was determined that the problem was with the meat supplier.

5. Imagine the surprise of five-year-old Jordan Willett of the UK when he poured a bowl of Golden Puffs breakfast cereal one morning in 2005, and out popped a snake! The two-foot long, nonvenomous corn snake was not inside the sealed cereal bag, so investigators are unsure how it got inside the cereal box.

6. In 2000, a two-year-old boy in the UK got the surprise of his life—and a stomachache—after munching on Burger King french fries that included a special treat—a fried lizard! The boy's family dutifully handed over the crispy lizard to the restaurant for further examination, and no lawsuit was filed.

7. In 2005, Clarence Stowers of North Carolina was savoring a pint of Kohl's frozen custard. Thinking that a chunk at the bottom of the dessert was candy, he decided to save it for last. How disappointed he must have been to discover that it wasn't candy, but was actually part of Kohl's Frozen Custard employee Brandon Fizer's index finger. What's more, Stowers wouldn't return the finger at first! He kept it as evidence for his lawsuit, and by the time he decided to give it back, it was too late to reattach it.

12 Facts About Pizza

✳ ✳ ✳ ✳

1. Since 1987, October has been officially designated National Pizza Month in the United States.

2. Approximately three billion pizzas are sold in the United States every year, plus an additional one billion frozen pizzas.

3. Pizza is a $30 billion industry in the United States.

4. Pizzerias represent 17 percent of all U.S. restaurants.

5. Ninety-three percent of Americans eat pizza at least once a month.

6. Women are twice as likely as men to order vegetarian toppings on their pizza.

7. About 36 percent of all pizzas contain pepperoni, making it the most popular topping in the United States.

8. The first known pizzeria, Antica Pizzeria, opened in Naples, Italy, in 1738.

9. More pizza is consumed during the week of the Super Bowl than any other time of the year.

10. On average, each person in the United States eats around 23 pounds of pizza every year.

11. The first pizzeria in the United States was opened by Gennaro Lombardi in 1895 in New York City.

12. The record for the world's largest pizza depends on how you slice it. According to *Guinness World Records,* the record for the world's largest circular pizza was set at Norwood Hypermarket in South Africa in 1990. The gigantic pie measured 122 feet 8 inches across, weighed 26,883 pounds, and contained 9,920 pounds of flour, 3,968 pounds of cheese, and 1,984 pounds of sauce. In 2005, the record for the world's largest rectangular pizza was set in Iowa Falls, Iowa. Pizza restaurant owner Bill Bahr and a team of 200 helpers created the 129-foot by 98.6-foot pizza from 4,000 pounds of cheese, 700 pounds of sauce and 9,500 sections of crust. The enormous pie was enough to feed the town's 5,200 residents ten slices of pizza each.

15 Countries with the Highest Coffee Consumption

❋ ❋ ❋ ❋

Country	Pounds of Coffee per Person per Year
1. Norway	23.6
2. Finland	22.3
3. Denmark	21.4
4. Sweden	17.2
5. Netherlands	15.7
6. Switzerland	15.4
7. Germany	12.6
8. Austria	12.1
9. Belgium	11.0
10. France	8.6
11. Italy	7.1
12. United States	6.6
13. Canada	5.3
14. Australia	4.4
15. Japan	3.1

POP STARS

20 Things You Didn't Know About Popcorn

❋ ❋ ❋ ❋

*High in fiber, low in fat, and a tiny demon in every kernel—
here are 20 things you didn't know about popcorn.*

1. Popcorn's scientific name is *zea mays everta,* and it is the only type of corn that will pop.

2. People have been enjoying popcorn for thousands of years. In 1948, popped kernels around 5,000 years old were discovered in caves in New Mexico.

3. It is believed that the Wampanoag Native American tribe brought popcorn to the colonists for the first Thanksgiving in Plymouth, Massachusetts.

4. Traditionally, Native American tribes flavored popcorn with dried herbs and spices, possibly even chili. They also made popcorn into soup and beer, and made popcorn headdresses and corsages.

5. Some Native American tribes believed that a spirit lived inside each kernel of popcorn. The spirits wouldn't usually bother humans, but if their home was heated, they would jump around, getting angrier and angrier, until eventually they would burst out with a pop.

6. Christopher Columbus allegedly introduced popcorn to the Europeans in the late 15th century.

7. The first commercial popcorn machine was invented by Charles Cretors in Chicago in 1885. The business he founded still manufactures popcorn machines and other specialty equipment.

8. American vendors began selling popcorn at carnivals in the late 19th century. When they began to sell outside movie theaters, theater owners were initially annoyed, fearing that popcorn would distract their patrons from the movies. It took a few years for them to realize that popcorn could be a way to increase revenues, and popcorn has been served in movie theaters since 1912.

9. Nowadays, many movie theaters make a greater profit from popcorn than they do from ticket sales, since, for every dollar spent on popcorn, around ninety cents is pure profit. Popcorn also makes moviegoers thirsty and more likely to buy expensive sodas.

10. What makes popcorn pop? Each kernel contains a small amount of moisture. As the kernel is heated, this water turns to steam. Popcorn differs from other grains in that the kernel's shell is not water-permeable, so the steam cannot escape and pressure builds up until the kernel finally explodes, turning inside out.

11. On average, a kernel will pop when it reaches a temperature of 347° F (175° C).

12. Unpopped kernels are called "old maids" or "spinsters."

13. There are two possible explanations for old maids. The first is that they didn't contain sufficient moisture to create an explosion; the second is that their outer coating (the hull) was damaged, so that steam escaped gradually, rather than with a pop. Good popcorn should produce less than 2 percent old maids.

14. Ideally, the moisture content of popcorn should be around 13.5 percent, as this results in the fewest old maids.

15. Popcorn is naturally high in fiber, low in calories, and sodium-, sugar-, and fat-free, although oil is often added during preparation, and butter, sugar, and salt are all popular toppings.

16. Americans consume 17 billion quarts of popped popcorn each year. That's enough to fill the Empire State Building 18 times!

17. Nebraska produces more popcorn than any other state in the country—around 250 million pounds per year. That's about a quarter of all the popcorn produced annually in the United States.

18. There are at least five contenders claiming to be the "Popcorn Capital of the World" due to the importance of popcorn to their local economies, and only one of them is in Nebraska. They are: Van Buren, Indiana; Marion, Ohio; Ridgway, Illinois; Schaller, Iowa; and North Loup, Nebraska.

19. Popped popcorn comes in two basic shapes: snowflake and mushroom. Movie theaters prefer snowflake because it's bigger. Confections such as caramel corn use mushroom because it won't crumble.

20. According to the *Guinness Book of World Records,* the world's largest popcorn ball measured 12 feet in diameter and required 2,000 pounds of corn, 40,000 pounds of sugar, 280 gallons of corn syrup, and 400 gallons of water to create.

45 Common Foods and the Number of Calories They Contain

❋ ❋ ❋ ❋

Despite what you hear from the purveyors of trendy fad diets,
specialty diet foods, and expensive weight-loss programs,
there is no secret to dropping pounds. You simply need to use
more calories than you consume. To put things into perspective,
here are the calorie counts for some typical foods—keep
in mind that the exact number of calories can vary.

Food	*Calories*
1. Apple, medium	72
2. Bagel	289
3. Banana, medium	105
4. Beer (regular, 12 ounces)	153
5. Bread (one slice, wheat or white)	66
6. Butter (salted, 1 tablespoon)	102
7. Carrots (raw, 1 cup)	52
8. Cheddar cheese (1 slice)	113
9. Chicken breast (boneless, skinless, roasted, 3 ounces)	142
10. Chili with beans (canned, 1 cup)	287
11. Chocolate-chip cookie (from packaged dough)	59
12. Coffee (regular, brewed from grounds, black)	2
13. Cola (12 ounces)	136
14. Corn (canned, sweet yellow whole kernel, drained, 1 cup)	180
15. Egg (large, scrambled)	102
16. Graham cracker (plain, honey, or cinnamon)	59
17. Granola bar (chewy, with raisins, 1.5-ounce bar)	193
18. Green beans (canned, drained, 1 cup)	40
19. Ground beef patty (15 percent fat, 4 ounces, pan-broiled)	193

Food	Calories
20. Hot dog (beef and pork)	137
21. Ice cream (vanilla, 4 ounces)	145
22. Jelly doughnut	289
23. Ketchup (1 tablespoon)	15
24. Milk (2 percent milk fat, 8 ounces)	122
25. Mixed nuts (dry roasted, with peanuts, salted, 1 ounce)	168
26. Mustard, yellow (2 teaspoons)	6
27. Oatmeal (plain, cooked in water without salt, 1 cup)	147
28. Orange juice (frozen concentrate, made with water, 8 ounces)	112
29. Peanut butter (creamy, 2 tablespoons)	180
30. Pizza (pepperoni, regular crust, one slice)	298
31. Pork chop (center rib, boneless, broiled, 3 ounces)	221
32. Potato, medium (baked, including skin)	161
33. Potato chips (plain, salted, 1 ounce)	155
34. Pretzels (hard, plain, salted, 1 ounce)	108
35. Raisins (1.5 ounces)	130
36. Ranch salad dressing (2 tablespoons)	146
37. Red wine (cabernet sauvignon, 5 ounces)	123
38. Rice (white, long grain, cooked, 1 cup)	205
39. Salsa (4 ounces)	35
40. Shrimp (cooked under moist heat, 3 ounces)	84
41. Spaghetti (cooked, enriched, without added salt, 1 cup)	221
42. Spaghetti sauce (marinara, ready to serve, 4 ounces)	92
43. Tuna (light, canned in water, drained, 3 ounces)	100
44. White wine (sauvignon blanc, 5 ounces)	121
45. Yellow cake with chocolate frosting (one piece)	243

Source: USDA National Nutrient Database for Standard Reference, Release 19 (2006)

SUPERSIZE ME, MY LIEGE
12 Items at a Feast of Henry VIII

✳ ✳ ✳ ✳

Henry VIII, who ruled England from 1509 until his death in 1547, was known for his voracious appetite. Portraits of Henry show a man almost as wide as he was tall. When he wasn't marrying, divorcing, or beheading his wives (he was on his sixth marriage when he died at age 58), this medieval ruler dined like a glutton.

He enjoyed banquets so much that he extended the kitchen of Hampton Court Palace to fill 55 rooms. The 200 members of the kitchen staff provided meals of up to 14 courses for the 600 people in the king's court. Here are some dishes served at a typical feast.

1. Spit-Roasted Meat

Spit-roasted meat—usually a pig or boar—was eaten at every meal. It was an expression of extreme wealth because only the rich could afford fresh meat year-round; only the very rich could afford to roast it, since this required much more fuel than boiling; and only the super wealthy could pay a "spit boy" to turn the spit all day. In a typical year, the royal kitchen served 1,240 oxen, 8,200 sheep, 2,330 deer, 760 calves, 1,870 pigs, and 53 wild boar. That's more than 14,000 large animals, meaning each member of the court was consuming about 23 animals every year.

2. Grilled Beavers' Tails

These tasty morsels were particularly popular on Fridays, when, according to Christian tradition, it was forbidden to eat meat. Rather conveniently, medieval people classified beavers as fish.

3. Whale Meat

Another popular dish for Fridays, whale meat was fairly common and cheap, due to the plentiful supply of whales in the North Sea, each of which could feed hundreds of people. It was typically served boiled or very well roasted.

4. Whole Roasted Peacock

This delicacy was served dressed in its own iridescent blue feathers (which were plucked, then replaced after the bird had been cooked), with its beak gilded in gold leaf.

5. Internal Organs

If you're squeamish, stop reading now. Medieval cooks didn't believe in wasting any part of an animal, and, in fact, internal organs were often regarded as delicacies. Beef lungs, spleen, and even udders were considered fit for a king and were usually preserved in brine or vinegar.

6. Black Pudding

Another popular dish—still served in parts of England—was black pudding. This sausage is made by filling a length of pig's intestine with the animal's boiled, congealed blood.

7. Boar's Head

A boar's head, garnished with bay and rosemary, served as the centerpiece of Christmas feasts. It certainly outdoes a floral display.

8. Roasted Swan

Roasted swan was another treat reserved for special occasions, largely because swans were regarded as too noble and dignified for everyday consumption. The bird was often presented to the table with a gold crown upon its head. To this day, English law stipulates that all mute swans are owned by the Crown and may not be eaten without permission from the Queen.

9. Vegetables

Perhaps the only type of food Henry and his court didn't consume to excess was vegetables, which were viewed as the food of the poor and made up less than 20 percent of the royal diet.

10. Marzipan

A paste made from ground almonds, sugar, and egg whites and flavored with cinnamon and pepper, marzipan was occasionally served at the end of a meal, although desserts weren't popular in England until the 18th century when incredibly elaborate sugar sculptures became popular among the aristocracy.

11. Spiced Fruitcake

The exception to the no dessert rule was during the Twelfth Night banquet on January 6, when a special spiced fruitcake containing a dried pea (or bean) was served. Whoever found the pea would be king or queen of the pea (or bean) and was treated as a guest of honor for the remainder of the evening.

12. Wine and Ale

All this food was washed down with enormous quantities of wine and ale. Historians estimate that 600,000 gallons of ale (enough to fill an Olympic-size swimming pool) and around 75,000 gallons of wine (enough to fill 1,500 bathtubs) were drunk every year at Hampton Court Palace.

12 Countries with the Highest Beer Consumption

Country	*Gallons per Person per Year*
1. Ireland	41.0
2. Germany	32.0
3. Austria	28.0
4. Belgium (tied)	26.0
5. Denmark (tied)	26.0
6. United Kingdom	25.5
7. Australia	23.5
8. United States	22.4
9. Netherlands (tied)	21.0
10. Finland (tied)	21.0
11. New Zealand	20.5
12. Canada	18.5

18 Countries with the Highest Wine Consumption

Country	Gallons per Person per Year
1. Italy	14.3
2. France	12.4
3. Switzerland	11.1
4. Austria	9.5
5. Denmark	8.5
6. Belgium	7.9
7. Germany	6.9
8. Australia	5.5
9. United Kingdom (tied)	5.3
10. Netherlands (tied)	5.3
11. New Zealand	5.0
12. Sweden	4.2
13. Ireland	3.4
14. Norway	2.9
15. Japan (tied)	2.6
16. Finland (tied)	2.6
17. Canada (tied)	2.6
18. United States	1.8

Favorite Pizza Toppings from 10 Countries

❋ ❋ ❋ ❋

Around the world, pizza toppings vary greatly, reflecting regional tastes, local foods, and cultural preferences. Take a look at some of the toppings that stack pizzas around the world.

1. **India**—pickled ginger, minced mutton, and *paneer* (a form of cottage cheese)

2. **Russia**—*mockba* (a combination of sardines, tuna, mackerel, salmon, and onions), red herring

3. Brazil—green peas

4. Japan—eel, squid, and *Mayo Jaga* (mayonnaise, potato, bacon)

5. France—flambé (bacon, onion, fresh cream)

6. Pakistan—curry

7. Australia—shrimp, pineapple, barbecue sauce

8. Costa Rica—coconut

9. Netherlands—"Double Dutch"—double meat, double cheese, double onion

10. United States—pepperoni, mushrooms, sausage, green pepper, onion, and extra cheese

I WOULDN'T EAT THAT IF I WERE YOU
7 Banned Foods

❋ ❋ ❋ ❋

The following is a list of some foods and beverages that have been banned either because the particular species is endangered or because, if ingested, they can seriously threaten the health, safety, and well-being of the consumer.

1. Japanese Puffer Fish

Also known as blowfish, these creatures are so named for their ability to inflate themselves to several times their normal size by swallowing water or air when threatened. Although the eyes and internal organs of most puffer fish are highly toxic, the meat is considered a delicacy in Japan and Korea. Still, nearly 60 percent of humans who ingest this fish die from *tetrodotoxin,* a powerful neurotoxin that damages or destroys nerve tissue. Humans need only ingest a few milligrams of this toxin for a fatal reaction to occur. Most puffer fish poisoning is the result of accidental consumption of other foods that are tainted with the puffer fish toxin rather than from the ingestion of puffer fish itself. Symptoms include rapid numbness and tingling of lips and mouth, which are generally resolved within hours to days if treated promptly.

2. Absinthe

The exact origin of absinthe is unknown, but this strong alcoholic liqueur was probably first commercially produced around 1797. It takes its name from one of its ingredients, *Artemisia absinthium*, which is the botanical name for the bitter herb known as wormwood. Green in color due to the presence of chlorophyll, it became an immensely popular drink in France by the 1850s. Said to induce creativity, produce hallucinations, and act as an aphrodisiac, the bohemian lifestyle quickly embraced it, and absinthe soon became known as *la fée verte* (the green fairy). But in July 1912, the Department of Agriculture banned absinthe in America for its "harmful neurological effects," and France followed in 1915.

3. Foie Gras

Foie gras, which literally means "fatty liver," is what actor Roger Moore calls a "delicacy of despair." When Moore discovered how geese were tortured to create the hors d'oeuvre, he was so appalled that he teamed up with PETA (People for the Ethical Treatment of Animals) and APRL (Animal Protection and Rescue League) to educate the public. In order to create foie gras, ducks and geese are painfully force-fed up to four pounds of food a day by cramming it down their throats through metal pipes until, according to Moore, "they develop a disease that causes their livers to enlarge up to ten times their normal size!" Investigations into foie gras farms have revealed such horrible, unabashed cruelty to animals that the dish has been banned in many countries and many parts of the United States.

4. Casu Marzu Maggot Cheese

Casu marzu, which means "rotting cheese" in Sardinian, is not just an aged and very smelly cheese, it is an illegal commodity in many places. Casu marzu is a runny white cheese made by injecting Pecorino Sardo cheese with cheese-eating larvae that measure about one-half inch long. Tradition calls for this cheese to be eaten with the maggots running through it. Sardinians claim these critters make the cheese creamier and that it's absolutely delicious. This cheese is widely, but not openly, eaten in Sardinia, even though the ban on it is only enforced sporadically.

5. Sassafras

Now recognized by the U.S. Department of Agriculture as a potential carcinogen, sassafras is the dried root bark of the sassafras tree native to eastern North America. Throughout history, sassafras has been used for making tea, as a fragrance for soap, a painkiller, an insect repellent, and a seasoning and thickener for many Creole soups and stews. But the best-known use of sassafras lies in the creation of root beer, which owes its characteristic flavor to sassafras extract. In 1960, the FDA banned the ingredient *saffrole*—found in sassafras oil—for use as an additive because in several experiments massive doses of sassafras oil were found to induce liver cancer in rats. It should come as no surprise that chemicals and artificial flavors are used to flavor root beer today.

6. Blackened Redfish

In 1980, New Orleans chef Paul Prudhomme publicized his recipe for blackened redfish, which is still very popular today. The recipe was so popular that it sparked a blackened redfish craze in the 1980s, which so severely threatened the redfish stock that the Commerce Department had to step in and close down fisheries in July 1986. In Florida, strict conservation measures were enforced for two years, and, to this day, the state requires that anglers keep only one redfish per day and release any that do not fall into the 18–27 inch limit, handling their catch as little as possible to assure that the fish survives upon release.

7. Ortolan

In the same cruel fashion as foie gras, this tiny bird has little to sing about, as historically it was horribly tortured before being eaten as a gastronomic treat by the aristocracy of France. Its fate was often to be captured, have its eyes poked out, and be put in a small cage, then force-fed until it grew to four times its normal size. Next the poor bird would be drowned in brandy, roasted, and eaten whole. Now considered a protected species in France, the ortolan is also in decline in several other European countries. Nevertheless, hunters still kill about 50,000 birds per year even though it is illegal to sell them.

15 Countries with the Highest Chocolate Consumption

✳ ✳ ✳ ✳

Country	*Pounds per Person per Year*
1. Switzerland	22.36
2. Austria	20.13
3. Ireland	19.47
4. Germany	18.04
5. Norway	17.93
6. Denmark	17.66
7. United Kingdom	17.49
8. Belgium	13.16
9. Australia	12.99
10. Sweden	12.90
11. United States	11.64
12. France	11.38
13. Netherlands	10.56
14. Finland	10.45
15. Italy	6.13

13 Countries with the Highest Ice Cream Consumption

✳ ✳ ✳ ✳

Country	Gallons per Person per Year
1. New Zealand	7.0
2. United States	4.9
3. Australia	4.7
4. Finland	3.7
5. Sweden	3.1
6. Canada	2.5
7. Italy (tied)	2.4
8. Ireland (tied)	2.4
9. Denmark	2.3
10. United Kingdom	2.0
11. Chile	1.5
12. Malaysia (tied)	0.5
13. China (tied)	0.5

17 Obscure Brands of Soda Pop

✳ ✳ ✳ ✳

*Americans drink 13 billion gallons of soft drinks every year.
But until the latter half of the 1800s, selection was limited.
The usual suspects for soda flavors were cola, orange, grape, root
beer, strawberry, and lemon-lime. Oh, how times have changed!
Some of the beverages listed below are still being produced, while
others are now only available in the big soda fountain in the sky.*

1. DraCola

This was a cola product made for "Halloween fans of all ages" by
Transylvania Imports. Yes, you can still find it and, no, it isn't blood-
flavored. DraCola is an ordinary cola-flavored beverage.

2. Aphrodite

Cherry-red with a fruit punch flavor, this discontinued soda featured a different quote from a famous screen siren (such as Mae West) on every bottle. In addition, Aphrodite's suggestive slogan was "Get Some Tonight." This soda came onto the scene in 2002 and only lasted a few years.

3. OK Soda

This soda had a forgettable taste but a legendary marketing campaign. Aimed at the too-cool-for-everything Generation X in the early 1990s, OK Soda purposely employed minimalist art and negative advertising to sell the drink. The Gen Xers didn't buy into the hype or the soda—which was a pretty run-of-the-mill, cola-flavored beverage—and OK was soon a thing of the past.

4. Celo Polka Cola

Created by the Sauk City, Wisconsin, Celo Bottling Company, Celo Polka Cola was presented to the world in 1991 to promote polka music and dancing. The jury's still out as to whether or not that worked, but you can order this cola-flavored beverage online and decide for yourself.

5. Whooppee Soda

"The Bottled Joy," a ginger ale-flavored soda, featured the innovative "Tilt-Top Cap." The best thing about this early 20th century soda was a contest offered by the company. Up to $500 in prizes were awarded to the 24 best letters in which consumers described their "saddest, most injurious or embarrassing experience in taking off the ... bottle crown cap."

6. Dr. Enuf

Since 1949, the Tri-City Beverage Corporation has been bottling this "vitamin-enriched lemon-lime soft drink" invented by Charles Gordon. Back in the day, Dr. Enuf was said to relieve people's "untold misery" from aches and pains, stomach disturbances, and general malaise. Dr. Enuf is still available from the manufacturer but doesn't appear on most supermarket shelves.

7. Leninade

With slogans like, "A taste worth standing in line for," and "A drink for the masses!" you can guess that there's some humor behind this "Simple Soviet Style Soda." Produced by the Lenin Company, the fruity taste pleased communists and noncommunists alike—so much so that you can still find it online.

8. Hemp Soda

Ah, the mid-1990s, when alternative music actually meant something and everyone was discovering hemp-based products. This "herbal" soda was produced in 1996 and featured a large hemp leaf on the can. The beverage can still be ordered online from the manufacturer "Designer Food."

9. Nesbitt's Orange Soda

The Nesbitt Orange Soda Company was founded in 1938 in Los Angeles and produced its famous beverage for 40 years. Real orange zest settles to the bottom of this classic orange soda that is still available online and in some stores.

10. Brain Wash Blue

If you have trouble placing the flavor of this soda, don't feel too bad. Jalapeño oil doesn't go into many mainstream beverages, which is perhaps why this small batch soda, courtesy of Skeleteens, hasn't hit it big. If you dare give it a try, it's available online.

11. Tab Clear

If you blinked in 1993, you missed Tab Clear. The Coca-Cola Company tried to hop on the clear-cola bandwagon, (remember Crystal Pepsi?) but less than a year after its introduction, Tab Clear was pulled. Original Tab is still going strong.

12. Flathead Lake Monster

The North American Beverage Company developed this line of boutique sodas and named them for a monster said to live in Flathead Lake, Montana. Flavors include Huckleberry and Wild White Grape, among others. Limited distribution has kept these sodas obscure, though the beverages have a solid fan base.

13. Gay Energy Cola Drink

In the never-ending quest to zero in on and exhaust the consumer habits of a particular demographic, POWER Drinks, S.L. produced this energy drink several years ago. If you find a can of this beverage, you should keep it as a collector's item—they don't make it anymore.

14. Pickle Juice "Sport"

This soda, conceived by Golden Beverages, Inc., isn't just the same color as pickle juice, it actually *tastes* like pickle juice, too. Carbonated pickle juice that is. Neither the Original Flavor nor the Sport flavor has sold well and, therefore, Pickle Juice is not easy to find in stores, but it is available online.

15. Orbitz

The folks at Clearly Canadian were so successful with their flavored sparkling water that they decided to take a risk. Possibly inspired by bubble teas found in Japan, Orbitz drinks featured gelatin balls floating in semi-colloidal, fruit-flavored water. Orbitz resembled a lava lamp and tasted like something you immediately never wanted to taste again.

16. Nuky Rose Soda

This light pink soda from the Florida-based Nuky Corporation smells and tastes like perfume. After all, it's made from rose petals.

17. Abali "Yogurt Original Flavor" Soda

Carbonated dairy products might be obscure to the Western world, but yogurt sodas are very popular in the Middle East, especially in Iran and Afghanistan. Most yogurt sodas are naturally carbonated, due to the magic of fermentation.

✳ ✳ ✳

"Part of the secret of success in life is to eat what you like and let the food fight it out inside."
—Mark Twain

Calories and Fat in 36 Favorite Fast Foods

Most health and fitness experts, as well as the USDA, agree that the recommended daily caloric intake varies from person to person, depending on an individual's age, gender, and activity level. But on average, experts recommend a 2,000-calorie diet with about 60 to 65 grams of fat per day. So, as you can see, some of the fast-food items on the following list contain half or nearly all of the daily requirements.

Food Item	*Calories*	*Fat (grams)*
1. Deluxe Breakfast Biscuit (McDonald's)	1,320	63
2. Double Whopper with cheese (Burger King)	990	64
3. Chocolate Shake (large, 22 ounces, Burger King)	950	29
4. Roast Turkey, Ranch & Bacon Sandwich (Arby's)	834	38
5. Baconator (Wendy's)	830	51
6. Onion Petals (large, Arby's)	828	57
7. TenderCrisp Chicken Sandwich (Burger King)	780	43
8. Nachos Bell Grande (Taco Bell)	770	44
9. Grilled Stuft Burrito (beef, Taco Bell)	680	30
10. Pepperoni Personal Pan Pizza (Pizza Hut)	640	29
11. Curly Fries (large, Arby's)	631	37
12. Chicken Club Sandwich (Wendy's)	610	31
13. French Fries (large, McDonald's)	570	30
14. Meatball Marinara (6-inch wheat sub, Subway)	560	24
15. Big Mac (McDonald's)	540	29
16. Tuna (6-inch wheat sub, Subway)	530	31

Food Item	Calories	Fat (grams)
17. Meat Lovers Hand-Tossed Pizza (1 slice, Pizza Hut)	490	27
18. Sausage, Egg, and Cheese Croissan'wich (Burger King)	470	32
19. Beef 'n' Cheddar Sandwich (Arby's)	445	21
20. Extra Crispy Chicken Breast (KFC)	440	27
21. Supreme Pan Pizza (1 slice, Pizza Hut)	440	23
22. Sweet & Spicy Wings (5, boneless, KFC)	440	19
23. Cheesy Tots (large, 12 pieces, Burger King)	430	24
24. Mozzarella Sticks (4 pieces, Arby's)	426	28
25. Burrito Supreme (beef, Taco Bell)	410	17
26. Cold Cut Combo (6-inch wheat sub, Subway)	410	17
27. Vanilla Frosty (medium, Wendy's)	410	10
28. Pepperoni Stuffed Crust Pizza (1 slice, Pizza Hut)	390	19
29. Asian Salad with Crispy Chicken (McDonald's)	380	17
30. Glazed Kreme Filled Doughnut (Krispy Kreme)	340	20
31. Original Recipe Thigh (KFC)	330	24
32. KFC Snacker (KFC)	320	16
33. Regular Roast Beef Sandwich (Arby's)	320	14
34. Hershey's Sundae Pie (Burger King)	310	19
35. Oven Roasted Chicken Breast (6-inch wheat sub, Subway)	310	5
36. Coca-Cola Classic (large, 32 ounces, McDonald's)	310	0

FOODS FIT FOR A... KING'S RANSOM
11 of the World's Most Expensive Foods

✳ ✳ ✳ ✳

Food is one of the basic needs that all living things
have in common. But all foods are not created equal, especially
in terms of price, as the following list illustrates.

1. Hamburger

At $99, the Double Truffle Hamburger at DB Bistro
Moderne in Manhattan gives new meaning to the term
whopper. The burger contains three ounces of rib meat
mixed with truffles and foie gras stuffed inside seven ounces of
sirloin steak and served on a Parmesan and poppy seed bun, with
salad and truffle shavings. For penny-pinchers and calorie counters,
the Single Truffle version is a mere $59.

2. Caviar

The world's most expensive caviar is a type of Iranian beluga called
Almas. Pale amber in color, it comes from sturgeons that are
between 60 and 100 years old, and a 3.9-pound container will set
you back $48,750.

3. Pie

In 2006, a chef in northwestern England created the world's most
expensive pie. Based on a traditional steak and mushroom pie, the
dish includes $1,000 worth of Wagyu beef fillet, $3,330 in Chinese
matsutake mushrooms (which are so rare that they are grown under
the watchful eyes of armed guards), two bottles of 1982 Chateau
Mouton Rothschild at a cost of about $4,200 each, as well as black
truffles and gold leaf. The pie serves eight with a total cost around
$15,900, or $1,990 per slice, which includes a glass of champagne.

4. Bread

Forget Poilâne's famous French sourdough at $19.50 a loaf. In
1994, Diane Duyser of Florida noticed that the toasted sandwich

she was eating appeared to contain an image of the Virgin Mary. She kept it for ten years (it never went moldy), before selling it to Canadian casino Goldenpalace.com for $28,000 in 2004.

5. Ice Cream Sundae

At $1,000, the Grand Opulence Sundae at New York's Serendipity 3 certainly lives up to its name. Made from Tahitian vanilla bean ice cream covered in 23-karat edible gold leaf and drizzled with Amedei Porcelana, the world's most expensive chocolate, this indulgence is studded with gold dragées and truffles and topped with dessert caviar.

6. Pizza

Americans love their pizza. And at $1,000 a pie (or $125 a slice) they better be able to put their money where their mouth is. The Luxury Pizza, a 12-inch thin crust, is the creation of Nino Selimaj, owner of Nino's Bellissima in Manhattan. To order this extravagant pizza, call 24 hours in advance because it is covered with six different types of caviar that need to be specially ordered. The pie is also topped with lobster, crème fraîche, and chives.

7. Boxed Chocolates

At $2,600 per pound, Chocopologie by Knipschildt Chocolatier of Connecticut, is the world's most expensive box of chocolates. The Chocolatier, opened in 1999 by Danish chef Fritz Knipschildt, also sells a decadent dark chocolate truffle with a French black truffle inside for a mere $250. But don't expect to just drop in and buy one on a whim... they're available on a preorder basis only.

8. Sandwich

Since the 19th century, the club sandwich has been a restaurant

staple. But thanks to English chef James Parkinson, the von Essen Platinum club sandwich at the Cliveden House Hotel near London is also

the world's most expensive sandwich at $197. Weighing just over a pound, the sandwich is made of the finest ingredients, including Iberico ham cured for 30 months, quail eggs, white truffles, semi-dried Italian tomatoes, and 24-hour fermented sourdough bread.

9. Omelette

For $1,000, this gigantic concoction comes stacked with caviar and an entire lobster encased within its eggy folds. Still, one might expect a seafood fork made of platinum and a few precious stones within to justify the price of a few eggs (albeit with a few added trappings). Nicknamed "The Zillion Dollar Lobster Frittata," the world's most "egg-spensive" omelette is the objet d'art of chef Emilio Castillo of Norma's restaurant in New York's Le Parker Meridien Hotel. A smaller version is also available for $100.

10. Spice

Saffron, the most expensive spice in the world, has sold in recent years for as much as $2,700 per pound! The price tag is so high because it must be harvested by hand and it takes more than 75,000 threads or filaments of the crocus flower to equal one pound of the spice! Most saffron comes from Iran, Turkey, India, Morocco, Spain, and Greece, and in the ancient world the spice was used medicinally and for food and dye. Prices vary depending on the quality and the amount, but high quality saffron has been known to go for as much as $15 per gram (0.035 ounces).

11. Cake

And the award for the most expensive food goes to... a fruitcake? Encrusted with 223 small diamonds, this cake (which is edible without the gems, of course) was for sale for an unbelievable $1.6 million in December 2005. One of 17 diamond-themed displays in a Japanese exhibit called "Diamonds: Nature's Miracle," the masterpiece took a Tokyo pastry chef six months to design and one month to create.

Chapter 8
TRANSPORTATION

DO YOU KNOW HOW FAST YOU WERE GOING?
13 Land and Water Speed Records

When it comes to speed, most people don't even think about it until a police officer asks if they know how fast they were going. But world speed records are kept for just about everything that goes. Here are some records for the world's fastest vehicles on land and sea.

1. Land Speed Record

The land speed record was set on October 15, 1997, by Andy Green, a British fighter pilot in the Royal Air Force. On Black Rock Desert, a dry lake bed in northwestern Nevada, Green's TurboSSC jet-propelled car reached a speed of 763.035 miles per hour, making him the first driver to reach supersonic speed (761 mph) and break the sound barrier. Green broke his own record of 714.144 miles per hour, which was set on September 25, 1997. The TurboSSC is powered by two after-burning Rolls-Royce Spey engines—the same engines used in the Phantom jet fighters Green flew for the RAF. The jet engines powering the TurboSSC burn 4.8 gallons of fuel per second and get about 0.04 miles per gallon.

2. Underwater Speed Records

Official underwater speed records—usually achieved by military submarines—are not kept due to the secrecy surrounding the capabilities of these warships. But in 1965, the USS *Albacore,* a Gato-class submarine, was clocked at 33 knots (38 mph), an unofficial underwater speed record. Claims of higher speeds have been made by submarine manufacturers but have not been officially measured. Russia's Akula-class submarine allegedly can travel at 35 knots (approximately 40 miles per hour) submerged, while the Alfa-class submarine it replaced was said to reach 44.7 knots (approximately 51.4 miles per hour) for short periods.

3. Fastest Person on Two Wheels

The fastest person on two wheels is motorcycle racer Chris Carr. On September 5, 2006, at the Bonneville Salt Flats in Utah—the site of many land speed records—Carr broke the motorcycle land speed record with an average speed of 350.8 miles per hour over two passes on a fixed-length course in two opposite-direction runs. Of the two passes, Carr's fastest was 354 miles per hour. He was riding the Number Seven Streamliner, a specially designed bike with a turbocharged V4 engine.

4. World's Fastest Speedboat

The world's fastest speedboat was actually built in the backyard of the man who set the record. On October 8, 1978, at Blowering Dam, Australia, motorboat racer Ken Darby captained the *Spirit of Australia* to a world record average speed of 318.75 miles per hour, breaking his own record of 290.313 miles per hour set the previous year. Darby designed and built the *Spirit of Australia* himself, using balsa wood, fiberglass, and a military surplus engine he bought for only $69. This is a dangerous sport—no other speedboat racer has clocked in at more than 300 miles per hour and survived.

5. Sailing Speed Record

The fastest sailing vessel, and the smallest, is the sailboard, a surfboard with a sail attached. Windsurfing world champion Finian Maynard of Ireland holds the world sailing speed record of 48.7 knots (about 56 miles per hour), set on a 500-meter course near Saintes Maries de la Mer, France, in April 2005. Maynard broke his own record of 46.82 knots (53.9 miles per hour), set on November 13, 2004.

6. Fastest Long-Distance Sailing Ship

According to the World Sailing Speed Record Council, the fastest long-distance sailing ship is the *Orange II*, a 125-foot-long catamaran. Piloted by French yachtsman Bruno Peyron, the crew of the

Orange II set the record on a transatlantic trip in July 2006, crossing the Atlantic at an average speed of 28 knots (about 32 miles per hour) and completed the trip in 4 days, 8 hours, 23 minutes, and 54 seconds. Peyron and the *Orange II* also own the round-the-world sailing record set on March 16, 2005. They circled the globe (27,000 nautical miles) in 50 days, 16 hours, and 20 minutes, with an average speed of 17.89 knots (around 20 miles per hour).

7. World's Fastest Trains

In the category of trains with wheels, the French TGV, a high-speed train, is the fastest in the world. On April 3, 2007, under test conditions, the high-speed train consisting of two engine cars and three double-decker passenger cars set the record of 357.2 miles per hour. In the category of magnetic levitation trains—where the cars float above a guidance track using powerful electric magnets—the Japanese JR-Maglev three-car train set a record of 361 miles per hour on December 2, 2003. But, without people onboard—and with rockets attached—railed vehicles can go much faster. On April 30, 2003, an unmanned four-stage rocket sled (a small railroad car with rockets strapped to it) reached a speed of 6,416 miles per hour at Holloman Air Force Base in New Mexico.

8. Bicycle Speed Records

Bicycles require human power to move forward, but that doesn't mean they can't move fast. The record for the fastest speed achieved on a regular (upright) bicycle belongs to Fred Rompelberg, who, in 1995, reached a speed of 166.944 miles per hour while being paced by a motor vehicle, which substantially reduced his wind resistance. The official record for an unpaced upright bicycle is 51.29 miles per hour over 200 meters set by Jim Glover in Vancouver in 1986. Recumbent bicycles—those funny-looking bikes where the rider sits in a reclined position with legs extended forward—are aerodynamically faster than conventional bicycles. Canadian cyclist Sam Whittingham set the recumbent bicycle speed record on October 5, 2002, reaching 81 miles per hour over 200 meters with a flying start and no pace vehicle.

9. Fastest Steam-Powered Vehicle

Probably the longest-running speed record belongs to a steam-powered vehicle, the Stanley Steamer. Between 1902 and 1927, these steam-powered automobiles were produced for the public by the Stanley twins—Francis and Freelan—through their Stanley Motor Carriage Company. In 1906, a Stanley Rocket driven by Fred Marriott set the world land speed record for all automobiles, reaching 127.7 miles per hour at the Daytona Beach Road Course in Florida. While the land speed record has been broken by cars with internal combustion or jet-powered engines, the Stanley Steamer still owns the record for steam-powered cars.

10. Fastest Electric (Battery-Powered) Vehicle

Electric cars are usually thought to be slow, but not the Buckeye Bullet. This electric (battery-powered) vehicle, designed and built by engineering students at Ohio State University, holds both the U.S. and international land speed records, which have different sets of rules. To set the international record, an electric car must run a 1-kilometer course twice in opposite directions within a one hour time period. On October 13, 2004, at the Bonneville Salt Flats, driver Roger Schroer set the new international land speed record of 271.737 miles per hour. To get the U.S. record, the vehicle had to be impounded for four hours between two qualifying runs so that it couldn't be repaired, adjusted, or tampered with. On October 15, 2004, the Buckeye Bullet, driven again by Schroer on the same course, set the U.S. land speed record at 314.958 miles per hour.

11. Fastest Roller Coaster

While it never leaves the park, Kingda Ka roller coaster at Six Flags Great Adventure amusement park in Jackson, New Jersey, is recognized as the world's fastest roller coaster. Opened in 2005, the Kingda Ka is a hydraulic launch rocket coaster that reaches its top speed of 128 miles per hour in just 3.5 seconds. Its 456-foot-tall tower is also the world's tallest for a coaster. Built by the Swiss ride manufacturer Intamin, the Kingda Ka uses an over-the-shoulder safety restraint system to keep riders in their seats, but there's no guarantee it will keep their lunch in their stomachs.

12. Fastest Diesel-Powered Vehicle

The word *diesel* used to conjure up images of smelly buses and slow-moving trucks, but that picture changed on August 23, 2006, when the JCB DIESELMAX diesel-powered car driven by Andy Green averaged 350 miles per hour over two runs at the Bonneville Salt Flats. On the first run, he hit 365.779 miles per hour. The JCB DIESELMAX was built by the British company JCB, which normally makes diesel-powered backhoes, loaders, and other types of construction equipment.

13. Fastest Lawn Mower

Most kids hate mowing the lawn, but that might change if their parents bought them this riding mower. On July 4, 2006, at the Bonneville Salt Flats, Bob Cleveland drove his specially-built lawn mower at an average speed of just over 80 miles per hour. Cleveland assembled the mower himself, using a Snapper lawn tractor with a 23-horsepower Briggs & Stratton V-twin modified engine and other custom accessories. At the time he set the record, Cleveland was an eight-time champion in the National Lawn Mower Racing Series.

8 Automotive Lemons

❋ ❋ ❋ ❋

Automakers aim for excellence with every new car they introduce, but sometimes things don't pan out as planned. The following is a sampling of automobiles that were branded "lemons."

1. 1958–1960 Edsel. Perhaps the most famous automotive flop, the Edsel wasn't a truly bad car. From an engineering standpoint, it was in step with most other brands of the late 1950s. Unfortunately, its wide-at-the-top, narrow-at-the-bottom vertical grille resembled a collar used to harness draft horses, giving it a controversial look. It also had the misfortune of hitting the market in September 1957 as an economic recession was brewing, slowing down sales of medium-priced cars. Then, too, promotion for the Edsel made it sound as if the car would revolutionize the industry when, mechanically, it really wasn't much different from other Fords and Mercurys. Ford stopped producing Edsels in November 1959.

2. 1962 Plymouth and Dodge. About 15 years before "downsizing" became the rage in Detroit, Chrysler tried it on its two lowest-priced makes. Unfortunately, this was still the era of "bigger is better." Chrysler exec William Newberg erroneously believed Chevrolet was going smaller for 1962 and ordered chief stylist Virgil Exner to trim the size of the '62 Plymouths and Dodges under development. However, scaling them down from the bigger cars they were intended to be ruined their proportions, and Exner was fired when the cars flopped.

3. 1975–1980 AMC Pacer. Had this disco-era compact come with the smooth, lightweight, GM-built rotary engine that was planned, perhaps the Pacer hatchback's styling would have seemed appropriately adventurous. But with a conventional powertrain, the Pacer was just plain odd. "America's first wide small car" ran a six-cylinder engine—and briefly a V8—after GM canceled its rotary program when the engine wouldn't meet emissions and fuel-mileage targets. It was roomy inside, but with its rounded body, large windows, hatchback, and no discernible trunk, the Pacer resembled a "fishbowl on wheels," making it the butt of many jokes.

4. 1981–1982 DeLorean DMC-12. When flamboyant John Z. DeLorean left General Motors in 1973, he did so intending to start a company to build an "ethical" sports car. He wound up with a movie prop and a world of financial trouble. The car was famous for its stainless-steel body and gull-wing doors—hinged at the top rather than the sides, resembling a gull in flight when open. Moviegoers remember it from *Back to the Future.* But poor quality control and tepid performance from its Renault-supplied V6 engine quickly tarnished its sexy image.

5. 1986–1991 Yugo GV. The Yugo originated from a plant that had been making Fiat-based cars since 1954. The GV, which reached America in mid-1985, was billed as the cheapest car on the market with a starting price of $3,990, compared to $5,340 for a Chevrolet Chevette, the lowest starting price for a domestic car. Soon owners knew why: little power, shoddy quality and reliability, and scary crashworthiness. The little hatchback was later joined by a convertible, but bankruptcy in the United States and civil strife back home in a disintegrating Yugoslavia ended things.

6. 1996–1998 Suzuki X-90. This little two-seater tried to make a sports car out of the Suzuki Sidekick. But the X-90 would have looked more at home in a circus, disgorging a steady stream of clowns. The compact SUV had a petite 86.6-inch wheelbase and a 95-horsepower four-cylinder engine. Noisy at highway speeds, the X-90 also had a bouncy ride, minimal cargo space, and tiny radio buttons that were nearly impossible to use in the dark.

7. 1996–2003 General Motors EV1. After talk of alternatives to the petroleum internal-combustion engine started gaining momentum in the 1980s, General Motors plugged in to the pursuit of electric technology. The EV1 was the result, and it was leased through certain Saturn dealers. However, it was a two-seat economy car with a luxury-car price, and it had limited range before it needed to be charged. (Range was severely limited in colder climates, which made the EV1 even more impractical in those areas.) Some lessees wanted to buy their EV1s, but GM, wary of future liability concerns, wouldn't sell.

8. 2001–2005 Pontiac Aztek. This was Pontiac's first stab at a "crossover" vehicle, a mix of car and sport-utility vehicle that was a new market segment at the beginning of the 21st century. Derived from Pontiac's Montana minivan platform, the Aztek suffered from incoherent, angular styling that was roundly criticized. From the rear, it looked tall, narrow, and ungainly. Off-road capability was limited in all-wheel-drive models, and interior materials and finish left something to be desired.

33 Cars Named After Animals

✳ ✳ ✳ ✳

Automakers are often inspired by the natural world when naming new vehicles. How many of these auto names do you recognize?

1. Barracuda (Plymouth)
2. Beetle (Volkswagen)
3. Bison (Chevrolet heavy-duty truck)
4. Blackhawk (Stutz)
5. Bluebird (Nissan/Datsun)
6. Bronco (Ford)
7. Charger (Dodge)
8. Cheetah (rare 1960s high-performance sports car)
9. Cobra (Shelby, Shelby-Ford)
10. Cougar (Mercury)
11. Fox (Audi, Volkswagen)
12. Gazelle (Singer)
13. Honey Bee (Nissan/Datsun)
14. Impala (Chevrolet)
15. Jaguar (outgrowth of S.S. Cars, formerly Swallow Sidecars, Ltd.)
16. Lark (Studebaker)
17. Marlin (AMC)
18. Mustang (Ford)
19. Pinto (Ford)
20. Rabbit (Volkswagen)
21. Ram (Dodge)
22. Road Runner (Plymouth)
23. Sable (Mercury)
24. Skylark (Buick)
25. Spider/Spyder (Porsche)
26. Stag (Triumph)
27. Sting Ray/Stingray (Chevrolet Corvette)
28. Super Bee (Dodge)
29. Thunderbird (Ford)

11 Design Innovations of Harley Earl

✳ ✳ ✳ ✳

Harley Earl, generally considered the father of American automotive design, was born in Los Angeles, California, in 1893. In the late 1920s, Earl's design talent caught the eye of General Motors Chairman Alfred Sloan, who offered him a position directing the styling of all GM car lines. Earl accepted, moved to Detroit, and soon wielded unprecedented control over GM's new product development. During Earl's 31-year career with the company, General Motors reigned supreme as an industry leader. Under his direction, designers and stylists pioneered countless innovations, such as the following, which propelled the company to the forefront of automotive design.

1. The Auto-Styling Studio

Prior to Earl's arrival in Detroit, cars were designed almost entirely by engineers who often showed little talent for attractive, cohesive forms. The Art and Colour Section (which Earl later renamed Styling) changed all that. GM's new division revolutionized the auto industry, and rival manufacturers soon developed styling studios of their own. A car's appearance became just as important as its mechanicals in Detroit's new product development process.

2. The Wraparound Windshield

The groundbreaking 1951 LeSabre concept car boasted an innovative new windshield design in which the glass curved sharply at the ends to meet the windshield pillars. This gave a futuristic look and a panoramic view. The design soon saw production on the 1953 Cadillac Eldorado and the 1953 Oldsmobile Fiesta and quickly became de rigueur on most American cars in the 1950s.

3. Model-Line Hierarchy

One of GM Chairman Alfred Sloan's great innovations was a model-line hierarchy of increasing price and status. The idea was that General Motors would have an appropriate product for consumers at each level of the automotive marketplace, and consumers would aspire to the next rung up the GM product ladder. Harley Earl's work dovetailed perfectly with this strategy, as he designed a natural progression of increasing style and prestige into Chevrolets, Pontiacs, Oldsmobiles, Buicks, and Cadillacs.

4. The Dream Car

Earl popularized the idea of the "dream car" or concept car, a one-off, non-production vehicle built for auto-show display. Earl's dazzling, futuristic dream cars forecast tomorrow's styling innovations and whet the car-hungry public's appetite for the "next big thing" in automotive design. Public reaction to the new designs was also used to gauge the popularity of future production models. Earl's 1938 Buick "Y-Job" was the first full-fledged dream car.

5. Clay Modeling

Even before he arrived at General Motors, Earl was a pioneer in the concept of taking a design from a two-dimensional drawing to a three-dimensional form by producing clay models of his creations. The use of clay as a modeling tool greatly simplified and sped up the design process by allowing designers to visualize shapes and forms that were difficult and time-consuming to create in steel.

6. Dagmars

Among the 1951 LeSabre dream car's many design innovations were large, bullet-shaped bumper guards. These protrusions, which were nicknamed "Dagmars" after a buxom TV personality of the day, became standard styling flourishes on 1950s Cadillacs.

7. The Chevrolet Corvette

Harley Earl put more than 45,000 miles on the LeSabre show car, using it as his personal car and driving it to automotive events. In September 1951, Earl took the LeSabre to a sports car race at

Watkins Glen, New York. Seeing the passion these enthusiasts had for their cars, most of which were imported, Earl decided America needed an affordable sports car of its own. The Corvette debuted at the New York Motorama in January 1953, and the rest is history.

8. Integrated Body Design

When Harley Earl first started out in automotive design, cars were a hodgepodge of disparate parts. Earl visualized a car as a cohesive whole and designed individual components so they would harmonize with the overall design of the car.

9. Tailfins

Earl was infatuated with aircraft design motifs and loved incorporating them into automotive designs. In particular, the twin-boom tail of the Lockheed P-38 Lightning caught his eye. The 1948 Cadillac was the first production car to receive these ornamental appendages, which sparked a trend that culminated in the skyrocketing fins of the 1959 Cadillac. Tailfins became more subdued each year and had mostly disappeared by the mid-1960s.

10. Copious Chrome

Chrome trim was a simple way to add visual pizzazz to cars, and Harley Earl was a master at effectively using this automotive bling. However, he eventually took the "more is better" approach, and by 1958, GM designers had gone overboard, piling on the brightwork until cars looked like gaudy, chrome-encrusted chariots. Detroit began toning down the chrome soon after.

11. Rear-Mounted Television Cameras

Earl loved automotive gadgetry. In place of rearview mirrors, the 1956 Buick Centurion show car boasted a functional TV camera that transmitted the rear view to a small screen on the dashboard. Rearview cameras that supplement rearview mirrors began showing up on SUVs and large luxury cars in the early 2000s. Earl was definitely ahead of his time.

17 Silly and Unusual Motorcycle Names

✻ ✻ ✻ ✻

Many companies hire expensive marketing firms to come up with catchy names for their products. Others just wing it. The following is a list of motorcycles burdened with monikers seemingly conjured up during a hallucinogenic road trip.

1. Adonis

Adorn your product with the name of a handsome Greek god and you better design something striking. A good place to start would be somewhere other than this 48-cc, early 1950s motorbike, essentially the 98-pound weakling of the motorcycle universe.

2. Anker

Here's an idea: Name your sporty motorcycle after an object used to render vehicles stationary. At least this 1950s German company didn't make boats.

3. Stahl

Perhaps this was not the best choice of name for an American bike built during the motorcycle's formative—and typically unreliable— years, in the early 1910s.

4. Satan

Perhaps the name given to these big single-cylinder bikes from the late 1920s was acceptable in its native Czechoslovakia, but it didn't go over well on this side of the pond. Since the make only lasted one year, they apparently had a devil of a time selling them.

5. Thor

Name a bike after the Norse god of thunder, and it better live up to its name—and the Thor did. First produced in 1907, Thors were big 76-cubic-inch (about 1250-cc) V-twin brutes that rivaled contemporary Harley-Davidsons for speed. But due to the competitive environment, Thor ceased motorcycle production by 1920.

6. Honda Dream

Japanese manufacturers have always leaned toward whimsical names for their machines, so it was hardly a surprise when the Dream became reality in the early 1960s. When this 305-cc bike arrived on American shores with its skirted fenders, stamped-steel frame and forks, and somewhat bulbous bodywork, typical '60s names like Venom, Tiger, or Commando hardly seemed appropriate, so the Dream was born. The Dream was a surprising success and sold under the Honda emblem for nearly ten years.

7. Snob

This 1920s German bike sported a lowly 155-cc single-cylinder engine that really gave it no reason to brag.

8. New Motorcycle

A midsize bike built in France during the 1920s, one can't help but imagine an Abbott and Costello-type routine:

"What's that?"

"A New Motorcycle."

"Duh...I know it's a new motorcycle. But what is it?"

"I just told you."

"All I know is it's a new motorcycle."

"Then why did you ask?"

9. Silver Pigeon

From 1946 to 1964, these scooters were quite popular in Japan, but it's hard to imagine the name would fly in the States.

10. Génial-Lucifer

Like *jumbo shrimp,* the two words just don't seem to go together. Nevertheless, this French builder of small-to-midsize motorcycles managed to tough it out for 28 years (1928–1956), which is more than can be said for most upstarts of the period.

11. Juncker

Blame it on the language barrier, but there's no way this small French bike of the 1930s would have sold very well in the States.

12. Sissy

An Austrian company chose this name to grace a mini-scooter that lasted only one year (1957). What were they thinking?

13. RIP

Seemingly doomed from the start, this English motorcycle company was born in 1905 and gone by 1909. May it rest in peace.

14. Flying Merkel

Ridiculous as its moniker sounds, this big American bike of the early 1900s lived up to its billing, as Flying Merkels set several speed records thanks to their advanced V-twin engines.

15. Harley-Davidson Fat Boy

One of Harley-Davidson's best sellers, the Fat Boy is a beefy motorcycle, originally offered in 1990 on the company's big softail frame with a large, 1340-cc V-twin engine and unique solid wheels. This bulky bike is still sold today in an even "fatter" 1584-cc form.

16. Whizzer Pacemaker

In the years after World War II, Whizzer offered a three-horse-power engine that could be bolted to a conventional bicycle to turn it into a rudimentary form of motorized transport. "Put a Whizzer on it!" trumpeted the ads, and thousands did. The company soon came out with a complete motorbike, the Whizzer Pacemaker, which some credit with starting the scooter revolution that led to the company's demise in the mid-1950s.

17. Wackwitz

Perhaps in its native Germany the name isn't so amusing, but this early '20s maker of small "clip on" engines (much like those sold by Whizzer) lasted only two years. And one can imagine why: "Put a Wackwitz on it!" just doesn't have the same ring.

7 Bizarre Foreign Vehicle Names

✳ ✳ ✳ ✳

1. Nissan Fairlady Z .... Japan 1970–Present
2. Flirt .... Italy 1913–1914
3. Humber Super Snipe .... Great Britain 1946–1967
4. Wartburg Knight .... East Germany 1966–1990
5. Geely PU .... China 2006
6. Beijing Jinggangshan .... China 1958–1960
7. Dri-Sleeve Moonraker .... Great Britain 1971–1972

LOST AT SEA
10 Items that Went Down with the *Titanic*

✳ ✳ ✳ ✳

When the opulent passenger liner RMS Titanic *was built
in 1912, it was declared by* Shipbuilder *magazine to be
"practically unsinkable." Unfortunately, the word* practically
turned out to be key. On the Titanic's *maiden voyage from
Southampton, England, to New York City, it hit an iceberg
and sank in just three hours. Of the 2,229 passengers and crew
onboard, only 713 survived. The ship has been a source of
fascination ever since, partly because of the many stories
associated with its sinking, but also because of the huge wealth
that went down with the ship and remains on the ocean floor
to this day. Here are some of the people and cargo that
were onboard that fateful day.*

1. Passengers

The ship carried 1,316 passengers—325 in first class, 285 in second class, and 706 in third class—of which 498 survived. Around two-thirds of first-class passengers survived, compared to around one-quarter of those in third class, mainly because, at some point after the collision, the gates to the third-class quarters were locked, denying those passengers access to lifeboats. Some of the more famous first-class passengers included millionaire Benjamin Guggenheim and his manservant, who both helped women and children into lifeboats before changing into their best clothes and preparing to "die like gentlemen," which they did. Also in first class was Lady Duff Gordon, a dress designer whose clientele included the British royal family. She and her husband survived, but they were later questioned why their lifeboat had been only half full. They were accused of bribing crew members to not allow more people into the boat. John Jacob Astor IV, the richest man in the world at the time, was also onboard. He assisted his pregnant wife, Madeleine, onto a lifeboat but was not allowed to board himself because officers were applying the principle of "women and children first." Madeleine survived, but John went down with the ship.

2. Crew

The *Titanic* had around 900 crew members, of whom 215 survived. These staff included the deck crew (responsible for sailing the ship), the engineering department (who kept the engines running), the victualing department (responsible for passenger comfort), restaurant staff, and musicians. As the ship was sinking, its two bands came together on the deck and played to keep the spirits of the passengers up. None of the band members survived.

3. Lifeboats

Famously, the *Titanic* had an inadequate number of lifeboats for the number of people it carried. In fact, it had just 20, with a total capacity of 1,178 people—about half the number onboard. The ship had been designed to hold 32 lifeboats (still not enough for everyone), but the owner, White Star Line, had been concerned that too many boats would spoil its appearance.

4. Food

With all those people onboard, it's not surprising that the ship contained incredible quantities of food. There were 75,000 pounds of fresh meat, as well as 15,000 pounds of fish, 25,000 pounds of poultry, and 2,500 pounds of sausages (around 40,000 sausages). Among other items, the ship carried 40 tons of potatoes and 1,750 pounds of ice cream—that's the weight of a full-grown elephant.

5. Drink

Passengers needed something to wash down all that food, so the *Titanic* carried 15,000 bottles of ale and stout, 1,000 bottles of wine, and 850 bottles of spirits, plus 1,200 bottles of soft drinks and mixers, such as lemonade, tonic water, and orange juice.

6. Tableware

Serving all that food and drink required 57,600 items of crockery, 29,000 pieces of glassware, and 44,000 pieces of cutlery. The cutlery alone would have weighed more than 4,000 pounds—about the weight of four cows!

7. Linen

The restaurants, cafés, kitchens, and bedrooms of the *Titanic* required so much linen that White Star Line built a large laundry close to the docks at Southampton, so that each time the ship docked, the dirty linen could quickly be unloaded and cleaned for the next voyage. The 200,000 individual items (not including items belonging to passengers) included 18,000 bedsheets, 6,000 tablecloths, 36,000 towels, and 45,000 table napkins.

8. Art

Perhaps unsurprisingly, considering the wealth of many of its passengers, the *Titanic* was carrying a number of works of art, all of which were lost when the ship sank. The most spectacular of these was a jeweled copy of *The Rubáiyát*, a collection of about 1,000 poems by the 11th-century Persian mathematician and astronomer Omar Khayyám. The binding of this incredibly luxurious book contained 1,500 precious stones, each set in gold. It had been sold at auction in March 1912 to an American bidder for £405 or around $1,900— 15 years worth of wages for a junior crew member on the *Titanic*.

9. Freight

One important function of the *Titanic* was to carry transatlantic mail. When the ship sank, there were 3,364 bags of mail and between 700 and 800 parcels onboard, contents unknown. Other cargo claimed as lost included 50 cases of toothpaste, a cask of china headed for Tiffany's, five grand pianos, and 30 cases of golf clubs and tennis rackets for A.G. Spalding. However, contrary to popular myth, the *Titanic* was not carrying an ancient Egyptian mummy that was believed to have cursed the ship.

10. Passenger Facilities

The sinking of the *Titanic* also meant the loss of some of the most opulent facilities ever seen on a cruise liner. These included the first-ever onboard heated swimming pool, a Turkish bath, first- and second-class libraries, and a veranda café with real palm trees. For communication, the ship had a Marconi wireless radio station to send and receive telegrams and a 50-phone switchboard complete with operator. The *Titanic* even had its own state-of-the-art infirmary and operating room staffed by two physicians. All of this was lost when the ship sank.

10 Most Frequently Stolen Autos

✳ ✳ ✳ ✳

1. 1991 Honda Accord
2. 1995 Honda Civic
3. 1989 Toyota Camry
4. 1994 Dodge Caravan
5. 1994 Nissan Sentra
6. 1997 Ford F150 Series
7. 1990 Acura Integra
8. 1986 Toyota Pickup
9. 1993 Saturn SL
10. 2004 Dodge Ram Pickup

Source: National Insurance Crime Bureau, 2006

Chapter 9
MUSIC

✳ ✳ ✳ ✳

I WANNA HOLD YOUR WORLD RECORD
25 of The Beatles' Top Singles

The story of The Beatles is truly epic. Not only did they create some of the most popular music in the history of rock 'n' roll, when Rolling Stone *magazine compiled its 500 Greatest Songs of All Time, The Beatles beat out everyone else with a whopping 23 songs on the list. For a week in 1964, John, Paul, George, and Ringo had 12 songs on* Billboard's Hot 100, *including the number one, two, three, four, and five songs. Nobody before or since has accomplished that feat. The following list is a sampling of the Fab Four's music arsenal with 25 of their biggest hits.*

1. "I Want to Hold Your Hand" (1963)
This song, which started the "British invasion," became the Fab Four's first number one tune in the States. It did pretty well elsewhere, too—it was their all-time best-selling single worldwide.

2. "She Loves You" (1963)
When this peppy song made its debut in America in September 1963, it didn't get much attention. But it was rereleased in January 1964 after the success of "I Want to Hold Your Hand," and this time it spent 15 weeks on U.S. charts, hitting number one on March 21.

3. "From Me to You" (1963)
The first number one for The Beatles in the UK, this song didn't make much of a splash in the States, reaching only number 41 upon its second release in 1964. However, across the pond it would mark the first of 11 number one singles, so they didn't have time to sulk about this tune, written by John and Paul while on a tour bus.

4. "Twist and Shout" (1964)

If you've ever rocked out to The Beatles' version of this Isley Brothers tune, you know that John's vocals are scratchy, growly, and decidedly different from other Beatles songs. During the recording session for their album *Please, Please Me,* John started to lose his voice. Producer Brian Epstein saved the recording for "Twist and Shout" till the very end. By then, John's voice was nearly shot and sounded strained—in fact, he shouted most of the song. The classic tune was recorded in one take not just because that was all John had left, but because it was pretty much perfect from the start.

5. "Can't Buy Me Love" (1964)

Pressure to create another huge hit after "I Want to Hold Your Hand" didn't phase The Beatles. This tune is one of the first songs ever to start with the chorus. The formula worked like a charm, creating another UK and U.S. number one.

6. "A Hard Day's Night" (1964)

This malapropism was uttered by Ringo, who often got American words and phrases mixed up. He was stating that the band had had a hard day, but then realized it was already evening. "A Hard Day's Night" became another number one for the band and served as the title for their documentary released the same year.

7. "I Feel Fine" (1964)

This song came out of some downtime between John and Ringo, who were playing with a riff John had come up with while working on "Eight Days a Week." "I Feel Fine" eventually went to number one in every major market. The song featured reverb—Jimi Hendrix and The Who were using feedback in their concerts at the time, but The Beatles were the first to commit the sound to vinyl.

8. "Eight Days a Week" (1965)

The title of this song was again based on a Ringo-ism; the drummer claimed that he had worked so hard, he had added another day to the week. Even though the song reached number one in the States, it wasn't a band favorite, and they seldom performed it live.

9. "Ticket to Ride" (1965)

The meaning behind this song is unclear—it could be about a prostitute, John getting his driver's license, or a girl walking out the door. Whatever the subject, it's a catchy tune that reached number one in both the UK and the United States.

10. "Help!" (1965)

John would later claim that he penned the lyrics to "Help!" after dealing with the pressures of being part of a group that was, as he so notoriously put it, "bigger than Jesus." He said that he wished the song could've been recorded at a slower tempo, but fans liked it just fine, making it another chart-topper for the band.

11. "Yesterday" (1965)

This melancholy tune about lost love reportedly came to Paul in a dream, so he worried that he'd unintentionally plagiarized another artist's work. He hadn't, and once he completed the lyrics, he recorded the song in the studio without the other three Beatles. The song reached number one in the United States, but the other band members were initially against its release in the UK.

12. "We Can Work It Out" (1965)

One of the Fab Four's fastest-selling singles, this moody Lennon-McCartney collaboration touched a nerve with struggling lovers everywhere. When The Beatles disbanded, this song took on an ironic and ominous overtone for the group that ultimately couldn't work things out.

13. "Day Tripper" (1965)

Though they fervently denied it for 40 years, Paul revealed in a 2005 interview that yes, "Day Tripper" is about drugs. At the time, nobody knew (or they didn't care) and this tune, released along with "We Can Work It Out" shot to number one right away.

14. "Nowhere Man" (1966)

This rather disturbing song, written by John about a man whose life is pointless and lonely, turned out to be somewhat autobiographical.

Lennon reportedly had to come up with another song for *Rubber Soul*, but after several hours of writing nothing, he gave up. As soon as he did, this song simply came to him. "Nowhere Man" only reached the number three spot in America.

15. "Paperback Writer" (1966)

This number one was penned by Paul after an aunt reportedly told him to write a song that wasn't about a girl. The song clips along at a fast pace and tells the story of an aspiring writer, possibly based on a book Ringo was reading at the time.

16. "Yellow Submarine" (1966)

Though Paul vehemently denied it, "Yellow Submarine" (the song that later inspired an animated movie of the same name) got a reputation for being about hallucinogenic drug use. Ringo sings lead vocals on this goofy-but-catchy song that hit number one in the UK and number two in the States.

17. "Eleanor Rigby" (1966)

This melancholy track further proved to the world that The Beatles were not just a flash in the pan. Paul wrote the lyrics to this song about "all the lonely people" and producer George Martin added a lush string score. It all meshed together to describe the loneliness of old age. It hit the top of the charts in the UK, but only made it to number 11 on U.S. charts.

18. "Hello, Goodbye" (1967)

Spending several weeks at number one on both the UK and U.S. charts, "Hello, Goodbye" was released around Christmastime 1967 and later on the *Magical Mystery Tour* album.

19. "With a Little Help from My Friends" (1967)

The cheers and applause that accompany this Ringo-led tune came from earlier recordings of The Beatles' live shows, since they were no longer touring when the song was recorded. The single wasn't a chart-topper, but it has a sweet message and a catchy melody that make it a classic Beatles fan favorite.

20. "Lady Madonna" (1968)

Before The Beatles left for India in 1969 (and changed directions musically) they recorded one last song for Parlophone/Capitol before releasing on their own label, Apple Records. "Lady Madonna" was that song, and it hit the top spot in the UK and reached number four in the States.

21. "Hey Jude" (1968)

Even though the lyrics don't exactly make sense, even though the song in its original version is over seven minutes long, even though it's technically a song about divorce, the song is beloved by many people. Written by Paul for John's son Julian during his parents' divorce, "Hey Jude" stayed at number one on U.S. charts for nine weeks, a record for any Beatles song. Across the pond, the full-length version of the song peaked at number one for two weeks.

22. "Come Together" (1969)

Originally written for Timothy Leary's short-lived gubernatorial campaign, "Come Together" was released on the *Abbey Road* album in 1969. The song was also the subject of a lawsuit by Chuck Berry's music publisher, who claimed that a line from one of Berry's songs had been stolen for use in The Beatles' tune. The suit was settled out of court. The song reached number one in the States and number four in the UK.

23. "Get Back" (1969)

The last song on the *Let It Be* album, this hard-driving rock tune tells the listener to "get back to where you once belonged." Since The Beatles did not release any more records together after *Let It Be,* this song was the end of the line, period. The single reached number one around the world and was the first Beatles tune to credit a fifth musician, Billy Preston on keyboards.

24. "Let It Be" (1970)

The *Let It Be* album, released in 1970 shortly after the band officially broke up, was the Fab Four's swan song. This single was a huge hit around the world, reaching number one in America and number two in the UK. Paul was inspired to write it following a dream he had of his mother (Mary), who died when he was 14. The song's theme of surrendering and letting go touched a chord with millions of fans. "Let It Be" is often played at funerals, due to its hopeful, farewell message.

25. "The Long and Winding Road" (1970)

This sad song about unrequited love, also released after The Beatles disbanded, would prove to be the group's last number one song in the United States. Paul reportedly wrote the song during a time when tensions were mounting among the band members.

WE LOVE YOU, TOO, U2
The Stories Behind 29 U2 Songs

❋ ❋ ❋ ❋

September 1976: A 14-year-old drummer posts a notice at school that he's looking to start a band. Rehearsals are held in his parent's kitchen in Dublin, and The Larry Mullen Band is born. The name didn't last, but more than 30 years and 22 Grammys later, the band, which would eventually be called U2, has proven it has what it takes to stay on top. The keys to U2's longevity include respect for each other and their fans; the ability to continuously reinvent themselves and their musical style; and powerful music with a message. But the meanings of most U2 songs are subject to interpretation. Bono is a genius at writing ambiguous lyrics, allowing listeners to decide what each song means to them. Read on to take a musical journey with the band that Time *magazine once named "Rock's Hottest Ticket."*

1. "I Will Follow" (1980)

This peppy '80s tune, released on the *Boy* album, is still as fresh today as when it debuted nearly three decades ago. The song is charged with Edge's gritty guitar riffs and Larry Mullen, Jr.'s pounding drum beat, still played with the intensity of an 18-year-old. According to Bono, the lyrics are about the unconditional love between mother (or God) and child. Whatever the child does, whatever his or her faults, a mother (or God) still loves her child.

2. "Out of Control" (1980)

Another toe-tapper from *Boy,* "Out of Control" has the distinction of being the first song the guys heard played on the radio. Bono wrote the lyrics in the wee hours of the morning following his eighteenth birthday. "It was one dull morning/I woke the world with bawling/I was so sad/They were so glad. . . " The song is about being born—or rather objecting to it—and feeling that you have no control over your life.

3. "Gloria" (1981)

No, it's not a cover of fellow Irishman Van Morrison's '60s hit. This one comes from U2's sophomore album, *October,* which was heavy-laden with references to religion and spirituality. Bono has said he had a difficult time writing the lyrics, so he turned it into a psalm, complete with verses in Latin. The music is quite edgy considering the subject matter, which is what makes it classic U2.

4. "Tomorrow" (1981)

Most U2 lyrics are pretty heavy. But with "Tomorrow," from *October,* Bono was truly speaking from the heart. When he was 14, his mother suffered a brain hemorrhage at her father's funeral and died a few days later. Bono would later state that the melancholy lyrics to "Tomorrow" were a description of her funeral.

5. "Sunday Bloody Sunday" (1983)

From the *War* album, "Sunday Bloody Sunday" is a powerhouse in the U2 canon, performed on every major tour since its debut. It's a classic U2 protest song about the Troubles in Northern Ireland. Larry's militaristic drumming and Edge's abrasive guitar drive the song, while Bono's powerful lyrics cry out "How long, how long must we sing this song?" The song, which reached number seven on *Billboard*'s Mainstream Rock chart in the '80s, has now become a global plea to end the violence that threatens the world today.

6. "New Year's Day" (1983)

This song, inspired by the solidarity movement in Poland, reached number two on *Billboard*'s Mainstream Rock chart. It was also the first U2 video to get major airplay on MTV, giving the band the exposure that would get them named "Band of the Eighties" by *Rolling Stone* magazine just two years later. During live shows, Edge takes control on this song, playing guitar and keyboard simultaneously in parts and also singing backup vocals.

7. "40" (1983)

Also from *War*, Bono based the lyrics of this bass-driven song on Psalm 40. Although the song was only released in Germany, it is a fan favorite that has frequently been used to close shows. When a show ends with "40," guitarist Edge and bassist Adam Clayton switch instruments, and the band members leave the stage one by one—first Bono, Adam, then Edge, leaving Larry alone onstage to perform a brief (but kickin') drum solo, as fans chant the chorus.

8. "Pride (In the Name of Love)" (1984)

Released on *The Unforgettable Fire* album, this song about Jesus ("one man betrayed with a kiss") and Martin Luther King, Jr., reached number two on *Billboard*'s Mainstream Rock chart. Bono gave his all recording "Pride," shouting the lyrics from the depths of his soul. But don't rely on Bono for a history lesson; the lyric referring to Dr. King ("Early morning, April four/Shot rings out in the Memphis sky...") is incorrect—King was actually killed around 6:00 P.M. Bono has since realized his mistake and now sings "Early evening, April four" in live shows.

9. "Bad" (1984)

From *The Unforgettable Fire* album, "Bad" was never released as a single, but it's a fan favorite that sometimes closes shows. As always, the lyrics are subject to much debate, but according to Bono, the song is about drug addiction, specifically heroin, which ran rampant in Dublin in the early '80s and had taken hold of one of his friends. Ever the perfectionist, Bono feels the song could've been better if he'd "finished" it. Most fans think it's a masterpiece as it stands.

10. "With or Without You" (1987)

This perpetual crowd-pleaser, released on the Grammy Award-winning album *The Joshua Tree,* was U2's first number one song in America. Some feel the song is about Jesus ("see the thorn twist in your side"); others think it's about romantic love and longing for someone you can't be with. The song is rife with symbolism, in both the lyrics and the music. Adam's bass is the pulse. Larry's drumming is the heartbeat. Edge's guitar chords represent the agony of a heart breaking. And Bono's voice and haunting lyrics are the personification of love and longing and the agony of unrequited love. When his voice cries out, you know he's not just reciting the words, but truly feeling the pain of loving someone he can't be with...and you feel that pain with him.

11. "I Still Haven't Found What I'm Looking For" (1987)

No dual meaning here—U2's second song to top U.S. charts, "I Still Haven't Found What I'm Looking For" is a gospel song about searching for and understanding one's spiritual beliefs. U2 even took a gospel choir with them to sing backup vocals during The Joshua Tree tour. Bono often says he's not satisfied with some of his recorded lyrics, so he tends to "rewrite" them during live performances. For example, the original lyric: "You broke the bonds/And you loosed the chains/Carried the cross of my shame/Oh my shame..." is now sung: "You broke the bonds/And you loosed the chains/Carried the cross/Took my shame/You took the blame...." The change is ever so slight, but it makes the song much deeper and more meaningful.

12. "Where the Streets Have No Name" (1987)

Although "Streets" didn't crack the top ten in the States, it's a fan favorite that was frequently used to open shows on The Joshua Tree tour. The lyrics were inspired by a trip Bono and his wife took to Ethiopia in the mid-1980s, during which they volunteered at a refugee camp orphanage. With Edge's distinctive scratchy chords, Larry's enthusiastic drumming, and Adam's deep bass holding it all together, even the band admits it's much better live.

13. "Desire" (1988)

With "Desire," released as the first single from the album *Rattle and Hum,* Bono parodies and criticizes evangelical preachers, politicians, and the greed ingrained in the landscape of 1980s America. But the lyrics can have a more carnal interpretation as well. Either way, the song was a hit, reaching number one on both *Billboard*'s Mainstream Rock and Modern Rock charts. The song also won a Grammy for Best Rock Performance, and it was U2's first song to reach the top of the charts in the UK.

14. "Angel of Harlem" (1988)

With "Angel of Harlem," U2 racked up another number one on *Billboard*'s Mainstream Rock chart. Recorded in Sun Studios in Memphis, Elvis's legendary music engineer Cowboy Jack Clement pitched in on this one, and it was all captured on film in the "rockumentary" *Rattle and Hum.* The song chronicles the band's arrival in America for their first tour in 1980 ("It was a cold and wet December day/When we touched the ground at JFK..."). It is also a tribute to Billie Holiday, the "Angel of Harlem."

15. "All I Want Is You" (1989)

Bono has said that "All I Want Is You," from *Rattle and Hum,* is dedicated to his wife, Ali. The poetic and symbolic lyrics describe his desire for true, unconditional love, and the promises his lover makes show the depth of her feelings. The song closed the *Rattle and Hum* movie, and much to the surprise of fans (because it seldom closes a live show), it was the last song played on the Vertigo tour, when it closed the show in Honolulu in December 2006.

16. "Mysterious Ways" (1991)

In the 1990s, U2 took a new musical direction, attempting to "chop down *The Joshua Tree*" by reinventing themselves with a funkier, more experimental sound on the album *Achtung Baby.* It must have worked because "Mysterious Ways," powered by Edge's abrasive guitar riffs and Bono's enigmatic lyrics, scored U2 another number one on both *Billboard*'s Mainstream Rock and Modern

Rock charts. Fans disagree over the song's meaning—some feel it's deeply spiritual, with references to John the Baptist, while others believe the lyrics are more sexual in nature, and others just think it's a funky dance groove.

17. "One" (1992)

Such a simple title, such a powerful lyric. Tensions were running high while recording *Achtung Baby*, and the band was reportedly on the brink of breaking up. "One" is the song that brought them back together, essentially saving the band. The lyrics can be interpreted in several ways: a gay son coming out to his father; a relationship in which a couple loves each other but have hurt each other too much to stay together; or Bono's rocky relationship with his own father. Whatever the meaning, the song reminds us that all humans are equal and that we need to help those less fortunate: "We're one, but we're not the same/We get to carry each other, carry each other." "One" topped *Billboard*'s Mainstream Rock and Modern Rock charts and has been played at every U2 concert since its debut on the ZooTV tour in 1992.

18. "Numb" (1993)

U2 got even more experimental with the album *Zooropa*. "Numb," the first single from that album, reached number two on *Billboard*'s Modern Rock chart. Edge takes lead vocals on this song, speaking the lyrics in a monotone voice with backup vocals by Bono and Larry Mullen, Jr.—a very rare occurrence for the drummer. Bono has said the lyrics symbolize information overload from the constant barrage of media coverage.

19. "Stay (Far Away, So Close)" (1993)

"Stay" is another example of a fan favorite that did not chart well, not breaking the top ten on any U.S. chart. The song, which appears on *Zooropa*, was written for the Wim Wenders' film *Far Away, So Close*. The song's meaning is debatable, but one take is that it's about a guardian angel who feels helpless that he can watch over the living person, but not really help them. Or perhaps it's about somebody caught in an abusive relationship. Fans love it, but it hasn't been played on tour since 2001.

20. "Please" (1997)

"Please" appeared on *Pop*, the band's most experimental and dance-oriented album to date, which band members agree needed a few more weeks to really polish it. "Please" is a song about terrorism and the Troubles in Northern Ireland, but the song and its prophetic lyrics ("September, streets capsizing... /Shards of glass, splinters like rain...") took on new meaning following 9/11. In recordings from the Popmart tour, Bono pours out his heart and soul, crying out "please, please," almost desperate, begging. But then, just as your heart starts to break for him, you hear the ping of Larry's drumstick against the cymbal as "Streets" takes off. It's like a security blanket or the voice of an old friend, and with the reassuring sounds of an old favorite, fans know all will be okay.

21. "Beautiful Day" (2000)

With the release of *All That You Can't Leave Behind*, U2 once again reinvented themselves, ditching their dance-oriented experimental phase and returning to their roots, albeit with a harder, rock-based sound. "Beautiful Day," the first single from the multiplatinum, Grammy Award-winning album, is a reminder that no matter how bad life can get, we should always be thankful for what we have. The song went to number five on *Billboard's* Modern Rock chart, and it secured three more Grammys for the Dublin lads—Song of the Year, Record of the Year, and Best Rock Performance.

22. "Stuck in a Moment You Can't Get Out Of" (2001)

"Stuck," the second single from *All That You Can't Leave Behind*, reached only number 35 on U.S. charts. Nevertheless, this in-your-face number earned the boys another Grammy for Best Pop Performance. Bono wrote the lyrics as a conversation he wishes he'd had with his friend Michael Hutchence to prevent the INXS singer from committing suicide in 1997. The lyrics are somewhat argumentative with Bono shouting: "You've got to get yourself together/You've got stuck in a moment and now you can't get out of it...." Still, the words are very powerful and uplifting, reminding the downtrodden that "It's just a moment/This time will pass."

23. "Elevation" (2001)

"Elevation," also from *All That You Can't Leave Behind,* climbed to number eight on *Billboard's* Modern Rock chart and won the band a Grammy for Best Rock Performance. This crowd-pleaser is even better live, so it's not surprising that it appeared in every concert on the Elevation and Vertigo tours. With Adam's head-bobbing bass line, Edge's grinding chords, and Larry's powerful drumming, "Elevation" is a rockin' tune that makes fans (and Edge) want to jump up and down during live shows. Some feel the song is simply about passion and sexuality. Others feel there is a deeper meaning and that Bono is referring to his spirituality when he sings the tune.

24. "Walk On" (2001)

"Walk On" scored U2 another Grammy for Record of the Year. This song was supposedly inspired by Aung San Suu Kyi, a nonviolent Burmese political activist who has been under house arrest off and on since 1989. But many people feel the song is a tribute to someone nearing the end of his life (possibly Bono's father), who realizes that love is really the most important, and only, thing to take on his journey. ("You're packing a suitcase for a place none of us has been/ A place that has to be believed to be seen..." and "Home...I can't say where it is but I know I'm going home.") During the Elevation tour dates after 9/11, the band took NYC firefighters and police officers on tour with them and brought them onstage during this song, which adopted a special meaning after the terrorist attacks.

25. "Vertigo" (2004)

"Vertigo" was the first single from *How to Dismantle an Atomic Bomb,* which is harder and more upbeat than their previous efforts. No mixed messages with this U2 powerhouse—"Vertigo" is an adrenalized rocker about an evening at a nightclub. The song reached number one on *Billboard's* Modern Rock chart, garnered the band two more Grammys (Best Rock Performance and Best Rock Song), and was featured in a commercial for Apple's iPod. The fellas had so much fun playing the song that it was played at every concert of the Vertigo tour—sometimes twice!

26. "Sometimes You Can't Make It on Your Own" (2005)

U2 racked up two more Grammys for Song of the Year and Best Rock Performance with "Sometimes," which is a tribute to the somewhat distant relationship Bono had with his father, who passed away in 2001. The song reaches a climax when, from the depths of his soul, Bono cries out, "You're the reason I sing/You're the reason why the opera is in me...," and fans are often moved to tears by his display of raw emotion.

27. "City of Blinding Lights" (2005)

U2 cleaned up at the 2005 Grammys, taking home five awards including Best Rock Song for "City" and Album of the Year and Best Rock Album for *How to Dismantle an Atomic Bomb*. Inspired by Bono's love for New York City and the band's love for their fans ("I miss you when you're not around"), this peppy, upbeat song quickly found a home as the opener on the Vertigo tour with Adam playing the opening notes on the keyboard.

28. "The Saints Are Coming" (2006)

U2 teamed up with Green Day for this cover of a 1970s punk rock song by The Skids. "Saints," one of two new songs on the compilation album *U2 18 Singles,* was recorded in the legendary Abbey Road studios in London where The Beatles recorded most of their albums. The song, which mentions New Orleans, storms, and flooding, took on new meaning when the two bands played it live when the New Orleans Saints returned to the Superdome for the first time following the devastation of Hurricane Katrina in 2005. This energetic and mighty rocker reached number one in Australia, Canada, and all over Europe, but didn't receive much airplay in the States.

29. "Window in the Skies" (2007)

Another new song from *U2 18 Singles,* this cheerful, snappy tune was also recorded at Abbey Road studios and has a slight "Beatles" sound to it. Although it didn't fare well on U.S. charts due to lack of airplay, it reached the top ten in many other parts of the world and became an instant fan favorite. Some argue that the lyrics are about romantic love, but most die-hard fans agree that this one is all about God's love and the grace, redemption, and forgiveness we receive by accepting his gift.

11 Bands Named After Places

❈ ❈ ❈ ❈

With all the pressure that comes with starting a band, who has time to labor over a name? The following musical groups decided to keep things simple and named themselves after a place.

1. Alabama

One of the best-selling country music acts of the 1980s continues to hold ground as one of the most commercially successful music groups ever. The four-piece group, named for their home state, might be known to noncountry listeners via their hit "If You're Gonna Play in Texas (You Gotta Have a Fiddle in the Band)."

2. Boston

When their self-titled debut album was released in 1976, members of the rock 'n' roll band Boston had no idea how popular their progressive new sound would be. The record would become one of the best-selling debut albums in U.S. history, selling more than 17 million copies. Boston's distinctive sound can be heard in songs such as "More Than a Feelin'" and "Don't Look Back."

3. Chicago

When Chicago formed in 1967, they actually called themselves Chicago Transit Authority. Trouble was, that was the name of the, uh, Chicago Transit Authority. The powers that be didn't want any

confusion about what was a rock band and what was a public transportation system, so they made the guys change their name. After
becoming Chicago, hits such as "25 or 6 to 4" and "Hard to Say I'm
Sorry" made the band a household name.

4. The E Street Band

Named after a street in New Jersey, The E Street Band garnered
major media attention while backing Bruce Springsteen in the
1980s, most notably on the Boss's mega-popular album *Born in the
U.S.A.*, which sold 15 million copies. But the band has played with
many other musical giants since they formed in 1972, including
Bob Dylan, David Bowie, and Aretha Franklin.

5. Europe

Swedish band Europe had a big influence on the heavy metal, hair-
band rock scene that was growing in the 1970s and 1980s. With hits
such as "Carrie" and "The Final Countdown" these rockers have
sold more than ten million albums worldwide and released a new
album, *Secret Society,* in 2006.

6. Kansas

The guitar-driven, boogie-rock sound of Kansas filled arenas and
stadiums at the height of their popularity. Hits such as "Dust in the
Wind" and "Carry on Wayward Son" made stars out of this Topeka-
based group in the late 1970s and early 1980s.

7. Sugarhill Gang

Named for the Sugar Hill section of Harlem, the Sugarhill Gang
was the first group to land a hip-hop song on *Billboard*'s Top
40 chart. The song was "Rapper's Delight" and it sold more than
eight million copies. Music hasn't been the same since.

8. Asia

Named for the vast continent, the supergroup Asia formed in
1981 and was made up of members of Yes; Emerson, Lake &
Palmer; King Crimson; and The Buggles. Known for their visually
graphic album covers, Asia topped the charts with early '80s hits
"Heat of the Moment" and "Don't Cry."

9. Backstreet Boys

Named after the Back Street Market, a shopping area in their hometown of Orlando, Florida, this mega-popular boy band took the world by storm in the late 1990s. With massive hits like "Quit Playin' Games (With My Heart)" and "I Want It That Way," the Backstreet Boys have sold more than 90 million albums worldwide.

10. All Saints

The lovely ladies of All Saints aren't saying that they're angels—with songs like "Bootie Call" and "I Know Where It's At," you probably could've guessed that. This UK girl group is named for All Saints Road, a street near the recording studio where several of the members got their start in the industry, singing backup vocals for various groups.

11. Bay City Rollers

In 1967, two brothers from Edinburgh, Scotland, formed a band called The Saxons, but they wanted a more American-sounding name, so they allegedly threw a dart at a map of the United States and when it landed on Bay City, Michigan, the Bay City Rollers were born. Known for boogie-worthy music that makes you want to take a spin around a roller rink, the Bay City Rollers reached the top of the U.S. charts in 1976 with their hit "Saturday Night."

17 Notable Super Bowl Halftime Shows

❉ ❉ ❉ ❉

1. Super Bowl XXV—1991............New Kids on the Block
2. Super Bowl XXVI—1992..........Gloria Estefan/Brian Boitano/ Dorothy Hamill
3. Super Bowl XXVII—1993.........Michael Jackson/3,500 local children
4. Super Bowl XXVIII—1994.......Clint Black/Tanya Tucker/ Travis Tritt/The Judds
5. Super Bowl XXIX—1995..........Tony Bennett/Patti LaBelle/Arturo Sandoval/Miami Sound Machine
6. Super Bowl XXX—1996............Diana Ross

12 One-Hit Wonders

✳ ✳ ✳ ✳

Who knows why an artist scores a hit once but never again. In some cases, the hit makers weren't even recording artists in the first place. Even if you weren't alive when some of these songs enjoyed their five minutes of fame, chances are you've heard them. Sing along as we remember these 12 one-hit wonders. *

1. "Harper Valley P.T.A." by Jeannie C. Riley (1968)

Better known as a country singer, Jeannie C. Riley became an overnight sensation with "Harper Valley P.T.A.," which topped both the pop and country charts. The song even spawned a variety show hosted by Riley in 1969, as well as a movie (1978) and television show (1981), both starring Barbara Eden.

2. "Spirit in the Sky" by Norman Greenbaum (1969)

Former Boston University coffeehouse musician Norman Greenbaum hit the top of the charts with "Spirit in the Sky." The record, which sold two million copies, soared to number three in the States and all the way to number one in the UK.

3. "Disco Duck" by Rick Dees (1976)

"Disco Duck," a satirical disco song by deejay Rick Dees, went all the way to number one in 1976. Dees may be a one-hit wonder as a recording artist, but other musical artists hope to gain his attention; he is known around the world for his Weekly Top 40 Countdown radio show. He was inducted into the Radio Hall of Fame in 1999 and even earned a star on Hollywood's Walk of Fame.

4. "Don't Give Up on Us Baby" by David Soul (1976)

In 1976, right in the middle of his hit TV show *Starsky & Hutch*, David Soul, aka "Hutch," traded his tough guy image for that of a sweet-voiced ballad singer and it paid off. "Don't Give Up on Us Baby" shot all the way to number one on U.S. charts. Afterward, he released several more albums that were much more popular in the UK than they were in the States. Today, Soul lives in England and works in theater.

5. "You Light Up My Life" by Debby Boone (1977)

Debby Boone, daughter of '50s icon Pat Boone, spent ten weeks on top of the charts with "You Light Up My Life." Who was she singing about? No mere mortal, it was God, according to Miss Boone. She may be a one-hit wonder on the pop charts, but Debby Boone has enjoyed a successful career as a stage actress and in the music biz with hits in both the country and Christian-music genres.

6. "Funkytown" by Lipps, Inc. (1980)

In 1980, a Minneapolis band named to poke fun at the concept of lip-synching spent four weeks at number one with their hit tune "Funkytown." The group had disbanded by 1983, but a few of the group's members lent their experience to Minneapolis's next big thing—Prince's band, The Revolution.

7. "Mickey" by Toni Basil (1982)

Singer/choreographer Toni Basil took this song all the way to number one on U.S. charts and number two in the UK. With its snappy beat, catchy tune, and peppy video, this '80s classic has become a favorite with cheerleaders.

8. "99 Luft Ballons" by Nena (1984)

This protest song by German artist Nena came along toward the end of the Cold War. Although versions in both German and English ("99 Red Balloons") were released in the States, the German version proved more popular, floating all the way to number two. However, Nena could not duplicate the song's success and has not had a hit single outside of Europe since.

9. "She's Like the Wind" by Patrick Swayze (1988)

Originally written for another movie, "She's Like the Wind" reached number three on *Billboard*'s Hot 100 after appearing in the blockbuster movie *Dirty Dancing* (starring Swayze and Jennifer Grey). The movie's sound track sold 11 million albums and remained on top of the charts for 18 weeks.

10. "Don't Worry, Be Happy" by Bobby McFerrin (1988)

From the album *Simple Pleasures,* this upbeat song was featured in the Tom Cruise movie *Cocktail.* The song stayed at number one for two weeks, making it the first a cappella song to top the *Billboard* Hot 100 chart. McFerrin continues to enjoy a successful career as a jazz musician and "Don't Worry, Be Happy" lives on in television and movies.

11. "I'm Too Sexy" by Right Said Fred (1992)

British brothers Fred and Richard Fairbrass and their friend Rob Manzoli wrote this "corker" of a song over a pot of tea. Without the help of a record company, they got the song played on top radio stations, and it became a hit in 30 countries, going all the way to number one in the United States. The group may be off the radar in the States, but they are still releasing albums and touring in Europe.

12. "Macarena" by Los del Rio (1996)

In 1996, Spanish group Los del Rio occupied the top of the U.S. charts for 14 weeks with their catchy tune "Macarena," which had sold 11 million copies by 1997. The song even had its own dance, sparking a trend amongst the line-dancing set. VH1 ranks this song number one on their list of 100 Greatest One-hit Wonders.

Artists deemed one-hit wonders in the United States based on song positions on Billboard *magazine's Hot 100 chart.*

ROMANCING THE STONES
19 of The Rolling Stones' Greatest Hits

✳ ✳ ✳ ✳

It all began in 1962 when a group of fresh-faced hipsters by the name of the Rollin' Stones performed at the Marquee in London. Nearly five decades, one added g, and countless groupies later, The Rolling Stones are still going strong. Here are 19 of their greatest hits.

1. "Time Is on My Side" (1964)

"Time Is on My Side," which appeared on the album *12×5*, is a cover of a song written by Jerry Ragovoy (Norman Meade) and first recorded by jazz trombonist Kai Winding and his Orchestra in 1963. It was the Stones' first top ten hit in the United States, peaking at number six and spending 13 weeks on the charts.

2. "(I Can't Get No) Satisfaction" (1965)

"(I Can't Get No) Satisfaction," from the *Out of Our Heads* album, was the band's first number one single in the United States and is arguably the Stones' best-known song, ranking number two on *Rolling Stone* magazine's 500 Greatest Songs of All Time. Mick Jagger once said of the song, "It was the song that really made The Rolling Stones, changed us from just another band into a huge, monster band."

3. "Get Off of My Cloud" (1965)

"Get Off of My Cloud," from the album *December's Children (And Everybody's)*, was written by Mick Jagger and Keith Richards. Although lyrically defiant and acrimonious, the song was penned in response to the band's instant popularity following "(I Can't Get No) Satisfaction."

4. "As Tears Go By" (1965)

"As Tears Go By," also from *December's Children (And Everybody's)*, was written by Jagger and Richards, but was made famous by Marianne Faithfull, who released a recording of the song in 1964 to rave reviews. The Stones performed their version of the song during their 1966 appearance on *The Ed Sullivan Show,* one of six visits the band made to that show.

5. "19th Nervous Breakdown" (1966)

In "19th Nervous Breakdown," from *Big Hits (High Tide and Green Grass)*, the Stones direct their ire at a spoiled young woman who is unable to appreciate life. The song went to number one in the UK and number two in the States.

6. "Paint It, Black" (1966)

"Paint It, Black," which appeared on the album *Aftermath,* is written from the viewpoint of a depressed man who wants to paint everything black to match his dour mood. "Paint It, Black" is among the band's most covered songs, including versions by Duran Duran, Judas Priest, Led Zeppelin, R.E.M., Rush, U2, and the London Symphony Orchestra.

7. "Mother's Little Helper" (1966)

"Mother's Little Helper" relies on a bit of metaphoric magic. The "helper" here does not refer to a cooperative little sprite running around mom's kitchen, but rather a "little yellow pill," as in: "Mother needs something today to calm her down/And though she's not really ill, there's a little yellow pill...." Things don't end happily for this mother, as the song ends: "No more running to the shelter of a mother's little helper/They just helped you on your way through your busy dying day."

8. "Ruby Tuesday" (1967)

"Ruby Tuesday," which appeared on *Between the Buttons,* is a favorite among Stones fans. Some say the lyrics were inspired by a free-spirited groupie that Keith Richards knew. True or not, the song reached number one in the States and number three in the UK.

9. "Jumpin' Jack Flash" (1968)

"Jumpin' Jack Flash," from the album *Through the Past Darkly (Big Hits Vol. 2),* has the distinct honor of being the only Rolling Stones song to inspire the title of a Whoopi Goldberg movie. The song reached number one in the UK and number three in the States, and also ranked number two on *Q* magazine's list of the 100 Greatest Guitar Tracks.

10. "Honky Tonk Women" (1969)

"Honky Tonk Women," also from *Through the Past Darkly (Big Hits Vol. 2),* is widely thought to be an homage to a prostitute. Aside from being one of the Stones' most popular songs, it also holds the distinction of being released in England the day after Stones founding member Brian Jones was found dead in his swimming pool.

11. "Brown Sugar" (1971)

"Brown Sugar" appeared on the *Sticky Fingers* album, but the Stones debuted the song live at Altamont, the 1969 free rock concert featuring a slew of hot bands and famously marred by violence, including the stabbing death of a fan during the Stones set. The meaning of the song is debatable, but some suggest it's about an interracial relationship or heroin addiction.

12. "Angie" (1973)

"Angie," from *Goats Head Soup,* is clearly about lost love. What's not clear is who did the loving—or the losing. Some say the lyrics are about David Bowie's wife, Angela, with whom Mick Jagger was close. Others think the song is about Keith Richards' lover, Anita Pallenberg, or possibly their daughter, Angela, who was born in 1972.

13. "Miss You" (1978)

"Miss You" appeared on the album *Some Girls.* The song, which reached number one in the States and number three in the UK, was reportedly inspired by Mick Jagger's deteriorating marriage with his first wife, Bianca.

14. "Beast of Burden" (1978)

"Beast of Burden" is also from the album *Some Girls.* In their 2003 book, *According to the Rolling Stones,* Keith Richards claims he wrote the song as a thank you to Mick for "shouldering the burden" in the studio while he was getting help for his drug habit.

15. "Emotional Rescue" (1980)

"Emotional Rescue," from the album of the same name, earned a mixed reception. While the song was an immediate commercial hit, soaring to number three on U.S. charts, critics and die-hard fans were less than enthusiastic about its disco-infused sound.

16. "Start Me Up" (1981)

"Start Me Up," off *Tattoo You,* often opens the Stones' live shows and was also used by Microsoft to kick-start its Windows 95 marketing campaign. Portions of the song were recorded in the bathroom of New York City's Power Station recording studio, famous for its "bathroom reverb" sound.

17. "Waiting on a Friend" (1981)

"Waiting on a Friend," also from *Tattoo You,* is a bit of a departure from the Stones' usual content. The relationships in the band supposedly inspired Jagger's lyrics, which discuss giving up women and booze for those friendships. Is that you, Mick?

18. "Undercover of the Night" (1983)

Another top ten song for the Stones, "Undercover of the Night" appeared on the album *Undercover.* It is one of only a few Stones songs with a political bent, tackling corruption in Central and South

America, with lyrics such as: "Hear the screams of Center 42/Loud enough to bust your brains out/The opposition's tongue is cut in two/Keep off the street 'cause you're in danger."

19. "Mixed Emotions" (1989)

"Mixed Emotions," appeared on the Stones' comeback album, *Steel Wheels,* released after Jagger and Richards had spent a few years working on their solo careers. The song, which reached number five on U.S. charts, is the Stones' last U.S. top ten single to date.

14 Notable Grand Ole Opry Performers

✳ ✳ ✳ ✳

Created in 1925 by station manager George Dewey Hay, the Grand Ole Opry began as a weekly radio program that featured traditional "country" music, including folk songs and classic mountain tunes. In 1939, the show moved to NBC radio where it reached tens of thousands of listeners across the country. During the 1950s, the Opry was one of the nation's favorite radio programs, and with every song played on the Opry stage broadcast to America, Nashville solidified its spot as the country music capital of the world. Here are a few major stars of the Opry.

1. Hank Williams

By the mid-1930s, Hank Williams's legendary music career was well underway and would astonish everyone for years to come. Despite 12 number one songs, including "Hey Good Lookin'," Williams battled alcoholism, which almost cost him a chance at the Opry. Producers couldn't bear not to feature Williams, however, and the country star joined the cast in 1949. He was called back for six encores the first time he performed. Williams died at age 29, from a heart attack, possibly brought on by drug and alcohol abuse.

2. Patsy Cline

From humble beginnings came Patsy Cline, one of the most recognizable voices in country music. In 1957, Cline made her first national television appearance on *Arthur Godfrey's Talent Scouts,* singing what would become her first hit song, "Walkin' After Midnight." Three years later, Cline achieved a lifelong dream when she became a member of the Opry. Tragically, however, Cline died in a plane crash in 1963, just five years after her popularity snowballed.

3. Minnie Pearl

An upper-class girl from Tennessee, Sarah Colley decided to skip the debutante balls and formal education to pursue the vaudeville circuit. Colley created the character of Minnie Pearl after witnessing the brassy demeanor of a mountain lady during an amateur comedy show in 1936. When she joined the Opry in 1940, 28-year-old Colley had no idea she would spend the next 50 years in show business performing as Minnie Pearl and wearing her trademark straw hat with the $1.98 price tag still attached.

4. Dolly Parton

As a young girl growing up in the heart of Appalachia, Dolly Parton sang like a bird and even wrote her own songs modeled after the folksy tunes she learned from her parents. After appearing on a televised talent show, she was booked at the Opry in 1959 at the tender age of 13. Parton recorded steadily during the 1960s, but it wasn't until 1967 that her career skyrocketed when she was cast on the *Porter Wagoner Show.* Parton has recently returned to her roots, recording several critically-acclaimed bluegrass albums.

5. Garth Brooks

Not one, not two, not three, but *four* of Garth Brooks's country records have each exceeded sales of ten million—he's the only male country star in history to achieve such a feat. Though he's currently retired, Brooks has sold more than 100 million records worldwide, and he even has a star on the Hollywood Walk of Fame for his work in movies and television. Hits such as "Friends in Low Places" have won him 2 Grammys, 11 Country Music Association Awards, and 24 Billboard Music Awards, but he claims that his membership in the Opry is his proudest career accomplishment.

6. Roy Acuff

In the 1930s and 1940s, no one sold more country music records than Roy Acuff. In 1938, this warbler became a regular performer and emcee on the Grand Ole Opry radio program. Known as the "King of Country Music," his performance of "The Great Speckled Bird" changed the Opry forever—until then singers usually played second fiddle to the band.

7. Deford Bailey

When Deford Bailey was growing up in rural Tennessee, his parents gave him a harmonica, and history was made. Bailey's ability with the "harp" was unrivaled, and after he moved to Nashville, a few lucky breaks got him gigs playing on radio shows. In 1927, those breaks helped him land a spot on the Opry—without a formal audition. Bailey was the first African-American included in the Opry cast and was one of the highest-paid stars of his day.

8. Loretta Lynn

Everyone's favorite "coal miner's daughter" joined the Opry after getting married, having four kids, and signing a recording contract—all before age 25. Lynn and her husband Mooney distributed (largely by hand) her first single, "I'm a Honky Tonk Girl," and through word of mouth and steady airplay, the single reached number 14 on the country charts in 1960. That impressive debut got Lynn her first appearance at the Opry that year, which boosted her career to the next level. She would go on to have dozens of megahits by blending her country girl image with some potent subject matter, such as birth control and deadbeat husbands. *Coal Miner's Daughter,* Lynn's autobiography, was made into an Academy Award-winning movie in 1980.

9. Johnny Cash

The people on this list are all titans of the country music world, but few are as well known as Johnny Cash, who has a place in both the Country Music Hall of Fame and the Rock and Roll Hall of Fame. The "Man in Black" joined the Opry in 1956 following the success of his hit single "I Walk the Line." But he only stuck around for two years. Though Cash would battle addiction, a bitter divorce, and several career missteps, his popularity surged in the 1960s and again in the 1990s before his death in 2003.

10. Willie Nelson

Rabble-rouser, political activist, gifted musician, and chart-topper Willie Nelson is probably one of the more controversial figures to grace the Opry stage and the country music scene. But his outspoken nature doesn't eclipse his musical ambition or talent. Between 1962 and 1993, Nelson racked up 20 number one hits, and 114 singles made it to the country and/or pop charts. A tireless advocate for the American farmer, the seventy-something Nelson has performed all over the world and recorded countless songs both on his own and with a dazzling lineup of collaborators, including Patsy Cline, Johnny Cash, and Waylon Jennings.

11. The Carter Family

Known as the First Family of Country Music, the Carter Family recorded more than 300 classic country songs that embodied the simple lyrics and harmonies that continue to define the genre. Various members of the family came and went in several incarnations of the group, and by the time the Carters got to the Opry around 1946, the now all-female group was billed as Mother Maybelle and the Carter Sisters. June Carter later married Johnny Cash and cowrote some of his biggest hits, including "Ring of Fire." Pete Seeger, Woody Guthrie, and Bob Dylan have all cited the Carter Family as influences in their careers and have covered Carter Family tunes.

12. "Uncle Dave" Macon

One of the first stars of the Opry, David Harrison Macon was one of the major catalysts behind country music's popularity. Southern folk music from the late 1800s and early 1900s might not have made the leap to radio, stage, and television had it not been for the magnetic quality of Uncle Dave and his performances. Macon played the banjo and sang at the Opry—which he had a hand in establishing—for more than 25 years. He was a workhorse of a musician and influenced players for decades to come.

13. Grandpa Jones

It's a good thing Louis Marshall Jones was a successful country artist for more than seven decades—it gave him time to grow into the nickname he was given at age 22 after being told he sounded "old and grouchy" on radio shows. The singer and banjo player, who was known as a country music purist, promised fans that he would "keep it country" while other styles influenced the genre. Jones' witty repartee made him a star on the TV show *Hee Haw,* and he was one of the few stars to celebrate 50 years on the Opry stage.

14. Elvis Presley

The most famous and successful name in modern music didn't actually fare very well when he appeared at the Opry in 1954. It was Presley's only performance at the Opry—the audience wasn't impressed by his raucous rockabilly style. An angry Presley left after the show, swearing never to return. Who could blame him? The Opry manager at the time told him to leave music forever and go back to driving a truck. Obviously, Elvis didn't take his advice and went on to break every music industry record there was.

9 Fictional Bands with Hit Songs

✳ ✳ ✳ ✳

Reaching the top ten or even the top 40 on the music charts is something that most bands can only dream of achieving after years of hard work. But the bands on this list didn't have to agonize over that because they weren't real bands in the first place. Check out these fictional hit makers, but be prepared to get at least one song stuck in your head.

1. The Chipmunks

The Chipmunks, a fictitious music group created by Ross Bagdasarian in 1958, consisted of three singing chipmunks: Alvin, the troublemaking frontman; Simon, the intellectual; and Theodore, the sweetheart. The trio was managed by their human "father," Dave Seville. In reality, Dave Seville was the stage name of Bagdasarian, who electronically sped up his own voice to create the higher-pitched squeaky voices of the chipmunks. This process was so new and innovative that it earned a Grammy for engineering in 1959. The Chipmunks released a number of albums and singles, with "The Chipmunk Song (Christmas Don't Be Late)" spending four weeks atop the charts in the late 1950s. They have also starred in their own cartoon series and animated films over the years.

2. The Monkees

Hey, hey…were the Monkees a real band or a fake? In 1965, auditions were held for "folk & roll musicians" to play band members on a new TV show called *The Monkees*. Actors Davy Jones and Micky Dolenz, and musicians Mike Nesmith and Peter Tork were chosen as The Monkees. The show won two Emmy Awards in 1967, and the band was so successful that they went on tour—with the Jimi Hendrix Experience as their opening act! The Monkees reached the top of the charts three times with hits "I'm a Believer," "Last Train to Clarksville," and "Daydream Believer." Although the show was canceled in 1968 and the band officially broke up in 1970, they have continued to record and tour with some or all of the original members.

3. The Archies

Stars of the comic strip *Archie* and the Saturday morning cartoon *The Archie Show,* The Archies were a garage band founded in 1968. Band members included Archie, Reggie, Jughead, Betty, and Veronica. Producer Don Kirshner gathered a group of studio musicians to perform the group's songs, the most popular being "Sugar, Sugar," which topped the pop charts in 1969 and was named *Billboard* magazine's song of the year, the only time a fictional band has ever claimed that honor. The Archies also reached the top 40 with "Who's Your Baby?," "Bang-Shang-A-Lang," and "Jingle Jangle."

4. The Kids from The Brady Bunch

Marcia, Marcia, Marcia...is that you singing? The music group known as The Kids from The Brady Bunch was made up of—who else—the young cast members from the mega-popular sitcom that originally aired from 1969 to 1974. During the show's run, the cast recorded several albums, including *Christmas With the Brady Bunch* and *Meet the Brady Bunch*. None of the songs topped the charts, but some fan favorites include, "Sunshine Day," "Time to Change," and "Keep On." All of the kids sang on the albums, and Barry Williams (Greg) and Maureen McCormick (Marcia) both pursued careers in music after the show ended.

5. The Partridge Family

The Partridge Family, a popular television show that aired in the early 1970s, focused on Shirley Partridge (Shirley Jones) and her brood of five children, who suddenly find themselves with a hit song. The show chronicled the family's life on the road performing gigs, as well as their home life. To promote the show, producers released a series of albums by The Partridge Family. Although the music was originally created by studio musicians with Jones singing backup, David Cassidy, who played eldest son Keith, quickly convinced producers to let him sing lead vocals. The show and the band became overnight sensations, making Cassidy a teen idol. The group's most popular hits included the show's theme song "C'Mon, Get Happy," "I Woke Up in Love This Morning," and "I Think I Love You," which spent three weeks at number one in late 1970.

6. The Blues Brothers

In April 1978, *Saturday Night Live* cast members John Belushi and Dan Aykroyd appeared on the show as The Blues Brothers. Dressed in black suits, fedoras, and sunglasses, Belushi sang lead vocals as "Joliet" Jake Blues while Aykroyd portrayed Elwood Blues, singing backup and playing harmonica. Their first album, *Briefcase Full of Blues,* went double platinum and reached number one on *Billboard*'s album chart. The record produced two top 40 hits with covers of Sam and Dave's "Soul Man" and The Chips' "Rubber

Biscuit." The Blues Brothers went on tour, even opening for The Grateful Dead in December 1978. In 1980, Belushi and Aykroyd starred in *The Blues Brothers,* a feature film that chronicled the life of the fictional duo. Belushi died in 1982, but The Blues Brothers live on with Jim Belushi (John's brother), John Goodman, and other guests stepping in to fill his shoes.

7. The Heights

The Heights, a TV show about a rock 'n' roll band of the same name, aired for only one season in 1992. By day, the characters worked blue-collar jobs, but at night they were The Heights. The series depicted the struggles of the band, as well as the romances among the characters, and a new song was performed each week. The show's theme song, "How Do You Talk to an Angel," which featured actor Jamie Walters on lead vocals, topped the charts in mid-November. Ironically, the show was canceled a week later.

8. The Wonders

When your band's name is The Oneders (pronounced The Wonders) and everybody calls you The Oh-nee-ders, it's time to change your name—even if you're just a fictional band. That's exactly what happened in the 1996 hit movie *That Thing You Do!,* written and directed by Tom Hanks. The film about a one-hit wonder band in the '60s starred Hanks, as well as Tom Everett Scott, Steve Zahn, and Liv Tyler. The band's hit song "That Thing You Do!" went as high as number 18 on *Billboard* charts and was nominated for an Oscar for Best Original Song. In addition, the sound track reached number 21 on *Billboard*'s album chart.

9. Gorillaz

Guinness World Records named Gorillaz the most successful virtual band after its 2001 debut album, *Gorillaz,* sold more than six million copies. Created in 1999 by Damon Albarn and Jamie Hewlett, this alternative rock band is made up of four animated characters: 2D, Murdoc, Noodle, and Russel. The band's second album, *Demon Days,* received five Grammy nominations in 2006, including a victory for Best Pop Collaboration with Vocals.

YOU USED TO BE CALLED *WHAT*?

Former Names of 17 Famous Bands

❋ ❋ ❋ ❋

Most famous bands had other names before they made it big. See if you can match the former names to these famous bands.

1. Cheap Trick	a. Angel and the Snake
2. U2	b. Atomic Mass
3. The Beatles	c. Tea Set
4. Styx	d. The Detours, The High Numbers
5. Queen	e. Tom and Jerry
6. Led Zeppelin	f. Feedback, The Hype
7. The Beach Boys	g. Golden Gate Rhythm Section
8. Green Day	h. Smile
9. KISS	i. Unique Attraction
10. The Who	j. Fuse
11. Def Leppard	k. The Tradewinds
12. Pink Floyd	l. Sweet Children
13. Boyz II Men	m. Mookie Blaylock
14. Blondie	n. The New Yardbirds
15. Simon and Garfunkel	o. Wicked Lester
16. Journey	p. The Pendletones
17. Pearl Jam	q. The Quarrymen, Johnny and the Moondogs

Answers: 1. *j;* 2. *f;* 3. *q;* 4. *k;* 5. *h;* 6. *n;* 7. *p;* 8. *l;* 9. *o;* 10. *d;* 11. *b;* 12. *c;* 13. *i;* 14. *a;* 15. *e;* 16. *g;* 17. *m*

IT'S A MADGE, MADGE WORLD
Madonna's 25 Most Popular Songs

❋ ❋ ❋ ❋

This fiery, petite Italian-American was born in 1958 in Bay City,
Michigan. From the start, Madonna Louise Veronica Ciccone
had big dreams, and at 19 she moved to New York City where she
began to make a name for herself as a singer and dancer.
Selling more than 200 million albums in a career that has spanned
more than two decades, "Madge" has stayed on top by constantly
reinventing herself. Though many disagree with some of her
artistic choices, the numbers don't lie: Billboard *magazine*
reports that Madonna's 2006 Confessions tour was the most
successful concert tour by a female artist in history.
Here are 25 of the biggest hits that put her on top.

1. "Holiday" (1983)

From her self-titled debut album, "Holiday" was the first of
Madonna's songs to make *Billboard's* Hot 100, peaking at number
16. It is now one of her signature songs.

2. "Borderline" (1984)

Madge's second single broke the top ten on U.S. charts, which was
impressive for a newcomer. In this video, look for a very young
John Leguizamo, who plays a friend of Madonna's boyfriend.

3. "Like a Virgin" (1984)

This song was Madonna's first number one on the *Billboard* Hot
100, probably due to her legendary appearance at the first ever
MTV Video Music Awards. Rolling around in a wedding dress,
Madonna sang this song and cemented a mutually beneficial relationship with music videos.

4. "Material Girl" (1985)

This song, which earned Madonna the moniker "the Material Girl,"
painted the singer as a girl who would rather have a rich boyfriend

than a love-struck one, although it was meant to parody the commercialism and greed of the '80s. "Material Girl," the second single from Madonna's *Like a Virgin* album, reached number two on U.S. charts, with the video imitating Marilyn Monroe's famous musical number "Diamonds Are a Girl's Best Friend."

5. "Crazy for You" (1985)

From the sound track of the film *VisionQuest,* "Crazy for You" was Madonna's second number one song. Madonna makes a cameo in the movie, belting out this tune in a nightclub scene.

6. "Into the Groove" (1985)

Coinciding with her role in the film *Desperately Seeking Susan,* this popular tune was remixed for use in a 2003 Gap ad starring Madonna and rapper Missy Elliott.

7. "Live to Tell" (1986)

Written and produced by Madonna and longtime collaborator Patrick Leonard, "Live to Tell" is the story of a woman facing a difficult decision. The song was written for the movie *At Close Range,* starring Sean Penn, Madonna's husband at the time. With this number one ballad, Madonna emerged as more mature, abandoning the street urchin look for that of a grown-up.

8. "Papa Don't Preach" (1986)

Another one of Madonna's more serious ballads, the song tells the story of a pregnant teen who has decided to have her child and raise it with her boyfriend. You'd think such a heavy topic wouldn't fly as a pop song, but this was another number one for Madonna in the summer of '86. Groups that had once condemned Madge now commended her for the song's antiabortion theme, although some were concerned that it glorified teen pregnancy.

9. "Open Your Heart" (1986)

In classic Madonna style, "Open Your Heart" was buoyed by a risqué video. In it, Madonna plays an exotic dancer who performs for a room that includes an underage boy. Plenty of people were outraged, but the song was another number one hit.

10. "Who's That Girl" (1987)

Nominated for a Grammy, "Who's That Girl" sped to number one in the summer of '87 when it appeared in the movie of the same name, starring Madonna. The movie didn't do so well, but the sound track went platinum. Other artists are included on the sound track, but this song and another Madonna hit, "Causing a Commotion," were the reasons most people picked it up.

11. "Like a Prayer" (1989)

"Like a Prayer," with its dramatic lyrics and gospel choir backup, is undoubtedly one of Madonna's biggest hits of all time. But the video, complete with burning crosses and Madonna making out with a black saint, was just a tad controversial. Pepsi had signed a deal to use Madonna and the song for a soda commercial, but they backed out when they saw the scandalous video. Still, the song topped the charts in every major music market in the world, and the video won an MTV Viewers Choice Award, sponsored by—you guessed it—Pepsi!

12. "Express Yourself" (1989)

A call to women everywhere to stick up for what they want, "Express Yourself" was a top-five hit around the world, peaking at number two in the States. The notorious conical bra made its debut in the video. Designed by Jean-Paul Gautier, the pink corset with the pointy cups was worn under a black suit in the video and throughout Madonna's Blonde Ambition Tour, as well.

13. "Cherish" (1989)

The third hit single off the *Like a Prayer* juggernaut, "Cherish" is a song that finds Madonna in an innocent frame of mind, singing about the joys of true love. The song reached number two in the States, her seventeenth single to reach the top ten on U.S. charts.

14. "Vogue" (1990)

There have been a few megahit dance crazes in American pop music history: The Twist, The Macarena, and Vogue to name a few. This song, from the *Dick Tracy: I'm Breathless* sound track, featured instructions on "vogue" dancing, an expressive style of dance popular in the underground gay clubs of New York City. Leave it to Madonna to make it a number one song.

15. "Justify My Love" (1990)

Madge teamed up with songwriters Ingrid Chavez and Lenny Kravitz to pen this steamy song, which became Madonna's ninth number one in the States. The video was so racy, MTV banned it! As a result, the "Justify My Love" video was the first video single ever released and it immediately sold out in stores everywhere.

16. "This Used to Be My Playground" (1992)

Madonna's tenth single to reach number one, this ballad was featured in the movie *A League of Their Own.* Madonna's performance in the movie was also well received by critics. The song wasn't included on the sound track, but it appeared on Madonna's ballad compilation, *Something to Remember,* released in 1995.

17. "Take a Bow" (1994)

Following the release of her controversial, best-selling book *Sex* (1992), Madonna experienced sagging chart positions. But "Take a Bow" changed all that. This farewell-to-love tune was a record breaker for Madonna, spending seven weeks at number one on U.S. charts.

18. "Frozen" (1998)

This single, which featured dark themes, eastern instruments, and techno beats, was a huge hit for the recently reinvented Madonna. "Frozen" reached number one or two in most major music markets, foretelling the enormous success of *Ray of Light,* the album on which it was featured.

19. "Ray of Light" (1998)

This techo-infused dance hit broke a record for Madonna, selling 73,000 singles in the first week of its release. The second track from her Grammy Award-winning album of the same name, "Ray of Light" was a massive club hit that received major remix attention from the most in-demand deejays. The single reached the top ten on charts the world over, peaking at number five in the States.

20. "Beautiful Stranger" (1999)

Another song-from-a-movie hit for Madonna, this bouncy tune was penned by Madonna and *Ray of Light* album coproducer William Orbit for the second Austin Powers movie, *Austin Powers: The Spy Who Shagged Me.* The song reached number 19 in the United States—even though it was never officially released—and it garnered the singer another Grammy.

21. "American Pie" (2000)

Don McLean's classic tune got the Madonna treatment for inclusion in the movie *The Next Best Thing.* The movie flopped, but the song did well—reaching number one in the UK, Canada, and Australia, among others. Oddly enough, although the song wasn't released in the States, it reached number 29 off airplay alone.

22. "Music" (2000)

"Music," Madonna's twelfth single to top U.S. charts was in the running for a Grammy for Record of the Year, but lost to "Beautiful Day" by U2. The video featured Madonna (five months pregnant at the time) and comedy star Sacha Baron Cohen. "Music" has been featured in all of Madonna's shows since its release.

23. "Don't Tell Me" (2000)

When "Don't Tell Me" went gold, Madonna tied The Beatles for second place for the most gold, platinum, or multiplatinum singles—a total of 24—trailing Elvis, who's way ahead of the pack with a whopping 52. "Don't Tell Me" made it to number four on U.S. charts, and the video shows Madge hanging out with cowboys and riding a mechanical bull. Yee-haw!

24. "American Life" (2003)

The first single off her highly criticized album of the same name, "American Life" lambasted the materialistic culture of America and the lack of satisfaction in the face of so much abundance. But

Americans weren't ready for a political statement from the woman who used to sing about the joys of sex. This single reached the top ten (and often number one spot) in much of Europe, as well as Canada and Japan, but only made it to number 37 on U.S. charts.

25. "Hung Up" (2006)

The first single off her album *Confessions on a Dance Floor,* "Hung Up" included an infectious sample from superstar dance group ABBA. A disco-fied Madonna emerged in this dance hit, signaling the return of the megastar after lukewarm album sales for *American Life.* "Hung Up" topped the charts in an unprecedented 41 countries, but peaked at number seven in the States.

IF YOU REMEMBER BEING AT WOODSTOCK, YOU PROBABLY WEREN'T THERE
All 32 Bands that Performed at Woodstock

✳ ✳ ✳ ✳

The Woodstock Music and Art Festival was held August 15–18, 1969, not in Woodstock but in Bethel, New York, 40 miles away. Woodstock was supposed to host the festival, but when rumors spread that attendance could reach a million people, the city backed out. Farmer Max Yasgur saved the concert by hosting the more than 500,000 attendees in his alfalfa field. With the huge crowd, there were shortages of food, water, and restrooms, but most revelers still enjoyed some of the best musical acts of the era. Here's the lineup from that fateful weekend.

1. Richie Havens

Richie Havens, a Greenwich Village folksinger, got the concert started around 5:00 P.M. on Friday, August 15. He played eight songs, including the memorable "Motherless Child," which he ended with the word *freedom* sung over and over. After Woodstock, Havens continued to tour and release albums, and in 1993 he performed at the inauguration ceremonies for President Bill Clinton.

2. Country Joe McDonald

Country Joe McDonald made an unscheduled appearance at Woodstock on Friday evening without his band, The Fish. McDonald's solo set included "I Find Myself Missing You," "I-Feel-Like-I'm-Fixin'-to-Die Rag," and the "Fish Cheer," a song where he usually spelled out the word *fish* with the audience, but at Woodstock he spelled another four-letter f-word instead.

3. John Sebastian

John Sebastian is best known as a founder of The Lovin' Spoonful, members of the Rock and Roll Hall of Fame. Sebastian wasn't scheduled to appear at the festival, but he played five songs, including "I Had a Dream" and "Rainbows Over Your Blues." In 1976, he had a number one single with the TV theme song *Welcome Back, Kotter.* Sebastian continues to record and tour and promotes a collection of the '60s greatest hits via infomercial.

4. Sweetwater

After three solo artists, Sweetwater—who pioneered the psychedelic rock/classical fusion style later picked up by Jefferson Airplane—was the first band to perform at the festival. They played eight songs, including "What's Wrong," "My Crystal Spider," and "Why Oh Why." After Woodstock, Sweetwater disbanded when lead singer Nansi Nevins was badly injured in a car accident.

5. The Incredible String Band

The Incredible String Band was a Scottish acoustic band that formed in the early '60s and later switched to psychedelic folk music. Their set of four songs included "The Letter" and "This Moment." The Incredible String Band broke up in 1974, reunited in 2003, and broke up again in 2006.

6. Bert Sommer

Bert Sommer was a folksinger and former member of the baroque-pop group the Left Banke. Sommer played ten songs at the festival, including "Jennifer," "Jeanette," and "America." He continued to record and perform until his death in 1990.

7. Tim Hardin

Tim Hardin was also a Greenwich Village folk musician and composer. During his hour-long set, Hardin performed only two songs—"Misty Roses" and "If I Were a Carpenter," which was a top ten hit for Bobby Darin. Hardin continued to record until 1973 and died of a heroin and morphine overdose in 1980.

8. Ravi Shankar

Bengali-Indian musician and composer Ravi Shankar is best known for teaching George Harrison to play the sitar. His work with Harrison and other rock stars landed him a gig at Woodstock, where he played five songs in the rain, including "Tabla Solo in Jhaptal." Today, his daughters Anoushka Shankar and Norah Jones are both successful musicians.

9. Melanie

Melanie, born Melanie Anne Safka-Schekeryk, made her first recording at age five and was successful in Europe with "Beautiful People," one of the two songs she performed at Woodstock. She later recorded "Lay Down (Candles in the Rain)" after being inspired by the Woodstock audience lighting candles during her set.

10. Arlo Guthrie

Prior to Woodstock, Arlo Guthrie—the son of folksinger and composer Woody Guthrie—was best known for his 18-minute-long song (and subsequent film) "Alice's Restaurant," which describes how he avoided the draft. Arlo played three songs at Woodstock, "Coming into Los Angeles," "Walking Down the Line," and "Amazing Grace." He continues to record and performed his song "City of New Orleans" at fund-raisers for victims of Hurricane Katrina.

11. Joan Báez

Day one at Woodstock closed with Joan Báez, probably the most famous folk and protest singer to perform at the festival. Báez performed 12 songs at Woodstock, including her hits "Joe Hill" and "Sweet Sir Galahad" and classics such as "Swing Low Sweet Chariot" and "We Shall Overcome." After more than 50 years in the music biz, Báez continues to record and perform songs about non-violence, civil and human rights, and the environment.

12. Quill

Day two at Woodstock kicked off around noon with the Boston band Quill. They had opened for several notable artists, including The Who, Sly & the Family Stone, The Grateful Dead, and Janis Joplin. At Woodstock, Quill played four songs, including "They Live the Life" and "Waitin' for You." After Woodstock, Quill released its first album, which fizzled, and the band broke up in 1970.

13. The Keef Hartley Band

The Keef Hartley Band, which mixed elements of jazz, blues, and rock, was one of the few British bands to play at Woodstock. Keef Hartley's career took off when he replaced Ringo Starr as the drummer for Rory Storm and The Hurricanes when Ringo joined The Beatles. At Woodstock, the band played eight songs, including "Spanish Fly" and "Rock Me Baby." Hartley recorded until the mid-1970s, and today he occasionally plays with John Mayall.

14. Santana

The career of Latin rock guitarist Carlos Santana got a major boost when concert producer Bill Graham convinced Woodstock promoters to book the band, even though they hadn't yet released an album. The band played seven songs, including "Waiting," "Jingo," and the 11-minute instrumental "Soul Sacrifice," which was considered a highlight of the festival. Although the 1970 album *Abraxas* reached number one on the album charts and sold more than four million copies, Carlos Santana wouldn't duplicate this success until the 1999 release of *Supernatural,* a collaboration with Eric Clapton, Wyclef Jean, and other artists. The album garnered nine Grammy Awards, including Album of the Year and Record of the Year for the song "Smooth" with Rob Thomas.

15. Canned Heat

Blues-rock/boogie band Canned Heat performed four songs at Woodstock, including "Goin' Up the Country" and "Let's Work

Together." In 1970, they brought in blues singer and guitarist John Lee Hooker to record the double album, "Hooker 'n' Heat." While many of the original members have died, Canned Heat has replaced them and continues to perform and record.

16. Mountain

The rock band Mountain was playing only its fourth live gig when it performed 13 songs at Woodstock, including "Stormy Monday," "Waiting to Take You Away," and "Theme for an Imaginary Western." Mountain broke up and re-formed a number of times after Woodstock and is currently back together and performing, but without founding member Felix Pappalardi, who was shot and killed by his wife on April 17, 1983.

17. Janis Joplin

Before her death from a heroin overdose in 1970, Janis Joplin made a huge impact on rock music with four albums and memorable performances. At Woodstock, she gave a spirited execution of ten songs including "To Love Somebody," "Try (Just a Little Bit Harder)," and "Piece of My Heart." Her biggest-selling album *Pearl*, released posthumously in 1971, featured her hit single "Me and Bobby McGee" and the a cappella song "Mercedes Benz."

18. Sly & the Family Stone

One of the first racially integrated bands, San Francisco's Sly & the Family Stone combined soul, funk, and psychedelia in its music. They played eight songs at Woodstock, including "Dance to the Music," "Stand!," "Everyday People," and "I Want to Take You Higher." Woodstock made the band popular, but Sly Stone's drug use brought them down. When the band was inducted into the Rock and Roll Hall of Fame in 1993, many of the founding members performed, but Sly, in a surprise appearance, accepted his award and disappeared. Then, during a Sly & the Family Stone tribute at the 2006 Grammy Awards, Sly joined the band in the middle of "I Want to Take You Higher," but left the stage before the song ended.

19. The Grateful Dead

The Grateful Dead was known for performing long live jams of their combination of rock, folk, bluegrass, blues, country, jazz, psychedelia, and gospel. Formed in San Francisco in 1965 by guitarist Jerry Garcia, The Grateful Dead performed four songs at Woodstock: "St. Stephen," "Mama Tried," "Dark Star/High Time," and "Turn on Your Love Light." The Grateful Dead continued to tour regularly for its "Deadhead" followers until Jerry Garcia died in August 1995. The remaining members disbanded, but later reunited to form The Other Ones and in 2003 renamed themselves The Dead.

20. Creedence Clearwater Revival

Heavily influenced by the swamp blues music that came out of Louisiana in the late '50s and early '60s, Creedence Clearwater Revival formed in the San Francisco Bay area in 1959. They hit their peak in early 1969, just in time for Woodstock. At the festival, they performed an 11-song set that included "Bad Moon Rising" and "Proud Mary." Their performance was not included in the Woodstock film or album, apparently because lead singer John Fogerty didn't like their performance. CCR broke up in 1972, but Fogerty emerged as a solo artist in the mid-1980s and continues to record and tour.

21. The Who

Woodstock was The Who's biggest performance since the release of their groundbreaking rock opera *Tommy*. Their 24-song set began around 3:00 A.M. and included many songs from *Tommy* as well as "I Can't Explain," "Shakin' All Over," and "My Generation." At the conclusion of their set, Pete Townshend slammed his guitar into the stage and threw it into the crowd. Drummer Keith Moon died in 1978 from a prescription drug overdose, and the group officially disbanded in 1983 but have reunited for various events and tours over the years. In 1990, The Who were inducted into the Rock and Roll Hall of Fame, and in 2006 founding members Townshend and Roger Daltrey released *Endless Wire* and returned to touring.

22. Jefferson Airplane

Jefferson Airplane's eight-song set took off at 8:00 A.M. on Sunday morning. This psychedelic rock band from San Francisco performed such hits as "Volunteers," "Somebody to Love," and "White Rabbit." After Woodstock, Jefferson Airplane continued to perform and record hits under different names, including Starship and Jefferson Starship The Next Generation. Jefferson Airplane was inducted into the Rock and Roll Hall of Fame in 1996.

23. Joe Cocker

After an all-night music marathon, Joe Cocker took the stage around 2:00 P.M. The English rock and blues musician performed five songs, including his version of The Beatles' song "With a Little Help from My Friends," as well as "Delta Lady" and "Some Things Goin' On." Cocker overcame problems with drug and alcohol abuse and continues to tour sporadically.

24. Country Joe and The Fish

After a rain delay lasting several hours, Country Joe returned, this time with his band The Fish, taking the stage around 6:00 P.M. They played four songs, including "Rock and Soul Music" and "Love Machine." In 2004, Country Joe formed the Country Joe Band with some of the original band members and went on tour.

25. Ten Years After

English blues-rock band Ten Years After performed five songs at Woodstock, including "Good Morning Little Schoolgirl," "Hear Me Calling," and "I'm Going Home." Between 1967 and 1974, Ten Years After recorded and released ten multimillion-selling albums, before breaking up in 1975. After their entire catalog was digitally remastered and rereleased in 2001, three of the founding members got back together and are again recording and touring.

26. The Band

Originally known as The Hawks, the careers of Canadian-American musicians The Band took flight when Bob Dylan recruited them as his backing band for his 1965–1966 world tour. They subsequently recorded four albums with Dylan. At Woodstock, their 11-song set included the songs "Tears of Rage," "Long Black Veil," and "Loving You Is Sweeter Than Ever." The Band broke up in 1976, then reformed in 1983 without founding guitarist and main songwriter Robbie Robertson. They are members of both the Canadian Music Hall of Fame and the Rock and Roll Hall of Fame.

27. Blood, Sweat & Tears

When they performed at Woodstock, jazz-rock band Blood, Sweat & Tears were still riding high from their 1969 Grammy win for Album of the Year for their self-titled sophomore album. The band's five-song set at Woodstock included "Spinning Wheel" and "Something Coming On." Blood, Sweat & Tears broke up and reformed a number of times and continues to tour.

28. Johnny Winter

Albino blues singer and guitarist Johnny Winter released his first album in 1968. He performed nine songs at Woodstock, including two with his brother Edgar Winter, also an albino blues singer. The set included "Johnny B. Goode," "I Can't Stand It," and "Tobacco Road." In 1977, Johnny produced Muddy Waters' Grammy Award-winning comeback album, *Hard Again.* In 1988, Johnny was inducted into the Blues Foundation Hall of Fame, and he continues to record and tour.

29. Crosby, Stills, Nash & Young

Folk rock supergroup Crosby, Stills, Nash & Young began their 16-song set around 3:00 A.M. Made up of former members of The Byrds, The Hollies, and Buffalo Springfield, Woodstock was only their second gig. Their nine-song acoustic set included "Suite: Judy Blue Eyes" and "Marrakesh Express." The electric set that followed included "Long Time Gone" and "Find the Cost of Freedom." They later recorded the song "Woodstock" to commemorate the festival, and for a while they rivaled The Beatles in terms of popularity. But their superegos caused the group to disband in mid-

1970. They've all enjoyed success as solo artists and have reunited in various configurations to record and tour over the years.

30. Paul Butterfield Blues Band

Paul Butterfield was a harmonica player and singer who brought the Chicago electric blues style to rock. The Paul Butterfield Blues Band's five-song set at Woodstock included "Everything's Gonna Be Alright," "Driftin'," and "Born Under a Bad Sign." Butterfield broke up the Blues Band in 1970 and formed a new group called Better Days. He performed solo in the late '70s and early '80s and died in 1987 from a drug and alcohol overdose.

31. Sha Na Na

By far the funniest band to perform at Woodstock was Sha Na Na, a group that covered doo-wop songs from the 1950s while clowning around in period outfits. At Woodstock—only the seventh gig of their career—they performed nine songs, including "Yakety Yak," "Wipe Out," and "At the Hop." At the time, Sha Na Na did not have a record deal, but they received one immediately afterward and went on to release more than 25 albums. From 1977 to 1982, the group even had its own hit TV show, and they continue to tour with some of the original members.

32. Jimi Hendrix

Perhaps the most influential guitarist in rock music history, Jimi Hendrix insisted on closing the show. He was scheduled to perform at midnight, but his set was delayed until around 8:00 A.M. Monday morning. By that time, the crowd, which once numbered more than 500,000, had dwindled to an estimated 80,000. Still, Hendrix played a 16-song set that featured hits such as "Foxy Lady," "Purple Haze," and "Hey Joe." He also played a striking and memorable rendition of "The Star-Spangled Banner." On September 18, 1970, Jimi Hendrix was found dead in London. It is believed that he asphyxiated on his own vomit following an overdose of sleeping pills. Hendrix was inducted into the Rock and Roll Hall of Fame in 1992 and the UK Music Hall of Fame in 2005.

25 Best-Selling Albums of All Time

✳ ✳ ✳ ✳

Title	Artist
1. Eagles/Their Greatest Hits 1971–1975	Eagles
2. Thriller	Michael Jackson
3. Led Zeppelin IV	Led Zeppelin
4. The Wall	Pink Floyd
5. Back in Black	AC/DC
6. Greatest Hits Volume I & Volume II	Billy Joel
7. Double Live	Garth Brooks
8. Come on Over	Shania Twain
9. The Beatles	The Beatles
10. Rumours	Fleetwood Mac
11. Boston	Boston
12. The Bodyguard (sound track)	Whitney Houston/ Various Artists
13. The Beatles 1967–1970	The Beatles
14. No Fences	Garth Brooks
15. Hotel California	Eagles
16. Cracked Rear View	Hootie & The Blowfish
17. Greatest Hits	Elton John
18. Physical Graffiti	Led Zeppelin
19. Jagged Little Pill	Alanis Morissette
20. The Beatles 1962–1966	The Beatles
21. Saturday Night Fever (sound track)	Bee Gees/Various Artists
22. Appetite for Destruction	Guns N' Roses
23. Dark Side of the Moon	Pink Floyd
24. Supernatural	Santana
25. Born in the U.S.A.	Bruce Springsteen

Source: Recording Industry Association of America

THE KING'S HIT PARADE
The Top 30 Songs of Elvis Presley

✳ ✳ ✳ ✳

You don't become "The King of Rock 'n' Roll" without your share of number one songs. Here are 30 of Elvis's chart-toppers.

1. "Heartbreak Hotel" (1956)
Released on January 27, 1956, this heart-wrenching tune was inspired by a suicide note printed in *The Miami Herald.* The tune didn't catch the public's attention until Elvis started appearing on television in the months following its release.

2. "Don't Be Cruel" (1956)
This was the first song that Elvis self-produced. And what a job he did! Not only did he rack up his second number one in three months, he also created a whole new style for himself—one characterized by a free, casual sound.

3. "Hound Dog" (1956)
This song was a blues classic long before anyone had heard of Elvis Presley. But it was the King's July 1956 TV appearances, in which he crooned to a real pup, that propelled it to the top of the pop charts. The machine-gun-like drumming of D. J. Fontana perfectly complemented Elvis's edgy vocals.

4. "Love Me Tender" (1956)
This song's tune came from a Civil War ballad called "Aura Lee." The lyrics were written for Elvis's first movie, also called *Love Me Tender.* The movie—a depiction of the notorious Reno Brothers Gang, was forgettable—the song was anything but!

5. "Too Much" (1957)
Released on January 4, 1957, "Too Much" brought to the forefront the talents of Elvis's supporting players, especially guitarist Scotty Moore. And, of course, the King sounds great, too!

6. "All Shook Up" (1957)

You can't help but dance to this great tune. Released in March 1957, it epitomizes the rock 'n' roll sound that energized teens all over the world. Listen for the sound of Elvis slapping his guitar.

7. "(Let Me Be Your) Teddy Bear" (1957)

Teddy bear sales went through the roof with this June 1957 hit. The song's popularity also helped get people into theaters to see Elvis's second movie, *Loving You.*

8. "Jailhouse Rock" (1957)

Jailhouse Rock marked Elvis's third foray into film and gave him another number one song. Even if the song hadn't been a hit, the movie's dance sequence alone would have made it memorable.

9. "Don't" (1958)

This ballad, written by Jerry Leiber and Mike Stoller, brilliantly conveyed the teen angst felt by the majority of Elvis's fan base. Elvis put his heart and soul into the lyrics, connecting on a personal level with listeners, and it was one of his personal favorites.

10. "Hard Headed Woman" (1958)

Released on June 10, 1958, this hit came out of the movie *King Creole,* which would be the last movie for Elvis until 1960, after his discharge from the army.

11. "One Night" (1958)

"One Night" was a hit for New Orleans blues musician Smiley Lewis just two years before Elvis covered it. The lyrics and overall sound were softened to appeal to a white teen audience.

12. "(Now and Then There's) A Fool Such as I" (1959)

Elvis liked this Hank Snow song so much that he covered it, adding his own special flavor. In fact, many people regard it as their favorite Elvis tune.

13. "A Big Hunk o' Love" (1959)

This song came from the only recording session that Elvis made while in the army. That session was also his first without his original backing band.

14. "Stuck on You" (1960)

Fans wondering if a post-army Elvis still had it could rest assured with the release of this easy-listening track. Yet, this Elvis was different—more mature and sophisticated.

15. "It's Now or Never" (1960)

Elvis's musical maturity is fully showcased in this ballad. Elvis had worked on developing his vocal range while in the army, and the operatic notes in this song demonstrate this new ability.

16. "Are You Lonesome Tonight?" (1960)

This old Al Jolson hit from 1927 just happened to be a favorite of the wife of Elvis's manager, Colonel Tom Parker. In fact, it was the only song that Parker specifically asked Elvis to sing.

17. "Surrender" (1961)

This hit was an adaptation of the Italian-Neapolitan ballad "Torna a Surriento," a hit song for Dean Martin, one of Elvis's inspirations.

18. "(Marie's the Name) His Latest Flame" (1961)

Released on August 8, 1961, this fun tune came from the writing team of Doc Pomus and Mort Shuman. The single was paired with "Little Sister," its mirror opposite in terms of style and mood.

19. "Can't Help Falling in Love" (1961)

This much-loved tune, which appeared in the movie *Blue Hawaii,* was actually based on an 18th-century French ballad. In the 1970s, Elvis often used the song as the closing number for his shows, including his final concert in June 1977.

20. "Good Luck Charm" (1962)

A lightweight, feel-good song that struck a chord, this tune epitomized the sound popular with teens of the early 1960s.

21. "She's Not You" (1962)

A beautiful ballad that Elvis sang with deep conviction, this song has the power to move and inspire.

22. "Return to Sender" (1962)

Not intended for a movie sound track, "Return to Sender" was so well received following its October 2, 1962, release that it soon found its way into *Girls! Girls! Girls!* Elvis sings with great intensity and enthusiasm, making for a very catchy three minutes.

23. "(You're the) Devil in Disguise" (1963)

After venturing into lightweight pop tunes, Elvis returned to his rock 'n' roll roots with this one—giving an intense, emotional performance.

24. "Wooden Heart" (1964)

Directly inspired by Elvis's army stint in Germany, this tune was adapted from a German children's song and was featured in Elvis's first post-army movie, *G.I. Blues.*

25. "Crying in the Chapel" (1965)

Elvis was passionate about singing gospel, and in 1960 he got the opportunity to record an entire gospel album. "Crying in the Chapel" was recorded during that session, but would not be released for another five years. A huge hit, it was definitely worth the wait.

26. "In the Ghetto" (1969)

After a four-year drought without a number one hit, Elvis was back with "In the Ghetto," his most socially responsible song. The haunting lyrics come together with Elvis's passionate expression to create an experience that will move the coldest of hearts.

27. "Suspicious Minds" (1969)

Released on August 26, 1969, this song has a similar feel to "In the Ghetto," which was recorded during the same session in Memphis. Both songs highlighted the now well-established maturity and emotional control that Elvis brought to his work.

28. "The Wonder of You" (1970)

By April 1970, Elvis was performing in Las Vegas, and "The Wonder of You" was the first hit to emerge from that phase of his career. After 14 years of number ones, he continued to push his vocal range, revealing new facets of his amazing gift.

29. "Burning Love" (1972)

"Burning Love" emerged during a very difficult period in Elvis's life. He lacked motivation, and his producer had to work hard to get him to record it. When he did record, he put the full measure of his angst into his music.

30. "Way Down" (1977)

Just a few months before he died, Elvis dragged himself into the studio for what would prove to be his final recording session. When the King died, this song was climbing the charts. His tragic death undoubtedly gave it a boost.

12 Unusual Band Names

❋ ❋ ❋ ❋

1. Aardvark Spleen
2. Barenaked Ladies
3. Dexy's Midnight Runners
4. Lavay Smith and Her Red Hot Skillet Lickers
5. Moby Grape
6. Ned's Atomic Dustbin
7. Nine Inch Nails
8. Squirrel Nut Zippers
9. Strawberry Alarm Clock
10. The Flying Burrito Brothers
11. Ugly Kid Joe
12. Vanilla Fudge

Chapter 10

HISTORY, POLITICS, AND WAR

✳ ✳ ✳ ✳

THE HISTORY BOOKS CAN'T BE WRONG...RIGHT?
10 Common Misconceptions

Don't believe everything you read in the history books. Many events that for centuries have been passed down as true have eventually been proven false. Some were originally based on fact, but all became twisted and embellished as they were told and retold like a game of telephone. None of the following really happened. Trust us...would we lie to you?

1. Lady Godiva's Naked Ride

Even if the Internet had existed during the Middle Ages, you wouldn't have been able to download nude pictures of Lady Godiva because she never actually rode naked through the streets of Coventry, England. Godiva was a real person who lived in the 11th century and she really did plead with her ruthless husband, Leofric, the Earl of Mercia, to reduce taxes. But no records of the time mention her famous ride. The first reference to her naked ride doesn't appear until around 1236, nearly 200 years after her death.

2. Sir Walter Raleigh's Cloak

The story goes that Sir Walter Raleigh laid his cloak over a mud puddle to keep Queen Elizabeth I from getting her feet wet. Raleigh did catch the queen's attention in 1581 when he urged England to conquer Ireland. The queen rewarded him with extensive landholdings in England and Ireland, knighted him in 1584, and named him captain of the queen's guard two years later. But an illicit affair with one of the queen's maids of honor in 1592 did him in. He was imprisoned in the Tower of London and ultimately beheaded for treachery. The story of the cloak and the mud puddle probably originated with historian Thomas Fuller, who was known for embellishing facts.

3. Nero Fiddled While Rome Burned

When asked who fiddled while Rome burned, the answer "Nero" will get you a zero. Legend has it that in A.D. 64, mad Emperor Nero started a fire near the imperial palace and then climbed to the top of the Tower of Maecenas where he played his fiddle, sang arias, and watched Rome flame out. But according to Tacitus, a historian of the time, Nero was 30 miles away, at his villa in Antium, when the fire broke out. Nero wasn't exactly a nice guy—he took his own mother as his mistress, then had her put to death. Despite this, historians believe that the fire was set by Nero's political enemies, who were right in thinking that it would be blamed on him. Actually, Nero was a hero, attempting to extinguish the blaze, finding food and shelter for the homeless, and overseeing the design of the new city.

4. The Forbidden Fruit

Both the apple and Eve get an undeserved bad rap in the story of Paradise. According to the Book of Genesis, Adam and Eve were evicted from Paradise for eating "the fruit of the tree which is in the midst of the garden." There's no mention of any apple! Some biblical scholars think it was a fig, since Adam and Eve dressed in fig leaves, while Muslim scholars think it may have been wheat or possibly grapes. Aquila Ponticus, a 2nd-century translator of the Old Testament, may have assumed that the apple tree in the Song of Solomon was the fruit-bearing tree in Genesis. Two centuries later, St. Jerome also linked the apple tree to the phrase "there wast thou corrupted" in his Latin translation of the Old Testament.

5. Cinderella Wore Glass Slippers

Ask anyone and they'll tell you that Cinderella wore glass slippers to the ball, but historians say that part of the legend isn't true. More than 500 versions of the classic fairy tale exist, dating back as far as the 9th century. In each account, Cinderella has a magic ring or magic slippers made of gold, silver, or some other rare metal, which are sometimes covered with gems but are never made of glass. In the earliest French versions, Cinderella wore *pantoufles en vair* or "slippers of white squirrel fur." In 1697, when French writer Charles Perrault wrote "Cendrillon," his version of the tale, the word *vair* had vanished from the French language. Perrault apparently assumed it should have been *verre*, pronounced the same as *vair*, but meaning "glass." Even a wave of the fairy godmother's magic wand couldn't make that mistake disappear, and it has been passed down ever since.

6. Abner Doubleday Invented Baseball

Contrary to popular belief, Abner Doubleday did not invent the game of baseball. In 1907, a committee was formed to document how baseball had originated. The committee concluded that in 1839, as a youngster in Cooperstown, New York, Abner Doubleday drew a diamond-shape diagram for a game he called "Town Ball." A great story, but merely a myth—especially considering Doubleday was attending West Point in 1839 and was never known to follow the game he supposedly invented. Today, it is generally accepted that Alexander Joy Cartwright, a New York bank teller and talented draftsman, invented the game. A plaque in the Baseball Hall of Fame credits him as "the Father of Modern Baseball," while Abner Doubleday has never been enshrined.

7. Witches Were Burned at the Stake in Salem

Although there really were witch trials in Salem, Massachusetts, in 1692, and 20 people were put to death, none of the accused were burned at the stake. Hanging was the method of execution, although one victim was crushed to death under heavy stones. Moreover, there's no evidence these people were practicing witchcraft or were possessed by the devil. Historians now believe that they, along with the townspeople who persecuted them, were suffering from mass hysteria. Others believe the accusers were afflicted with a physical illness, possibly even hallucinating after eating tainted rye bread.

8. "Let Them Eat Cake"

She probably said a lot of things she later regretted, but Marie Antoinette never suggested hungry French mothers who had no bread should eat cake. In 1766, Jean Jacques Rousseau was writing his "Confessions" when he quoted the famous saying of a great princess, which was incorrectly attributed to Marie Antoinette, Queen of France and wife of Louis XVI. But Marie Antoinette couldn't have made the statement because in 1766, she was only 11 years old. Historians now believe that Rousseau's "great princess" may have been Marie Thérèse, the wife of Louis XIV, who reigned more than 75 years before Louis XVI and Marie Antoinette.

9. The Great Wall of China Is Visible from the Moon

You can see a lot of things while standing on the moon, but the Great Wall of China isn't one of them. In his 1938 publication, *Second Book of Marvels,* Richard Halliburton stated that the Great Wall was the only human-made object visible from the moon. However, the Great Wall is only a maximum of 30 feet wide and is about the same color as its surroundings, so it's barely visible to the naked eye while orbiting Earth under ideal conditions, much less from the moon, which is about 239,000 miles away.

10. Ben Franklin Discovered Electricity

Benjamin Franklin did not discover electricity when his kite was struck by lightning in 1752. In fact, electricity was already well known at the time. Instead, Franklin was trying to prove the electrical nature of lightning. During a thunderstorm, as Franklin flew a silk kite with a metal key near the end of the string, he noticed the fibers on the line standing up as though charged. He touched the key and felt a charge from the accumulated electricity in the air, not from a lightning strike. This was enough evidence to prove his theory that lightning was electricity. Had the kite been struck by lightning, Franklin would likely have been killed as was Professor Georg Wilhelm Richmann of St. Petersburg, Russia, when he attempted the same experiment a few months later.

27 Silly Presidential Nicknames

✳ ✳ ✳ ✳

President	Nickname
1. James Monroe	Last Cocked Hat
2. John Quincy Adams	Old Man Eloquent
3. Martin Van Buren	The Little Magician; Martin Van Ruin
4. John Tyler	His Accidency
5. Zachary Taylor	Old Rough and Ready
6. Millard Fillmore	His Accidency
7. James Buchanan	The Bachelor President; Old Buck
8. Andrew Johnson	King Andy; Sir Veto
9. Ulysses S. Grant	Useless; Unconditional Surrender
10. Rutherford B. Hayes	Rutherfraud Hayes; His Fraudulency
11. James Garfield	The Preacher; The Teacher President
12. Grover Cleveland	Uncle Jumbo; His Obstinacy
13. Benjamin Harrison	Little Ben; White House Iceberg
14. William McKinley	Wobbly Willie; Idol of Ohio
15. Woodrow Wilson	The Schoolmaster
16. Warren Harding	Wobbly Warren
17. Herbert Hoover	The Great Engineer
18. Harry Truman	The Haberdasher
19. John F. Kennedy	King of Camelot
20. Lyndon B. Johnson	Big Daddy
21. Richard M. Nixon	Tricky Dick
22. Gerald Ford	The Accidental President
23. Jimmy Carter	The Peanut Farmer
24. Ronald Reagan	Dutch; The Gipper; The Great Communicator
25. George H. W. Bush	Poppy
26. Bill Clinton	Bubba; Slick Willie; The Comeback Kid
27. George W. Bush	Junior; W; Dubya

6 Political Scandals

✳ ✳ ✳ ✳

Political scandals in the United States have been around since the birth of the nation and don't show any signs of going away, much to the satisfaction of late-night comedians and talk show hosts. Who needs soap operas when real life in Washington is so scandalous? Check out these infamous political scandals.

1. Teapot Dome Scandal

The Teapot Dome Scandal was the largest of numerous scandals during the presidency of Warren Harding. Teapot Dome is an oil field reserved for emergency use by the U.S. Navy located on public land in Wyoming. Oil companies and politicians claimed the reserves were not necessary and that the oil companies could supply the Navy in the event of shortages. In 1922, Interior Secretary Albert B. Fall accepted $404,000 in illegal gifts from oil company executives in return for leasing the rights to the oil at Teapot Dome to Mammoth Oil without asking for competitive bids. The leases were legal but the gifts were not. Fall's attempts to keep the gifts secret failed, and, on April 14, 1922, *The Wall Street Journal* exposed the bribes. Fall denied the charges, but an investigation revealed a $100,000 no-interest loan in return for leases that Fall had forgotten to cover up. In 1927, the Supreme Court ruled that the oil leases had been illegally obtained, and the U.S. Navy regained control of Teapot Dome and other reserves. Fall was found guilty of bribery in 1929, fined $100,000, and sentenced to one year in prison. He was the first cabinet member imprisoned for his actions while in office. President Harding was not aware of the scandal at the time of his death in 1923, but it contributed to his administration being considered one of the most corrupt in history.

2. Chappaquiddick

Since being elected to the Senate in 1962, Edward M. "Ted" Kennedy has been known as a liberal who champions causes such as education and health care, but he has had less success in his personal life. On July 18, 1969, Kennedy attended a party on Chappaquiddick Island in Massachusetts. He left the party with 29-year-old Mary Jo Kopechne, who had campaigned for Ted's late brother Robert. Soon after the two left the party, Kennedy's car veered off a bridge and Kopechne drowned. An experienced swimmer, Kennedy said he tried to rescue her but the tide was too strong. He swam to shore, went back to the party, and returned with two other men. Their rescue efforts also failed, but Kennedy waited until the next day to report the accident, calling his lawyer and Kopechne's parents first, claiming the crash had dazed him. There was speculation that he tried to cover up that he was driving under the influence, but nothing was ever proven. Kennedy pleaded guilty to leaving the scene of an accident, received a two-month suspended jail sentence, and lost his driver's license for a year. The scandal may have contributed to his failed presidential bid in 1980, but it didn't hurt his reputation in the Senate. In April 2006, *Time* magazine named him one of "America's 10 Best Senators."

3. Watergate

Watergate is the name of the scandal that caused Richard Nixon to become the only U.S. president to resign from office. On May 27, 1972, concerned that Nixon's bid for reelection was in jeopardy, former CIA agent E. Howard Hunt, Jr., former New York assistant district attorney G. Gordon Liddy, former CIA operative James W. McCord, Jr., and six other men broke into the Democratic headquarters in the Watergate Hotel in Washington, D.C. They wiretapped phones, stole some documents, and photographed others. When they broke in again on June 17 to fix a bug that wasn't working, a suspicious security guard called the Washington police, who arrested McCord and four other burglars. A cover-up began to destroy incriminating evidence, obstruct investigations, and halt any spread of scandal that might lead to the president. On August 29, Nixon announced that the break-in had been investigated and that no one in the White House was involved. Despite his efforts to hide his involvement, Nixon was done in by his own tape recordings, one of which revealed that he had authorized hush money paid to Hunt. To avoid impeachment, Nixon resigned on August 9, 1974. His successor, President Gerald Ford, granted him a blanket pardon on September 8, 1974, eliminating any possibility that Nixon would be indicted and tried. *Washington Post* reporters Bob Woodward and Carl Bernstein helped expose the scandal using information leaked by someone identified as Deep Throat, a source whose identity was kept hidden until 2005, when it was revealed that Deep Throat was former Nixon administration member William Mark Felt.

4. Wilbur Mills

During the Great Depression, Wilbur Mills served as a county judge in Arkansas and initiated government-funded programs to pay medical and prescription drug bills for the poor. Mills was elected to the House of Representatives in 1939 and served until 1977, with 18 of those years as head of the Ways and Means Committee. In the 1960s, Mills played an integral role in the creation of the Medicare program, and he made an unsuccessful bid for president in the 1972 primary. Unfortunately for Mills, he's best known for one of Washington's juiciest scandals. On October 7, 1974, Mills' car was stopped by police in West Potomac Park near the Jefferson Memorial. Mills was drunk and in the back seat of the car with an Argentine stripper named Fanne Foxe. When the police approached, Foxe fled the car. Mills checked into an alcohol treatment center and was reelected to Congress in November 1974. But just one month later, Mills was seen drunk onstage with Fanne Foxe. Following the incident, Mills was forced to resign as chairman of the Ways and Means Committee and did not run for reelection in 1976. Mills died in 1992, and despite the scandal, several schools and highways in Arkansas are named for him.

5. The Iran-Contra Affair

On July 8, 1985, President Ronald Reagan told the American Bar Association that Iran was part of a "confederation of terrorist states." He failed to mention that members of his administration were secretly planning to sell weapons to Iran to facilitate the release of U.S. hostages held in Lebanon by pro-Iranian terrorist groups. Profits from the arms sales were secretly sent to Nicaragua to aid rebel forces, known as the contras, in their attempt to overthrow the country's democratically-elected government. The incident became known as the Iran-Contra Affair and was the biggest scandal of Reagan's administration. The weapons sale to Iran was authorized by Robert McFarlane, head of the National Security Council (NSC), in violation of U.S. government policies regarding terrorists and military aid to Iran. NSC staff member Oliver North arranged for a portion of the $48 million paid by Iran to be sent to the contras, which violated a 1984 law banning this type of aid. North and his secretary Fawn Hall also shredded critical documents. President Reagan repeatedly denied rumors that the United States had exchanged arms for hostages, but later stated that he'd been misinformed. He created a Special Review Board to investigate. In February 1987, the board found the president not guilty. Others involved were found guilty but either had their sentences overturned on appeal or were later pardoned by George H. W. Bush.

6. The Keating Five

After the banking industry was deregulated in the 1980s, savings and loan banks were allowed to invest deposits in commercial real estate, not just residential. Many savings banks began making risky investments, and the Federal Home Loan Bank Board (FHLBB) tried to stop them, against the wishes of the Reagan administration, which was against government interference with business. In 1989, when the Lincoln Savings and Loan Association of Irvine, California, collapsed, its chairman, Charles H. Keating, Jr., accused the FHLBB and its former head Edwin J. Gray of conspiring against him. Gray testified that five senators had asked him to back off on the Lincoln investigation. These senators—Alan Cranston of California, Dennis DeConcini of Arizona, John Glenn of Ohio, Donald Riegle of Michigan, and John McCain of Arizona—became known as the Keating Five after it was revealed that they received a total of $1.3 million in campaign contributions from Keating. While an investigation determined that all five acted improperly, they all claimed this was a standard campaign funding practice. In August 1991, the Senate Ethics Committee recommended censure for Cranston and criticized the other four for "questionable conduct." Cranston had already decided not to run for reelection in 1992. DeConcini and Riegle served out their terms but did not run for reelection in 1994. John Glenn was reelected in 1992 and served until he retired in 1999. John McCain continues his work in the Senate, and in February 2007 announced his bid for the 2008 Republican presidential nomination.

23 Military Awards Won by Audie Murphy

❊ ❊ ❊ ❊

Audie Murphy was the most decorated U.S. soldier during World War II. He received 33 awards, including 5 awards from France and Belgium and every decoration of valor that the United States offered. After the war, he pursued a successful movie career, starring in films such as The Red Badge of Courage, The Unforgiven, *and* To Hell and Back, *based on his autobiography. Murphy won each of the following awards—some of them more than once.*

1. Medal of Honor
2. Distinguished Service Cross
3. Silver Star with First Oak Leaf Cluster
4. Legion of Merit
5. Bronze Star with V Device and First Oak Leaf Cluster
6. Purple Heart with Second Oak Leaf Cluster
7. U.S. Army Outstanding Civilian Service Medal
8. Good Conduct Medal
9. Distinguished Unit Emblem with First Oak Leaf Cluster
10. American Campaign Medal
11. European-African-Middle Eastern Campaign Medal
12. World War II Victory Medal

13. Army of Occupation with Germany Clasp
14. Armed Forces Reserve Medal
15. Combat Infantry Badge
16. Marksman Badge with Rifle Bar
17. Expert Badge with Bayonet Bar
18. French Fourragere
19. French Legion of Honor, Grade of Chevalier
20. French Croix de Guerre with Silver Star
21. French Croix de Guerre with Palm
22. Medal of Liberated France
23. Belgian Croix de Guerre 1940 Palm

6 of the World's Greatest Missing Treasures

❄ ❄ ❄ ❄

*They were fantastic examples of opulence, decadence,
and splendor. People marveled at their beauty, drooled over their
excess, and cowered at their power. And now they're gone.
But where are they? And what happened to them?*

1. The Amber Room

Described as the eighth wonder of the world by those who saw it,
the Amber Room is certainly the most unique missing treasure in
history. It was an 11-foot-square hall consisting of large wall panels
inlaid with several tons of superbly designed amber, large gold-leaf-
edged mirrors, and four magnificent Florentine mosaics. Arranged
in three tiers, the amber was inlaid with precious jewels, and glass
display cases housed one of the most valuable collections of Prus-
sian and Russian artwork ever assembled. Created for Prussia's
King Friedrich I, and given to Russian czar Peter the Great in 1716,
it was located at Catherine Palace, near St. Petersburg. Today, the
Amber Room would be valued at more than $142 million.

When Adolf Hitler turned his Nazi war machine toward Russia,
the keepers of the Amber Room got nervous. They tried to move it,
but the amber began to crumble, so they tried to cover it with wall-

paper. They were unsuccessful and when the Nazis stormed Leningrad (formerly called St. Petersburg) in October 1941, they claimed it and put it on display in Konigsberg Castle during the remaining war years. But, when Konigsberg surrendered in April 1945, the fabled treasure was nowhere to be found. The Amber Room was never seen again. Did the Soviets unwittingly destroy their own treasure with bombs? Was it hidden in a now lost subterranean bunker outside the city? Or was it destroyed when Konigsberg Castle burned shortly after the city surrendered? We'll probably never know for sure. But fortunately for lovers of opulence, the Amber Room has been painstakingly recreated and is on display in Catherine Palace.

2. Blackbeard's Treasure

The famous pirate Blackbeard only spent about two years (1716–1718) plundering the high seas. Within that time, however, he amassed some serious wealth. While the Spanish were busy obtaining all the gold and silver they could extract from Mexico and South America, Blackbeard and his mates waited patiently, then pounced on the treasure-laden ships as they sailed back to Spain.

Blackbeard developed a fearsome reputation as a cruel and vicious opportunist. His reign of terror centered around the West Indies and the Atlantic coast of North America, with headquarters in both the Bahamas and North Carolina. His end came in November 1718, when British Lieutenant Robert Maynard decapitated the pirate and hung his head from the bowsprit of his ship as a grisly trophy.

But what happened to the vast treasure that Blackbeard had amassed? He acknowledged burying it but never disclosed the location. But that hasn't stopped countless treasure hunters from trying to get their hands on it. Blackbeard's sunken ship, *Queen Anne's Revenge,* is believed to have been discovered near Beaufort, North Carolina, in 1996, but the loot wasn't onboard. Possible locations for the hidden stash include the Caribbean Islands, Virginia's Chesapeake Bay, and the caves of the Cayman Islands.

3. Treasures of Lima

In 1820, Lima, Peru, was on the edge of revolt. As a preventative measure, the viceroy of Lima decided to transport the city's fabulous wealth to Mexico for safekeeping. The treasures included jeweled stones, candlesticks, and two life-size solid gold statues of Mary holding the baby Jesus. In all, the treasure filled 11 ships and was valued at around $60 million.

Captain William Thompson, commander of the *Mary Dear,* was put in charge of transporting the riches to Mexico. But the viceroy should have done some research on the man to whom he handed such fabulous wealth because Thompson was a pirate, and a ruthless one at that. Once the ships were well out to sea, he cut the throats of the Peruvian guards and threw their bodies overboard.

Thompson headed for the Cocos Islands, in the Indian Ocean, where he and his men allegedly buried the treasure. They then decided to split up and lay low until the situation had calmed down, at which time they would reconvene to divvy up the spoils. But the *Mary Dear* was captured, and the crew went on trial for piracy. All but Thompson and his first mate were hanged. To save their lives, the two agreed to lead the Spanish to the stolen treasure. They took them as far as the Cocos Islands and then managed to escape into the jungle. Thompson, the first mate, and the treasure were never seen again.

Since then over 300 expeditions have tried—unsuccessfully—to locate the treasures of Lima. The most recent theory is that the treasure wasn't buried on the Cocos Islands at all, but on an unknown island off the coast of Central America.

4. Pharaohs' Missing Treasure

When Howard Carter found the tomb of Tutankhamen in Egypt's Valley of the Kings in 1922, he was mesmerized by the splendor of the artifacts that the young king took to the afterlife. Attached to the burial chamber was a treasury with so many jewels and other artifacts that it took Carter ten years to fully catalog them. However, when the burial chambers of more prominent pharaohs were unearthed in the late 19th century, their treasure chambers were virtually empty. It is common knowledge that tomb robbers had been busy in the tombs over the centuries, but the scale of the theft required to clean out the tombs of the kings is beyond petty criminals. So, where is the vast wealth of the pharaohs buried in the Valley of the Kings?

Some scholars believe that the treasures were appropriated by the priests who conducted reburials in the Valley of the Kings during the period of the early 20th and late 21st Egyptian dynasties (425–343 B.C.). Pharaohs were not averse to reusing the funeral splendors of their ancestors, so this may have been carried out with official sanction. One particular ruler, Herihor, has been the focus of special attention. Herihor was a high court official during the reign of Ramses XI. Upon Ramses' death, Herihor usurped the throne, dividing up the kingdom with a coconspirator, his son-in-law Piankh. Herihor placed himself in charge of reburial proceedings at the Valley of the Kings, affording himself ample opportunity to pilfer on a grand scale. His tomb has never been found. When and if it is, many scholars believe that the missing treasures of many of Egypt's pharaohs will finally see the light of day.

5. The Ark of the Covenant

To the ancient Israelites, the Ark of the Covenant was the most sacred thing on Earth. The central and paramount object of the Hebrew nation, this ornate chest was, according to the Bible, designed by God. Measuring 44 inches long, 26 inches wide, and 26 inches high, the chest was made of acacia wood, overlaid inside and out with pure gold, and surrounded by an artistic gold border. Mounted on the solid gold cover were two golden cherubs, one at each end of the cover facing each other, with heads bowed and wings extending upward.

The Ark served as a holy archive for the safekeeping of sacred relics, including the two stone tablets of the Ten Commandments. As a historical and religious treasure, the Ark and its contents were absolutely priceless.

In 607 B.C., Jerusalem, the capital city of the Israelite kingdom of Judah and home of Solomon's Temple, where the Ark was housed, was besieged and overthrown by the Babylonians. In a terrible slaughter, more than a million people were killed, with the survivors driven off into captivity. Seventy years later, when the Israelites returned to rebuild the city, the Ark of the Covenant was gone. What happened to this priceless relic has been the subject of intense speculation ever since.

It is widely believed that the Ark was hidden by the Hebrews to keep it from the Babylonians. Possible locations for its hiding place range from Mount Nebo in Egypt to Ethiopia to a cave in the heart of Judah. Yet, if the Ark was hidden, why was it not recovered when the Israelites returned to Jerusalem and rebuilt the temple? Others believe that the Ark was destroyed by the rampaging Babylonians. Still another explanation put forth by the faithful is that God miraculously removed the Ark for safekeeping by means of divine intervention.

6. Montezuma's Treasure

The Spanish decimation of the Aztec empire in Mexico came to a head on July 1, 1520. After mortally wounding Emperor Montezuma, Hernando Cortés and his men were besieged by enraged Aztec warriors in the capital city of Tenochtitlán. After days of fierce fighting, Cortés ordered his men to pack up the vast treasures of Montezuma in preparation for a night flight, but they didn't get far before the Aztecs fell upon them. The ensuing carnage filled Lake Tezcuco with Spanish bodies and the stolen treasures of Montezuma. The terrified army had thrown the booty away in a vain attempt to escape with their lives. The hoard consisted of countless gold and silver ornaments, along with a huge array of jewels.

Cortés and a handful of his men got away with their lives and returned a year later to exact their revenge. When the inhabitants of Tenochtitlán got wind of the approaching invaders, they buried the remains of the city's treasure in and around Lake Tezcuco to prevent it from falling prey to the gold-crazed Spanish. Today, a vast treasure trove remains hidden beneath nearly five centuries of mud and sludge on the outskirts of Mexico City, the modern day incarnation of Tenochtitlán. Generations of treasure seekers have sought the lost hoard without success. A former president of Mexico even had the lake bed dredged, but no treasure was found.

TAKE A NUMBER...
17 People in Line for the Presidency

✳ ✳ ✳ ✳

It's common knowledge that if the president of the United States dies or is removed from office, the vice president takes over. But what happens if the V.P. is unavailable? President Harry Truman signed into law the Presidential Succession Act of 1947, placing the Speaker of the House second in line for the presidency and creating the following order of successors to the White House.

1. Vice President
2. Speaker of the House of Representatives
3. President Pro Tempore of the Senate
4. Secretary of State
5. Secretary of the Treasury
6. Secretary of Defense
7. Attorney General
8. Secretary of the Interior
9. Secretary of Agriculture
10. Secretary of Commerce
11. Secretary of Labor
12. Secretary of Health and Human Services
13. Secretary of Housing and Urban Development
14. Secretary of Transportation
15. Secretary of Energy
16. Secretary of Education
17. Secretary of Veterans Affairs

Heights and Zodiac Signs of 42 Presidents

❋ ❋ ❋ ❋

President	Height	Zodiac Sign
1. George Washington	6' 2"	Pisces
2. John Adams	5' 7"	Scorpio
3. Thomas Jefferson	6' 2"	Aries
4. James Madison	5' 4"	Pisces
5. James Monroe	6' 0"	Taurus
6. John Quincy Adams	5' 7"	Cancer
7. Andrew Jackson	6' 1"	Pisces
8. Martin Van Buren	5' 6"	Sagittarius
9. William Henry Harrison	5' 8"	Aquarius
10. John Tyler	6' 0"	Aries
11. James Polk	5' 8"	Scorpio
12. Zachary Taylor	5' 8"	Sagittarius
13. Millard Fillmore	5' 9"	Capricorn
14. Franklin Pierce	5' 10"	Sagittarius
15. James Buchanan	6' 0"	Taurus
16. Abraham Lincoln	6' 4"	Aquarius
17. Andrew Johnson	5' 10"	Capricorn
18. Ulysses S. Grant	5' 8"	Taurus
19. Rutherford B. Hayes	5' 8"	Libra
20. James Garfield	6' 0"	Scorpio
21. Chester Arthur	6' 2"	Libra
22. Grover Cleveland	5' 11"	Pisces
23. Benjamin Harrison	5' 6"	Leo
24. William McKinley	5' 7"	Aquarius
25. Theodore Roosevelt	5' 10"	Scorpio
26. William Howard Taft	6' 0"	Virgo
27. Woodrow Wilson	5' 11"	Capricorn
28. Warren Harding	6' 0"	Scorpio
29. Calvin Coolidge	5' 10"	Cancer

President	Height	Zodiac Sign
30. Herbert Hoover	5' 11"	Leo
31. Franklin Delano Roosevelt	6' 2"	Aquarius
32. Harry Truman	5' 9"	Taurus
33. Dwight Eisenhower	5' 10"	Libra
34. John F. Kennedy	6' 0"	Gemini
35. Lyndon B. Johnson	6' 3"	Virgo
36. Richard M. Nixon	5' 11"	Capricorn
37. Gerald Ford	6' 0"	Cancer
38. Jimmy Carter	5' 9"	Libra
39. Ronald Reagan	6' 1"	Aquarius
40. George H. W. Bush	6' 2"	Gemini
41. Bill Clinton	6' 2"	Leo
42. George W. Bush	5' 11"	Cancer

IT'S A LONG WAY FROM THE BRAIN TO THE MOUTH
9 Political Slips of the Tongue

✳ ✳ ✳ ✳

Presidents and other politicians have a lot to say and not much time to say it; in their haste, the message often gets lost on its way from the brain to the mouth and comes out in funny, embarrassing, and memorable quotes. Here are some favorites.

1. **Ronald Reagan:** As president, Reagan sometimes veered from his carefully written speeches with disastrous results. In 1988, when trying to quote John Adams, who said, "Facts are stubborn things," Reagan slipped and said, "Facts are stupid things." Not known as an environmentalist, Reagan said in 1966, "A tree is a tree. How many more do you have to look at?" His most famous blooper came during a microphone test before a 1984 radio address when he remarked, "My fellow Americans, I am pleased to tell you I just signed legislation which outlaws Russia forever. The bombing begins in five minutes."

2. Al Gore: Al Gore served as vice president under Bill Clinton from 1993 to 2001. During the 1992 campaign, he asked voters skeptical of change to remember that every Communist government in Eastern Europe had fallen within 100 days, followed by, "Now it's our turn here in the United States of America." Gore has often been incorrectly quoted as saying that he invented the Internet, but his actual comment in 1999 was, "During my service in the United States Congress, I took the initiative in creating the Internet."

3. Richard Nixon: Richard M. Nixon was the 37th president of the United States, serving from 1969 to 1974. He is the only U.S. president to have resigned from office. Famous for telling reporters, "I am not a crook," Nixon once gave this advice to a political associate, "You don't know how to lie. If you can't lie, you'll never go anywhere." Nixon couldn't cover up Watergate and he couldn't cover up bloopers like that either.

4. Richard J. Daley: Mayor Richard J. Daley served as the undisputed leader of Chicago during the turbulent 1960s. The Democratic National Convention was held in Chicago in August 1968, but with the nation divided by the Vietnam War and the assassinations of Martin Luther King, Jr., and Robert F. Kennedy fueling animosity, the city became a battleground for antiwar protests, which Americans witnessed on national television. When confrontations between protesters and police turned violent, Daley's blooper comment reflected the opinion of many people: "The police are not here to create disorder, they're here to preserve disorder."

5. Texas House Speaker Gib Lewis: A true slow-talkin' Texan, many of Texas House Speaker Gib Lewis's famous bloopers may have influenced his colleague, future president George W. Bush. While closing a congressional session, Lewis's real feelings about his peers slipped out when he said, "I want to thank each and every one of you for having extinguished yourselves this session." He tried to explain his problems once by saying, "There's a lot of uncertainty that's not clear in my mind." He could have been describing his jumbled reign as Texas speaker when he commented, "This is unparalyzed in the state's history."

6. **Dan Quayle:** Before President George W. Bush took over the title, Dan Quayle was the reigning king of malaprops. Serving one term as vice president from 1989 to 1993, Quayle's slips of the tongue made him an easy but well-deserved target for late-night talk shows. His most famous blunder came in 1992 when, at an elementary school spelling bee in New Jersey, he corrected student William Figueroa's correct spelling of *potato* as p-o-t-a-t-o-e. Quayle didn't really help the campaign for reelection when, at a stop in California, he said, "This president is going to lead us out of this recovery."

7. **Spiro Agnew:** Spiro Theodore Agnew served as vice president from 1969 to 1973 under President Nixon, before resigning following evidence of tax evasion. This slip expressed his true feelings on this matter, "I apologize for lying to you. I promise I won't deceive you except in matters of this sort." Agnew also didn't endear himself to poor people in 1968 when he commented, "To some extent, if you've seen one city slum, you've seen them all."

8. **George W. Bush:** Reflecting about growing up in Midland, Texas, President George W. Bush said in a 1994 interview, "It was just inebriating what Midland was all about then." Back in those days, Dubya was known to be a heavy drinker, so misspeaking the word *invigorating* was a real Freudian slip. During his time in the White House, the junior Bush has had enough malaprops to give a centipede a serious case of foot-in-the-mouth syndrome.

9. **George H. W. Bush:** With Dan Quayle as his vice president, the bloopers of President George H. W. Bush sometimes got overshadowed, but he still managed some zingers. While campaigning in 1988, he described serving as Ronald Reagan's vice president this way, "For seven and a half years I've worked alongside President Reagan. We've had triumphs. Made some mistakes. We've had some sex…uh…setbacks." When it comes to presidents 41 and 43, you could say that the slip doesn't fall far from the tongue.

Chapter 11
DEATH

* * * *

I WOULDN'T GO IN THERE IF I WERE YOU!
8 Famous People Who Died in the Bathroom

When these people said they had to go, they weren't kidding!
All of these people ended their time on Earth in the bathroom—
some accidentally, others intentionally. One thing is for certain—
none of them got a chance to wash their hands before leaving!

1. Elvis Presley

On January 8, 1935, Elvis Presley, the King of Rock 'n' Roll, was born in Tupelo, Mississippi. He was discovered in Memphis by Sun Records founder Sam Phillips, who was looking for a white singer with an African-American sound and style. Elvis catapulted to fame following three appearances on *The Ed Sullivan Show* in 1956 and 1957. Although he was pushed off the charts by The Beatles and the rest of the British invasion in the early 1960s, he still sold more than a billion records in his lifetime, more than any other recording artist in history. His movie career kept him in the public eye until his comeback album in 1968, and in the 1970s, he sold out shows in Las Vegas as an overweight caricature of his former self. Elvis's addiction to prescription drugs was well known, and on August 16, 1977, he was found dead on the bathroom floor in his Graceland mansion. A vomit stain on the carpet showed that he had become sick while seated on the toilet and had stumbled to the spot where he died. A medical examiner listed the cause of death as cardiac arrhythmia caused by ingesting a large number of drugs.

2. Lenny Bruce

Controversial comedian Lenny Bruce was born Leonard Alfred Schneider in October 1925. Bruce was famous in the 1950s and 1960s for his satirical routines about social themes of the day, including politics, religion, race, abortion, and drugs. His use of profanity—rarely done at that time—got him arrested numerous times. He was eventually convicted on obscenity charges, but was freed on bail. On August 3, 1966, Bruce, a known drug addict, was found dead in the bathroom of his Hollywood Hills home with a syringe, a burned bottle cap, and other drug paraphernalia. The official cause of death was acute morphine poisoning caused by an accidental overdose.

3. Elagabalus

Scandalous 3rd-century Roman emperor Elagabalus married and divorced five women, including a Vestal Virgin (a holy priestess), who under Roman law should have been buried alive for losing her virginity. Elagabalus also may have been bisexual. Objecting to his sexual behavior and his habit of forcing others to follow his religious customs, his grandmother Julia Maesa and aunt Julia Avita Mamaea murdered Elagabalus and his mother (Julia Maesa's own daughter) in the emperor's latrine. Their bodies were dragged through the streets of Rome and thrown into the Tiber River.

4. Robert Pastorelli

Born in 1954, actor and former boxer Robert Pastorelli was best known as Candace Bergen's housepainter on the late '80s sitcom *Murphy Brown*. He had numerous minor roles on television and also appeared in *Dances with Wolves, Sister Act 2,* and *Michael*, as well as a number of made-for-TV movies. Pastorelli struggled with drug use and in 2004 was found dead on the floor of his bathroom of a suspected heroin overdose.

5. Orville Redenbacher

Orville Redenbacher, founder of the popcorn company that bears his name, was born in 1907, in Brazil, Indiana. Millions came to know him through his folksy television commercials for the specialty popcorn he invented. He sold the company to Hunt-Wesson Foods in 1976, but remained as a spokesperson until September 20, 1995, when he was found dead in a whirlpool bathtub in his condominium, having drowned after suffering a heart attack.

6. Claude François

Claude François was a French pop singer in the 1960s who had a hit with an adaptation of Trini Lopez's folk song "If I Had a Hammer." On March 11, 1978, François' obsession with cleanliness did him in when he was electrocuted in the bathroom of his Paris apartment as he tried to fix a broken lightbulb while standing in a water-filled bathtub.

7. Albert Dekker

Actor Albert Dekker, who appeared in *Kiss Me Deadly, The Killers,* and *Suddenly, Last Summer,* was blacklisted in Hollywood for several years for criticizing anticommunist Senator Joe McCarthy. Dekker later made a comeback, but in May 1968, he was found strangled to death in the bathroom of his Hollywood home. He was naked, bound hand and foot, with a hypodermic needle sticking out of each arm and obscenities written all over his body. The official cause of death was eventually ruled to be accidental asphyxiation.

8. Jim Morrison

Born on December 8, 1943, Jim Morrison was best known as the lead singer for The Doors, a top rock band in the late 1960s. His sultry looks, suggestive lyrics, and onstage antics brought him fame, but drug and alcohol abuse ended his brief life. On July 3, 1971, Morrison was found dead in his bathtub in Paris. He reportedly had dried blood around his mouth and nose and bruising on his chest, suggesting a massive hemorrhage brought on by tuberculosis. The official report listed the cause of death as heart failure, but no autopsy was performed because there was no sign of foul play.

✻ ✻ ✻

Our death is not an end
if we can live on in our children
and the younger generation.
For they are us, our bodies are only
wilted leaves on the tree of life.
—Albert Einstein

TOO YOUNG TO DIE
59 Famous People Who Died Before Age 40

✲ ✲ ✲ ✲

1. Jessica Dubroff (7)—Pilot—Plane crash—1996
2. Heather O'Rourke (12)—Child actor—Bowel obstruction—1988
3. Anne Frank (15)—Dutch-Jewish author—Typhus in concentration camp—1945
4. Ritchie Valens (17)—Rock 'n' roll singer—Plane crash—1959
5. Eddie Cochran (21)—Rockabilly musician—Auto accident—1960
6. Aaliyah (22)—R&B singer—Plane crash—2001
7. Buddy Holly (22)—Rock 'n' roll singer—Plane crash—1959
8. Freddie Prinze (22)—Comedian/actor—Suicide—1977
9. River Phoenix (23)—Actor—Drug overdose—1993
10. Selena (23)—Mexican-American singer—Homicide—1995
11. James Dean (24)—Actor—Auto accident—1955
12. Otis Redding (26)—Soul singer—Plane crash—1967
13. Brian Jones (27)—British rock guitarist—Drug-related drowning, possibly homicide—1969
14. Janis Joplin (27)—Rock/soul singer—Heroin overdose—1970
15. Jim Morrison (27)—Rock singer—Heart attack, possibly due to drug overdose—1971
16. Jimi Hendrix (27)—Rock guitarist/singer—Asphyxiation from sleeping pill overdose—1970
17. Kurt Cobain (27)—Grunge rock singer/guitarist—Gunshot and lethal dose of heroin, presumed suicide—1994
18. Reggie Lewis (27)—Basketball player—Heart attack—1993
19. Brandon Lee (28)—Actor—Accidental shooting on the set of *The Crow*—1993
20. Shannon Hoon (28)—Rock singer—Drug overdose—1995
21. Hank Williams (29)—Country musician—Heart attack, possibly due to an accidental overdose of morphine and alcohol—1953
22. Andy Gibb (30)—Singer—Heart failure due to cocaine abuse—1988
23. Jim Croce (30)—Singer/songwriter—Plane crash—1973
24. Patsy Cline (30)—Country music singer—Plane crash—1963
25. Sylvia Plath (30)—Poet and author—Suicide—1963

26. Brian Epstein (32)—Beatles manager—Drug overdose—1967
27. Bruce Lee (32)—Martial arts actor—Possible allergic reaction—1973
28. Cass Elliot (32)—Singer—Heart attack brought on by obesity—1974
29. Karen Carpenter (32)—Singer and musician—Cardiac arrest from anorexia nervosa—1983
30. Keith Moon (32)—Rock drummer—Overdose of medication—1978
31. Carole Lombard (33)—Actor—Plane crash—1942
32. Chris Farley (33)—Comedian/actor—Overdose of cocaine and heroin—1997
33. Darryl Kile (33)—Major League Baseball pitcher—Coronary heart disease—2002
34. Jesus Christ (33)—Founder of Christianity—Crucifixion—A.D. 30
35. John Belushi (33)—Comedian/actor—Overdose of cocaine and heroin—1982
36. Sam Cooke (33)—Soul musician—Homicide—1964
37. Charlie Parker (34)—Jazz saxophonist—Pneumonia and ulcer, brought on by drug abuse—1955
38. Dana Plato (34)—Actor—Prescription drug overdose—1999
39. Jayne Mansfield (34)—Actor—Auto accident—1967
40. Andy Kaufman (35)—Comedian/actor—Lung cancer—1984
41. Josh Gibson (35)—Negro League baseball player—Stroke—1947
42. Stevie Ray Vaughan (35)—Blues guitarist—Helicopter crash—1990
43. Bob Marley (36)—Reggae musician—Melanoma that metastasized into lung and brain cancer—1981
44. Diana, Princess of Wales (36)—British royal—Auto accident—1997
45. Marilyn Monroe (36)—Actor—Barbiturate overdose—1962
46. Bobby Darin (37)—Singer/actor—Complications during heart surgery—1973
47. Lou Gehrig (37)—Major League Baseball player—Amyotrophic lateral sclerosis (ALS)—1941
48. Michael Hutchence (37)—Rock singer—Hanged, possibly suicide—1997
49. Sal Mineo (37)—Actor—Homicide—1976
50. Florence Griffith Joyner (38)—Olympian/sprinter—Possible asphyxiation during epileptic seizure—1998

51. George Gershwin (38)—Composer—Brain tumor—1937
52. Harry Chapin (38)—Singer/songwriter—Auto accident—1981
53. John F. Kennedy, Jr. (38)—Journalist/publisher—Plane crash—1999
54. Roberto Clemente (38)—Major League Baseball player—Plane crash—1972
55. Sam Kinison (38)—Comedian—Auto accident caused by drunk driver—1992
56. Anna Nicole Smith (39)—Model/actor—Accidental prescription drug overdose—2007
57. Dennis Wilson (39)—Rock 'n' roll drummer—Drowning due to intoxication—1983
58. Malcolm X (39)—Militant civil rights leader—Assassination—1965
59. Martin Luther King, Jr. (39)—Civil rights activist/minister—Assassination—1968

A TISKET, A TASKET, WHAT'S IN THAT CASKET!
5 People Buried with Strange Objects

❋ ❋ ❋ ❋

No one is sure what happens to us after we die, so many people like to leave this world prepared for anything by having odd or unusual objects buried with them. Some may have special meaning, some may be helpful, but others are just hard to figure out. Here are a few ideas to help you plan what to take on your own trip to the great beyond.

1. Tutankhamen (King Tut)

Tutankhamen, better known as King Tut, was an Egyptian pharaoh who ruled from 1333 B.C. to 1324 B.C. When his tomb was discovered by Howard Carter in 1923, the event received worldwide press coverage. Thousands of items were found buried with King Tut, including a solid gold mask that covered the head of the mummified king, hundreds of gold figurines, a small chair made of ebony inlaid with ivory, jewelry, ornamental vases, weapons, and enough seeds to plant a large garden.

2. Reuben John Smith

Before he died in 1899, Reuben John Smith of Buffalo, New York, made sure that he would spend eternity in comfort. He was buried in a leather recliner chair with a checkerboard sitting on his lap. Smith also requested that he be dressed in a hat and warm coat with the key to the tomb inside his coat pocket.

3. Humphrey Bogart

Legendary actor Humphrey Bogart appeared in 75 movies, many of them classics like *The Maltese Falcon, Casablanca, The Treasure of the Sierra Madre,* and *The African Queen,* for which he won an Oscar for Best Actor. In 1944, he starred in *To Have and Have Not* with Lauren Bacall, who became his fourth wife. A famous line from the movie, delivered by Bacall to Bogart, was, "If you need anything, just whistle." So when Bogart died in 1957, Bacall placed a whistle inscribed with the line inside the silver urn with his ashes.

4. Sandra Ilene West

When California socialite Sandra Ilene West died in 1977 from a drug overdose, she was buried in San Antonio, Texas, in her 1964 Ferrari 330 America. She asked to be clad in her favorite lace nightgown with the driver's seat positioned at a comfortable angle. West and her car were placed in a large box, which was covered with cement to discourage vandals.

5. Harry "The Horse" Flamburis

In 1977, Harry "The Horse" Flamburis, president of the Daly City, California, Hells Angels motorcycle club, was shot with his arms and legs bound together and his eyes and mouth taped shut. When he was buried, more than 150 Hells Angels members surrounded the cemetery on their bikes. Three months later, the Angels returned to the cemetery with Harry's motorcycle in tow. They placed the chopper on top of Harry's coffin and reburied him.

15 Most Common Causes of Death in the United States

✳ ✳ ✳ ✳

Where you live has a good deal to do with how you will die. In the United States, the top two causes of death are responsible for more than 50 percent of the annual death toll. In the world at large, there's a lot more variety in how you meet your Maker.

Cause	Percent of total
1. Diseases of the heart	28.5
2. Malignant tumors	22.8
3. Cerebrovascular diseases	6.7
4. Chronic lower respiratory diseases	5.1
5. Accidents (unintentional injuries)	4.4
6. Diabetes mellitus	3.0
7. Influenza and pneumonia	2.7
8. Alzheimer's disease	2.4
9. Nephritis, nephrotic syndrome, and nephrosis	1.7
10. Septicemia (blood poisoning)	1.4
11. Suicide	1.3
12. Chronic liver disease and cirrhosis	1.1
13. Primary hypertension and hypertensive renal disease	0.8
14. Parkinson's disease (tied)	0.7
15. Homicide (tied)	0.7

Source: CDC/NHS, National Vital Statistics System

✳ ✳ ✳

"The fear of death follows from the fear of life. A man who lives fully is prepared to die at any time."
—Mark Twain

WERE THEY REALLY OF SOUND MIND AND BODY?
9 Strange Last Wills and Testaments

✳ ✳ ✳ ✳

*A will is supposed to help surviving family and friends
dispose of your estate after you've passed away. Many people use
it as an opportunity to send a message from beyond the grave,
either by punishing potential heirs with nothing or perhaps by
giving away something fun or unusual to remember them by.
Where there's a will, there's a way, so make sure you have
a good will before you go away for good.*

1. Harry Houdini

Harry Houdini, born in 1874, was considered the greatest magician and escape artist of his era, and possibly of all time. When he died in 1926 from a ruptured appendix, Houdini left his magician's equipment to his brother Theodore, his former partner who performed under the name Hardeen. His library of books on magic and the occult was offered to the American Society for Psychical Research on the condition that J. Malcolm Bird, research officer and editor of the ASPR Journal, resign. Bird refused and the collection went instead to the Library of Congress. The rabbits he pulled out of his hat went to the children of friends. Houdini left his wife a secret code—ten words chosen at random—that he would use to contact her from the afterlife. His wife held annual séances on Halloween for ten years after his death, but Houdini never appeared.

2. Marie Curie

Born in Russian-occupied Poland in 1867, Marie Curie moved to Paris at age 24 to study science. As a physicist and chemist, Madame Curie was a pioneer in the early field of radioactivity, later becoming the first two-time Nobel laureate and the only person to win Nobel Prizes in two different fields of science—physics and chemistry. When she died in 1934, a gram of pure radium, originally received as a gift from the women of America, was her only property of substantial worth. Her will stated: "The value of the element being too great to transfer to a personal heritage, I desire to will the gram of radium to the University of Paris on the condition that my daughter, Irene Curie, shall have entire liberty to use this gram...according to the conditions under which her scientific researches shall be pursued." Element 96, Curium (Cm), was named in honor of Marie and her husband, Pierre.

3. William Randolph Hearst

Multimillionaire newspaper magnate William Randolph Hearst was born in San Francisco in 1863. When he died in 1951, in accordance with his will, his $59.5 million estate was divided into three trusts—one each for his widow, sons, and the Hearst Foundation for Charitable Purposes. Challenging those who claimed he had children out of wedlock, Hearst willed anyone who could prove "that he or she is a child of mine...the sum of one dollar. I hereby declare that any such asserted claim...would be utterly false." No one claimed it. The book-length will included the disposition of his $30 million castle near San Simeon, California. The University of California could have had it but decided it was too expensive to maintain, so the state government took it, and it is now a state and national historic landmark open for public tours.

4. Jonathan Jackson

Animal lover Jonathan Jackson died around 1880. His will stipulated that: "It is man's duty as lord of animals to watch over and protect the lesser and feebler." So he left money for the creation of a cat house—a place where cats could enjoy comforts such as bedrooms, a dining hall, an auditorium to listen to live accordion music, an exercise room, and a specially designed roof for climbing without risking any of their nine lives.

5. S. Sanborn

When S. Sanborn, an American hatmaker, died in 1871, he left his body to science, bequeathing it to Oliver Wendell Holmes, Sr., (then a professor of anatomy at Harvard Medical School) and one of Holmes's colleagues. The will stipulated that two drums were to be made out of Sanborn's skin and given to a friend on the condition that every June 17 at dawn he would pound out the tune "Yankee Doodle" at Bunker Hill to commemorate the anniversary of the famous Revolutionary War battle. The rest of his body was "to be composted for a fertilizer to contribute to the growth of an American elm, to be planted in some rural thoroughfare."

6. John Bowman

Vermont tanner John Bowman believed that after his death, he, his dead wife, and two daughters would be reincarnated together. When he died in 1891, his will provided a $50,000 trust fund for the maintenance of his 21-room mansion and mausoleum. The will required servants to serve dinner every night just in case the Bowmans were hungry when they returned from the dead. This stipulation was carried out until 1950, when the trust money ran out.

7. James Kidd

James Kidd, an Arizona hermit and miner, disappeared in 1949 and was legally declared dead in 1956. His handwritten will was found in 1963 and stipulated that his $275,000 estate should "go in a research for some scientific proof of a soul of a human body which leaves at death." More than 100 petitions for the inheritance were dismissed by the court. In 1971, the money was awarded to the American Society for Psychical Research in New York City, although it failed to prove the soul's existence.

8. Eleanor E. Ritchey

Eleanor E. Ritchey, heiress to the Quaker State Refining Corporation, passed on her $4.5 million fortune to her 150 dogs when she died in Florida in 1968. The will was contested, and in 1973 the dogs received $9 million. By the time the estate was finally settled its value had jumped to $14 million but only 73 of the dogs were still alive. When the last dog died in 1984, the remainder of the estate went to the Auburn University Research Foundation for research into animal diseases.

9. Janis Joplin

Janis Joplin was born in Port Arthur, Texas, on January 19, 1943. In her brief career as a rock and blues singer, she recorded four albums containing a number of rock classics, including "Piece of My Heart," "To Love Somebody," and "Me and Bobby McGee." Known for her heavy drinking and drug use, she died of an overdose on October 4, 1970. Janis made changes to her will just two days before her death. She set aside $2,500 to pay for a posthumous all-night party for 200 guests at her favorite pub in San Anselmo, California, "so my friends can get blasted after I'm gone." The bulk of her estate reportedly went to her parents.

15 Most Common Causes of Death in the World

✳ ✳ ✳ ✳

Cause	Percent of total
1. Ischemic heart disease	12.6
2. Cerebrovascular diseases	9.7
3. Lower respiratory infections (e.g. pneumonia)	6.8
4. HIV/AIDS	4.9
5. Chronic obstructive pulmonary disease	4.8
6. Diarrheal diseases	3.2
7. Tuberculosis	2.7
8. Malaria (tied)	2.2
9. Cancer of trachea/bronchus/lung (tied)	2.2
10. Road traffic accidents	2.1
11. Childhood diseases	2.0
12. Other unintentional injuries (tied)	1.6
13. Hypertensive heart disease (tied)	1.6
14. Suicide (tied)	1.5
15. Stomach cancer (tied)	1.5

Source: WHO's World Health Report

7 Strange Ways to Die

✳ ✳ ✳ ✳

Most of us strive to lead an interesting life, but some stake a place in history by dying in an unusual way. Some of the people on this list were just in the wrong place at the wrong time, while others met their ends at the hands of enemies who were particularly vindictive in their creativity. Either way, the cause of death on some of these death certificates could be listed as cruel irony.

1. So funny it hurts. The fatal guffaw struck Alex Mitchell, a 50-year-old English bricklayer on March 24, 1975, while he and his wife watched his favorite TV sitcom, *The Goodies.* Mitchell found a sketch called "Kung Fu Kapers" so hilarious that he laughed for 25 minutes straight, until his heart gave out and he died. Mitchell's wife sent the show a letter thanking the producers and performers for making her husband's last moments so enjoyable.

2. The tortoise in the air. Those flying monkeys in *The Wizard of Oz* were scary enough to frighten even the toughest kid on the block, but did you ever think you'd have to worry about flying tortoises? Greek playwright Aeschylus probably didn't, but according to the story, he was killed when an eagle or a bearded vulture dropped a tortoise on his bald head after mistaking his noggin for a stone in an attempt to crack open the tortoise's shell.

3. Deadly twist. Isadora Duncan was one of the most famous dancers of her time. Her fans marveled at her artistic spirit and expressive dance moves, and she is credited with creating modern dance. But it was another modern creation that prematurely ended her life. She was leaving an appearance on September 14, 1927, when her trademark long scarf got caught in the wheel axle of her new convertible. She died of strangulation and a broken neck at age 50.

4. A terrible taste. War is hell, but ancient wars were particularly brutal. After the Persians captured the Roman emperor Valerian during battle around A.D. 260, Persia's King Shapur I is said to have humiliated Valerian by using him as a footstool. But it only got worse for the Roman. After Valerian offered a king's ransom for his release, Shapur responded by forcing molten gold down his prisoner's throat, stuffing him with straw, and then putting him on display, where he stayed for a few hundred years.

5. Too long in the tooth. Sigurd I of Orkney was a successful soldier who conquered most of northern Scotland in the 9th century. Following a fever-pitched victory in A.D. 892 against Maelbrigte of Moray and his army, Sigurd decapitated Maelbrigte and stuck his opponent's head on his saddle as a trophy. As Sigurd rode with his trophy head, his leg kept rubbing against his foe's choppers. The teeth opened a cut on Sigurd's leg that became infected and led to blood poisoning. Sigurd died shortly thereafter.

6. An unfair way to go. Mark Twain once said, "Golf is a good walk spoiled," and although many a duffer has spent a frustrating couple of hours on the links, few actually die as a result. In 1997, Irishman David Bailey was not so lucky. Bailey was retrieving an errant shot from a ditch when a frightened rat ran up his pant leg and urinated on him. The rat didn't bite or scratch the golfer, so even though his friends kept telling him to shower, Bailey didn't think much of the encounter and kept playing. His kidneys failed two weeks later, and he died. The cause was leptospirosis, a bacterial infection spread by rodents, dogs, or livestock that is usually mild but can cause meningitis, pneumonia, liver disease, or kidney disease.

7. Fantasy meets harsh reality. Many people who like playing video games or online computer games do so to escape the pressures of the real world for a bit. But when that escapism is taken too far, gamers can leave the real world altogether. That's what happened to South Korean Lee Seung Seop in August 2005. Lee was an industrial repair technician, but he had quit his job to spend more time playing Internet games. Lee set himself up at a local Internet café and played a game for nearly 50 hours straight, taking only brief breaks to go to the bathroom or nap. Exhaustion, dehydration, and heart failure caused Lee to collapse, and he died shortly thereafter at age 28.

8 Stars Who Died During the Filming of a Movie

✳ ✳ ✳ ✳

Long after their time is up, movie stars live on through DVDs and cable reruns. But the stars on this list died before completing a project, leaving directors in an emotional and logistical bind, and forever attaching a dark footnote to a movie's history. In some cases the movie was canceled, in others the star was recast, while in others production moved forward with some creative editing.

1. John Candy

Funnyman John Candy, known for portraying portly, lovable losers in movies such as *Stripes, Uncle Buck,* and *Planes, Trains & Automobiles,* died of a massive heart attack on March 4, 1994, during the filming of *Wagons East.* A body double was used to replace Candy, and the film—a comedy set in the Wild West—was released later that summer. The movie was widely panned by critics as an unworthy farewell to Candy, who was just 43 when he died.

2. Marilyn Monroe

Blonde bombshell Marilyn Monroe, famous for her film roles, multiple marriages, and memorable serenading of President Kennedy, died on August 5, 1962, before she could finish filming *Something's Got to Give.* The comedy, directed by George Cukor and also starring Cyd Charisse and Dean Martin, had been plagued with conflict from the start. At one point, Monroe was even fired. But Martin refused to work with any actress other than Monroe, so the famous beauty was rehired. Before Monroe could resume her role, however, she was found dead in her Brentwood, California, home, the result of an overdose of barbiturates. *Something's Got to Give* was scrapped, but parts of the unfinished film were included in a 2001 documentary titled *Marilyn: The Final Days.*

3. River Phoenix

River Phoenix, a young actor who shot to stardom after appearing in Rob Reiner's *Stand by Me*, was near the end of filming *Dark Blood* when he died of a drug overdose on Halloween 1993 at age 23. The movie, a dark tale about a widower (Phoenix) living on a nuclear testing site, was subsequently canceled because Phoenix's presence was crucial to several yet-to-be-shot scenes. Phoenix was also slated to film *Interview with the Vampire* with Tom Cruise. His role was taken over by Christian Slater, who donated his salary from the film to a charity in Phoenix's honor.

4. Paul Mantz

To Paul Mantz, stunt flying was a natural calling, and the legendary aviator even lost his spot at the U.S. Army flight school when he buzzed a train filled with high-ranking officers. Mantz landed a role in 1932's *Air Mail*, in which he flew a biplane through a hangar not much bigger than the aircraft itself. He appeared in numerous films through the years, including *For Whom the Bell Tolls, Twelve O'Clock High*, and *The Wings of Eagles*. On July 8, 1965, Mantz was killed while performing a stunt for *The Flight of the Phoenix*. Flying over an Arizona desert site, Mantz's plane struck a hill and broke into pieces, killing the famous aviator immediately. Because the majority of the movie had already been shot, filmmakers were able to substitute another plane for some remaining close-ups and *The Flight of the Phoenix* was released later that year.

5. Vic Morrow

Vic Morrow, a tough-talking actor known for his role in the TV series *Combat!* as well as a string of B-movies, was killed in July 1982, in a tragic accident on the set of *Twilight Zone: The Movie*. The script called for the use of both a helicopter and pyrotechnics—a combination that would prove lethal. When the pyrotechnics exploded, the helicopter's tail was severed, causing it to crash. The blades decapitated Morrow and a child actor, and another child actor was crushed to death. Although the filmmakers faced legal action from the accident, the project was completed and the movie was released in June 1983. It performed poorly at the box office, based partially on the controversy surrounding the accident.

6. Oliver Reed

Oliver Reed, as famous for drinking and partying as he was for acting, died in a pub on May 2, 1999, before he could finish filming Ridley Scott's epic *Gladiator.* Reed, who was 61, collapsed on the floor of a bar in Malta and died of a heart attack. Most of his scenes in *Gladiator* had already been shot when he died, but Scott had to digitally re-create Reed's face for a few remaining segments. The Internet Movie Database estimated the cost of the digital touch-ups at $3 million. When *Gladiator* was released in 2000, it grossed more than $187 million in the United States alone and snared five Oscars, including Best Picture.

7. Steve Irwin

Steve Irwin, aka "The Crocodile Hunter," was in the Great Barrier Reef to film a documentary titled *The Ocean's Deadliest* when he was struck by a stingray and killed on September 4, 2006. Irwin, a 44-year-old Australian wildlife expert, was known for his daredevil stunts involving animals and could frequently be seen handling poisonous snakes and wrestling crocodiles on his Animal Planet TV show. Because of bad weather, Irwin was actually taking a break from filming his documentary at the time of the stingray attack, instead taping some snorkeling segments for a children's show. *The Ocean's Deadliest* aired in January 2007.

8. Brandon Lee

Brandon Lee, an aspiring actor and the son of martial arts star Bruce Lee, was killed in a freak accident on the set of *The Crow* on March 31, 1993. Lee, who was 28 at the time, was playing a character who gets shot by thugs upon entering his apartment. Tragically, the handgun used in the scene had a real bullet lodged in its barrel, which was propelled out by the force of the blank being shot. Lee was hit in the abdomen and died later that day. The

movie was nearly complete at the time of the shooting, but a stunt double was needed to complete a few remaining scenes, and Lee's face was digitally superimposed onto the stunt double's body.

CARVED IN STONE
11 Memorable Epitaphs

✻ ✻ ✻ ✻

They might be six feet under, but a good epitaph means they'll never been forgotten. Here are some of our favorite gravestone inscriptions.

1. Mel Blanc: "That's all folks!"
Arguably the world's most famous voice actor, Mel Blanc's characters included Bugs Bunny, Porky Pig, Yosemite Sam, and Sylvester the Cat. When he died of heart disease and emphysema in 1989 at age 81, his epitaph was his best-known line.

2. Spike Milligan: "Dúirt mé leat go raibh mé breoite."
The Gaelic epitaph for this Irish comedian translates as, "I told you I was ill." Milligan, who died of liver failure in 2002 at age 83, was famous for his irreverent humor showcased on TV and in films such as *Monty Python's Life of Brian.*

3. Joan Hackett: "Go away—I'm asleep."
The actor, who was a regular on TV throughout the 1960s and 1970s, appearing on shows such as *The Twilight Zone* and *Bonanza,* died in 1983 of ovarian cancer at age 49. Her epitaph was copied from the note she hung on her dressing room door when she didn't want to be disturbed.

4. Rodney Dangerfield: "There goes the neighborhood."
This comedian and actor died in 2004 from complications following heart surgery at age 82. His epitaph is fitting for this master of self-deprecating one-liners, best known for his catchphrase, "I don't get no respect."

5. Ludolph van Ceulen: "3.14159265358979323846264338327950 288..."

The life's work of van Ceulen, who died from unknown causes in 1610 at age 70, was to calculate the value of the mathematical constant pi to 35 digits. He was so proud of this achievement that he asked that the number be engraved on his tombstone.

6. George Johnson: "Here lies George Johnson, hanged by mistake 1882. He was right, we was wrong, but we strung him up and now he's gone."

Johnson bought a stolen horse in good faith but the court didn't buy his story and sentenced him to hang. His final resting place is Boot Hill Cemetery, which is also "home" to many notorious characters of the Wild West, including Billy Clanton and the McLaury brothers, who died in the infamous gunfight at the O.K. Corral.

7. John Yeast: "Here lies Johnny Yeast. Pardon me for not rising."

History hasn't recorded the date or cause of John Yeast's death, or even his profession. We can only hope that he was a baker.

8. Lester Moore: "Here lies Lester Moore. Four slugs from a 44, no Les, no more."

The date of birth of this Wells Fargo agent is not recorded, but the cause of his death, in 1880, couldn't be clearer.

9. Jack Lemmon: "Jack Lemmon in..."

The star of *Some Like It Hot*, *The Odd Couple*, and *Grumpy Old Men* died of bladder cancer in 2001 at age 76.

10. Hank Williams: "I'll never get out of this world alive."

The gravestone of the legendary country singer, who died of a heart attack in 1953 at age 29, is inscribed with several of his song titles, of which this is the most apt.

11. Dee Dee Ramone: "OK...I gotta go now."

The bassist from the punk rock band The Ramones died of a drug overdose in 2002, at age 49. His epitaph is a reference to one of the group's hits, "Let's Go."

Chapter 12

MONEY & BUSINESS

✳ ✳ ✳ ✳

WILL THAT BE CREDIT OR DEBIT?

Daily U.S. Consumption for 12 Items

Living in the United States has its perks. If you want to brush your teeth, you can buy a toothbrush. If you outgrow your pants, you can shop for a new pair. If you need a soy latte and a Twinkie, you can get those pretty easily, too. America is definitely "the land of plenty," and the statistics that follow offer a glimpse of how many goods U.S. consumers use every day and how much they spend on them. The numbers may surprise you....

1. Movie Tickets—3.8 million

If the average cost of a movie is $7, Americans spend about $26.6 million a day at movie theaters. Take that number times 365, and the industry rakes in $9.7 billion annually, which doesn't include profits from popcorn, soda sales, or DVDs.

2. Greeting Cards—19.2 million

There's a card for every occasion—heck, there's a card for occasions you didn't even know existed! Between birthday, holiday, and "just because" cards, Americans show loved ones they care by spending $7.5 billion a year on greeting cards.

3. Denim Jeans—641,000 pairs

Since Levi Strauss invented blue jeans in 1873, Americans have loved the fashionable pants. Whether you're buying a pair of generic jeans at a discount store or plunking down $300 for designer denim, the blue-jeans industry is big business in the United States. Today, the average price of a pair of jeans comes to about $60, which means Americans spend about $38.5 million on denim pants every day, or $14 billion annually.

4. Domestic Beer Kegs—975,000

Where there's a big celebration, or a bar, there are kegs of beer. Kegs of premium beer can get into the $200 range, but we're talking about good ol' American macro-brews. These average $60 per keg, so Americans spend about $58.5 million on them. Consumers down around 356 million kegs per year, which works out to more than $21 billion per year.

5. Pampers—300,000 packs

Pampers has the market cornered on the needs of new parents and sells its Jumbo pack (56 diapers) for around $13. Americans spend $3.9 million a day—$1.4 billion a year—keeping baby bottoms dry.

6. Cosmetic Procedures—20,000

Liposuction alone boasts about 1,000 procedures a day, and Botox injections have hit the 5,000-a-day mark. Whether you're going in for a tummy tuck or an eye lift, you can expect to pay an average of $1,700 for an appointment with a plastic surgeon. This means that the American cosmetic surgery industry makes about $34 million a day or $12.4 billion every year.

7. Axe Body Spray—28,876 cans

Priced around $5 per can, this deodorizer for frat boys and jocks pulls in approximately $145,000 every day. Guys are spending about $53 million a year to smell nice—and the ladies thank them for it.

8. Starbucks Coffee—153,424 pounds

The little Seattle coffee shop that could is now an internationally recognized trademark that rivals McDonald's when it comes to brand identification and customer loyalty. Americans like their Starbucks so much that the company orders around 56 million pounds of coffee beans every year.

9. Oreo Cookies—205,000 bags

An 18-ounce package of the iconic chocolate cookie filled with vanilla frosting is going to set a person back about $3.99. That means Americans spend nearly $818,000 every day, or about $300 million each year, on their beloved Oreos.

10. Cigarettes—1.1 billion

With huge campaigns by antitobacco activists and health organizations across the country, Americans smoke a lot less than they did in the past. Still, the tobacco industry is a juggernaut, selling more than 400 billion smokes a year. With the average cost of a pack at $3.50, the U.S. spends $70 billion a year on cigarettes.

11. Krispy Kreme Doughnuts—1.9 million

This statistic refers to the Original Glazed variety of Krispy Kremes, served piping hot at various spots along the daily commute. If each doughnut costs 79 cents, Krispy Kreme businesses pull in more than $1.5 million a day on Original Glazed doughnuts alone. That's not including crullers, jelly-filled doughnuts, or coffee.

12. iPods—88,163

The iPod is essentially a portable hard drive with headphones. Apple CEO Steve Jobs and his team of savvy engineers revolutionized the entire music industry with the iPod. A 30-gigabyte iPod that holds 7,500 songs and 40 hours of video costs $249. The price goes up from there, depending on added features, or skip the video and the price goes down. Still, on average, that's about $18 million a day and more than $6.4 billion a year—music to Apple's ears.

9 Most Successful Fast-Food Chains

❈ ❈ ❈ ❈

Americans spend more money on fast food than on movies, music, books, magazines, and newspapers combined. The rapid growth of this $240 billion industry over the last 30 years has been the result of economic shifts that have forced more women to work outside the home. Here are the top nine fast-food chains and how they stack up worldwide.

1. Subway

Almost everyone recognizes Jared Fogle as the poster boy for Subway's healthy, low-fat diet. He lost 245 pounds in a year by eating two Subway sandwiches per day and walking. Subway was founded in 1965 by 17-year-old college freshman Fred DeLuca and family friend Dr. Peter Buck. Today there are more than 27,000 restaurants in 85 countries, employing more than 150,000 people. With worldwide sales totaling more than $9 billion annually, Subway serves nearly 2,800 sandwiches and salads in the United States every 60 seconds. If all the sandwiches made by Subway in a year were placed end to end, they would wrap around the world an estimated six times.

2. McDonald's

Originally founded by Dick and Mac McDonald as a barbecue drive-in in the 1940s, the McDonald's Corporation now boasts annual profits of more than $21 billion. Known for its signature french fries, the corporation trains more new workers annually than the U.S. Army, and an estimated one in eight Americans has worked for McDonald's. In 1968, McDonald's operated about 1,000 restaurants worldwide, but today it has more than 31,000.

3. Pizza Hut

In 1958, brothers Dan and Frank Carney of Wichita, Kansas, founded Pizza Hut. Now based in Dallas, this restaurant chain specializes in American-style pizza along with side dishes such as buffalo wings, bread sticks, and garlic bread. Pizza Hut is the world's largest pizza chain, operating more than 12,500 stores in 100 countries and employing 140,000 people. With $5.3 billion in annual sales in the United States alone, the company rakes in more than its nearest competitors—Domino's and Papa John's—combined.

4. Burger King

In December 1954, James McLamore and David Edgerton opened the first Insta Burger King in Miami, Florida. The restaurant was based on an assembly line production system inspired by a visit to the McDonald brothers' hamburger stand. Today, Burger King has more than 11,000 restaurants in 65 countries. With an average annual income of $11.2 billion, the chain employs more than 340,000 employees and serves 11 million customers a day.

5. KFC

Kentucky Fried Chicken was the brainchild of Harland Sanders, who opened his first restaurant during the Great Depression in a gas station in Corbin, Kentucky. In the 1930s, Sanders developed his secret recipe of 11 herbs and spices, which has been touted as one of the best-kept secrets in the world and to this day is locked in a vault in Louisville. Colonel Sanders, as he was known, sold his empire for $2 million in 1964. Today, KFC is a $10.3 billion franchise with more than 11,000 restaurants in 80 countries. The company employs 750,000 people who serve more than a billion "finger lickin' good" chicken meals each year.

6. Wendy's

Dave Thomas opened the first Wendy's—named for his daughter—in Columbus, Ohio, in 1969. In 1970, Thomas introduced the drive-thru window, an innovation that allowed customers to purchase food without leaving their cars. The chain's passion for customer service and quality products has remained unchanged throughout the years. Today, with an annual income of $3.7 billion, Wendy's has more than 9,900 restaurants and 58,000 employees.

7. Domino's Pizza

Brothers Tom and James Monaghan started the first Domino's Pizza in 1960 in Ypsilanti, Michigan, when they purchased a pizza store called DomiNick's for $500. A year later, Tom became the restaurant's sole owner when James traded his share of the business for a Volkswagen Beetle. Tom renamed the store Domino's Pizza and it soon became one of the world's leading pizza chains with more than 8,000 stores in 50 countries. Serving in excess of one million customers a day, Domino's employs more than 140,000 people and brings in an annual income of $1.4 billion.

8. Taco Bell

Glen Bell opened the first Taco Bell in Downey, California, in 1962. In 1964, the first franchise was granted, and in 1969, Taco Bell went public on the stock market. Every year since 2001, company sales have increased 6 percent, and today, sales total more than $1.8 billion. Taco Bell maintains more than 6,000 restaurants worldwide, employing 143,000 workers.

9. Arby's

Founded in Ohio in 1964 by Forest and Leroy Raffel, the name Arby's is a play on R.B., an abbreviation for Raffel Brothers and also for roast beef, the restaurant's specialty. Always ahead of its time, in 1991, Arby's became the first fast-food chain to introduce a light menu, adding three sandwiches and four salads, all of which were under 300 calories and 94 percent fat free. In 1994, the chain banned smoking in all of its restaurants. Arby's currently employs more than 82,000 people at 3,500 stores worldwide and brings in $1.8 billion annually.

10 Most Dangerous Jobs in America

✳ ✳ ✳ ✳

Before you complain about punching the time clock, read this list for some perspective. Maybe the coffee stinks and you don't like your boss, but at least the threat of death or injury isn't perpetually hanging over your head. The order may change from year to year, but these are typically the most dangerous jobs in America.

1. Logger
2. Pilot
3. Fisher
4. Iron/Steel Worker
5. Garbage Collector
6. Farmer/Rancher
7. Roofer
8. Electrical Power Installer/Repairer
9. Sales, Delivery, and Other Truck Driver
10. Taxi Driver/Chauffeur

9 Odd Things Insured by Lloyds of London

✳ ✳ ✳ ✳

*Average people insure average things like cars, houses,
and maybe even a boat. Celebrities insure legs, voices, and some
things you might not want to examine if you're a claims adjuster.
Here are a few unusual things insured by the famous
Lloyds of London over the years.*

1. In 1957, world-famous food critic Egon Ronay wrote and published the first edition of the *Egon Ronay Guide to British Eateries.* Because his endorsement could make or break a restaurant, Ronay insured his taste buds for $400,000.

2. In the 1940s, executives at 20th Century Fox had the legs of actress Betty Grable insured for $1 million each. After taking out the policies, Grable probably wished she had added a rider to protect her from injury while the insurance agents fought over who would inspect her when making a claim.

3. While playing on Australia's national cricket team from 1985 to 1994, Merv Hughes took out an estimated $370,000 policy on his trademark walrus mustache, which, combined with his 6' 4" physique and outstanding playing ability, made him one of the most recognized cricketers in the world.

4. Representing the Cheerio Yo-Yo Company of Canada, 13-year-old Harvey Lowe won the 1932 World Yo-Yo championships in London and toured Europe from 1932 to 1935. He even taught Edward VIII, the Prince of Wales, how to yo-yo. Lowe was so valuable to Cheerio that the company insured his hands for $150,000!

5. From 1967 to 1992, British comedian and singer Ken Dodd was in *The Guinness Book of Records* for the world's longest joke-telling session—1,500 jokes in three and a half hours. Dodd has sold more than 100 million comedy records and is famous for his frizzy hair, ever-present feather duster, and extremely large buckteeth. His teeth are so important to his act that Dodd had them insured for $7.4 million, surely making his insurance agent grin.

6. During the height of his career, Michael Flatley—star of *Riverdance* and *Lord of the Dance*—insured his legs for an unbelievable $47 million. Before becoming the world's most famous Irish step dancer, the Chicago native trained as a boxer and won the Golden Gloves Championship in 1975, undoubtedly dazzling his opponents with some extremely fast and fancy footwork.

7. The famous comedy team of Bud Abbott and Lou Costello seemed to work extremely well together, especially in their famous "Who's on First?" routine. But to protect against a career-ending argument, they took out a $250,000 insurance policy over a five-year period. After more than 20 years together, the team split up in 1957—not due to a disagreement, but because the Internal Revenue Service got them for back taxes, which forced them to sell many of their assets, including the rights to their many films.

8. Rock and Roll Hall of Famer Bruce Springsteen is known to his fans as The Boss, but Springsteen knows that he could be demoted to part-time status with one case of laryngitis. That's why in the 1980s he insured his famous gravelly voice for $6 million. Rod Stewart has also insured his throat and Bob Dylan his vocal cords to protect themselves from that inevitable day when they stop blowin' in the wind.

9. Before rock 'n' roll, a popular type of music in England in the 1950s was skiffle, a type of folk music with a jazz and blues influence played on washboards, jugs, kazoos, and cigar-box fiddles. It was so big at the time that a washboard player named Chas McDevitt tried to protect his career by insuring his fingers for $9,300. It didn't do him much good because skiffle was replaced by rock 'n' roll, washboards by washing machines, and McDevitt by McCartney.

JUST PICTURE EVERYONE IN THEIR UNDERWEAR
18 Tips for Public Speaking

✳ ✳ ✳ ✳

If this were a list of the human race's greatest fears, public speaking would be right at the top. Whether it's forgetting your lines or realizing you have a tail of toilet paper hanging out of your pants, fear of public speaking really boils down to fear of being ridiculed, rejected, and publicly humiliated. But don't worry—with the following tips, you'll be fine!

1. Watch the Masters

If you've got a speech or presentation in your future, start looking for what makes successful public speakers so successful. Note their styles and habits and keep them in mind as good examples.

2. Fix Up, Look Sharp

If you're in a position where public speaking is required, let's hope you've already got a handle on the importance of personal grooming. If not, take heed: The better you look, the more ready and professional you'll feel. A lot of people are going to be looking at you—make sure you look your best.

3. Hello, Room. Nice to Meet You.

If at all possible, check the specs of the room where you'll be speaking. Is it football stadium big or conference room big? What about the sound system? If you'll be using a microphone, it's a good idea to test it out beforehand. The more familiar you are with your environment, the more comfortable you'll be at the podium.

4. Sober Up

If your speaking engagement is at a social function (i.e. wedding, reunion), it might seem like a good idea to guzzle as much liquid courage as you can before your speech. But listening to a sincere speech from someone who's nervous is much better than listening to incoherent babble from someone who's loaded.

5. Know Your Material

Winging it is *not* a good idea when you've got a speech to make. While going with the flow and being flexible is smart, trusting yourself to be brilliant without any preparation is something even the pros don't attempt. Do your research. Know your topic and what you're going to say about it and how you'd like to say it. The more you know, the more confident you'll be up there.

6. Practice, Practice, Practice

Once you're prepared, go through the speech. Then read it again. Then again. And then once more. Practice in front of a mirror. Practice to your dog. Grab a friend or family member and practice in front of a real human being. Every time you go through your presentation, you're adding another layer of "I know this stuff."

7. Visualize Yourself Being Fabulous

Negative thinking will get you nowhere but down in the dumps. If you believe that you'll be great, you will be. If you think you're going to fail, you probably will. It's as simple as that.

8. Know Your Audience

To whom are you speaking? If they're colleagues, they probably want to learn something from you. If they're friends, they're likely looking to be entertained. If it's a judge, well, he or she wants to be convinced. Know who your audience is and tailor your speech and delivery to them. Give them what they want!

9. Relax!

We're usually our own worst critics. If you forget to read a sentence off your notes, it's doubtful anyone will know. If you skip forward to the next image on the projector by mistake, no one's going to run you out of town. Don't worry. It's not life or death, it's just a speech.

10. Don't Give It Away

If it really, truly makes you feel better to announce to the room that you're *so* nervous before you begin, go ahead. But your speech will have a lot more weight if you don't. Chances are good that you're the only one who knows you're shaking in your boots—why show the cracks in your armor? Let them believe you have it under control, even if you don't feel like you do.

11. Slow Your Roll

One of the biggest indicators of nervousness is the lightning-fast talker. You might have the best speech ever written, but if no one can understand what you're saying, it doesn't matter. Pace yourself and remember to speak at a normal (or even slightly slower) pace when you're speaking publicly.

12. The Eyes Have It

People trust people who look them in the eye, so look at your audience when you're speaking to them. Don't look at the floor—there's nothing down there. Don't look solely at your notes—the audience will think you haven't prepared. You appear more confident when your head is up, which puts your audience at ease and allows you to take command of the room.

13. Go On, Be Funny!

Who doesn't like to laugh a little? You don't have to be a comedian, but a few lighthearted comments can help humanize you to your audience. Win them over with a smile and a well-timed clever remark, if you can. But be advised, too many jokes can weaken the validity of a presentation.

14. Your Errors Are Okay

So you tripped on the microphone cord. So what? So you said *macro* when you meant *micro* somewhere in your speech. So you accidentally said the name of your sister's ex-boyfriend during your toast instead of the name of her new husband—so what! Everyone makes mistakes. Acknowledge them and move on.

15. Keep It Short, Please

Even the president's State of the Union Address is only around an hour. Know what's expected of you and deliver that—and no more. We've all been tortured by a speaker who goes on and on, caring little for the audience's interest or comfort level. Don't be one of those speakers—always leave them wanting more.

16. It's SO Not About You

The more you can take the focus off yourself, the better. After all, it's not likely you're being asked to give a presentation of your life story. So concentrate on the message and find freedom in just being the messenger.

17. Fake It 'Til You Make It

The old saying "fake it 'til you make it" is actually pretty good advice. Even if you have zero confidence in yourself, try acting like you do. The longer you fake it, the more comfortable it will feel, until, voilà, you're a bona fide confidence machine.

18. Be Yourself

We're all human. We're all a little afraid of the podium, the microphone, or the boardroom. Despite what you may believe, people don't want you to fail. They ultimately want to see you succeed. Give them what they want by just being the best *you* you can be.

CHARITY BEGINS WITH A FEW BILLION DOLLARS
10 Largest Foundations in the World

❋ ❋ ❋ ❋

Some people who have more money than they can possibly spend in a lifetime make a valiant effort and just keep spending. Others take a more philanthropic approach, setting up foundations to distribute their wealth in areas such as education, medicine, or technology. It's never too late to start planning your own foundations, so here are some facts about the world's largest.

1. Bill & Melinda Gates Foundation

Believing that "every life has equal value," Microsoft cofounder Bill Gates and his wife Melinda established their foundation in 2000 with $106 million. The foundation's goals include improving health care and education, fighting extreme poverty, and providing increased access to information technology. In June 2006, Warren

Buffett, the world's second richest person (behind Gates), pledged ten million shares of his company's stock (worth nearly $31 billion) to the Bill & Melinda Gates Foundation. As of April 2006, the foundation's endowment exceeded $33 billion, which means that to keep its charitable status, it must make approximately $1.65 billion in annual charitable contributions. In addition to his ample financial gifts, Bill Gates has also pledged his time to the foundation, announcing that he will phase out of his managerial role at Microsoft by July 2008 to focus on charity work.

2. Wellcome Trust

The Wellcome Trust was founded in London in 1936 on the death of pharmaceuticals mogul Henry Wellcome. The mission of the Wellcome Trust is to promote research, improve human and animal health, and improve the understanding of science and medicine. As of September 2005, Wellcome's endowment was approximately $23.2 billion, making it the largest charitable foundation in Great Britain and the second largest in the world.

3. Howard Hughes Medical Institute

The Howard Hughes Medical Institute was founded in 1953 by aviator, moviemaker, and millionaire industrialist Howard Hughes to promote medical research and education. The initial endowment consisted of 75,000 shares of Hughes Aircraft stock. After Hughes' death in 1976, the endowment quickly grew from $4 million in 1975 to $15 million in 1978. During this time, the institute became more involved with genetics, immunology, and molecular biology. Another increase in the endowment occurred in the mid-1980s when General Motors purchased Hughes Aircraft, and by September 2005, it had reached nearly $15 billion.

4. Lilly Endowment

In 1937, Lilly Endowment, Inc., was established by Josiah K. Lilly, Sr., and his sons with stock from Eli Lilly pharmaceuticals company. While the endowment, which now totals $10.8 billion, is 13 percent of the company's stock, the foundation is separate from the pharmaceuticals company. The foundation's primary recipients are in community development, education, and religion. The Lilly Endowment is the largest private foundation in the United States to contribute mostly to local projects, with 60 to 70 percent of its annual funds going to charities in its home state of Indiana.

5. Ford Foundation

Founded in 1936 by Edsel Ford and two Ford Motor Company executives, the purpose of the Ford Foundation was to fund scientific, educational, and charitable projects. Today, the foundation's mission includes promoting democracy, improving education, and reducing poverty. In its early years, the foundation supported National Educational Television, which was replaced by the Public Broadcasting Service in 1970. At the end of 2006, the foundation's endowment was approximately $12 billion. In that year alone, the foundation gave out nearly $530 million in grants for projects focused on community and economic development, education, media, arts, peace, social justice, and human rights.

6. Robert Wood Johnson Foundation

The Robert Wood Johnson Foundation was established in 1936 by Robert Wood Johnson II, the son of Johnson & Johnson founder Robert Wood Johnson and later a World War II army general. The foundation focuses primarily on improving the health of all Americans by helping to provide quality health care at a reasonable cost, improving the quality of care for people with chronic illnesses, promoting healthy lifestyles, and reducing the problems caused by substance abuse. With an endowment estimated at $9.4 billion, the Robert Wood Johnson Foundation made $403 million in grants in 2006 to support these causes.

7. W. K. Kellogg Foundation

Believing that "all people have the inherent capacity to effect change in their lives, in their organizations, and in their communities," breakfast cereal magnate Will Keith Kellogg founded the W. K. Kellogg Foundation in June 1930. Throughout his lifetime,

Kellogg donated more than $66 million in Kellogg stock and other investments to the endowment, which today has assets of more than $7.8 billion. During the 2005–2006 fiscal year, the W. K. Kellogg Foundation funded $329 million in grants, including $39 million to areas devastated by Hurricane Katrina.

8. William and Flora Hewlett Foundation

Hewlett-Packard cofounder Bill Hewlett and his wife Flora formed the William and Flora Hewlett Foundation in 1966 to address social and environmental issues. With more than $8 billion in assets, the Hewlett Foundation donates approximately $300 million annually. The foundation distributes grants worldwide in the areas of global development, education, performing arts, reproductive health, and environmental issues. It also funds programs to aid underprivileged communities in the San Francisco area where the foundation has its headquarters.

9. Robert Bosch Foundation

The Robert Bosch Stiftung (Robert Bosch Foundation) was established in Germany in 1964 to fulfill the philanthropic and social pursuits of Robert Bosch, founder of the automotive parts company Robert Bosch GmbH. Today, the foundation has an endowment of approximately $6.9 billion, of which 92 percent is stock in Robert Bosch GmbH. In 2005, the foundation distributed around $75 million in grants to promote education, international understanding, science and research, and health and humanitarian aid. The foundation also operates three health and research facilities in Germany.

10. The David & Lucile Packard Foundation

In 1964, David Packard, the other half of the Hewlett-Packard team, and his wife Lucile Salter Packard established the David & Lucile Packard Foundation. The foundation's mission is "to improve the lives of children, enable the creative pursuit of science, advance reproductive health, and conserve and restore earth's natural systems." The foundation's endowment is approximately $6.2 billion and it awarded $224 million in grants in 2006.

The World's 10 Fastest-Growing Economies

✳ ✳ ✳ ✳

Country	Growth Rate Percentage
1. Equatorial Guinea	18.9
2. China	9.2
3. Ireland	6.5
4. Vietnam	6.0
5. Sudan	5.6
6. Maldives	5.4
7. Chile	5.2
8. Guyana	5.0
9. Myanmar	4.8
10. South Korea	4.7

Source: United Nations Human Development Report, 2002

HAPPY DAYS, INDEED
Grocery Store Prices for 14 Items in 1957

✳ ✳ ✳ ✳

*Maybe Father knew best in 1957, but he probably didn't have
a clue about how much Mother forked over at the grocery story
for his tuna noodle casserole. He made about $4,494 a year, paid
about $20,000 for his house, $2,500 for his Ford, and roughly
27 cents a gallon to fill 'er up. Let's see how deep Mother had
to dig into her pocketbook at the grocery store checkout.*

1. Milk

Back in 1957, milk was $1 per gallon. Today, we have a lot more
choices when standing in the dairy aisle, but whether whole, 2 percent, 1 percent, skim, or soy, milk sets us back about $3.49 when it's
not on sale.

2. TV Dinner

A Swanson TV dinner cost just 75 cents in 1957. With classics like *Wagon Train* and *American Bandstand* shown in 39.5 million homes, TV trays were popping up all over the place. Today, a frozen chicken and corn tray will set you back $2.99.

3. Tang

Tang Breakfast Crystals were launched in America in 1957 for around 50 cents a jar. In 1965, the *Gemini 4* astronauts got this powdered vitamin C powerhouse for free on their space mission and all of the following Gemini and Apollo missions. Today, anyone can buy Tang for $3.39 for a 12-ounce canister.

4. Ground Beef

To make that delicious meatloaf, Mother shelled out 30 cents for a pound of hamburger in 1957. Today, we pay considerably more for our ground beef—$4.09 per pound!

5. Butter

When they weren't cooking with lard or shortening, American women of 1957 opted for butter at 75 cents a pound. These days, we're more likely to count fat grams and opt for margarine or other butter substitutes. In any case, at about $3.99 a pound, we don't pay with just our arteries to enjoy good old-fashioned butter today.

6. Syrup

In 1957, you could douse a stack of flapjacks with pure Vermont maple syrup because it only cost 33 cents for 12 ounces. At $9.36 for 12 ounces of the real stuff today, we have to go a little lighter on the sap. But these days it's much less expensive to grab an imitation. You can get 12 ounces of Aunt Jemima for $1.89.

7. Campbell's Tomato Soup

It's no wonder Campbell's tomato soup has always been a family favorite. People have been wallowing in its creamy comfort for generations. To make it even more soothing, in 1957 a can only set you back a dime! Today, it's still an affordable form of therapy, and it costs only a buck.

8. Gum

Gum chompers had a few choices back in 1957. There was Juicy Fruit, Wrigley's Spearmint, and Dubble Bubble, to name a few. You could pretty much chew until your jaw hurt at just 19 cents for 6 packs (30 pieces). Today, in addition to the dental bills, it costs about $1.19 for a 6-pack of gum.

9. Broccoli

In 1957, in a world in which the word *fiber* was mostly used to discuss fabrics, a bunch of broccoli only cost 23 cents. Today's health conscious crowd pays a little more to munch this super food—around $1.79 per bunch.

10. Eggs

In 1957, a dozen eggs cost a mere 55 cents. For those who aren't quite ready to pour an omelette from a pint-size container of artificial eggs, you can still crack the good old-fashioned, incredible, edible egg for $2.99 a dozen.

11. Iceberg Lettuce

Iceberg lettuce used to rule the refrigerator's produce bin—it only cost 19 cents per head in 1957! Salad makers these days reach for romaine, red leaf, and endive, just to name a few. Iceberg still has its loyal followers, but they can now plan on paying $1.49 per head.

12. Nabisco Saltines

Nabisco saltines can settle an upset stomach, and, at 25 cents for a 16-ounce package in 1957, that's better than medicine. But today, the same size box will set you back $2.69.

13. Pot Roast

Pot roasts brought families to the table most Sundays in 1957, and it cost 69 cents a pound for that roast. Today, it's harder to get busy families together, but when they do, the cook can expect to pay $4.59 per pound.

14. Canned Corn

The "Ho Ho Ho, Green Giant" jingle wasn't born until 1959, but cooks in 1957 reached for a can of corn with his jolly green likeness for about 14 cents per 27-ounce can. Today, 95 cents will get you a 15-ounce can.

8 Memorable Ad Campaigns

❋ ❋ ❋ ❋

Some commercial messages last only for the 30 seconds that they exist in real time, while others linger with us for decades. Here are some amusing ads that have stood the test of time.

1. Coca-Cola: "The pause that refreshes" (1929)

With the advent of the Great Depression, corporate America worried that sales would suffer. Not so with Coca-Cola, whose ads depicted carefree people and an idealized view of American life when real life was rather dreary. During the first year of the campaign, sales actually doubled! The economy may have been depressed, but "the pause that refreshes" appears to have been just what Americans needed to lift their spirits.

2. Clairol: "Does she... or doesn't she?" (1956)

"... Only her hairdresser knows for sure." When there's only one female employee in the copywriting department, you give her a shot at the product geared toward women. Shirley Polykoff, who coined the phrase that jump-started the home hair-coloring industry, felt that a woman had the right to change her hair color without everybody knowing about it. The campaign lasted for 15 years, and Clairol's sales increased by 413 percent in the first six years!

3. Volkswagen: "Think Small" (1959)

In 1959, art director Helmut Krone and copywriter Julian Koenig came up with this "less is more" message geared toward car buyers. Like the VW Beetle, the ads were simple and uncluttered, featuring photos of the car against a plain background. Can you sell a car with a headline that reads "Lemon"? Sure! In the ad, Volkswagen was pointing out that the car in the photo didn't make it off the assembly line because one of the many inspectors found a blemish. "We pluck the lemons; you get the plums," was the slogan.

4. McDonald's: "You deserve a break today" (1971)

In 1970, Needham, Harper & Steers successfully pitched an upbeat, catchy melody to McDonald's, but they struggled with the lyrics. Noticing that the word *break* continuously surfaced in focus groups, copywriter Keith Reinhard finally wrote the perfect lyrics for the jingle. Within the next few years, global sales jumped from $587 million to $1.9 billion. The song was named the top jingle of the 20th century by *Advertising Age*.

5. Miller Lite Beer: "Tastes great, less filling" (1974)

This campaign peppered with ex-jocks contained more than 200 commercials, and its lively debate entertained sports fans for nearly two decades. Is Miller Lite good because of the taste or because you can drink a ton of it and still have room for nachos? During the first five years of the campaign, sales of Miller Lite took off from just under 7 million barrels a year to more than 31 million barrels, breaking the all-time record for beer makers. A guy's gotta be full after that!

6. Federal Express: "Fast Talker" (1982)

These memorable ads are breathtaking . . . literally, you might gasp for air when watching the TV spots. When writer Patrick Kelly and art director Mike Tesch discovered John Moscitta, Jr., who could speak more than 500 words a minute, they knew he would be perfect for ads for the overnight delivery service. When director Joe Sedelmaier put his quirky spin on the concept, the spots were discussed around watercoolers across the country.

7. Apple Computer: "1984" (1984)

This is the TV spot that made the Super Bowl about more than just football. Based on George Orwell's book *1984,* the commercial pitted the new Macintosh computer against the totalitarian control of Big Brother and the Thought Police (represented by other computer companies). Depicting an apocalyptic view of the future, the ad opened with a zombielike crowd fixated on a huge screen, then an Amazon woman entered and hurled a hammer into the screen, shattering it. The ad's creators, Lee Clow and Steve Hayden, won every advertising award that year for this venerable commercial.

8. Nike: "Just Do It" (1988)

When ad exec Dan Wieden met with a group of Nike employees to talk about a new ad campaign, he told them, "You Nike guys... you just do it." The result was one of the most effective taglines in advertising history. During the first ten years of this award-winning campaign, Nike's percent of the sport shoe market shot up from 18 to 43 percent. Today, the Nike name is so recognizable that it doesn't even need to appear in the advertising. Only the iconic "swoosh" is needed.

LOST IN TRANSLATION

12 Items that Would Need a Name Change to Sell in America

❊ ❊ ❊ ❊

The meanings of many foreign words get lost in translation when converted into English. But the English names of the following products would probably benefit from a name change if they want to be successful in the United States.

1. Cream Collon

Glico's Cream Collon is a tasty cookie from Japan. The small cylindrical wafers wrapped around a creamy center actually do resemble a cross section of a lower intestine filled with cream. An ad says to "Hold them between your lips, suck gently, and out pops the filling." Yum! Glico's Cream Collon can be ordered on the Internet.

2. Ass Glue

Ass glue is made from fried donkey skin and is considered a powerful tonic by Chinese herbalists, who use it to fortify the body after illness, injury, or surgery. If you have a dry cough, a dry mouth, or are irritable, you can find ass glue at most Chinese herb shops.

3. Mini-Dickmann's

Mini-Dickmann's, a German candy made by Storck, is described as a "chocolate foam kiss." Available in milk, plain, or white chocolate, Mini-Dickmann's are only an inch and a half long. Too embarrassed to be seen with a box of Mini-Dickmann's? Try Super-Dickmann's, the four-inch variety. Both sizes are available from Storck USA.

4. Kockens Anis

If you think *anis* sounds funny, you'll laugh even harder when you see Kockens Anis in Swedish grocery stores. Anis is aniseed, a fragrant spice used in baking, and Kockens is the brand name. While aniseed is found in most U.S. grocery stores, don't ask for the Kockens brand because it's not available and could get you coldcocked.

5. Aass Fatøl

On those rare hot days, Norwegians like to quench their thirst with a cold bottle of Aass Fatøl beer. The word *fatøl* appears on many Scandinavian beer labels and means "cask." This beer comes from the Aass Brewery, the oldest brewery in Norway. If you'd like to get some Aass, it's imported in the United States.

6. Big Nuts

Big Nuts is a chocolate-covered hazelnut candy from the Meurisse candy company in Belgium. For those who like candy that makes a statement, Big Nuts is available online.

7. Dickmilch

Dairy cases in Germany are the place to find *dickmilch,* a traditional beverage made by Schwalbchen. In German, *dickmilch* means "thick milk" and is made by keeping milk at room temperature until it thickens and sours. Called sour milk in the United States, it's a common ingredient in German and Amish baked goods.

8. Pee Cola

If you're asked to take a cola taste test in Ghana, one of the selections may be a local brand named Pee Cola. The drink was named after the country's biggest movie star Jagger Pee, star of *Baboni: The Phobia Girl*. Don't bother looking for a six-pack of Pee to chug because it's not available in the United States.

9. Golden Gaytime

Street's Golden Gaytime is toffee-flavored ice cream dipped in fine chocolate and crunchy cookie pieces and served on a stick. Also available in a cone, Golden Gaytime is one of many Street's ice cream treats sold in Australia but not in the United States. One memorable advertising slogan remarks: "It's so hard to have a Gaytime on your own."

10. Piddle in the Hole

Take a Piddle in the Hole at a pub in England and you'll be drinking a beer from the Wyre Piddle Brewery. Made in the village of Wyre Piddle, the brewery also makes Piddle in the Wind, Piddle in the Dark, and Piddle in the Snow. Before you run out for a Piddle, it's only available in the UK.

11. Shito

Shito is a spicy hot chili pepper condiment that, like ketchup in the United States and salsa in Mexico, is served with most everything in Ghana. There are two versions: a spicy oil made with dried chili pepper and dried shrimp; and a fresh version made from fresh chili pepper, onion, and tomato. Shito appears as an ingredient in Ghanaian recipes but hasn't found a market in the United States.

12. Fart Juice

While it may sound like an affliction caused by drinking it, Fart Juice is a potent potable in Poland. Made from the leftover liquid from cooking dried beans, this green beverage could pass for a vegetable juice and is probably a gas to drink, but it's not available in the United States.

Chapter 13
BOOKS

❋ ❋ ❋ ❋

9 Surprising Banned Books

In a world where sex, violence, and murder rule the television airwaves, it's hard to imagine that classic books such as Harper Lee's To Kill a Mockingbird *and John Steinbeck's* The Grapes of Wrath *were ever banned for objectionable content. Read on to find out why the following seemingly innocent tales have been banned in various locales.*

1. *Fahrenheit 451* by Ray Bradbury

Ray Bradbury reportedly wrote this novel in the basement of the UCLA library—on a pay-by-the-hour typewriter. Ironically, the story examines censorship, but unbeknownst to Bradbury, his publisher released a *censored* edition in 1967, nixing all profanity so the book would be safe for distribution in schools. A school in Mississippi banned the book in 1999 for the use of the very words Bradbury insisted be put back into the book when it was reprinted.

2. The *Where's Waldo?* Series by Martin Hanford

Who wants to look for Waldo when there are so many more interesting things to see in the pages of these colorful, oversized children's books? Waldo-mania swept the country in the mid-1990s, but schools in Michigan and New York wiped out Waldo because "on some of the pages there are dirty things." These "dirty things" included a topless lady on the beach. It's just a hunch, but if you can find her, Waldo's probably not far away. . . .

3. The *American Heritage Dictionary*

As recently as 1987, a school district in Anchorage, Alaska, went straight to the source of their problem and banned the whole darned dictionary. They didn't approve of the inclusion of certain slang usage for words like *bed* and *knockers*.

4. *The Complete Fairy Tales of The Brothers Grimm* by Jacob and Wilhelm Grimm

Those Grimm boys sure knew how to push the envelope. Most of the fairy tales we learned as kids are watered-down versions of classic Grimm stories such as *Little Red Riding Hood* and *Hansel and Gretel*. In the original works, however, there was more blood and fewer happy endings. Concerned parents have been contesting the literary merit—and age-appropriateness—of the Grimm Brothers' work since it was first published in the early 1800s.

5. *The Diary of a Young Girl* by Anne Frank

You're probably thinking, "I can see why this book might not be appropriate for youngsters, what with the baffling subject matter—how do you explain anti-Semitism and the Holocaust to anyone, much less a sixth-grader?" Unfortunately, that's not why a school in Alabama banned this book. Their reasoning? They just felt it was "a real downer."

6. The *Harry Potter* Series by J. K. Rowling

Wizards, magic spells, ghosts, and clever kids who outsmart adults—Rowling's dizzyingly popular series about a young magician with funny glasses is a treasure trove of "questionable content" for a surprising number of parents and teachers around the world.

7. *The Adventures of Tom Sawyer* by Mark Twain

No one can deny that Tom Sawyer is a bit of a troublemaker, and you could say the book somewhat glorifies running away from home, but was it really bad enough to ban? Libraries in New York and Colorado banned Twain's adventurous tale soon after the book came out, claiming Tom Sawyer was a protagonist of "questionable character." Tom would probably approve of the controversy.

8. *Steal This Book* by Abbie Hoffman

Sixties political activist Abbie Hoffman was cheeky as usual when naming his guide to governmental overthrow. The book was banned in Canada, and many stores in the United States refused to carry it for fear the title would prompt customers to shoplift. Had they carried the book, it would've been banned for other reasons—Hoffman describes how to make a pipe bomb, steal credit cards, and grow marijuana.

9. *Forever* by Judy Blume

Lots of authors tackle touchy topics such as divorce, racism, and death. Judy Blume did, too, only the novels she wrote were for young adults. Blume has always felt the issues that kids deal with on a daily basis are the ones they want to read about. When she published *Forever* in 1975, parents and teachers everywhere were steaming mad about the story of a girl and her boyfriend who decide to have premarital sex. The book is still being challenged in school libraries today.

17 Unusual Book Titles

❋ ❋ ❋ ❋

1. *How to Avoid Huge Ships* by John W. Trimmer
2. *Scouts in Bondage* by Michael Bell
3. *Be Bold with Bananas* by Crescent Books
4. *Fancy Coffins to Make Yourself* by Dale L. Power
5. *The Flat-Footed Flies of Europe* by Peter J. Chandler
6. *101 Uses for an Old Farm Tractor* by Michael Dregni
7. *Across Europe by Kangaroo* by Joseph R. Barry
8. *101 Super Uses for Tampon Applicators* by Lori Katz and Barbara Meyer
9. *Suture Self* by Mary Daheim
10. *The Making of a Moron* by Niall Brennan
11. *How to Make Love While Conscious* by Guy Kettelhack
12. *Underwater Acoustics Handbook* by Vernon Martin Albers
13. *Superfluous Hair and Its Removal* by A. F. Niemoeller
14. *Lightweight Sandwich Construction* by J. M. Davies
15. *The Devil's Cloth: A History of Stripes* by Michel Pastoureaut
16. *How to Be a Pope: What to Do and Where to Go Once You're in the Vatican* by Piers Marchant
17. *How to Read a Book* by Mortimer J. Adler and Charles Van Doren

20 Best-Selling Children's Books of All Time

❋ ❋ ❋ ❋

Title/Author	Number of Copies Sold
1. *The Poky Little Puppy* by Janette Sebring Lowrey (HC)	14,898,341
2. *Charlotte's Web* by E. B. White (PB)	9,899,696
3. *The Outsiders* by S. E. Hinton (PB)	9,695,159
4. *The Tale of Peter Rabbit* by Beatrix Potter (HC)	9,380,274
5. *Tootle* by Gertrude Crampton (HC)	8,560,277
6. *Green Eggs and Ham* by Dr. Seuss (HC)	8,143,088
7. *Harry Potter and the Goblet of Fire* by J. K. Rowling (HC)	7,913,765
8. *Pat the Bunny* by Dorothy Kunhardt (HC)	7,562,710
9. *Saggy Baggy Elephant* by Kathryn and Byron Jackson (HC)	7,476,395
10. *Scuffy the Tugboat* by Gertrude Crampton (HC)	7,366,073
11. *The Cat in the Hat* by Dr. Seuss (HC)	7,220,982
12. *Tales of a Fourth Grade Nothing* by Judy Blume (PB)	7,131,648
13. *Love You Forever* by Robert Munsch (PB)	6,970,000
14. *Where the Red Fern Grows* by Wilson Rawls (PB)	6,754,308
15. *Island of the Blue Dolphins* by Scott O'Dell (PB)	6,636,267
16. *Harry Potter and the Sorcerer's Stone* by J. K. Rowling (PB)	6,631,807
17. *Are You There, God? It's Me, Margaret* by Judy Blume (PB)	6,478,427
18. *Shane* by Jack Schaeffer (PB)	6,397,270
19. *The Indian in the Cupboard* by Lynne Reid Banks (PB)	6,394,587
20. *A Wrinkle in Time* by Madeleine L'Engle (PB)	6,393,523

° *HC=Hardcover; PB=Paperback*

Source: Publisher's Weekly, 2001

14 Best-Selling Books Repeatedly Rejected by Publishers

✳ ✳ ✳ ✳

Novelists spend years developing their craft, editing and reediting their work, agonizing over the smallest word, often to be rejected by publisher after publisher. The following famous books and authors were turned down by publishers at least 15 times before they became household names.

1. *Auntie Mame* by Patrick Dennis

Based on his party-throwing, out-of-control aunt, Patrick Dennis's story defined in 1955 what Americans now know as "camp." However, before Vanguard Press picked it up, 15 other publishers rejected it. Within years, *Auntie Mame* would not only become a hit on Broadway, but a popular film as well. Dennis became a millionaire and, in 1956, was the first author in history to have three books simultaneously ranked on *The New York Times* best seller list.

2. *Jonathan Livingston Seagull* by Richard Bach

Richard Bach has always said that this story, told from the point of view of a young seagull, wasn't written but channeled. When he sent out the story, Bach received 18 rejection letters. Nobody thought a story about a seagull that flew not for survival but for the joy of flying itself would have an audience. Boy, were they wrong! Macmillan Publishers finally picked up *Jonathan Livingston Seagull* in 1972, and that year the book sold more than a million copies. A movie followed in 1973, with a sound track by Neil Diamond.

3. *Chicken Soup for the Soul* by Jack Canfield and Mark Victor Hansen

Within a month of submitting the first manuscript to publishing houses, the creative team behind this multimillion dollar series got turned down 33 consecutive times. Publishers claimed that "anthologies don't sell" and the book was "too positive." Total number of rejections? 140. Then, in 1993, the president of Health Communications took a chance on the collection of poems, stories, and tidbits of encouragement. Today, the 65-title series has sold more than 80 million copies in 37 languages.

4. *Kon-Tiki* by Thor Heyerdahl

With a name like Thor, adventure on the high seas is sort of a given, isn't it? In 1947, Heyerdahl took a crew of six men on a 4,300-mile journey across the Pacific Ocean. But not on a cruise ship—their vessel was a reproduction of a prehistoric balsawood raft, and the only modern equipment they carried was a radio. Heyerdahl wrote the true story of his journey from Peru to Polynesia, but when he tried to get it published, he couldn't. One publisher asked him if anyone had drowned. When Heyerdahl said no, they rejected him on the grounds that the story wouldn't be very interesting. In 1953, after 20 rejections, *Kon-Tiki* finally found a publisher—and an audience. The book is now available in 66 languages.

5. *The Peter Principle* by Laurence Peter

In 1969, after 16 reported rejections, Canadian professor Laurence Peter's business book about bad management finally got a green light from Bantam Books. Within one year, the hardcover version of *The Peter Principle* was in its 15th reprint. Peter went on to write *The Peter Prescription, The Peter Plan,* and the unintentionally amusing *The Peter Pyramid: Will We Ever Get to the Point?* None of Peter's follow-up books did as well as the original, but no one can deny the book's impact on business publishing.

6. *Dubliners* by James Joyce

It took 22 rejections before a publisher took a chance on a young James Joyce in 1914. They didn't take too big of a chance—only 1,250 copies of *Dubliners* were initially published. Joyce's popularity didn't hit right away; out of the 379 copies that sold in the first year, Joyce himself purchased 120 of them. Joyce would go on to be regarded as one of the most influential writers of the 20th century. *Dubliners,* a collection of short stories, is among the most popular of Joyce's titles, which include *A Portrait of the Artist as a Young Man, Finnegans Wake,* and *Ulysses.*

7. *Lorna Doone* by Richard Doddridge Blackmore

You know you've done well when you've got a cookie named after your novel's heroine. Not only does Nabisco's Lorna Doone cookie remind us of Blackmore's classic, there are nearly a dozen big-screen or TV versions of the story, as well. This Devonshire-set romance of rivalry and revenge was turned down 18 times before being published in 1889. Today, Blackmore is considered one of the greatest British authors of the 19th century, though his popularity has waned over time.

8. *Zen and the Art of Motorcycle Maintenance* by Robert Pirsig

Pirsig's manuscript attempts to understand the true meaning of life. By the time it was finally published in 1974, the book had been turned down 121 times. The editor who finally published *Zen and the Art of Motorcycle Maintenance* said of Pirsig's book, "It forced me to decide what I was in publishing for." Indeed, *Zen* has given millions of readers an accessible, enjoyable book for seeking insight into their own lives.

9. *M*A*S*H* by Richard Hooker

Before the television series, there was the film. Before the film, there was the novel. Richard Hooker's unforgettable book about a medical unit serving in the Korean War was rejected by 21 publishers before eventually seeing the light of day. It remains a story of courage and friendship that connects with audiences around the world in times of war and peace.

10. *Carrie* by Stephen King

If it hadn't been for Stephen King's wife Tabitha, the iconic image of a young girl in a prom dress covered in pig's blood would not exist. King received 30 rejections for his story of a tormented girl with telekinetic powers, and then he threw it in the trash. Tabitha fished it out. King sent his story around again and, eventually, *Carrie* was published. The novel became a classic in the horror genre and has enjoyed film and TV adaptations as well. Sometimes all it takes is a little encouragement from someone who believes in you.

11. *Gone With the Wind* by Margaret Mitchell

The only book that Margaret Mitchell ever published, *Gone With the Wind* won her a Pulitzer Prize in 1937. The story of Scarlett O'Hara and Rhett Butler, set in the South during the Civil War, was rejected by 38 publishers before it was printed. The 1939 movie made of Mitchell's love story, which starred Clark Gable and Vivien Leigh, is the highest grossing Hollywood film of all time (adjusted for inflation).

12. *A Wrinkle in Time* by Madeleine L'Engle

The publishing house of Farrar, Straus and Giroux was smart enough to recognize the genius in L'Engle's tale for people of all ages. Published in 1962, the story was awarded the prestigious Newbery Medal the following year. *Wrinkle* remains one of the best-selling children's books of all time, and the story of precocious children and the magical world they discover was adapted for television in 2001. Still, L'Engle amassed 26 rejections before this success came her way.

13. *Heaven Knows, Mr. Allison* by Charles Shaw

In 1952, Crown Publishing Group in New York took a chance on the story of a shipwreck in the South Pacific. Shaw, an Australian author, was rejected by dozens of publishers on his own continent, and by an estimated 20 British publishing firms, too. By 1957, this humorous tale was made into a movie starring Deborah Kerr and Robert Mitchum. The story and the movie are considered war classics and garnered several Academy Award nominations, including one for Best Writing.

14. *Dune* by Frank Herbert

This epic science-fiction story was rejected by 23 publishers before being accepted by Chilton, a small Philadelphia publisher. *Dune* quickly became a success, winning awards such as the Hugo Award for Best Novel in 1966. *Dune* was followed by five sequels, and though none did as well as the original, a film version of the book starring rock star Sting did quite well and remains a cult favorite.

27 Largest American Libraries

✳ ✳ ✳ ✳

Library	*Number of Volumes*
1. Library of Congress	30,011,748
2. Harvard University	15,555,533
3. Boston Public Library	15,458,022
4. Yale University	12,025,695
5. University of Illinois–Urbana	10,370,777
6. County of Los Angeles Public Library	10,117,319
7. University of California–Berkeley	9,985,905
8. Columbia University	9,277,042
9. Public Library of Cincinnati and Hamilton County	9,148,846
10. University of Texas–Austin	8,937,002
11. Stanford University	8,200,000
12. University of Michigan	8,133,917
13. University of California–Los Angeles	8,064,896
14. University of Wisconsin–Madison	7,911,834
15. Cornell University	7,644,371
16. Detroit Public Library	7,572,562
17. University of Chicago	7,363,549
18. Indiana University	7,241,929
19. University of Washington	6,639,850
20. University of Minnesota	6,587,430
21. Queens Borough Public Library	6,557,823
22. Princeton University	6,495,597
23. Los Angeles Public Library	6,393,429
24. Free Library of Philadelphia	6,307,978
25. Ohio State University	5,936,434
26. Chicago Public Library	5,891,661
27. New York Public Library	5,879,441

Source: American Library Association

18 Famous Sidekicks

✳ ✳ ✳ ✳

As fearless, funny, or heroic as a protagonist may be, everyone needs a hand from time to time. Many of the leading men and women in literature, television, and cinema have had a trusty sidekick. See if you can match these faithful friends.

1. Don Quixote	a. Little John
2. Snoopy	b. Boo Boo
3. Ken Hutchinson	c. Babe
4. Fred Flintstone	d. Tinkerbell
5. D. J. Tanner	e. Ed McMahon
6. Archie Andrews	f. Ethel Mertz
7. Dorothy Gale	g. Goose
8. Robin Hood	h. Scooby-Doo
9. Yogi Bear	i. Tonto
10. Maverick	j. Jughead Jones
11. Peter Pan	k. Kimmy Gibbler
12. Batman	l. Dave Starsky
13. Shaggy	m. Barney Rubble
14. Paul Bunyan	n. Toto
15. Sherlock Holmes	o. Robin
16. Johnny Carson	p. Sancho Panza
17. Lucy Ricardo	q. Dr. Watson
18. The Lone Ranger	r. Woodstock

Answers: 1. p; 2. r; 3. l; 4. m; 5. k; 6. j; 7. n; 8. a; 9. b; 10. g; 11. d; 12. o; 13. h; 14. c; 15. q; 16. e; 17. f; 18. i

21 Best-Selling Books of All Time

✳ ✳ ✳ ✳

Title/Author	Copies Sold (millions)
1. The Bible by Various Authors	5,000–6,000
2. *Quotations from Chairman Mao Zedong* by Mao Zedong	900
3. The Qur'an by Muhammed	800
4. *Xinhua Zidian* Author Unknown	400
5. *The Book of Mormon* by Joseph Smith, Jr.	120
6. *Harry Potter and the Sorcerer's Stone* by J. K. Rowling	107
7. *And Then There Were None* by Agatha Christie	100
8. *The Lord of the Rings* by J.R.R. Tolkien	100
9. *Harry Potter and the Half-Blood Prince* by J. K. Rowling	65
10. *The Da Vinci Code* by Dan Brown	65
11. *Harry Potter and the Chamber of Secrets* by J. K. Rowling	60
12. *The Catcher in the Rye* by J. D. Salinger	60
13. *Harry Potter and the Goblet of Fire* by J. K. Rowling	55
14. *Harry Potter and the Order of the Phoenix* by J. K. Rowling	55
15. *Harry Potter and the Prisoner of Azkaban* by J. K. Rowling	55
16. *Ben Hur: A Tale of the Christ* by Lew Wallace	50
17. *Heidi's Years of Wandering and Learning* by Johanna Spyri	50
18. *The Alchemist* by Paulo Coelho	50
19. *The Common Sense Book of Baby and Child Care* by Dr. Benjamin Spock	50
20. *The Little Prince* by Antoine de Saint-Exupéry	50
21. *The Mark of Zorro* by Johnston McCulley	50

18 Memorable Character Names from the Works of Charles Dickens

✳ ✳ ✳ ✳

Born near London in 1812, Charles Dickens suffered many hardships throughout his life. Like many of the characters he would later create, Dickens stayed for a time in a workhouse, witnessed the death of several family members, and fell in and out of love a few times. All of this went into classic stories such as Oliver Twist, A Christmas Carol, *and* Great Expectations. *Dickens's characters typically had colorful names; the following list offers a sampling of these unusual and unique character names.*

1. Harold Skimpole (*Bleak House*)

This cheapskate claims he knows nothing about money management and uses that as an excuse to never pay for anything. Some claim Dickens modeled Skimpole after Leigh Hunt, another writer of the time, which, not surprisingly, caused a bit of animosity.

2. Sloppy (*Our Mutual Friend*)

One of Dickens's many orphan characters, Sloppy lives with Betty Higden and is taken in by the Boffin family. The noble Sloppy later has a hand in exposing nasty Silas Wegg.

3. Wopsle (*Great Expectations*)

Wopsle is a parish clerk when we meet him in this classic story, but he doesn't stay one for long. Choosing to become an actor, he changes his name to Waldengarver.

4. Polly Toodle (*Dombey and Son*)

Polly Toodle is Little Paul Dombey's nurse who gets fired after taking him to visit her dingy apartment in London's poorest area. Jolly and plump, Polly is a ray of hope in the face of poverty and hardship.

5. The Squeers (*Nicholas Nickleby*)

Wackford Squeers is the patriarch of this conniving, weasely pack. The Squeers run Dotheboys Hall, an orphanage for unwanted boys whom they mistreat horribly. Daughter Fanny, son Wackford, Jr., and the missus are each more cruel than the last.

6. Luke Honeythunder (*The Mystery of Edwin Drood*)

As with most of Dickens's characters, Luke Honeythunder's name fits him well. Described as boisterous and overbearing, this philanthropist is the guardian of Neville and Helena Landless.

7. Tulkinghorn (*Bleak House*)

This unscrupulous lawyer to the Dedlock family learns of Lady Dedlock's secret past and tries to take advantage of it. It doesn't end well for him—he is eventually murdered by her maid.

8. Bumble (*Oliver Twist*)

A petty officer in the workhouse where Oliver spends much of his time, Bumble symbolizes Dickens's contempt for the workhouse system.

9. Silas Wegg (*Our Mutual Friend*)

This street vendor is a gold digger after the Boffin family fortune. He tries to swindle the family when he's hired to read to Mr. Boffin, but Sloppy later exposes Wegg's ulterior motives.

10. Dick Swiveller (*The Old Curiosity Shop*)

Though the name sounds a little on the sinister side, this character is not a villain. Swiveller wants to marry the sweet and pretty Nell Trent but ends up with the Marchioness instead. He and the Marchioness expose the evil Brasses, Swiveller inherits money from his aunt, and the couple lives happily ever after.

11. Paul Sweedlepipe (*Martin Chuzzlewit*)

An eccentric barber, landlord, and bird lover, this character later inspired *A Christmas Carol*. Themes of greed and false honor run through *Martin Chuzzlewit* and also appear in the tale of Ebenezer Scrooge, published the following year.

12. Caroline "Caddy" Jellyby (*Bleak House*)

This sympathetic young woman is neglected by her mother, claiming, "I'm pen and ink to ma." Caddy ends up leaving home and marrying Prince Turveydrop.

13. Smike (*Nicholas Nickleby*)

The title character in this beloved story rescues Smike from the evil Squeers. As it turns out, Smike is Nickleby's cousin. Unfortunately, this is discovered after Smike has died from the Squeers' cruelty.

14. Mr. Sowerberry (*Oliver Twist*)

Oliver Twist runs away to London after being mistreated and abused by this ugly, cruel undertaker.

15. Uriah Heep (*David Copperfield*)

Uriah Heep, the antagonist of this novel, is one of literature's most wicked villains. Scheming and hypocritical, he plans to ruin Copperfield's friend Agnes Wickfield but is ultimately undone by Mr. Micawber.

16. Pumblechook (*Great Expectations*)

The great expectations of Pip, the main character and another Dickensian orphan, come from this rotund, loud-breathing guardian who takes Pip to wealthy and eccentric spinster Miss Havisham.

17. John Podsnap (*Our Mutual Friend*)

Dickens coined the term *podsnappery* to describe middle-class pomp and complacency. John Podsnap embodied this undesirable trait. Apparently, he was modeled after Dickens's first biographer, John Forster.

18. Lucretia Tox (*Dombey and Son*)

Described as tall, lean, and sad, Lucretia is friends with Mrs. Louisa Chick. Mrs. Chick has a brother named Paul. Lucretia is in love with Paul. Paul has a wife. Paul's wife dies. Lucretia hopes to marry Paul. Paul doesn't want Lucretia. Lucretia remains loyal, despite her broken heart. Classic Dickens.

10 Countries with the Most Readers

✳ ✳ ✳ ✳

Country	Avg. Hours Spent Reading per Week
1. India	10.7
2. Thailand	9.4
3. China	8.0
4. Philippines	7.6
5. Egypt	7.5
6. Czech Republic	7.4
7. Russia	7.1
8. Sweden (tied)	6.9
9. France (tied)	6.9
10. Hungary	6.8

15 Must-Read Books

✳ ✳ ✳ ✳

Throughout time, literary appetites have been sated with a slew of masterpieces that have brought readers to the depths of despair and the heights of elation, opened a world of possibilities, and challenged them to contemplate the meaning of life. As Ralph Waldo Emerson said of books, "They are for nothing but to inspire." Here are 15 that everyone should read at least once.

1. The Diary of a Young Girl by Anne Frank

First published in 1947, *The Diary of a Young Girl* chronicles the life of a Jewish girl while she and her family hide from the Nazis during World War II. The diary is the work of a deep, insightful mind, and the reader cannot help but be deeply affected by its poignancy. A few months after penning the last line of the diary, Anne died of typhus at age 15 while a prisoner at the Bergen-Belsen camp. The camp was liberated by Allied troops just a few weeks later.

2. *Crime and Punishment* by Fyodor Dostoevsky

Crime and Punishment, a psychological thriller first published in 1866, depicts the story of a murder from the killer's point of view. The novel illustrates the killer's fiendish game of cat and mouse with an implacable detective, but the real genius lies in the description of the inner turmoil that eats away at the murderer. As a bonus, the reader gets a history lesson on prerevolutionary Russia.

3. *The Adventures of Huckleberry Finn* by Mark Twain

According to Ernest Hemingway, *The Adventures of Huckleberry Finn* is the book that spawned all modern American literature. First published in 1884, it is the tale of a young rascal who teams up with a runaway slave. Together they travel down the Mississippi River, becoming embroiled in a series of adventures that expose them to the harsh realities of the American South. Despite the antiracist tenor of the book, it has repeatedly been banned as racist—it uses the "n-word" 212 times. Nevertheless, the book reveals the hypocrisy of racism like few books before or since.

4. *Cujo* by Stephen King

Cujo shows master horror writer King at the top of his game. First published in 1981, it tells the story of the middle-class Trenton family, whose domestic problems are dwarfed when a rabid St. Bernard goes a-huntin'. The novel occasionally allows the reader to see things from the perspective of the canine killer, especially during the three-day onslaught of Donna Trenton and her young son as they remain cooped up in a stalled Ford Pinto.

5. *Charlotte's Web* by E. B. White

First published in 1952, *Charlotte's Web* is a simple tale that has delighted millions of readers for decades. What would happen if a spider could weave words into her webs? The answer provides the plot for one of the best-selling children's books of all time. But don't be fooled—this story has plenty for adults, too. The struggle to save Wilbur the pig's life provides the canvas on which important themes such as the meaning of friendship, the cycle of life and death, and the power of loyalty are explored.

6. *The Great Gatsby* by F. Scott Fitzgerald

Written in the 1920s, *The Great Gatsby* studies the loss of the American Dream in an era of material excess. Set during the period of unrestrained prosperity that Fitzgerald dubbed "the Jazz Age," the story revolves around the sordid deeds of wealthy young Jay Gatsby and his inner circle of flunkies, led by Nick Carraway. Carraway, representing the reader's conscience, exposes the hypocrisy and futility of the materialistic lifestyle—an urgent message especially today.

7. *The Grapes of Wrath* by John Steinbeck

An American classic first published in 1939, *The Grapes of Wrath* is a story of survival and human dignity, courage and hope. It chronicles the life of the Joad family, poor Oklahoma farmers who set out at the height of the Great Depression for greener pastures in California. They ultimately discover, however, that promises of the good life are empty. The novel emphasizes the need for cooperative, rather than individual, solutions to the challenges facing society.

8. *Animal Farm* by George Orwell

Animals on a farm overthrow their human oppressors and establish a socialist state in George Orwell's *Animal Farm*. This modern fable, first published in 1945, is an allegory of the Soviet way of life. What starts out as an egalitarian society quickly degenerates into a state of terror where the pigs rule with an iron fist. The dangers the book warns about are not limited to socialism, reminding readers that absolute power leads to complete corruption.

9. *All Quiet on the Western Front* by Erich Maria Remarque

All Quiet on the Western Front was first published in 1929 and within 18 months had sold 2.5 million copies. Remarque, a German veteran of World War I, tells the story of Paul Bäumer, a German soldier who arrives on the battlefield with an idealistic vision of war. His illusions are quickly shattered as he is inexorably led to the conclusion that all war is pointless. No other novel so graphically portrays the horror and futility of war—a message that still needs to be heard today.

10. *To Kill a Mockingbird* by Harper Lee

Published in 1960, *To Kill a Mockingbird* is the only novel that Harper Lee has ever written, and it garnered her a Pulitzer Prize for Fiction. Set in a sleepy southern town during the Great Depression, the book is the first person account of a year in the life of young Scout Finch. During the year, two important things happen: Scout, her brother, and a friend try to out Boo Radley, a spooky recluse who lives next door; and Scout's father, the town lawyer, defends a black man against a rape charge. These two story lines are brilliantly woven together and ultimately combine to reveal a powerful and moving message.

11. *Fahrenheit 451* by Ray Bradbury

In the world of Bradbury's *Fahrenheit 451*, firemen don't put out fires, they start them—to burn books. As relevant today as when it was published in 1953, the novel shows what life would be like under a totalitarian regime in which all critical thought is suppressed. The main character is Guy Montag, a fireman (i.e. book burner) who sees his work as noble and beneficial to society. His confidence takes a hammering with the death of his wife and a subsequent relationship with a teenage girl who is full of curiosity about the world. Her disappearance is the catalyst that gradually transforms Montag into an advocate of free thought—he even starts to read books.

12. *The Lord of the Rings* by J.R.R. Tolkien

The Lord of the Rings by J.R.R. Tolkien was first published in three volumes between 1954 and 1955. The book is a sequel to Tolkien's earlier work *The Hobbit,* published in 1937. The central character is Frodo, a hobbit entrusted with a magical ring that is the source of power for the evil Sauron. The fate of Middle Earth ebbs and flows through page after page of spectacular fantasy, epic battles, and, ultimately, the triumph of good over evil. Perhaps the most powerful message of the book is its conclusion, which shows that although good has triumphed, evil has left a permanent mark in the world.

13. *Oliver Twist* by Charles Dickens

"Please sir, I want some more." This famous line was spoken by the orphan Oliver Twist in Charles Dickens's book of the same name. First published in 1838, *Oliver Twist* is a social novel, revealing the stark reality of 19th-century workhouses and the treatment of poor and underprivileged children. Oliver spends his first nine years on a baby farm—a place where orphans were sold to the highest bidder—then he transfers to the workhouse. After six months of drudgery, he loses a bet and faces up to the cook with his famous request. The fallout has him parceled off to various brutes before setting off for London. On the way he meets a colorful character known as the Artful Dodger. It's a great adventure as well as an important reminder to protect society's most innocent and vulnerable members.

14. *The Lord of the Flies* by William Golding

In *The Lord of the Flies,* a group of young boys are stranded on a deserted island and forced to govern themselves. The results are chaotic and deadly. Golding's story presents an allegory about human nature, individual welfare, and the value of communal living. The book was first published in 1954 and, although it sold only 3,000 copies in its first year, it had become a best seller by 1960.

15. The Bible

The Bible, made up of 66 separate books, is the most influential collection of books in human history and, by far, the best-selling book of all time. It has influenced some of the world's greatest art, literature, and music and has had a significant impact on law. Esteemed by scholars and extolled for its literary style, the Bible's effect on the lives of people in all strata of society has been particularly profound, inspiring a remarkable degree of loyalty in many of its readers. Some have even risked death just to read it. The Bible is the most translated, most quoted, and most respected book in Western society and probably the most controversial book in the world, surviving bans, burnings, and violent opposition.

Chapter 14
TELEVISION

✳ ✳ ✳ ✳

18 Memorable TV Theme Songs

A great TV theme song can tell you everything you need to know about a show in less than a minute. Better yet, if you can sing a few lines at work the next day and everyone joins in, you know you're on to something worth watching!

1. "Where Everybody Knows Your Name" (*Cheers*)

Written by Judy Hart Angelo and Gary Portnoy (and sung by him, too), this comforting tune conjures up images of a place where the lonely and downtrodden can find a friend to lean on, where people can forget about their troubles for a while, and, yes, "where everybody knows your name." And that's exactly what *Cheers* did for 275 episodes from 1982 to 1993.

2. "Love Is All Around" (*Mary Tyler Moore*)

Songwriter Sonny Curtis wrote and performed the empowering theme song for this trailblazing show about women's lib and the single life of spunky career woman Mary Richards. The opening sequence showed a fresh-faced Mary as she arrives in her new city and tosses her beret into the air out of the pure excitement of starting a new life. The original lyrics contemplated "...you might just make it after all," but after the first season, when it was clear that Mary would be a success, the lyrics were changed to "...you're gonna make it after all!" The bubbly and upbeat song has even been covered by Joan Jett & The Blackhearts and Sammy Davis, Jr.

3. "Theme Song from The Brady Bunch" (*The Brady Bunch*)

Series creator Sherwood Schwartz collaborated with composer Frank DeVol to come up with the much-repeated theme song that describes what happens when a second marriage merges two families and six children under one roof. The song alone is memorable, but so is the opening sequence, which divided the screen into nine squares, one for each family member, including the housekeeper Alice. On the left, we saw the three daughters "...All of them had hair of gold, like their mother. The youngest one in curls." The right side introduced the three sons, who with their father made "...four men, living all together. Yet they were all alone." Who sang the song, you ask? The cast, of course!

4. "Ballad of Gilligan's Isle" (*Gilligan's Island*)

All you have to do is listen to the theme song—it's all there! But here it is in a coconut shell: Five passengers went on a boating expedition that was supposed to last only three hours, but there was a storm, and the S.S. *Minnow* shipwrecked. The Skipper, his goofy first mate, and the passengers set up house on an island and made various futile attempts to be rescued. True *Gilligan's Island* aficionados know that there were two versions of the theme song, which was written by George Wyle and the show's creator Sherwood Schwartz. The first version specifically mentions five of the cast members, then lumps two other characters together, referring to them as "the rest." But Bob Denver (aka Gilligan) thought the song should be rewritten to include "The Professor and Mary Ann." Denver may have played the doofus on camera, but he used his star power to get equal billing for his fellow cast mates. He truly was everyone's "little buddy."

5. "Meet the Flintstones" (*The Flintstones*)

During the first two seasons there was no theme song! Then show creators William Hanna and Joseph Barbera wrote lyrics for a tune by Hoyt Curtin. The show, which took place in the prehistoric town of Bedrock, was a parody on contemporary suburbia. There were no brakes on cars, just bare feet to slow things down. Cameras were primitive—birds feverishly chiseled slabs of rock to capture various images. And instead of a garbage disposal, people just kept a hungry reptile under the sink. Still, it was a "yabba-dabba-doo time. A dabba-doo time." In fact, it was a "...gay old time!"

6. "I'll Be There for You" (*Friends*)

Written and performed by The Rembrandts, "I'll Be There for You" pretty much sums up the premise of these loyal friends who supported each other through life's ups and downs. The intensely popular sitcom showed just how funny it is to be in your twenties (eventually thirties), single, and living in New York City. Three guys and three girls formed a special bond as they roomed together, sometimes dated each other, and always entertained audiences worldwide. The song wasn't intended to be a full-length track, but eventually the band went back into the studio and recorded a longer version of the song, which topped U.S. charts and reached number two in the UK.

7. "Those Were the Days" (*All in the Family*)

Longing for a less complicated time, "Those Were the Days" was written by Charles Strouse and Lee Adams and was performed at the family piano by bigoted, blue-collar Archie Bunker and his screechingly off-key "dingbat" wife Edith. In the show, which aired from 1971 to 1979, staunchly conservative Archie is forced to live with a liberal when his "little goil" Gloria and her husband Michael move in with the Bunkers. The resulting discussions shed light on two sides of politics and earned Michael the nickname "Meathead."

8. "Theme from The Addams Family" (*The Addams Family*)

TV and film composer Vic Mizzy wrote the music and engaging lyrics that helped to describe the "creepy...kooky...mysterious...spooky...and all together ooky" Addams Family. The show takes a peek at the bizarre family: Gomez and Morticia, their children Pugsley and Wednesday, Cousin Itt, Uncle Fester, and servants Lurch and Thing, who all live together in a musty castle. The show lasted only two seasons, but it lives on in pop culture through reruns, cartoons, movies, and video games.

9. "Theme to Happy Days" (*Happy Days*)

Bill Haley and His Comets recorded a new version of their hit "Rock Around the Clock" for the theme song of the show about the middle-class Cunningham family and their life in Milwaukee in the 1950s and 1960s. After two seasons, the song "Theme to Happy Days," composed by Charles Fox and Norman Gimbel and performed by Truett Pratt and Jerry McClain, moved from the show's closing song to the opener. The song was released as a single in 1976 and cracked *Billboard*'s top five. The final season of the show featured a more modern version of the song led by Bobby Avron, but it was unpopular with fans.

10. "Making Our Dreams Come True" (*Laverne & Shirley*)

Factory workers never had so much fun! Laverne and Shirley were two kooky girls who were introduced to TV audiences on *Happy Days* and ended up with their own hit show. They got into all kinds of trouble but always made it look like fun. The upbeat theme song was written by Charles Fox and Norman Gimbel and sung by Cyndi Grecco. The lyrics were empowering, but perhaps the most repeated line over the years was a mix of Yiddish and German words: "Schlemiel! Schlemazl! Hasenpfeffer Incorporated!"

11. "Sunny Day" (*Sesame Street*)

Sesame Street was the first TV show to merge entertainment and learning for the preschool set and is largely responsible for children starting kindergarten knowing their letters, numbers, and colors. The show, which airs in more than 120 countries, has won more than 100 Emmy Awards, making it the most award-winning TV series of all time. The cheerful and idyllic theme song was written by Joe Raposo, Jon Stone, and Bruce Hart, but the singers are all children. Or at least they were when the show debuted in 1969!

12. "Theme from The Monkees" (*The Monkees*)

Here they come.... The original "prefab" four, The Monkees were a mix of zany actors and musicians cast as a rock band for the 1960s TV show of the same name. "Theme from The Monkees" was written by Bobby Hart and Tommy Boyce, and once the band members were cast, they recorded the song. The band was so successful that they went on tour and three of their songs reached number one on

U.S. charts. The show only lasted two seasons, but The Monkees are now best known for their musical success and occasionally get together for reunion tours.

13. "The Fishin' Hole" (*The Andy Griffith Show*)

When *The Andy Griffith Show* debuted in 1960, Sheriff Andy Taylor became one of TV's first single dads when his wife died and left him to raise their young son Opie in the small town of Mayberry. Aunt Bea came to town to help out, and Deputy Barney Fife helped keep small-town crime at bay. The result was an endearing slice of Americana that still lives on in syndication. The show's theme song was written by Earle Hagen and Herbert Spencer and is memorable but not for the lyrics—there are none! The melody is carried by a lone whistler (Hagen) and accompanies footage of Andy and Opie heading off together for some quality time fishing.

14. "The Love Boat" (*The Love Boat*)

The Love Boat was just one of producer Aaron Spelling's offerings that dominated TV sets in the '70s and '80s. Love was definitely exciting and new every week when the *Pacific Princess* cruise ship set sail with a new set of passengers and a new set of challenges! Paul Williams and Charles Fox wrote the theme song, and for the first eight years, Jack Jones provided the vocals, but in 1985 Dionne Warwick recorded her version for the show. With lyrics such as "Set a course for adventure, your mind on a new romance..." people were hooking up all over the Pacific seaboard.

15. "Ballad of Jed Clampett" (*The Beverly Hillbillies*)

When hillbilly Jed Clampett struck oil while hunting on his land, he packed up his family and moved where the other rich people lived—Beverly Hills, California, of course! His beautiful and usually barefoot daughter Elly May attracted a lot of attention as did pretty much everything about the Clampett family. Series creator Paul Henning wrote the "Ballad of Jed Clampett," which was performed by bluegrass musicians Flatt and Scruggs. After the show debuted in 1962, the song made it to number 44 on the pop charts and all the way to number one on the country charts.

16. "I Love Lucy" (*I Love Lucy*)

One of the most popular TV shows ever produced, *I Love Lucy* starred Lucille Ball as zany redhead Lucy Ricardo and Desi Arnaz as her husband, Cuban bandleader Ricky. Lucy and her reluctant neighbor and best friend, Ethel Mertz, were always involved in one harebrained scheme or another during this classic's six-year run. The show's theme song, written by Harold Adamson and Eliot Daniel, is most recognizable in its instrumental version, but the song does have lyrics. During a 1953 episode in which Lucy believes everyone has forgotten her birthday, Ricky croons "I love Lucy, and she loves me. We're as happy as two can be...."

17. "A Little Help from My Friends" (*The Wonder Years*)

Set in the late 1960s and early 1970s, *The Wonder Years* chronicled the life of teenager Kevin Arnold as he grows up in suburbia in a middle-class family during this turbulent time. During the opening credits, the theme song, "A Little Help from My Friends," plays alongside "home movies" of Kevin and his family and friends. Hardly recognizable as the classic Beatles tune, Joe Cocker's cover of the song is much slower and in a different key, but was reportedly loved by the Fab Four themselves.

18. "Generation" (*American Dreams*)

In this family drama, the Pryor family faces the social and political issues of the 1960s, while teenager Meg Pryor and her friend Roxanne are regular dancers on *American Bandstand,* which sets the show to the sound track of the '60s. The theme song, "Generation," written and performed by Tonic's Emerson Hart, takes listeners back to a time when life was much simpler and safer. With lyrics like "we just want to dance all night..." and "...This might be the only time around...," the song inspired a "seize the day" attitude. The show had an extremely loyal fan base, but poor time slots assigned by NBC resulted in low ratings, and the show was unexpectedly axed following the third season-ending cliffhanger, which left fans disappointed and longing for more.

16 Popular TV Shows of the 1950s

❋ ❋ ❋ ❋

1. *I Love Lucy*
2. *You Bet Your Life*
3. *Gunsmoke*
4. *I've Got a Secret*
5. *Dragnet*
6. *The Jack Benny Program*
7. *The Adventures of Ozzie and Harriet*
8. *The Milton Berle Show*
9. *The Honeymooners*
10. *Leave It to Beaver*
11. *The Ed Sullivan Show*
12. *The Donna Reed Show*
13. *Father Knows Best*
14. *Make Room for Daddy (The Danny Thomas Show)*
15. *Have Gun, Will Travel*
16. *The Lone Ranger*

10 Longest-Running TV Shows

❋ ❋ ❋ ❋

The first television drama aired in 1928, but it wasn't until after World War II that TV really took off. Today, satellite and cable options provide a TV smorgasbord. Although many news programs and soap operas have lasted longer, we've narrowed this list down to longest-running dramas and sitcoms in television history. Grab the remote and take a trip down TV's memory lane.

1. Gunsmoke (1955–1975)

Gunsmoke tops the list as the longest-running dramatic series in network television history with 635 episodes. Set in Dodge City, Kansas, during the 1870s, *Gunsmoke* began as a radio program in

1952, switched to the land of visual entertainment in 1955, and finally ended its 20-year run in 1975.

2. *Lassie* (1954–1972)

Running for 588 episodes, *Lassie* centered around a loyal canine companion who rescued her human family from various predicaments. Over the years, Lassie was portrayed by nine different male dogs, all descendants of the original Lassie, whose real name was Pal. During the show's run, Lassie had various owners, most notably Timmy and Jeff. Only three dogs have a star on the Hollywood Walk of Fame—Lassie, Rin Tin Tin, and Strongheart.

3. *Death Valley Days* (1952–1970)

In 1952, *Death Valley Days,* which aired as a radio show from 1930 to 1945, evolved into a successful TV show that lasted 18 seasons. A host introduced each of the 451 episodes, which were based on actual pioneer stories that took place in southeastern California and western Nevada during the late 1800s. Future President Ronald Reagan and country singer Merle Haggard were among the hosts during the show's run.

4. *The Adventures of Ozzie and Harriet* (1952–1966)

What began as a radio program in 1944 became a movie (*Here Come the Nelsons*) in 1952 and then a successful television program that ran for 435 episodes. In this wholesome show, the characters played themselves—Ozzie and Harriet Nelson and their two sons, David and Ricky. Ozzie's roots were in music, so when Ricky's talent started to emerge, Ozzie wrote it into the story line, ending each show with a performance by his younger son. These weekly, televised performances helped skyrocket Ricky onto the pop charts, making him a teen idol as well as a successful recording artist.

5. *Bonanza* (1959–1973)

Airing for 430 episodes, this Western was set in the mid-1800s on a Nevada ranch called "The Ponderosa." The show revolved around the life of Ben Cartwright and his sons Adam, Hoss, and Little Joe (played by Michael Landon). *Bonanza* was the first series to tape all of its shows in color, and it held the number one spot on the Nielsen ratings chart from 1964 to 1967.

6. *The Simpsons* (1989–????)

With more than 400 episodes (and counting), the most successful animated family in the history of TV has been going strong since 1989. Creator Matt Groening parodies the average (albeit dysfunctional) American family with buffoonish, yet lovable Homer Simpson, his wife Marge, their brilliant daughter Lisa, bad-seed son Bart, and baby Maggie. There are enough interesting factoids about this show to make a book of its own! For starters, snagging a voice-over gig to play oneself on the show is a real show-biz coup. Even rock bands like U2, Smashing Pumpkins, and Aerosmith have contributed their likenesses and voices to the effort.

7. *Law & Order* (1990–????)

With 390 episodes (and counting) under its belt since it premiered in 1990, the key to this show's success may lie in its ever-revolving cast. None of the original actors remain on the show, and most cast members only stick around a couple of seasons. Still, the show must go on, and the New York City Police Department and District Attorney's office have their hands (and squad cars and jail cells) full as they clean up the streets of Manhattan on this award-winning drama. Halfway through each episode, the focus shifts from investigation to prosecution of the same case.

8. *My Three Sons* (1960–1972)

For 380 episodes and 12 seasons, Americans stepped into the world of widower Steve Douglas and—you guessed it—his three sons: Mike, Robbie, and Chip. When Mike left the show after the 1965 season, a younger boy named Ernie was adopted so that the title would still work! Uncle Charley moved in to help with cooking, cleaning, and homework. Fred MacMurray, who played the father, was also a star of Disney movies, so in order for him to do both, he shot all of his *My Three Sons* scenes for an entire season at once. The rest of the scenes were shot later and the episodes were then pieced together. But as the boys grew and their hairstyles changed, this arrangement caused problems with continuity.

9. *Dallas* (1978–1991)

You'd think life on a Texas oil ranch and mansion named "Southfork" would be sublime, but not so for this feuding bunch. For 357 episodes, *Dallas* revolved around the wealthy Ewing family— oil baron and patriarch Jock Ewing, his wife Miss Ellie, and their sons JR, Bobby, and black sheep Gary. When JR was shot in the finale of the third season, "Who Shot JR?" mania swept across the country—and much of the world. But viewers had to wait until four episodes into the new season to find out who pulled the trigger. The episode titled "Who Done It?" was the second most-watched show in the history of television.

10. *Knots Landing* (1979–1993)

These were the original desperate housewives. (In fact, Nicollette Sheridan was among the cast!) The show's premise centered on Gary Ewing (from *Dallas*) and his lovely bumpkin wife Valene, who moved to California. Their neighbors included a host of dysfunctional families and through marriages, affairs, births, stolen babies, murders, novels, new business enterprises, and even a televangelist brother, this show kept viewers watching for 344 episodes.

20 Popular TV Shows of the 1960s

❋ ❋ ❋ ❋

1. *Candid Camera*
2. *The Andy Griffith Show*
3. *Bonanza*
4. *The Red Skelton Show*
5. *Gunsmoke*
6. *The Lucy Show*
7. *Gomer Pyle U.S.M.C.*
8. *The Beverly Hillbillies*

9. *The Dick Van Dyke Show*
10. *Gilligan's Island*
11. *My Three Sons*
12. *Lassie*
13. *The Munsters*
14. *Bewitched*
15. *Green Acres*
16. *Get Smart*
17. *Batman*
18. *Family Affair*
19. *The Twilight Zone*
20. *I Dream of Jeannie*

10 Puppets that Made it Big on Television

❊ ❊ ❊ ❊

Puppets have a special place in television history. Many of the first shows broadcast starred ventriloquist dummies, hand puppets, and marionettes. Although animation has replaced many puppet shows, the Muppets and others carry on the tradition.

1. Charlie McCarthy

Charlie McCarthy will forever be remembered as the best-known dummy on radio. As a teenager in the late 1910s, ventriloquist Edgar Bergen purchased the wooden dummy, and they became partners until Bergen's death in 1978. Following a successful appearance on singer Rudy Vallee's radio program in 1936, Edgar and Charlie were given their own show, which remained on the air until 1956. No one listening could see that Charlie was dressed in a top hat, cape, and monocle, nor could they see that Bergen's lips often moved when Charlie spoke. Fans didn't seem to mind, even when the pair appeared on television and in movies. Their success was a result of the hilarious and somewhat risqué (for the time) conversations that Charlie had with stars like actress Mae West and comedian W. C. Fields. In 1938, Bergen won an honorary Oscar for his creation of Charlie. The award was a wooden statuette.

2. Kukla, Fran, and Ollie

Kukla, Fran, and Ollie was a children's show that first hit the airwaves in 1947. Kukla, the leader of the group, resembled a clown but wasn't one; Ollie was Oliver J. Dragon, a feisty dragon with one tooth; and Fran was not a puppet but a big sister figure who kept the two in line. Rounding out the cast were other puppets, including Madame Ooglepuss, a former opera diva; Beulah Witch; and Fletcher Rabbit. Although the show was originally created for children, it quickly became more popular with adults for the character development and humor.

3. Farfel and Danny O'Day

Farfel, the long-eared shaggy dog, and Danny O'Day were puppets who appeared in many TV commercials for Nestle's Quik. Danny O'Day sang "N-E-S-T-L-E-S, Nestle's makes the very best..." and Farfel responded with "Chawk-lit!" Along with ventriloquist Jimmy Nelson, the trio reached national prominence in the 1950s when they joined the *Texaco Star Theater* starring Milton Berle.

4. Topo Gigio

Created in 1958 by artist Maria Perego, Topo Gigio, a friendly mouse with huge ears, was the star of a children's television show in Italy in the early 1960s. Immensely popular in his home country, Topo Gigio became a worldwide sensation after his appearance on *The Ed Sullivan Show* in 1963. A fixture of Italian pop culture, Topo Gigio still performs regularly at festivals in Italy.

5. Howdy Doody

The Howdy Doody Show, hosted by "Buffalo Bob" Smith, was a groundbreaking children's television show that aired from 1947 through 1960. Howdy Doody was a blue-eyed, red-haired, freckle-faced marionette, whose name originated from the expression "howdy do," a variation of the greeting "How do you do?" Each episode of the show began with Buffalo Bob asking the audience, "What time is it?" to which they would enthusiastically respond, "It's Howdy Doody time!" Howdy Doody is now on display at the Smithsonian's National Museum of American History.

6. Andy Pandy

Andy Pandy, a marionette who lived in a picnic basket, starred in the British children's television show of the same name, which first aired in 1950. Andy's sidekick was a teddy bear named Teddy, and rag doll Looby Loo only appeared when the two weren't around. In 2002, the show was revived using stop-motion animation rather than puppets, and some new characters were added, including Missy Hissy, a snake; Tiffo, a dog; and Orbie, a yellow and blue ball.

7. Lamb Chop

Lamb Chop is a sweet sock puppet sheep created by comedian and ventriloquist Shari Lewis in 1957. During the 1960s, Lamb Chop appeared on Lewis's musical-comedy television show. In 1992, Lewis created *Lamb Chop's Play-Along,* a children's show for PBS that won five Emmy Awards. Shari Lewis died in 1998, but her daughter Mallory has kept Lamb Chop alive for her many fans.

8. Bert and Ernie

Created by the legendary Jim Henson, Bert and Ernie are two Muppets that have appeared on the long-running PBS children's television show *Sesame Street* since its debut in 1969. Bert and Ernie are something of an "odd couple" with the impish and naive Ernie often frustrating the rational and practical Bert. Despite misconceptions surrounding their living situation, *Sesame Street* execs contend that Bert and Ernie are not homosexual, they're simply roommates, and the pair continues to be a fan favorite. Ernie even released a record, "Rubber Duckie," which reached the top 40 on *Billboard* charts in 1970.

9. Triumph the Insult Comic Dog

Resembling a rottweiler, Triumph the Insult Comic Dog is a rubbery hand puppet featured on *Late Night with Conan O'Brien.*

Triumph speaks with an Eastern European accent, puffs on a cigar, and his trademark catchphrase is "...for me to poop on!"—usually spoken to negate a compliment that precedes it, such as "You're the best...for me to poop on!" Since his debut in a 1997 comedy skit about the Westminster Kennel Club dog show, Triumph has been tossing insults at guests in the style of comedian Don Rickles.

10. Kermit the Frog

Kermit the Frog actually began life in 1955 as a lizard-like creature. Kermit, who was created by legendary muppeteer Jim Henson, was made from two ping-pong balls (for eyes) and a discarded green coat. By 1969, Kermit had transformed into a frog, and that year he landed a recurring part on *Sesame Street,* a role that would make him a household name. By far one of the most popular puppets of all time, Kermit has appeared on several television shows, including *The Muppet Show.* He has also starred in movies, such as *The Muppets Take Manhattan,* recorded songs ("Bein' Green" and "The Rainbow Connection"), and even guest-hosted *The Tonight Show.* You've come a long way from the swamp, Kermy!

21 Popular TV Shows of the 1970s

✳ ✳ ✳ ✳

1. *M*A*S*H*
2. *All in the Family*
3. *Sanford and Son*
4. *Hawaii Five-O*
5. *Happy Days*
6. *Maude*
7. *Laverne & Shirley*
8. *Mary Tyler Moore*
9. *The Brady Bunch*
10. *The Jeffersons*
11. *Three's Company*
12. *Alice*

13. *One Day at a Time*
14. *Good Times*
15. *Little House on the Prairie*
16. *Starsky and Hutch*
17. *The Waltons*
18. *The Partridge Family*
19. *The Carol Burnett Show*
20. *Welcome Back, Kotter*
21. *Charlie's Angels*

CHECK OUT THESE DRAMA QUEENS
11 Longest-Running Daytime Soap Operas

✳ ✳ ✳ ✳

"Soaps" have been around since the 1930s when Proctor &
Gamble produced 15-minute episodes of love and drama for radio.
Allegedly, the term soap opera *was coined because these shows*
were sponsored by a company that made cleansers. By the early
1950s, soap operas had switched over to television, and daytime
TV had no shortage of offerings. As you'll see, captivating story
lines and characters are the keys to longevity on daytime televi-
sion. If you're curious about the shortest-running soap, it was
NBC's These Are My Children, *which lasted only 24 days in 1949.*

1. (The) Guiding Light (1952–????)

Not only is *Guiding Light* the longest-running soap, at more than
15,000 episodes (and still going), it is also the longest-running non-
news program in U.S. television history. Like many of the oldest
soaps, *Guiding Light* began in 1937 as a radio program before making the transition to television on June 30, 1952. Originally, the soap
took place in the fictional town of Five Points, then Selby Flats,
and revolved around the Bauer family. Now, it's the Spauldings,
Coopers, and Lewises who are in the limelight. During the 1960s,
The was dropped from the show's title to make it sound more contemporary. One of the show's more bizarre story lines involved

cloning longtime character Reva Lewis from one of her own frozen eggs! Once the clone was born, she was given aging serum so that she would grow up fast. But she was evil and attempted to take Reva's place.

2. *As the World Turns* (1956–????)

Set in Oakdale, a fictional midwestern town, *As the World Turns* has been immensely popular since it debuted on April 2, 1956. The show is more reality-based than other soaps, but people do come back from the dead, and children grow up far faster than in real life, as is the norm for the soap world. The first soap opera to use a two-family setup, *As the World Turns* pitted a middle-class family against a wealthy, but troubled, family. The Hughes family remains as the middle-class hero, but the wealthy family was originally the Lowells, now it's the Munsons. After more than 13,000 episodes, the world is still turning, and this soap is still going strong.

3. *General Hospital* (1963–????)

Named the "Greatest Soap Opera of all Time" by *TV Guide* in 2003, *General Hospital* has won the Daytime Emmy for Outstanding Drama series nine times—more than any other soap! *General Hospital* began its run on ABC on April 1, 1963, the very same day that NBC launched its rival medical drama *The Doctors*. Today, the show revolves around the Spencers, the Cassidines, mobster Sonny Corinthos, and the wealthy Quartermaine family. The pairing of adventuresome Luke and Laura in the late '70s sparked the trend of the soap opera super couple. Set in fictional Port Charles, New York, most scenes take place at the docks, or, where else... General Hospital. Throughout the show's history, *General Hospital* has been a jumping-off point for several notable performers, including Demi Moore, Rick Springfield, John Stamos, and Ricky Martin.

4. *Days of Our Lives* (1965–????)

"Like sands through the hourglass..." faithful viewers have been watching *Days of Our Lives* since it debuted on November 8, 1965. *Days* takes place in the fictional midwestern town of Salem, with most scenes shot at University Hospital or the Brady Pub. Today, Salem is home to the respectable Horton and Brady families, as well as the evil DiMeras. Since the show debuted more than 40 years ago, matriarch Alice Horton has been portrayed by award-winning actor Frances Reid. In the 1980s, the "Salem Stalker" and "Salem Slasher" brought romantic adventure to the forefront, while in the 1990s, Dr. Marlena Evans-Black (Deidre Hall) was possessed by the devil.

5. *One Life to Live* (1968–????)

When *One Life to Live* originally aired on July 15, 1968, the wealthy Lord family was pitted against the middle-class Woleks and Rileys and the Siegels, the first Jewish family on a daytime drama. Now it's the Buchanans, Rapaports, Gannons, and Cramers who see most of the action. They live in Llanview, Pennsylvania, a fictional suburb of Philadelphia. Llanview residents have seen cults, time travel, and out-of-body experiences. Incidentally, Llanview is only a 30-minute drive from another fictional soap town: *All My Children's* Pine Valley. As such, there have been several story line crossovers since both soaps are on ABC.

6. *All My Children* (1970–????)

The brainchild of soap opera creator, writer, and producer Agnes Nixon, *All My Children* has been taking risks since its introduction on January 5, 1970. Set in fictional Pine Valley, Pennsylvania, this soap deals with serious issues and over the years has broached controversial topics such as abortion, drugs, homosexuality, rape, and even the Vietnam War. One of only two actors who have remained on the show for its entire run, Susan Lucci was nominated for a Daytime Emmy for 18 years in a row without a win for her role as Erica Kane. But Lucci was finally victorious in 1999.

7. *The Young and the Restless* (1973–????)

The Young and the Restless took to the small screen on March 26, 1973, and more than 10,000 episodes later, it shows no signs of letting up. Home for *Y&R* characters is Genoa City, Wisconsin, a fictional version of a real village. The TV town is a hotbed of corporate intrigue and grandeur, pitting two wealthy families—the Newmans and the Abbotts—against each other. One of *Y&R's* most outrageous characters, Sheila Carter Grainger Forrester Warwick (Kimberlin Brown) has switched babies, tried to burn her own mother alive, used paternity results as blackmail, shot people, lived in a mental institution, and escaped from a mental institution by convincing someone to have plastic surgery and take her place. She is currently presumed dead, but in soap world that means nothing—look for her to menace again! With story lines like that, it's no wonder that *Y&R* has held the top spot in the ratings war since 1988.

8. *Search for Tomorrow* (1951–1986)

For the show's entire run, from September 3, 1951 to December 26, 1986, *Search for Tomorrow* followed the life of heroine Joanne Gardner. Joanne and her friends lived in the fictional town of Henderson, and many scenes took place at her kitchen table over a cup of coffee. In the mid-1980s, in a last-ditch attempt to bring up ratings before cancellation, the entire town was wiped out in a flood, but even that didn't do the trick. By 1986, NBC decided that searching for tomorrow wasn't nearly as exciting as juicy topics like government scandals, so after 9,130 episodes, the soap was axed in favor of a glitzy new show called *Capitol.*

9. *Another World* (1964–1999)

The subject of abortion isn't exactly unheard of today, but in 1964, it was groundbreaking to say the least. During its first year on the air, *Another World* came on strong with a bold and risky story line in which a teen has an illegal abortion and ends up a sterile, acquitted murderer who marries her lawyer. In the early days, *Another World,* which is set in the fictional town of Bay City, started out pitting a middle-class branch and an upper-class branch of the Matthews family against each other. Later, the Randolph, Cory, and Hudson families became part of the show's fabric, but in 1999, after 8,891 episodes, *Another World* was canceled.

10. *Love of Life* (1951–1980)

When *Love of Life* first aired on September 24, 1951, it did not take commercial breaks. The show was owned by a company called American Home Products and licensed to CBS, so there was no need to break for commercials. Goods from American Home Products were hawked either before or after the show. The show was first set in fictional Barrowsville, then it moved to suburban Rosehill, New York. The show revolved around the relationship between the good Vanessa Dale and her evil sister Meg Dale Harper. Christopher Reeve's first major role was that of Meg's son Ben Harper, from 1974 to 1976. After ratings plummeted, the show ended abruptly with a cliffhanger on February 1, 1980, and since the show was canceled, fans were really left hanging... forever.

11. *The Edge of Night* (1956–1984)

From its debut on April 2, 1956, through the 1960s, *The Edge of Night* was consistently one of the top-ranking soaps on television. Known for its well-staged action sequences shot on location rather than on sets, most of the show's story lines took place in the fictional town of Monticello and centered around Assistant District Attorney Mike Karr and his love interest Sarah Lane. In 1978, *The Edge of Night*'s audience was nearly 50 percent male! This is probably because the soap didn't have a traditional love and drama theme; it was intended to be a daytime version of *Perry Mason*. After bouncing around different networks and time slots, the show was canceled for good in December 1984, after more than 7,400 episodes.

27 Popular TV Shows of the 1980s

✳ ✳ ✳ ✳

1. *Diff'rent Strokes*
2. *Dallas*
3. *The Cosby Show*
4. *Cheers*
5. *The Golden Girls*

6. *Dynasty*
7. *Murder, She Wrote*
8. *Who's the Boss?*
9. *Simon & Simon*
10. *Falcon Crest*
11. *Family Ties*
12. *A Different World*
13. *The Wonder Years*
14. *Facts of Life*
15. *Magnum P.I.*
16. *The A-Team*
17. *Knots Landing*
18. *Growing Pains*
19. *Moonlighting*
20. *Alf*
21. *L.A. Law*
22. *Trapper John, M.D.*
23. *Matlock*
24. *Miami Vice*
25. *Silver Spoons*
26. *thirtysomething*
27. *Mama's Family*

BUT WAIT... THERE'S MORE!
11 Items Sold by Ron Popeil

❋ ❋ ❋ ❋

Before there was QVC, there was Ron Popeil, an inventor who became a multimillionaire by pitching labor-saving, albeit unusual, devices on TV. But wait...there's more! Here are some of Ron Popeil's famous and infamous products.

1. Veg-O-Matic: Popeil learned to be a pitchman from his father, Samuel, who was also an inventor and salesman of kitchen gadgets such as the Chop-O-Matic, which later became Ron's Veg-O-Matic and together sold more than 11 million units. The Chop-O-Matic was introduced in the mid-1950s at the amazing low price of $3.98. Ron renamed it the Veg-O-Matic and pitched it as "the greatest kitchen appliance ever made...."

2. **Pocket Fisherman:** Popeil advertised this device as "the biggest fishing invention since the hook...and still only $19.95." The handle was a mini tackle box containing a hook, line, and sinker... worms were up to you since it didn't come with a pocket shovel. The Pocket Fisherman was invented in 1963 by Ron's father after he was nearly injured by the tip of a fishing pole. Today's version sells for $29.99 and has a double-flex rod hinge that unfolds to a fully extendable position. Together, both versions of the Pocket Fisherman have sold more than two million units.

3. **Mr. Microphone:** Launched in 1978, Mr. Microphone was a low-power FM modulator that turned radios into annoying precursors of the karaoke machine. The TV commercial featured Popeil's daughter and her boyfriend driving a convertible and using Mr. Microphone, which made one wonder why he didn't follow this invention up with Mr. Earplugs. Maybe it helped that he sold more than a million of them at $19.95.

4. **Smokeless Ashtray:** The Smokeless Ashtray was a tiny device that promised to suck up the smoke coming from cigars and cigarettes before it filled the room, and in the 1970s, Ron sold more than a million of these contraptions at $19.95 each. With most smoking being done outside today, the Smokeless Ashtray has been replaced by something less expensive—wind.

5. **Inside-the-Shell Egg Scrambler:** Not one of Popeil's best sellers, but here's how it works: A bent pin pierces the eggshell, rotates inside it, and creates perfectly scrambled eggs and yolk-free hard-boiled eggs. Only about 150,000 have sold at $19.95.

6. **Dial-O-Matic:** If the Chop-O-Matic and Veg-O-Matic don't cut veggies small enough that the kids can't recognize them, the Dial-

O-Matic will. This food slicer debuted in the mid-1950s, preceding the modern food processor, and, at the original price of $3, took a much smaller slice out of the family budget. The Dial-O-Matic has sold two million units and is still available—now for $29.95—and can still turn hundreds of potatoes into french fries in minutes.

7. **Automatic Pasta Maker:** This gadget allows you to make 12 different shapes of preservative-free homemade pasta in just five minutes! You can even use it to make homemade sausage. Since 1993, more than one million people have purchased the Automatic Pasta Maker for $159.95.

8. **GLH Formula Number 9 Hair System:** Got a bald spot? Ron Popeil can fix it with the GLH Formula Number 9 Hair System. Great Looking Hair isn't real hair but a spray that matches your hair color, thickens thinning hair, and covers bald spots. More than one million cans have sold for only $9.95 for the spray or $19.95 for the spray, shampoo, and finishing shield.

9. **Showtime Rotisserie and BBQ Oven:** Introduced in 1998, the Showtime Rotisserie and BBQ Oven is by far Ron Popeil's most successful product to date. He has sold seven million units in three different models: the $99.95 Compact Rotisserie, the $159.80 Standard Rotisserie, and the $209.75 Pro Rotisserie. Popeil's pitch for the Showtime Rotisserie is "Set it and forget it!," which has been repeated so many times in infomercials that it's impossible to forget.

10. **Electric Food Dehydrator:** Introduced in 1965 at $59.95, Ron Popeil called it "the most famous food dehydrator in the world!" The sun might disagree with that claim, but the Electric Food Dehydrator, which brought Popeil back from semiretirement, currently comes with five trays and sells for $39.95.

11. **Solid Flavor Injector:** Resembling a syringe with a large plastic "needle," this gadget is used to inject fillings such as dried fruit, small vegetables, nuts, chocolate chips, and candy into foods such as hams, roasts, cupcakes, and pastries. At just $14.95, it won't cost you a fortune to add a bit of flair and pizzazz to your food.

10 Favorite Cartoons of Animator Chuck Jones

❋ ❋ ❋ ❋

Academy Award-winning animator Chuck Jones (1912–2002) directed and created iconic cartoon figures such as Bugs Bunny, Porky Pig, Daffy Duck, Pepé Le Pew, and Roadrunner. His animated TV specials include Rikki-Tikki-Tavi *and* How the Grinch Stole Christmas. *In the following list, compiled in 1984, Jones discussed his favorites among the cartoons he directed.*

1. "One Froggy Evening" (1955)

"It was a difficult cartoon to do, and I'm most proud of the fact that the difficulty and effort doesn't show in the product."

2. "What's Opera, Doc?" (1957)

"We took 14 hours and cut it down to six minutes. We played the music straight—we had a sixty-piece orchestra."

3. "Feed the Kitty" (1952)

"A pugnacious dog is overcome with love for a kitten. It's just one of my favorites."

4. "A Bear for Punishment" (1951)

"This was an Archie Bunker story before its time, and we had a great cast, Bea Benaderet, Billy Bletcher, and Stan Freberg."

5. "Duck Amuck" (1953)

"Daffy has a long fight with the person drawing the cartoon. I had always wanted to do a story like that. It was a challenge, but it sure was fun."

6. "Duck Dodgers in the 24½th Century" (1953)

"Naturally, this was a Buck Rogers satire. We did a lot of experimenting. We did this in 1953, before there was a Cape Canaveral—we didn't even know what rockets were. You know, our cartoon looks just like Cape Canaveral. I'm often kidded that I'm the one who really designed Cape Canaveral."

7. "For Scent-Imental Reasons" (1949)

"This won an Academy Award in 1949. The star was Pepé Le Pew, and this is one of my favorites because I admire Pepé so much. Really, I want to be just like he was in this cartoon."

8. "Whoa, Be-Gone!" (1958)

"I had to include a Roadrunner picture in this list. The Roadrunner has no dialogue, so it crosses all international borders. This is my favorite Roadrunner."

9. "The Dot and The Line" (1965)

"It's quite an unusual picture, and it won an Academy Award in 1965. This is the plot: A line falls in love with a dot, and a dot falls in love with a squiggle. I got this idea from a book by Norton Juster."

10. "The Scarlet Pumpernickel" (1950)

"Daffy tries to sell a script to Jack Warner. We had all the characters in this one, and we really had the opportunity to play with Daffy's character. It was a lot of fun."

REASONS TO LOSE THE REMOTE
9 Famous TV Flops

✳ ✳ ✳ ✳

Everyone loved Lucy, and most even loved Raymond, but much of TV heaven is littered with the carcasses of shows that looked great on the drawing board but flopped miserably on the small screen. Check out this list of some memorable flops and decide how many episodes you might have watched before tuning out.

1. Supertrain

If you can find romance on *The Love Boat*, why not on a train? The show *Supertrain* was filled with reasons why not, derailing after airing on NBC from February to May 1979. Actors such as Tony Danza, Vicki Lawrence, and Joyce DeWitt hopped onboard the

Supertrain to cavort in an Olympic-size swimming pool, gym, and discotheque while traveling more than 200 miles per hour. The original million-dollar, large-scale model electric train set with cameras attached crashed during its first demonstration, but nobody at the network saw this as a bad sign. The show suffered from poor reviews and low ratings, and the high production costs combined with the U.S. boycott of the 1980 Summer Olympics (which cost NBC millions in ad revenue), nearly bankrupted the network.

2. Pink Lady and Jeff

Pink Lady and Jeff aired for six weeks in 1980 and made network executives see red. The show combined musical numbers by a Japanese female singing duo called Pink Lady and sketch comedy starring comedian Jeff Altman. The show was produced by Sid and Marty Krofft, famous for creating the landmark children's series *H. R. Pufnstuf* and *The Donny and Marie Show,* and special guests included Sid Caeser, Sherman Hemsley, Blondie, and Jim Varney. The girls knew very little English and had to learn their song lyrics and lines phonetically, one reason why critics said *sayonara.*

3. The Chevy Chase Show

Chevy Chase, one of the original cast members of *Saturday Night Live,* was unable to use his humorous pratfalls to save *The Chevy Chase Show,* a weeknight talk show that was canceled in 1993 after only five weeks and is often referred to as "The Edsel of Television." Chase later appeared in a commercial for Doritos, in which he made a humorous reference to the show.

4. Cop Rock

Cop Rock might have done better if it was called *Rock Around the Cop,* but the combination musical/police drama went down the donut hole in 1990 after only 11 episodes. Even with a theme song by Randy Newman and scripts written by Steven Bochco (creator of *Hill Street Blues*), *Cop Rock* still bombed due to scenes such as a jury singing a gospel song "He's Guilty." Bochco later redeemed himself with *NYPD Blue.*

5. You're in the Picture

Jackie Gleason was famous for saying "How sweet it is," but a game show he hosted called *You're in the Picture* wasn't so sweet at all. The first and only episode aired live on January 20, 1961, and featured celebrity contestants sticking their heads into a scene painted on plywood, and then trying to guess what the scene was by asking Gleason questions. After the disaster aired, Gleason convinced CBS to let him go on the next week and apologize to viewers under the title *The Jackie Gleason Show.* He did and *The Jackie Gleason Show* aired for eight more weeks as a talk show before the network pulled the plug for good.

6. Me and the Chimp

Working with animals on television is always a risk, something *That Girl* costar Ted Bessell found out when he shared top billing with a chimpanzee. From January to May 1972, *Me and the Chimp* was produced by Tom Miller and Garry Marshall, who later went on to create *Happy Days* and *Laverne & Shirley.* The show centered around a family who found a chimp wandering around the neighborhood and decided to keep it hidden from their neighbors. Bessell was able to change the original working title from *The Chimp and I,* so at least he was the top banana.

7. Turn-On

On February 5, 1969, *Turn-On,* became the first show to get canceled before the premier episode had finished airing. Created by Ed Friendly and George Schlatter, producers of *Rowan & Martin's Laugh-In,* this show utilized a barrage of "hi-tech" media such as computer graphics, animation, signs flashing sexual innuendos, and electronically distorted, synthesized music. Guests included Tim Conway, who later did a long run on *The Carol Burnett Show,* but *Turn-On* was turned off by most everyone who tuned in.

8. Who's Your Daddy?

The popular '90s slang phrase *Who's your daddy?* eventually appeared in everything from movies to a country music song by

Toby Keith. That didn't help a 2005 reality show on Fox called *Who's Your Daddy?*, which was canceled after one episode. The show took a woman who had been adopted as an infant and placed her in a room with eight men, one of whom was her biological father. If she chose the correct man as her father, they would win a big cash prize; if she chose the wrong man, the money would go to him instead. The show was blasted by adoption rights organizations, so Fox decided not to broadcast the other five episodes that had been produced.

9. *My Mother the Car*

My Mother the Car, typically named the worst TV show of all time, aired on NBC from 1965 to 1966. It starred Jerry Van Dyke as the owner of a 1928 Porter convertible possessed by his deceased mother (Ann Sothern), whose voice came out of the car radio. Although written by Allan Burns and Chris Hayward, who had success with *The Munsters*, the show was panned by critics. Still, *My Mother the Car* managed to survive a year, but in the end, a country that loved a talking horse just wasn't ready for a talking car.

16 Popular TV Shows of the 1990s

✳ ✳ ✳ ✳

1. *Beverly Hills, 90210*
2. *Home Improvement*
3. *Seinfeld*
4. *Friends*
5. *NYPD Blue*
6. *Frasier*
7. *ER*
8. *The Simpsons*
9. *Roseanne*
10. *Mad About You*
11. *Married with Children*
12. *Murphy Brown*
13. *Full House*

14. *Saved by the Bell*
15. *Sisters*
16. *The X Files*

"AND THE SURVEY SAYS…"
Television's 11 Longest-Running Game Shows

✳ ✳ ✳ ✳

Quiz shows first became popular in the age of radio, but when television was introduced, TV game shows became inextricably woven into American pop culture. Hundreds of game shows have come and gone since the first TV game show, Truth or Consequences, *hit the airwaves in 1950, but some, like those that follow, had the magic formula and ran for years.*

1. The Price Is Right

"Come on down!" Why does this relic from the 1970s still grab high daytime ratings more than 35 years after it debuted? With an agreeable host, contestants plucked from the audience, 80 different games like Plinko and Hi-Lo, and big prizes (motor homes, cars, trips, and furniture), there's something for everyone. The show, which debuted in 1972 and made Bob Barker a TV legend during his 35 years as host, is actually a revival of an earlier incarnation of the show, which aired from 1956 to 1965.

2. Wheel of Fortune

Since 1975, contestants have been spinning the wheel and risking bankruptcy to guess letters and complete the puzzle on the board. Contestants can buy a vowel and vie to be the first to solve the puzzle. The bonus round allows winners to add cars, trips, and up to $100,000 in cash to their winnings. Before Pat Sajak and Vanna White took the reins in the early 1980s, Chuck Woolery and Susan Stafford hosted the show. Dubbed "America's game," *Wheel* frequently goes on tour across the country and features celebrity and charity versions of the show as well.

3. Jeopardy!

Answer: This game show was ranked first in the Nielsen ratings for quiz shows for more than 1,000 weeks. Question: What is *Jeopardy*? With 27 Daytime Emmy Awards and 37 million viewers weekly, *Jeopardy* has dug its heels into television history. Current host Alex Trebek gives the answers to three contestants who buzz in to provide the questions. In 2004, contestant Ken Jennings racked up an unprecedented 74-game winning streak, earning more than $2.5 million on the show before he stumbled, making him the winningest contestant in game show history. The current show has been on the air since 1984 and is a revival of the original, which ran from 1964 to 1975.

4. Truth or Consequences

This show originally aired as a radio quiz show starting in 1940, then crossed over to television in 1950. The show asked contestants to answer obscure, often trick, questions, then, if they couldn't answer, made them suffer the "consequences"—often embarrassing or silly stunts. Bob Barker hosted the show from 1956 to 1975, but the show never quite recovered after his departure. The show ran off and on for about 20 seasons from 1950 to 1978 and had a short-lived revival in the late '80s.

5. What's My Line?

In *What's My Line?*, four celebrity panelists tried to guess the occupation (or "line" of work) of a fifth, secret contestant by asking only "yes" or "no" questions. During the third round, panelists were blindfolded and challenged to guess the identity of a "Mystery Guest." The original run of the show (which paid players for appearances, since prize money never exceeded $50) ran from 1950 to 1967, but since then several revivals have been launched. Celebrity guests have included author Gore Vidal, actor Jane Fonda, and singer Bobby Darin.

6. I've Got a Secret

An old parlor game, "Secret, Secret, Who's Got the Secret?," was the inspiration for this classic quiz show that originally aired from

1952 to 1967. The host introduced the contestant and asked them to whisper their "secret" into his ear. The secret was shown on-screen for at-home viewers, but celebrity panelists had to try to guess the secret by asking questions. Each time the panelist guessed incorrectly, the player was paid $20 with a whopping $80 maximum payout. In recent years, the show was revived on the Game Show Network with secrets that are much racier than they were in the 1950s.

7. *Hollywood Squares*

Mere mortals got a chance to play with celebrities in this game show based on tic-tac-toe. Nine Hollywood stars sit in separate, open-faced cubes that make up the board. The stars are asked questions by the host, and contestants judge whether or not their answers are true or false in order to put an *X* or *O* in the square. Prize winnings got larger and larger over the years, with one jackpot reaching $100,000. But the game was really a vehicle for the comedic banter between the host and the celebrities. Between the original version, which aired from 1966 to 1981, and its many reincarnations, *Squares* has featured celebrities such as Vincent Price, Joan Rivers, Whoopi Goldberg, Paul Lynde, Martin Mull, and Alf.

8. *Concentration*

The game show genre took a beating during the 1950s when it was revealed that several shows were rigged and contestants were given the answers in advance. Though they were later implicated in the quiz show scandals, producers Jack Barry and Dan Enright created a solid game with *Concentration*. The hit show survived the tumult of the scandals, airing from 1958 to 1973. The game was based on two concepts: a children's game known as "Memory," and a word puzzle that was revealed when matching cards were removed from the board. The show survived in syndication for some time and enjoyed a revival in 1987 that lasted approximately five years.

9. *Let's Make a Deal*

Monty Hall was the archetypal game show host in this long-running favorite that required contestants to have a little intuition and a lot of luck. The show involved contestants making a "deal" with Hall and selecting prizes that could be real or bogus. But what really made the show stand apart was the costumes that contestants wore. In the first days of the show, contestants wore everyday clothes until someone came to the show wearing a crazy costume to get the attention of producers—immediately, a tradition was born. From then on, contestants on *Let's Make a Deal* wore nutty outfits in order to be singled out to participate. Several revivals have been attempted, but fans of the show seem to prefer reruns of the original, which ran from 1963 to 1977.

10. *To Tell the Truth*

On this show, a team of celebrity panelists heard a story and then had to determine which of three contestants was associated with the story. Payoffs were based on the contestants' ability to fool the panel and weren't large by today's standards: Each incorrect guess from the panel paid the challengers $250 for a possible $1,000. But if the entire panel was correct, the challengers split $150. The show's original run lasted from 1956 to 1968, and the game that asked, "Will the real John Doe please stand up?" has enjoyed several reincarnations.

11. *You Bet Your Life*

This unique program was modeled after Groucho Marx's radio series of the same name, in which contestants answered questions for prize money. The audience was clued into the "secret word," but the contestant was not. If the contestant could answer the questions and come up with the secret word, a duck (a nod to Groucho's classic film *Duck Soup*) would descend from the ceiling and deliver $100 in prize money. Marx hosted the show during its original run from 1950 to 1961. Later versions hosted by Buddy Hackett and Bill Cosby were unable to match the success of the original.

✳ ✳ ✳

"You have to learn the rules of the game. And then you have to play better than anyone else."
—Albert Einstein

12 Hollywood Celebrities Who Have Made Ads in Japan

✳ ✳ ✳ ✳

Hollywood celebrities have been crossing the Pacific to make commercials in Japan for decades. It's a quick, easy way for celebs to make a buck without harming their reps back in the States, thanks to secrecy clauses that prevent Japanese companies from disclosing the endorsements. But with the success of YouTube and similar sites, many of these commercials are now available worldwide on the Web. The spots make for hilarious viewing, and you can be sure the stars are laughing all the way to the bank.

1. Arnold Schwarzenegger

If Arnold Schwarzenegger is to be believed, inhaling a cup of Nissin instant noodles will provide you with enough strength to swing really heavy-looking bronze pots back and forth with ease. Or, you can melt away your stress with a can of Hop's Beer. Or tap into your superhero-worthy powers with a jolt of Vfuyy energy drink. The bodybuilder/actor/governor of California endorsed these Japanese products in commercial spots from the 1990s.

2. Nicolas Cage

Maybe it happened while filming *Leaving Las Vegas*...or maybe *Honeymoon in Vegas.* Either way, at some point, Nicolas Cage was bit by the gambling bug, so much so that he felt the need to shill for Sankyo, the manufacturer of *pachinko* machines. Similar to slot machines, the devices can be found in casinos across Japan. Ads from the late 1990s feature a wild-eyed Cage so obsessed by his pachinko fever that he's having trouble functioning day to day!

3. Cameron Diaz

There's something about Aeon English Schools that made Cameron Diaz want to sing their praises. Aeon, a private institute with more than 300 schools in Japan, has also received a boost from Celine Dion, Ewan McGregor, and Mariah Carey. In the Diaz spots (which aired in 2000 and 2001), the bubbly star of *Charlie's Angels* and *There's Something About Mary* looks fresh-faced and innocent as she repeats the word *believe* over and over in front of a series of different backgrounds. Aeon posters featuring Diaz's mug were also plastered around Japanese cities during the same time.

4. Harrison Ford

What do hiking near a volcano, dining at a sushi restaurant, sitting in a steam room, and jetting around on an airliner have in common? They all go great with Kirin beer, according to Harrison Ford. The man who turned both Han Solo and Indiana Jones into household names lent his visage to this refreshing lager in at least five different TV commercials, plus a print ad, during the mid-1990s.

5. Anne Hathaway

The Princess Diaries, a tale of an ugly duckling turned royal beauty, made its way into Japanese movie theaters in 2002. Shortly afterward, the film's star, Anne Hathaway, made her way into Japanese living rooms via commercials for the Lux line of hair and beauty products. Hathaway joins a lofty list of Lux lovelies, which includes Catherine Zeta-Jones, Penelope Cruz, and Charlize Theron. Hathaway's spots trade on her princess rep, with the actress dressed in ethereal white and appearing to float through life as weightless as her styling mousse.

6. Jodie Foster

Jodie Foster appears to choose her movie roles carefully, opting for edgy roles that prick audience sensibilities: *The Silence of the Lambs, The Accused,* and *Panic Room,* to name a few. Her commercial résumé is a little less selective. From the mid-1990s to 2000, Foster pitched Keri beauty products, Pasona temp agency, Mt. Rainier iced coffee, and Honda, all the while smiling like she hadn't a care in the world. Clarice Starling, we hardly recognize ye.

7. Bruce Willis

After *Moonlighting*, but before the Demi Moore split, Bruce Willis spent a lot of time in the Far East. In the early 1990s, the man who gave us four *Die Hard* films and lots of movies with numbers in their titles (*The Fifth Element, The Sixth Sense, The Whole Nine Yards*) pitched Maki jewelry stores, Georgia coffee drinks, Eneos gas stations, Subaru, and Post drinking water in a can.

8. Madonna

Madonna is no stranger to endorsements, having appeared in Gap, H&M, and Versace ads in the United States. In Japan, the material girl could be seen plugging Shochu rice beverages in ads that ran in 1995 and 1996. The spots show Madge slaying both a giant dragon and an evil wizard before enjoying a glass of the drink and announcing, "I'm pure." Okay... if you say so!

9. Britney Spears

There are many sides to Britney Spears—pop star, mom, Paris Hilton's BFF, and, oddly enough, the face of Go-Go Tea. Brit appeared in ads for the iced tea beverage dressed as a '60s go-go girl, complete with white patent leather boots and some killer dance moves The ads ran until early 2003, when the singer was "not a girl, not yet a woman."

10. Sharon Stone

Many Americans weren't introduced to Sharon Stone until 1992's *Basic Instinct.* But Japanese audiences got a glimpse of the soon-to-be A-list actor in the late '80s when she appeared in ads for Vernal cosmetics. Dressed in a gray business suit, a brunette Stone looked sharp but offered not a hint of the upcoming sultry, villainous role that would forever seal her place in cinematic history.

11. Ashley Judd

Ashley Judd is *thrilled* to be driving a Honda Primo, and she can barely contain her enthusiasm in the 2000 commercial that has her coining the phrase "Hondaful life." The actor, famous for roles in *De-Lovely* and *Kiss the Girls* and infamous for her family squabbles

with sister Wynonna and mom Naomi, sports a bouncy, blonde 'do
and catches the eye of everyone in these bubbly spots.

12. Richard Gere

It's not cheap to be a Buddhist humanitarian, and Richard Gere is
a famously generous one. Perhaps that's why he appears in ads for
such entities as Mt. Rainier coffee drinks, Tokyo Towers real estate
development, and Dandy House clothing. The actor has appeared
in Dandy House commercials as recently as December 2006.

22 Popular TV Shows of the 2000s

✳ ✳ ✳ ✳

1. *Grey's Anatomy*
2. *CSI*
3. *Law & Order*
4. *Who Wants to Be a Millionaire*
5. *Survivor*
6. *The Apprentice*
7. *Desperate Housewives*
8. *Everybody Loves Raymond*
9. *American Idol*
10. *Will & Grace*
11. *The Sopranos*
12. *Sex and the City*
13. *King of Queens*
14. *The West Wing*
15. *Ally McBeal*
16. *Lost*
17. *Dancing with the Stars*
18. *24*
19. *Scrubs*
20. *The Amazing Race*
21. *The Office*
22. *Fear Factor*

FROM LOVE IN THE AFTERNOON
TO DARLINGS OF THE ACADEMY
17 Celebrities Who Started on Soap Operas

❋ ❋ ❋ ❋

If you ever catch some vintage soap opera footage, you may see
a few familiar faces. Here are some of today's hottest stars
who got their start on daytime dramas.

1. Demi Moore

For her first 19 years, her name was Demetria Guynes, but then
she married musician Freddy Moore and took the name that most
recognize today. In 1982, Demi beat out thousands of actors for the
role of Jackie Templeton on *General Hospital.* She was an instant
sensation as a sassy reporter who went to great lengths to get a
scoop. She left daytime TV in 1983, eventually starring in feature
films, such as *Ghost, Indecent Proposal,* and *A Few Good Men.*

2. Ricky Martin

This hottie was "Livin' La Vida Loca" in *General Hospital's* Port
Charles as Miguel Morez. As a fab example of typecasting, Martin
was tapped to play a Latino singer. He had long, curly hair and
steamed up the afternoons from 1994 to 1995. Today he's far from
Port Charles; in fact, this Grammy Award-winning artist spends
much of his free time working for children's charities.

3. Kathleen Turner

As a child, Mary Kathleen Turner traveled the world because her
father was a U.S. foreign service officer. During that time, the
Turner family lived in Canada, Cuba, London, Venezuela, and
Washington, D.C. By age 23, she shed her first name and got her
first big break in show business on *The Doctors.* From 1978 to
1979, Kathleen played trampy Nola Dancy, a girl from the wrong
side of the tracks who married someone from the right side. Then,
in 1981, she debuted on the big screen as a sizzling temptress in
Body Heat.

4. David Hasselhoff

The man listed in *Guinness World Records* as the "most watched TV star in the world" got his start on daytime television. Between 1975 and 1982, Hasselhoff could be seen on *The Young and the Restless* as Dr. Snapper Foster, who was put through college by his poor mother and manicurist sister (Jill Abbott, who is still on the show). After seven years, Hasselhoff left daytime TV without knowing what would come next. But he didn't have to wonder for long—NBC President Brandon Tartikoff asked him to play the lead (opposite a talking car) in a new show called *Knight Rider.* By 1989, the phenomenon known as *Baywatch* hit the airwaves with Hasselhoff at the helm as lead actor and executive producer.

5. Meg Ryan

Before she was the queen of romantic comedies, Meg Ryan was tangled up in a love triangle on *As the World Turns.* From 1982 to 1984, the spunky actor portrayed good girl Betsy Stewart, who was in love with blue-collar Steve Andropolous. Her stepfather didn't approve, so Betsy married unscrupulous Craig Montgomery instead. But true love prevailed when Betsy left Craig and married Steve in May 1984. Their happiness didn't last, but so it goes in the soap world. Ryan's movie career took off when she left the show, and her starring role in *When Harry Met Sally* in 1989 solidified her place as a leading lady.

6. Teri Hatcher

Voted by her 1982 high school class as "Girl Most Likely to Become a Solid Gold Dancer," Hatcher took a different direction and studied math in college. Her classmates might have been onto something, however, because she soon left college life and, in 1985, found a job as a dancing mermaid on *The Love Boat.* From 1986 to 1987, she was cast on *Capitol* as Angelica Clegg, a congressman's wife. But Hatcher didn't stick around for long; in 1987, she started to appear in several prime-time TV shows, such as *Night Court* and *L.A. Law.* By 1993, she landed her first major role—as Lois Lane on the series *Lois & Clark: The New Adventures of Superman.*

7. Christopher Reeve

Speaking of Superman... Long before he was characterized personally and professionally as a "man of steel," Christopher Reeve played devilishly handsome and selfish Ben Harper on *Love of Life* from 1974 to 1976. His character was married to two women from the same town at the same time! His wives eventually exposed him for the cad that he was, and he ended up in prison. Perhaps leading a double life on screen is why, in 1978, a casting director got the idea to make him a secretive superhero in *Superman.*

8. Kevin Bacon

This prolific actor had a small role in *National Lampoon's Animal House* before his 1979 TV debut on *Search for Tomorrow.* Then, from 1980 to 1981, he played a troubled teen on *Guiding Light.* Since then, Bacon has been involved in so many entertainment projects that there's even a game called "Six Degrees of Kevin Bacon," in which almost everyone in Hollywood is somehow linked to him. These days, in addition to acting, Kevin and his brother make music and tour as The Bacon Brothers.

9. Ray Liotta

The tough guy who later played a succession of gangsters, Liotta launched his career as lovable hero Joey Perrini on *Another World* from 1978 to 1981. A few years after Liotta's love-struck character left the soap, Robert De Niro suggested him for Martin Scorsese's disturbing film *GoodFellas* as mobster kingpin Henry Hill.

10. Kelsey Grammer

After a childhood marred with tragedy, Shakespeare-loving Allen Kelsey Grammer found himself at the esteemed Julliard School. After playing JFK's brother-in-law Stephen Smith on a 1983 TV miniseries, Grammer landed a spot on *Another World* as ER physician Dr. Canard from 1984 to 1985. The same year he was tapped to play a different kind of doctor—psychiatrist Frasier Crane on *Cheers.* His finicky character was so successful that he went on to star in the multi-Emmy Award-winning sitcom *Frasier.*

11. Marisa Tomei

After attending Boston University for a year, perky actor Marisa Tomei landed a role on *As the World Turns*. From 1983 to 1985, she played airhead Marcy Thompson. Her character accused a man of sexual harassment, then went on to marry a prince, Lord Stewart Cushing. He swept Marcy away to England where they lived happily ever after as Lord and Lady Cushing.

12. Tommy Lee Jones

From 1971 to 1975, this future Oscar winner played a bad seed on *One Life to Live*. As Dr. Mark Toland, Jones portrayed a moody man married to a frigid wife. The combination played out as a recipe for disaster, until finally, he was murdered by a woman while he was running from the law.

13. James Earl Jones

Before he was Darth Vader in *Star Wars*, even before he was nominated for an Oscar for his role in *The Great White Hope*, James Earl Jones played doctor. Soap opera doctor, that is! First he was Dr. Jerry Turner on *As the World Turns* and then Dr. Jim Frazier on *The Guiding Light*, both in 1966. Many fans recognize his deep voice from his famous line in *Star Wars*, when he said to Luke Skywalker, "I am your father." But in 1966, he was probably warming up that voice with lines like "Where's my stethoscope?"

14. Rick Springfield

In 1968, young Aussie singer/guitarist Rick Springfield (born Richard Springthorpe) was hired by a private promoter to visit military bases in Vietnam and entertain troops. By 1972, he lived in Hollywood, continued making music, and had branched out into acting. From 1981 to 1983, he played a sweetie pie named Dr. Noah Drake on *General Hospital*, breaking hearts all over the fictional town of Port Charles. He never stopped touring with his band, however, and his song "Jessie's Girl" won him a Grammy for Best Male Vocal Performance in 1982. Still touring and releasing CDs, Rick Springfield is another one of daytime TV's musical claims to fame.

15. Cicely Tyson

This highly acclaimed actor got her start on *The Guiding Light* in 1966. She originated the role of nurse Martha Frazier. On the show, her husband, Dr. Jim Frazier, was played by Billie Dee Williams and later, James Earl Jones. Tyson was plucked from the hospital set when producers chose her for a film called *The Comedians*. Her cast mates in the film were an impressive lot: Richard Burton, Elizabeth Taylor, Alec Guinness, Peter Ustinov, and Lillian Gish. Throughout her career, Cicely Tyson has been known for portraying strong African-American women.

16. Larry Hagman

In 1957, more than 20 years before the entire nation pondered the question "Who shot JR?," a young Larry Hagman played Curt Williams on *Search for Tomorrow*. Then, from 1961 to 1963, he played a lawyer by the name of Ed Gibson on *The Edge of Night*. By 1965, Hagman was starring in *I Dream of Jeannie*. But once he put on his cowboy hat to play unscrupulous oilman JR Ewing on *Dallas* starting in 1978, all of his other characters seemed to fade away.

17. Susan Sarandon

Politically active and outspoken, even as a teenager, Susan Sarandon landed a spot on the runway as a Ford model. But it was her role as Patrice Kahlman on the soap *A World Apart* that put her on the small screen from 1970 to 1971. She moved to *Search for Tomorrow* in 1972 and played a murderous drifter named Sarah Fairbanks. Sarandon left the show the same year, and in 1975 she appeared in the cult classic *The Rocky Horror Picture Show*. During the next 20 years, Sarandon was nominated for five Oscars before finally bringing one home in 1995 for her part in *Dead Man Walking*, which was directed by her partner Tim Robbins.

Chapter 15

SCIENCE & NATURE

✳ ✳ ✳ ✳

IT CAME FROM OUTER SPACE

10 Memorable Meteor Crashes

Every day hundreds of meteors, commonly known as shooting stars, can be seen flying across the night sky. Upon entering Earth's atmosphere, friction heats up cosmic debris, causing streaks of light that are visible to the human eye. Most burn up before they ever reach the ground. But if one actually survives the long fall and strikes Earth, it is called a meteorite. Here are some of the more memorable meteor falls in history.

1. The Ensisheim Meteorite, the oldest recorded meteorite, struck Earth on November 7, 1492, in the small town of Ensisheim, France. A loud explosion shook the area before a 330-pound stone dropped from the sky into a wheat field, witnessed only by a young boy. As news of the event spread, townspeople gathered around and began breaking off pieces of the stone for souvenirs. German King Maximilian even stopped by Ensisheim to see the stone on his way to battle the French army. Maximilian decided it was a gift from heaven and considered it a sign that he would emerge victorious in his upcoming battle, which he did. Today bits of the stone are located in museums around the world, but the largest portion stands on display in Ensisheim's Regency Palace.

2. The Tunguska Meteorite, which exploded near Russia's Tunguska River in 1908, is still the subject of debate nearly 100 years later. It didn't leave an impact crater, which has led to speculation about its true nature. But most scientists believe that around 7:00 A.M. on June 30 a giant meteor blazed through the sky and exploded in a huge ball of fire that flattened forests, blew up houses, and scorched people and animals within 13 miles. Scientists continue to explore the region, but neither a meteorite nor a crater have ever been found. Conspiracy theorists contend that what actually hit Earth that day was an alien spaceship or perhaps even a black hole.

3. Michelle Knapp was idling away at her Peekskill, New York, home on October 9, 1992, when a loud crash gave her a start. When she ran outside to investigate, she found that the trunk of her red Chevy Malibu had been crushed by a football-size rock that passed through the car and dug a crater into her driveway. When Michelle alerted police, they impounded the stone and eventually handed it over to the American Museum of Natural History in Manhattan. Turns out the meteor was first spotted over Kentucky, and its descent was caught on more than a dozen amateur videotapes. As for Michelle's Malibu, it was purchased by R. A. Langheinrich Meteorites, a private collectors group, which has taken the car on a world tour of museums and scientific institutions.

4. In terms of casualties, a red Malibu is nothing compared to an entire population, but many scientists believe that a meteorite was responsible for the extinction of the dinosaurs. The theory holds that approximately 65 million years ago, a six-mile-wide asteroid crashed into Earth, causing a crater about 110 miles across and blowing tons of debris and dust into the atmosphere. Scientists believe the impact caused several giant tsunamis, global fires, acid rain, and dust that blocked sunlight for several weeks or months, disrupting the food chain and eventually wiping out the dinosaurs. The theory is controversial, but believers point to the Chicxulub Crater in Yucatan, Mexico, as the striking point of the asteroid. Skeptics say the crater predates the extinction of dinosaurs by 300,000 or so years. Others believe dinosaurs may have been wiped out by several distinct asteroid strikes, rather than just the widely credited Chicxulub impact. Scientists will likely be debating this one for centuries, or at least until another gigantic asteroid strikes Earth and wipes us all out.

5. As Colby Navarro sat at his computer on March 26, 2003, he had no idea that a meteorite was about to come crashing through the roof of his Park Forest, Illinois, home, strike his printer, bounce off the wall, and land near a filing cabinet. The rock, about four inches wide, was part of a meteorite shower that sprinkled the Chicago area, damaging at least six houses and three cars. Scientists said that before the rock broke apart, it was probably the size of a car. Thank heaven for small favors.

6. The Hoba Meteorite, found on a farm in Namibia in 1920, is the heaviest meteorite ever found. Weighing in at about 66 tons, the rock is thought to have landed more than 80,000 years ago. Despite its gargantuan size, the meteorite left no crater, which scientists credit to the fact that it entered Earth's atmosphere at a long, shallow angle. It lay undiscovered until 1920 when a farmer reportedly hit it with his plow. Over the years, erosion, vandalism, and scientific sampling have shrunk the rock to about 60 tons, but in 1955 the Namibian government designated it a national monument, and it is now a popular tourist attraction.

7. Santa had to compete for airspace on Christmas Eve 1965, when Britain's largest meteorite sent thousands of fragments showering down on Barwell, Leicestershire. Museums immediately started offering money for fragments of the rock, causing the previously sleepy town to be inundated with meteorite hunters and other adventurers from around the world. Decades later, the phenomenon continues to captivate meteorite enthusiasts, and fragments can often be found for sale online.

8. Arizona would be short one giant hole in the ground if it wasn't for a 160-foot meteorite landing in the northern desert about 50,000 years ago, which left an impact crater about a mile wide and 570 feet deep. Known today as the Barringer Crater, or Meteor Crater, the site is now a popular tourist attraction. Scientists believe the meteorite that caused the crater was traveling about 28,600 miles per hour when it struck Earth, causing an explosion about 150 times more powerful than the Hiroshima atomic bomb. The meteorite itself probably melted in the explosion, spreading a mist of molten nickel and iron across the surrounding landscape.

9. At 186 miles wide, Vredefort Dome in South Africa is the site of the biggest impact crater on Earth. And at an estimated two billion years old, it makes the Chicxulub Crater look like a spring chicken. Today, the original crater, which was caused by a meteorite about six miles wide, is mostly eroded away, but what remains is a dome created when the walls of the crater slumped, pushing up granite rocks from the center of the meteorite strike.

10. Second in size only to the Vredefort Dome, the Sudbury Basin is a 40-mile-long, 16-mile-wide, 9-mile-deep crater caused by a giant meteorite that struck Earth about 1.85 billion years ago. Located in Greater Sudbury, Ontario, the crater is actually home to about 162,000 people. In 1891, the Canadian Copper Company began mining copper from the basin, but it was soon discovered that the crater also contained nickel, which is much more valuable, so the miners changed course. Today, the International Nickel Company operates out of the basin and mines about 10 percent of the world's nickel supply from the site.

9 Countries with the Worst Drinking Water

❋ ❋ ❋ ❋

Country	Daily Amount of Organic Water Pollutant (kg)
1. China	6,088,663
2. United States	1,968,196
3. India	1,556,371
4. Japan	1,279,287
5. Germany	1,020,145
6. Indonesia	753,657
7. Brazil	629,406
8. United Kingdom	604,821
9. Italy	495,973

Source: World Bank

SHAKE, RATTLE, AND ROLL
12 of the Most Destructive Earthquakes

✳ ✳ ✳ ✳

Every year, earthquakes cause thousands of deaths, either directly or due to the resulting tsunamis, landslides, fires, and famines. Quakes occur when a fault (where Earth's tectonic plates meet) slips, releasing energy in waves that move through the ground. Scientists measure the strength of tremors on the Richter scale, which assigns magnitude in numbers, like 6.0 or 7.2. A 5.0 tremor is equivalent to a 32-kiloton blast, nearly the explosive power of the atomic bomb dropped on Nagasaki in 1945! Going one whole number higher—such as from 5.0 to 6.0—reflects a tenfold increase in the amplitude of waves. Here are some of the most destructive earthquakes in recent history.

1. Missouri: December 16, 1811

The New Madrid fault—near where Missouri, Kentucky, Arkansas, and Tennessee meet—witnessed an 8.0 or greater magnitude quake nearly 200 years ago. The shaking spread so far that church bells reportedly rang in Boston, more than 1,500 miles away! It had dramatic effects on the area's geography, lifting up land enough to make the Mississippi River appear to flow upstream. Fortunately, the sparsely populated area suffered only one death and minimal property damage.

2. San Francisco: April 18, 1906

The Great San Francisco Earthquake—a 7.8 magnitude tremor—brought down structures across the Bay Area. In San Francisco, buildings crumbled, water mains broke, and streetcar tracks twisted into metal waves. But the majority of the 3,000 deaths and $524 million in property damage came from the massive post-tremor fire, which spread rapidly across the city in the absence of water to quell the flames. People as far away as southern Oregon and western Nevada felt the shaking, which lasted nearly a minute.

3. Southern USSR: October 5, 1948

This earthquake in Ashgabat, Turkmenistan, killed around 110,000 people, more than two-thirds of the city's population at the time. The 7.3 magnitude rumbling reduced much of the city to rubble and was one of the most devastating quakes to hit Central Asia. In 2002, the government of Turkmenistan commemorated the devastating event by issuing special coins featuring images of President Suparmurat Niyazov and his family members—most of whom died in the 1948 quake.

4. Southern Chile: May 22, 1960

The strongest earthquake ever recorded—9.5 on the Richter scale—was actually a succession of large quakes that struck southern Chile over the span of a few hours. A catastrophic tsunami ensued, severely ravaging the Chilean coast before rushing across the Pacific to pulverize Hawaii. In Chile, landslides, flooding, and the eruption of the Puyehue volcano less than two days later followed in the wake of the quake. All told, there were more than 5,700 deaths and $675 million in property damage in Chile, as well as Alaska, Hawaii, Japan, and the Philippines.

5. Alaska: March 28, 1964

The most powerful tremor in U.S. history—lasting three minutes and measuring 9.2 on the Richter scale—struck Prince William Sound in Alaska. Only 15 people died in the quake itself, but the resulting tsunami, which reached more than 200 feet high at Valdez inlet, killed 110 more people and caused $311 million in property damage. The city of Anchorage was hit particularly hard, with 30 downtown blocks suffering heavy damage.

6. Peru: May 31, 1970

A 7.9 magnitude quake just off the western coast of South America caused more than $500 million in damage and killed 66,000 Peruvians, with building collapses responsible for most of the deaths. Scientists say the South American tectonic plate continues to drift westward into the Pacific Ocean crustal slab, so additional serious earthquakes along the continent's coast are likely.

7. China: July 27, 1976

This quake, a 7.5 on the Richter scale, was one of many major tremors over the years along the "Ring of Fire," a belt of heavy seismic activity around the Pacific Ocean. It struck Tangshan, then a city of one million people near China's northeastern coast. Official Chinese figures indicate around 250,000 deaths, but other estimates are as high as 655,000.

8. Central California: October 18, 1989

The Loma Prieta quake—which struck the San Francisco area as game three of the 1989 World Series was just about to begin in Candlestick Park—killed 63 people and caused property damage of approximately $6 billion. At 6.9 on the Richter scale, it was the strongest shake in the Bay Area since 1906. Al Michaels, an ABC announcer in the ballpark for the game, was later nominated for an Emmy for his live earthquake reports.

9. Southern California: January 17, 1994

The 6.7 magnitude Northridge tremor left 60 people dead and caused an estimated $44 billion in damage. The rumbling damaged more than 40,000 buildings in four of California's most populated and expensive counties: Los Angeles, Orange, Ventura, and San Bernardino. The earthquake, which was felt as far away as Utah and northern Mexico, luckily struck at 4:30 A.M., when most people were not yet populating the region's crowded freeways, office buildings, and parking structures, many of which collapsed.

10. Japan: January 17, 1995

This massive quake in Kobe, Japan, measured 6.9 on the Richter scale. It killed more than 5,000 people and caused in excess of $100 billion in property loss, making it the most costly earthquake in history. The staggering expense was largely due to the collapse of, or damage to, more than 200,000 buildings in the high cost-of-living area. Coincidentally, the Kobe quake—or the Great Hanshin Earthquake, as it is most commonly known in Japan—occurred on the first anniversary of the Northridge tremor.

11. Indonesia: December 26, 2004

This massive earthquake just off the west coast of the island of Sumatra, and the tsunami that followed, killed at least 230,000 (and perhaps as many as 290,000) people in 12 countries—including about 168,000 in Indonesia alone. It registered 9.1 on the Richter scale and will long be remembered for the devastating waves that brought fatalities to countries all around the Indian Ocean. Scientists say the tremor was so strong that it wobbled Earth's rotation on its axis by almost an inch.

12. Pakistan: October 8, 2005

This earthquake, which registered 7.6 on the Richter scale and was felt across much of Pakistan and northern India, killed more than 80,000 people, injured almost 70,000, and destroyed thousands of structures. Landslides, rockfalls, and crumbled buildings left an estimated four million people homeless and cut off access to some areas for several days.

Top 9 Oil-Producing Countries

✻ ✻ ✻ ✻

There are 83 million barrels of oil produced in the world every day. The following list breaks down production by country.

Country	*Barrels per Day (millions)*
1. Saudi Arabia	9.475
2. Russia	9.400
3. United States	7.610
4. Iran	3.979
5. China	3.631
6. Mexico	3.420
7. Norway	3.220
8. Canada	3.135
9. Venezuela	3.081

Source: CIA World Factbook 2007

DO YOU KNOW WHAT'S IN YOUR MAKEUP BAG?
12 Odd Beauty Products Throughout History

❋ ❋ ❋ ❋

Before there were department store counters and drugstores, there were homemade cosmetics that often had some pretty funky ingredients. Even today, you might be surprised to learn what's in the items you throw into your makeup kit. But be forewarned— what we do for beauty can get pretty ugly . . . and dangerous.

1. Ambergris

Ambergris—a highly flammable, waxy substance with a sweet, earthy odor—comes from the intestines of whales and is used in perfume manufacturing. Prior to the 18th century, men and women molded ambergris into beads that were worn as an aromatic necklace. Although whales excrete the substance naturally (it's jokingly called whale barf), synthetic ambergris is now made to prevent the slaughter of whales for this highly sought-after product.

2. Wax

Wax is a common ingredient in many hair products and facial cosmetics today, but the men and women of ancient Egypt used wax more creatively. They would stick a cone of pomade, or scented ointment, on the top of their head, and over time, their body heat would melt the wax and give off a pleasant aroma.

3. Kohl

Often made from soot, kohl was used for black eyeliner in ancient Egypt, North Africa, the Middle East, and Greece. Although kohl served to protect the eyes against the harsh sun and certain eye infections, some forms of the pigment contain lead—not exactly a safe ingredient. Lead poisoning can induce insanity and death.

4. Carmine

The cochineal bug is a bright red insect that hangs out mostly on cacti in places such as Peru, Chile, Mexico, and the Canary Islands. For centuries, these bugs have been crushed for the carminic acid they produce, which is used to make a bright red dye called carmine. A common ingredient in lipsticks, rouges, and eye shadow, the dye is also synthetically produced today.

5. Guanine

Crystals of guanine, a compound made from fish scales and guano (the excrement of bats and sea birds), refract light in a lovely, pearly way. Guanine gives beauty products, such as shampoo, nail polish, and shimmering lotions, their shiny, glittery appearance.

6. Boar Bristles

All hairbrushes are not created equal, at least, according to fans of the boar bristle hairbrush. Boar bristle is scaly in texture, making it effective for cleaning the hair shaft, follicle, and scalp, and distributing oil along the hair shaft. Boars needn't be harmed for their bristles, just sheared like sheep. Boar bristle brushes can be found in fine salons and online for around $35.

7. Chitosan

Chitosan oligosaccharide is made from chitin, a starch found in the skeletons of shrimp, crabs, and other shellfish, and helps maintain moisture in facial cleansers and creams. Not only does it keep the stuff in the tube damp, this substance keeps skin moisturized, too.

8. Hooves and Feathers

Gelatin and keratin are animal by-products derived from the hair, hooves, horns, skin, bones, and feathers of animals such as cows, chickens, and horses. These ingredients have long been included in shampoos and conditioners as binding agents.

9. Propolis

Also called "bee glue," propolis is a brownish resin collected by bees from tree buds and bark to fill crevices and varnish the hive. Due to its antiseptic, anti-inflammatory, and anesthetic properties, bee glue can be found in many "all natural" lip balms, cosmetics, lotions, shampoos, conditioners, and toothpastes. But be careful—just because a product is "all natural" doesn't mean it's safe for everyone. Allergic reactions to propolis are fairly common.

10. Silk

For centuries, women in Japan have been utilizing silk in clothing and cosmetics. There are 18 amino acids in silk, making it a natural moisturizer readily absorbed by the skin. Silkworms produce silk naturally, and it's only the real stuff that provides any benefits to skin—synthetic silk has none of those properties.

11. Civet

The civet, which looks like a cat but is more closely related to the mongoose, has sacs near its anus that create secretions harvested for perfume. The process of obtaining the secretions is painful for civets, so animal rights activists have succeeded in reducing this practice. Fortunately, synthetic materials provide the same stuff without harming the animals.

12. Londinium Powder

Japanese women of the Heian era (around A.D. 800–1200) used londinium, a lead-based powder, mixed with water to create a thin paste they applied to their faces. As with lead-based eyeliners in other parts of the world, this stuff was not very good for those who used it. Lead is easily absorbed by the body and can quickly cause many health problems and even death.

10 Destructive Hurricanes in Recent Times

✳ ✳ ✳ ✳

What begin as thunderstorms off the west coast of Africa can become hurricanes by the time they reach the Caribbean and the southeastern United States. Between 80 and 100 of these systems develop each year from June to November, but usually only a handful evolve into hurricanes that impact the United States. Check out some of nature's most catastrophic hurricanes.

1. Galveston, Texas: September 1900

Climatologist Isaac Cline dismissed the notion that a hurricane could devastate the island city of Galveston, but when he noticed unusually heavy swells from the southeast, he drove his horse and buggy along the beach warning people to move to the mainland. Unfortunately, Cline's initially cavalier attitude about the storm may have played a part in the huge loss of life—between 8,000 and 12,000 deaths—because less than half the population evacuated and some people came from Houston just to watch. The U.S. Weather Bureau ranked the storm a category 4 hurricane with wind speeds measured at 100 miles per hour before the measuring device blew away. Other records say winds peaked around 145 miles per hour. The hurricane wiped out about three-quarters of the city and caused nearly $20 million in damages.

2. Florida Keys and Corpus Christi, Texas: September 1919

This was the only Atlantic hurricane to form in 1919, but it was a monster! With winds reaching 140 miles per hour, the category 4 storm originally made landfall in Key West, Florida, but continued over the warm waters of the Gulf of Mexico and struck again in Corpus Christi—now downgraded to category 3, but with a 12-foot storm surge. The storm cost more than $22 million in damages and killed between 600 and 900 people—many of them passengers on ten ships lost in the Gulf of Mexico. Coincidentally, a boy named Bob Simpson survived the Corpus Christi leg of the storm, sparking his interest in hurricanes and eventually leading him to codevelop the Saffir-Simpson scale used to measure hurricane strength.

3. Okeechobee Hurricane: September 1928

Reaching category 5 strength when it slammed Puerto Rico, the storm then hit Palm Beach, Florida, with 150-mile-per-hour winds and little warning. Coastal residents were prepared, but 40 miles inland at Lake Okeechobee, the massive rainfall that accompanied the storm crumbled a six-foot-tall mud dike around the lake. The storm cost $100 million in damages and killed more than 1,800 people, although some estimates list the death toll as high as 4,000.

4. The Great Labor Day Storm: September 1935

In little more than 24 hours, this storm went from a category 1 to a category 5, where it remained when it struck the Florida Keys, making it the first hurricane of such intensity to strike the United States. With wind speeds reaching 200 miles per hour and a 15-foot storm surge, this cataclysmic hurricane caused $6 million in damages. Of the more than 420 people killed in the storm, about 260 of them were World War I veterans who were in the region building bridges as part of President Roosevelt's New Deal. The flimsy camps that housed the veterans were no match for this wicked storm, and the train sent to rescue them was blown off the tracks.

5. The New England Hurricane: September 1938

Normally, hurricanes thrive on the warm, tropical waters along the southeastern coast of the United States. But this storm had other plans, striking the northeastern United States instead. With winds gusting at more than 100 miles per hour, the eye of this hurricane struck Long Island, New York, but winds and massive rainfall wreaked havoc in Massachusetts, Connecticut, and Rhode Island, and caused damage in Montreal as well. Dubbed the "Long Island Express," the storm killed 700 people, injured 700 more, and caused $306 million in damages. It also brought a 12- to 16-foot storm surge that destroyed more than 8,000 homes and 6,000 boats.

6. Hurricane Camille: August 1969

With wind gusts exceeding 200 miles per hour and a 20-foot storm surge, Camille was the second category 5 hurricane to hit the United States. The massive storm struck along the mouth of the Mississippi River and flattened nearly everything along Mississippi's coastline. After pounding the Gulf Coast, Camille moved inland and caused heaving flooding and landslides in Virginia. In total, Camille caused more than $1.4 billion in damages and 259 deaths.

7. Hurricane Hugo: September 1989

The strongest hurricane to hit the United States since Camille, Hugo struck near Charleston, South Carolina, as a category 4 storm with winds surpassing 135 miles per hour and a 20-foot storm surge. Hugo was also responsible for an estimated 85 deaths and $7 billion in damage, making it the costliest hurricane at the time.

8. Hurricane Andrew: August 1992

The third category 5 storm to hit U.S. shores and the first severe hurricane to hit southern Florida in 27 years, Hurricane Andrew brought along 145 mile per hour winds (with gusts up to 170 miles per hour) and a 17-foot storm surge. The day after Andrew ravaged southern Florida, it moved across to Louisiana, weakening to category 3 status but still packing 120 mile per hour winds. Andrew left 44 dead and caused $26.5 billion in damage, mostly in Florida. Around 250,000 people were left homeless, more than 700,000 insurance claims were filed, and even the coral reefs off the Florida coast sustained damage as far down as 75 feet.

9. Hurricane Ivan: September 2004

Ivan was the fourth major hurricane of the busy 2004 season. At one time a category 5 storm, by the time Ivan struck at Gulf Shores, Alabama, it had weakened to category 3 status with wind speeds reaching 130 miles per hour. But Ivan was the storm that wouldn't die! After devastating much of the Florida panhandle, Ivan dumped water across the southeastern United States, then drifted over the Atlantic Ocean. Once back over the water, Ivan built enough energy to loop around to the south, move across the Florida peninsula, and pick up steam over the Gulf of Mexico—again! Here, the remnants of the storm intensified and made landfall as a tropical storm along the coast of Louisiana. When Ivan finally dissipated over Texas, the storm had left 121 people dead and had caused more than $19 billion in damages.

10. Hurricane Katrina: August 2005

The year 2005 was another busy year for hurricanes, and Katrina, the fifth hurricane of the season, was one that will go down in history. Katrina made landfall near Buras-Triumph, Louisiana, with winds reaching 125 miles per hour before devastating the entire Gulf Coast of Mississippi. But all eyes were on New Orleans, situated below sea level and surrounded by rivers and lakes. So when Katrina made landfall slightly to the east, people in "The Big Easy" breathed a sigh of relief since it appeared that Mississippi had borne the major brunt of the storm. But that changed a few hours later when the massive rainfall and storm surge caused Lake Pontchartrain to flood. When the city's levee system was breached in several places, 80 percent of New Orleans was left under water. The rest of the nation watched via television as residents stayed on rooftops in the scorching heat for days awaiting rescue. The U.S. government was severely criticized for its delayed reaction in sending aid. Katrina's wrath took more than 1,800 lives and hundreds are still missing. With more than $81 billion in damages, Katrina was the most expensive natural disaster in U.S. history.

Top 13 Oil-Consuming Countries

The world consumes about 82.6 million barrels of oil a day, nearly as much as is produced on a daily basis. Here's how the top oil consumers stack up.

Country	*Barrels per Day (millions)*
1. United States	20.730
2. China	6.534
3. Japan	5.578
4. Germany	2.650
5. Russia	2.500
6. India	2.450
7. Canada	2.294
8. South Korea	2.149
9. Brazil	2.100
10. France (tied)	1.970
11. Mexico (tied)	1.970
12. Italy	1.881
13. Saudi Arabia	1.845

Source: CIA World Factbook 2007

TAKE A CUE FROM DOROTHY AND TOTO
15 Tornado Safety Tips

❈ ❈ ❈ ❈

Funnel clouds have been observed on every continent except Antarctica. The United States has significantly more than the rest of the world because of low-lying geography and a climate that breeds strong thunderstorms. With wind speeds up to 320 miles per hour, tornadoes kill about 60 people every year in the United States when uprooted trees and debris turn into deadly missiles. Check out the list below and get prepared!

1. Determine the best locations for shelter at home and work.
The safest location is always a basement, below the deadly wind and projectile objects. If you can't go underground, find a small interior room or hallway on the lowest level of the building.

2. Conduct tornado safety drills with your family.
Make learning quick and fun, and children will remember the basics of what to do, especially if you go through the motions several times. Just as most kids know what to do if their clothes are on fire, the same drill could be applied for tornado safety—instead of "Stop, drop, and roll" try "Run, duck, and cover!"

3. Prepare an emergency supply kit.
Experts recommend that each person (and pet) has supplies for at least three days, including bottled water (two quarts per person, per day), nonperishable food, and a first-aid kit that includes prescription items as well as aspirin and antacids. Make sure you have tools such as a can opener, utility knife, wrench (for turning power valves), whistle, battery-powered radio, several flashlights, and batteries. Each person will need blankets, clothing, rain gear, and heavy-soled shoes or boots. Lastly, stash away some cash and a copy of credit cards, passports, social security cards, phone numbers, and insurance information. Once a year, check your supplies and determine if family needs have changed.

4. Make an inventory of your possessions.

For insurance purposes, videotape or photograph everything you would need to replace in case you lose it all. When you're sure that you've included everything, keep the inventory somewhere away from the premises, such as a safe-deposit box.

5. Know how your community sends its warnings.

If it's a siren, stay inside and take cover. Know where the designated shelters are in the buildings where you and your family spend time.

6. Know the difference between a "watch" and a "warning."

There's a big difference in the danger level between the two terms used during stormy weather. A watch simply means that conditions are favorable for a tornado to develop. Be alert, but you don't need to take shelter. If there's a warning, a tornado has been spotted. When a warning is posted for your area, take shelter immediately.

7. Stay away from windows.

At 320 miles per hour, shards of glass can be deadly. You can eliminate this risk if you make sure your shelter area is free of windows. If this isn't possible, protect yourself with a heavy blanket.

8. Don't bother opening windows.

It's true that air pressure equalizes when there's an opening in the building, but the American Red Cross says that it's far more important to get to safety than to open windows. If there's flying debris, the windows will most likely break on their own!

9. Get in position.

Once you're in your shelter, find a sturdy piece of furniture, such as a workbench or table, and stay under it. Curl into a ball on the floor, and lock your hands behind your head to protect it from flying debris. If you can't find a table to get under, crouch under a door frame because the beams will offer some protection.

10. Mobile home residents need to take extra precautions.

If you live in a mobile home, never try to ride out a severe thunderstorm at home; go to a prearranged shelter. As a last resort, go outside and lie flat on the ground using your hands and arms to protect your head. It might be hard to believe that you're safer outside, but since your mobile home isn't built into the ground, it can be picked up and turned into an airborne missile.

11. What if you're in a public building?

The first choice is always a basement or lower level. If that isn't an option, avoid wide-open spaces such as cafeterias or auditoriums—there's just not enough physical support for you there. Look for an inside hallway, or a small closet or bathroom (with no windows).

12. What if you're in a vehicle?

Never try to outrun a tornado. Get out of your vehicle and try to get inside a building. If there isn't time, lie down flat in a ditch or any low-lying area away from the vehicle. (Hiding below an underpass isn't safe because you're still exposed to flying debris.) Use your hands and arms to protect your head.

13. What if you're outdoors?

Finding a building is your best bet, but if there's no time, follow the same instructions as above.

14. What to do when the storm has passed.

Treat injuries with your first-aid kit, but don't attempt to move anyone who is severely injured. Use the phone only for emergencies, such as calling for an ambulance. Then, listen to the radio for emergency information. If the building you are in is damaged, beware of broken glass and downed power lines as you evacuate. Check on neighbors who might need assistance, but otherwise stay out of the way so that emergency crews can do their work.

15. Beware of fire hazards.

Never strike a match until you're sure you haven't had a gas leak. Anything that holds gas can rupture and be vulnerable to explosions if you see (or smell) leakage after a storm. If you think there might be a gas leak, open all doors and get out of the house. Also watch out for severed electrical wires, which can spark debris piles. Check appliances to see if they are emitting smoke or sparks.

15 Greatest Oil Reserves by Country

❋ ❋ ❋ ❋

Country	Proved Reserves (billion barrels)
1. Saudi Arabia	262.7
2. Canada	178.9
3. Iran	132.5
4. Iraq	112.5
5. Kuwait	101.5
6. United Arab Emirates	97.8
7. Kuwait	96.5
8. Venezuela	75.2
9. Russia	74.4
10. Libya	42.0
11. Nigeria	36.2
12. Kazakhstan	26.0
13. Angola	25.0
14. United States	22.4
15. China	16.1

Source: CIA World Factbook, 2007

9 Things Invented or Discovered by Accident

❋ ❋ ❋ ❋

We tend to hold inventors in high esteem, but often their discoveries were the result of an accident or twist of fate. This is true of many everyday items, including the following surprise inventions.

1. Play-Doh

One smell most people remember from childhood is the odor of Play-Doh, the brightly-colored, nontoxic modeling clay. Play-Doh was accidentally invented in 1955 by Joseph and Noah McVicker while trying to make a wallpaper cleaner. It was marketed a year later by toy manufacturer Rainbow Crafts. More than 700 million pounds of Play-Doh have sold since then, but the recipe remains a secret.

2. Fireworks

Fireworks originated in China some 2,000 years ago, and legend has it that they were accidentally invented by a cook who mixed together charcoal, sulfur, and saltpeter—all items commonly found in kitchens in those days. The mixture burned and when compressed in a bamboo tube, it exploded. There's no record of whether it was the cook's last day on the job.

3. Potato Chips

If you can't eat just one potato chip, blame it on chef George Crum. He reportedly created the salty snack in 1853 at Moon's Lake House near Saratoga Springs, New York. Fed up with a customer who continuously sent his fried potatoes back, complaining that they were soggy and not crunchy enough, Crum sliced the potatoes as thin as possible, fried them in hot grease, then doused them with salt. The customer loved them and "Saratoga Chips" quickly became a popular item at the lodge and throughout New England. Eventually, the chips were mass-produced for home consumption, but since they were stored in barrels or tins, they quickly went stale. Then, in the 1920s, Laura Scudder invented the airtight bag by ironing together two pieces of waxed paper, thus keeping the chips fresh longer. Today, chips are packaged in plastic or foil bags or cardboard containers and come in a variety of flavors, including sour cream and onion, barbecue, and salt and vinegar.

4. Slinky

In 1943, naval engineer Richard James was trying to develop a spring that would support and stabilize sensitive equipment on ships. When one of the springs accidentally fell off a shelf, it continued moving, and James got the idea for a toy. His wife Betty came up with the name, and when the Slinky made its debut in late 1945, James sold 400 of the bouncy toys in 90 minutes. Today, more than 250 million Slinkys have been sold worldwide.

5. Saccharin

Saccharin, the oldest artificial sweetener, was accidentally discovered in 1879 by researcher Constantine Fahlberg, who was working at Johns Hopkins University in the laboratory of professor Ira Remsen. Fahlberg's discovery came after he forgot to wash his hands before lunch. He had spilled a chemical on his hands and it, in turn, caused the bread he ate to taste unusually sweet. In 1880, the two scientists jointly published the discovery, but in 1884, Fahlberg obtained a patent and began mass-producing saccharin without Remsen. The use of saccharin did not become widespread until sugar was rationed during World War I, and its popularity increased during the 1960s and 1970s with the manufacture of Sweet'N Low and diet soft drinks.

6. Post-it Notes

A Post-it note is a small piece of paper with a strip of low-tack adhesive on the back that allows it to be temporarily attached to documents, walls, computer monitors, and just about anything else. The idea for the Post-it note was conceived in 1974 by Arthur Fry as a way of holding bookmarks in his hymnal while singing in the church choir. He was aware of an adhesive accidentally developed in 1968 by fellow 3M employee Spencer Silver. No application for the lightly sticky stuff was apparent until Fry's idea. The 3M company was initially skeptical about the product's profitability, but in 1980, the product was introduced around the world. Today, Post-it notes are sold in more than 100 countries.

7. Silly Putty

It bounces, it stretches, it breaks—it's Silly Putty, the silicone-based plastic clay marketed as a children's toy by Binney & Smith, Inc. During World War II, while attempting to create a synthetic rubber substitute, James Wright dropped boric acid into silicone oil. The result was a polymerized substance that bounced, but it took several years to find a use for the product. Finally, in 1950, marketing expert Peter Hodgson saw its potential as a toy, renamed it Silly Putty, and a classic toy was born! Not only is it fun, Silly Putty also has practical uses—it picks up dirt, lint, and pet hair; can stabilize wobbly furniture; and is useful in stress reduction, physical therapy, and in medical and scientific simulations. It was even used by the crew of *Apollo 8* to secure tools in zero gravity.

8. Microwave Ovens

The microwave oven is now a standard appliance in most American households, but it has only been around since the late 1940s. In 1945, Percy Spencer was experimenting with a new vacuum tube called a magnetron while doing research for the Raytheon Corporation. He was intrigued when the candy bar in his pocket began to melt, so he tried another experiment with popcorn. When it began to pop, Spencer immediately saw the potential in this revolutionary process. In 1947, Raytheon built the first microwave oven, the Radarange, which weighed 750 pounds, was 5½ feet tall, and cost about $5,000. When the Radarange first became available for home use in the early 1950s, its bulky size and expensive price tag made it unpopular with consumers. But in 1967, a much more popular 100-volt, countertop version was introduced at a price of $495.

9. Corn Flakes

In 1894, Dr. John Harvey Kellogg was the superintendent of the Battle Creek Sanitarium in Michigan. He and his brother Will Keith Kellogg were Seventh Day Adventists, and they were searching for wholesome foods to feed patients that also complied with the Adventists' strict vegetarian diet. When Will accidentally left some boiled wheat sitting out, it went stale by the time he returned. Rather than throw it away, the brothers sent it through rollers, hoping to make long sheets of dough, but they got flakes instead. They toasted the flakes, which were a big hit with patients, and patented them under the name Granose. The brothers experimented with other grains, including corn, and in 1906, Will created the Kellogg's company to sell the corn flakes. On principle, John refused to join the company because Will lowered the health benefits of the cereal by adding sugar.

Chapter 16
TRAVEL

✳ ✳ ✳ ✳

12 Strange Tourist Attractions

Jaunting around America and Canada can be a visual adventure. But to truly experience the kitschy side, sometimes you need to meander the back roads. That's where you'll find giant roadside statues, fascinating collections, and these unusual attractions.

1. World's Largest Ball of Twine

Determining the world's largest ball of twine can be difficult. But the hands-down winner in the solo winder category has to be the nearly 9-ton 11-foot-tall hunk of string on display in Darwin, Minnesota. Francis Johnson spent four hours a day between 1950 and 1979 rolling the ball. He used a crane to hoist the ever-expanding ball as it grew, to ensure uniform wrapping.

Another ball in the running is the 1,300-mile-plus length of string originally rolled by Frank Stoeber of Cawker City, Kansas. From 1953 until his death in 1974, Stoeber diligently wound this twine ball. Every August, Cawker City hosts a festival during which anyone can add a bit of twine to the ball, so it now outweighs the one in Darwin, but it has had more than one person working on it.

2. Coral Castle

The Coral Castle was the brainchild of Edward Leedskalnin, who was jilted by his fiancée the day before their wedding. Crushed by the rejection, Leedskalnin moved from his home in Latvia and set out to build a monument to his lost love. The result was the Coral Castle in Homestead, Florida. Without any outside help or heavy machinery, the distraught lover sculpted more than 1,100 tons of coral into marvelous shapes. The entry gate alone is made of a single coral block weighing nine tons. The fact that Leedskalnin was barely five feet tall and weighed only 100 pounds adds to the feat.

3. Paul Bunyan Statues

There are enough Paul Bunyan statues around the continent to delight any teller of tall tales. Representations of the big fella— known for his ability to lay down more trees in a single swath of his ax than any contemporary logging firm—can be found wherever there have been logging camps. One of the most memorable statues is located in Bangor, Maine, the lumberjack's alleged birthplace, where a 31-foot-tall, 37,000-pound Paul shows off his ax and scythe. Other statues, such as those in Klamath, California, and Bemidji, Minnesota, show Bunyan accompanied by his faithful companion, Babe the blue ox.

4. Corn Palace

The city of Mitchell, South Dakota, proudly calls itself the "Corn Capital of the World," and it even has a palace in which to celebrate. The Mitchell Corn Palace, originally constructed in 1892, is now an auditorium with Russian-style turrets and towers and murals that local artists create each year out of corn and other South Dakota grains. After the annual fall harvest, pigeons and squirrels are allowed to devour the palace's murals until the next year when the process begins anew.

5. Jolly Green Giant Statue

Ho, ho ho! The Jolly Green Giant remains the towering symbol of the Green Giant food company, located in Blue Earth, Minnesota. Since 1979, the 55-foot-tall statue, who sports a size 78 shoe, honors the third-most-recognized advertising icon of the 20th century.

6. Lucy the Elephant

Looming 65 feet over the beach at Margate, New Jersey, Lucy the Elephant is the only example of "zoomorphic architecture" left in the United States. With staircases in her legs leading to rooms inside, the wide-eyed elephant was originally built in 1881 as a real-estate promotion. Over the years Lucy has served as a summer home, a tavern, a hotel, and a tourist attraction. Relocation in 1970 spared Lucy from demolition, and she received a loving face-lift and restoration in 2000.

7. Albert, the World's Largest Bull

Located in Audubon, Iowa, Albert, the world's largest bull, stands 30 feet tall and weighs in at 45 tons... of concrete. Named after local banker Albert Kruse, the monster Hereford statue was built in the 1960s for Operation T-Bone Days, an event held each September to honor the days when local cattle would board trains to the Chicago stockyards. As an interesting side note, Albert's internal steel frame is made from dismantled Iowa windmills.

8. World's Largest Hockey Stick and Puck

Leave it to hockey-hungry Canadians to build the world's largest hockey stick and puck. The stick, which is made of Douglas fir beams reinforced with steel, is 205 feet long, weighs 61,000 pounds, and is 40-times larger than life-size. It was created for Expo '86 in Vancouver, British Columbia, before being sent to Duncan, where it has been a popular tourist attraction since 1988.

9. Chuck the Channel Cat

Chuck the Channel Cat flips his tail at visitors cruising past his statue in Selkirk, Manitoba. Erected in 1986, the two-ton, 25-foot-tall monument to the area's enormous catfish greets visitors with a smile. Chuck's mission: to help promote Selkirk as the "Catfish Capital." It's a well-deserved title—anglers on the Red River regularly reel in catfish up to 30-plus pounds.

10. Superman Statue

Metropolis, in far southern Illinois, has nothing to fear these days because Superman lives there. In 1972, the town decided to capitalize on its famous name and subsequently adopted the moniker, "Hometown of Superman." A seven-foot-tall statue was erected in 1986, only to be replaced in 1993 by a more impressive 15-foot bronze monument. In 2008, a statue of Lois Lane will be erected next to her hunky beau in Superman Square.

11. Crazy Horse Memorial

The Crazy Horse Memorial in Crazy Horse, South Dakota, is a labor of love that sculptor Korczak Ziolkowski began in 1948 to honor the great Native American leader. Ziolkowski's life's work (until his passing in 1982), the sculpture is likely the most ambitious roadside project ever undertaken. Ziolkowski's family continues the project, but the statue remains very much a work in progress. The carving is a depiction of the legendary warrior on horseback and will measure 641 feet long by 563 feet high when completed.

12. House on the Rock

Resting atop a 60-foot stone formation in Spring Green, Wisconsin, the House on the Rock is one of the best-known architectural oddities in the United States. Built by eccentric artist Alex Jordan in the 1940s, the House on the Rock was his vacation home before being turned into a museum in 1961. Jordan sold the building in the early 1980s, but it continues to grow as a tourist attraction. With 14 unique and lavishly decorated rooms—including the Infinity Room, with 3,264 windows—and a surrounding complex that houses a miniature circus and the world's largest carousel, the House on the Rock is at once wacky, tacky, innovative, and elegant.

YOU'RE FROM *WHERE*?
23 Silly City Names

✳ ✳ ✳ ✳

1. Bird-in-Hand, Pennsylvania
2. What Cheer, Iowa
3. Ding Dong, Texas
4. Elbow, Saskatchewan
5. Monkeys Eyebrow, Kentucky
6. Flin Flon, Manitoba
7. Goofy Ridge, Illinois
8. Hell, Michigan
9. Intercourse, Pennsylvania
10. Joe Batt's Arm, Newfoundland
11. Cut and Shoot, Texas
12. Jackass Flats, Nevada

22 Romantic Kissing Spots in America

❈ ❈ ❈ ❈

What makes a place romantic enough to inspire a long, passionate kiss? The answer differs for all couples, but one universal answer seems to apply: Being together in beauty— whether in a natural setting or a creation of the human imagination—can certainly help affections flow freely.

1. Verde Hot Springs, Arizona

Hot passions won't cool off at these secluded hot springs. Wintertime water temperatures reach 96° F and soar higher in summer. Soak in pools fit for two, or in seclusion underneath cliff overhangs.

2. Mendocino Headlands State Park, California

If the town of Mendocino wasn't tantalizing enough for romance, there's the adjacent state park where kissing spots are as common as tidal pools. Explore gentle pathways leading along rugged coastline to secluded beaches, hidden grottoes, and sea arches. On foggy days, a cool mist caresses cheeks and lips, so snuggle up to stay warm.

3. San Juan Skyway (U.S. 550 between Durango and Ridgway), Colorado

Reach the height of romance on this high and mighty scenic loop in south central Colorado. The 14 summits along the route—all above 14,000 feet—lead lovers toward the sky and to unsurpassed vistas. Even at lower elevations, there's no romantic letdown. The old mining towns of Durango, Telluride, and Silverton—all mother lodes of romantic ambience—highlight this 236-mile stretch of highway.

4. Amelia Island, Florida

A sun-kissed beach certainly qualifies as a smooching spot, but if lovers want more drama, Amelia Island delivers. More than just sand and surf, the island increases the pucker-up potential with delights of the Deep South: gnarled oak trees dripping with Spanish moss, footbridges crisscrossing windswept dunes, and wide, unspoiled Atlantic beaches. Study the birds and the bees while kayaking through gentle tidal creeks where egrets and herons await.

5. Na Pali Coast State Park, Hawaii

Heaven and Earth merge at this exquisite state park, located on the untamed northern side of Kauai. Journeying by foot (the only way to go) into the verdant rainforests and deep valleys flanked by mile-high cliffs is like stepping into untouched Hawaii. There's nothing here but you and nature. Whisper "Aloha" to each other at one of the secret crescent beaches that dot the shoreline, many perfect for a little au naturel action.

6. Chicago's Navy Pier Ferris Wheel, Illinois

Take to the sky to smooch! Nighttime is prime time to whirl around, snuggled together on a swinging seat, and view Chicago's fabulous skyline from this 150-foot-tall Ferris wheel.

7. Cumberland Falls, Kentucky

Bring a flashlight, hold hands, and venture deep into the woods to cast your eyes upon a romantically rare and unforgettable moonbow. A moonbow is a lunar rainbow that occurs at night, and Cumberland Falls (dubbed the "Niagara of the South") serves up this optical phenomenon on clear, moon-bathed nights. There's no pot o' gold at the bow's end, but the romantic reward of a moonlit kiss should prove satisfying enough.

8. Haakwood State Forest Campground, Michigan

Howl at the moon and snuggle under the stars for a bit of rugged romance in this remote part of the state. For a taste of civilization, hop into the car and drive along Lake Michigan's coastline to watch the sun's last show of the day.

9. Ruins of Windsor, Mississippi

Hauntingly romantic and oh-so-southern, the largest antebellum mansion in Mississippi still captivates lovers despite its ruined status. Twenty-three massive Corinthian columns are all that remain of this Civil War survivor. (A careless smoker caused the mansion's demise in 1890.) Stroll the lush grounds together and imagine days "gone with the wind"... and fire.

10. Meadville Ghost Town, Nebraska

No spooks out here, just simple solitude, a slice of history, and a charming general store. Meadville isn't exactly easy to reach, but therein lies its quiet allure. Once you've made it, explore the blacksmith shop, farmhouse, and the 1890 cabin used by newlyweds in the days before honeymoon suites. At the renovated general store—the only business for miles—warm up by the wood-burning stove, sip wine, and share an old-fashioned smooch.

11. Valley of Fire, Nevada

Spark the romantic kindling in this tiny, fiery desert state park, located an hour from Las Vegas. Hide in the narrow arroyos, cuddle underneath overhanging rock formations, or spread out on the slickrock with only lizards to keep you company. There are numerous hiking trails, many with peekaboo views of Lake Mead.

12. Pitcher Mountain Trail, New Hampshire

Grab a small jug of New Hampshire's famous cider in nearby Stoddard, then stroll past blueberry fields and grazing Scottish Highland cattle to reach the summit of Mount Pitcher. The bald, flat mountaintop boasts the "softest rock in New Hampshire" for picnics and offers head-twirling views of the Presidential Range, the Berkshires, and Vermont foothills. The 15-minute hike is easily accessible, and encountering another couple is considered a crowd.

13. Cape May, New Jersey

When it comes to wooing your beloved, Cape May delivers all that's needed. During the day, stroll together through the area's numerous gardens and wildlife sanctuaries or beachcomb for Cape May's famous "diamonds"—pieces of quartz polished by the waves. Savor the romance with a horse-drawn carriage ride through the gaslit streets of the old Victorian town.

14. White Sands National Monument Moonlight Walk, New Mexico

Moonlight has never before exerted such an attraction for lovers. When the moon's out in full force, these gypsum sand formations—the largest in the world—glow. Stroll hand-in-hand under the brilliant New Mexico night sky and steal a kiss under the approving eye of the man in the moon.

15. Lake Metigoshe, North Dakota

Straddling the U.S.–Canadian border, Lake Metigoshe is as far north as you'll get in the state...making it the prime place to watch the northern lights dance or the Milky Way sparkle while bundled together in a blanket. There are no crowds to interfere with romance and no bright city lights to hinder stargazing.

16. The Richland Carousel, Ohio

Love makes the world go 'round, so keep on spinning by kissing aboard one of the carousel's ornate animals. This indoor merry-go-round keeps hearts and hands toasty in the winter, and, when things heat up in the summer, an airy breeze cools lovers as they twirl into the sunset.

17. McConnell's Mill Bridge in McConnell's Mill State Park, Pennsylvania

Back in horse-and-buggy days, a young fella could steal plenty of kisses as he and his sweetie rode underneath a long covered bridge, hence the nickname "kissing bridges." Pennsylvania boasts 213 such bridges, and a favorite is McConnell's Mill Bridge spanning scenic Slippery Rock Creek. At 96 feet long, there are plenty of kisses to be had while slowly traveling through.

18. Providence Athenaeum, Rhode Island

Amidst the library stacks, there's romance and history...but not just in the books. Edgar Allan Poe spent hours hidden away in this 1838-era building reading poems to his love, Sarah Whitman. Choose your favorite love poem and tuck back into the stacks together for some riveting recitation of passionate passages.

19. Landsford Canal State Park, South Carolina

It's not Venice, and canoes aren't gondolas, but you can glide along with the same romantic notions at this charming state park. Canoe the Catawba River canals or simply stroll along the riverside trails. Whichever mode of transport suits your style, the surroundings won't cease to amaze. Stone bridges, canal locks, and an old mill add a touch of history, while the rare spider lilies that bloom along the rocky shoals give a sense of the exotic.

20. McDonald Observatory, Texas

Like everything else in Texas, the night sky is big...and up in these parts it's darker than cowboy coffee—choice conditions for stargazing and kissing. At this remote observatory, starry-eyed lovers intent on romance can look toward the heavens for some unexpected celestial surprises but also find earthly delights. Relish romantic moments far from civilization (the nearest major town is 160 miles away), and be sure to wish upon a lone star.

21. Barboursville Vineyards, Virginia

Raise a toast to the state motto—"Virginia is for Lovers"—at this vineyard and winery nestled in the foothills of the Blue Ridge

Mountains. As if sipping wine at a lovely vineyard wasn't enough to captivate your romantic attention, there are also enchanting ruins to explore. The remains of an early 19th-century mansion designed by Thomas Jefferson are tucked away in the boxwoods.

22. American Camp, San Juan Island, Washington

Duck out of sight into secluded, sheltered coves or hide together in the tall grass. No one will see you, except for perhaps one of the rabbits. American Camp at the windswept southern end of San Juan Island doesn't let up on spectacular scenery or hidden spots. Find your own little beach and savor views of the Olympic Peninsula and Cascade Mountains. Between kisses, watch for orcas breaching in Puget Sound.

30 Countries and Their Currency

❊ ❊ ❊ ❊

1. Algeria.............................. Algerian dinar (DZD)
2. Argentina .... Argentine peso (ARS)
3. Brazil.............................. real (BRL)
4. Bulgaria........................... lev (BGL)
5. Chile.............................. Chilean peso (CLP)
6. China.............................. renminbi (yuan) (CNY)
7. Denmark............................ Danish krone (DKK)
8. Ecuador .... U.S. dollar (USD)
9. Guatemala.......................... quetzal (GTQ), U.S. dollar (USD)
10. Hungary .... forint (HUF)
11. Indonesia .... Indonesian rupiah (IDR)
12. Iran............................... Iranian rial (IRR)
13. Iraq............................... new Iraqi dinar (NID)
14. Japan .... yen (JPY)
15. Nigeria .... naira (NGN)
16. Panama .... balboa (PAB); U.S. dollar (USD)
17. Peru............................... nuevo sol (PEN)
18. Poland............................. zloty (PLN)

7 Wonders of the Natural World

✳ ✳ ✳ ✳

Each of the following sites captures the imagination with its natural power and beauty. And they have one thing in common: Nothing made by humans can approach their majestic dignity.

1. Grand Canyon

The Grand Canyon in northwestern Arizona was formed by the erosive power of the weather and the Colorado River and its tributaries as they scoured away billion-year-old rocks. Although known to Native Americans for thousands of years, the vast gorge was not discovered by the first Spanish explorers until 1540. Grand Canyon National Park was established in 1919, preserving the more than 1.2 million acres of colorful cliffs and waterways that are home to 75 species of mammals, 50 species of reptiles and amphibians, 25 species of fish, and more than 300 species of birds. The canyon stretches 277 miles, with some sections reaching a mile deep and 18 miles across. More than five million visitors view the canyon annually, often hiking or riding mules down to the canyon floor, while the more adventurous opt for boating or rafting the Colorado River through the canyon.

2. Aurora Borealis (Northern Lights)

The aurora borealis (also called the northern lights) consists of awe-inspiring twirls of light in the sky, caused by "solar wind"—electrically charged particles interacting with Earth's magnetic field. The aurora borealis can be up to 2,000 miles wide, but it fluctuates in size, shape, and color, with green being the most common color close to the horizon while purples and reds appear higher. Named after Aurora, Roman goddess of dawn, and Boreas, Greek god of the north wind, these ribbons of color are best viewed in northern climates like Alaska, but have been seen as far south as Arizona.

3. Mount Everest

Mount Everest, part of the Himalayan Mountains between Nepal and Tibet, was formed about 60 million years ago due to the shifting of Earth's rocky plates. Named after Sir George Everest, a British surveyor-general of India, Everest is the highest mountain on Earth, looming some 29,035 feet high and growing a few millimeters every year. Climbing Everest isn't easy, due to avalanches, strong winds, and thin air. Nevertheless, in 1953, Edmund Hillary and Sherpa Tenzing Norgay were the first climbers to reach the peak. More than 700 others have done so since, with at least 150 persons dying on their quest.

4. Paricutin

Paricutin provides one of nature's best lessons in how volatile Earth is. Exploding out of a Mexican cornfield in 1943, Paricutin was the first known volcano to have witnesses at its birth. Within a year, the cone had grown to more than 1,100 feet high. The flow eventually spread over 10 square miles, engulfing the nearby towns of Paricutin and San Juan Parangaricutiro. The eruptions ceased in 1952, and the cone now soars 1,345 feet high.

5. Victoria Falls

Victoria Falls, originally called Mosi-oa-Tunya ("smoke that thunders"), was named after Queen Victoria of England in 1855. The raging waters of the Zambezi River pour 19 trillion cubic feet of water per minute into a gorge that is 1.25 miles wide and 328 feet deep, making this the largest curtain of falling water in the world. Located between Zambia and Zimbabwe, Victoria Falls is flanked by national parks and is now one of the world's greatest tourist attractions, with resorts, hiking trails, and observation posts springing up around it. White-water rafting at the foot of the falls makes for a thrilling adventure.

6. Great Barrier Reef

The Great Barrier Reef blankets 137,600 square miles and extends a dramatic 1,242 miles along Australia's northeastern coast, making it the largest group of reefs in the world. The reef began forming more than 30 million years ago and is made up of the skeletons of marine polyps. Four hundred species of living polyps can also be found there, along with 1,500 species of fish, as well as crabs, clams, and other sea life. The area is an Australian national park and is visited by two million tourists a year.

7. Giant Sequoia Trees

Ancient giant sequoia trees are nature's ever-growing wonders. Giant sequoias grow naturally on the western slopes of California's Sierra Nevada Mountains at elevations from 5,000 to 7,000 feet. Some are as tall as a 26-story building, with their trunks spanning up to 100 feet and the bark on the older specimens reaching two to four feet thick. California's Sequoia National Park is home to several noteworthy giants, including the General Sherman, which is the world's largest tree by volume, measuring 274.9 feet high, almost 103 feet around, and comprising 52,508 cubic feet of wood. Giant sequoia trees are estimated to be between 1,800 and 2,700 years old. Depending on the tree and where it is situated, giant sequoias can grow up to two feet in height every year, producing almost 40 cubic feet of additional wood each year.

✳ ✳ ✳

"In all things of nature there is something of the marvelous."
—Aristotle, *Parts of Animals*

TWO NATIONS DIVIDED BY A COMMON LANGUAGE
27 American Terms and Their British Equivalents

❋ ❋ ❋ ❋

American Term	British Term
1. ballpoint pen	biro
2. toilet paper	bog roll
3. umbrella	brolly
4. fanny pack	bum bag
5. cotton candy	candy floss
6. french fry	chip
7. plastic wrap	clingfilm
8. zucchini	courgette
9. potato chip	crisp
10. checkers	draughts
11. thumbtack	drawing pin
12. busy signal	engaged tone
13. soccer	football
14. astonished	gobsmacked
15. sweater	jumper
16. elevator	lift
17. restroom	loo
18. truck	lorry
19. ground beef	mince
20. diaper	nappy
21. mailbox	pillar box
22. bandage (Band-Aid)	plaster
23. baby carriage/stroller	pram
24. collect call	reverse-charge call
25. aluminum can	tin
26. to go drastically wrong	to go pear-shaped
27. complain	whinge

A SAVVY TRAVELER'S GUIDE TO MANNERS
13 Examples of Good (and Bad) Manners Around the World

✳ ✳ ✳ ✳

Sit up straight. Say please and thank you. Don't put your elbows on the table. Most of us were drilled from an early age in proper manners and etiquette. But once you leave your home country, things get a bit complicated. Here are some examples of how other cultures do things differently.

1. In China, Taiwan, and much of the Far East, belching is considered a compliment to the chef and a sign that you have eaten well and enjoyed your meal.

2. In most of the Middle and Far East, it is considered an insult to point your feet (particularly the soles) at another person, or to display them in any way, for example, by resting with your feet up.

3. In most Asian countries, a business card is seen as an extension of the person it represents; therefore, to disrespect a card—by folding it, writing on it, or just shoving it into your pocket without looking at it—is to disrespect the person who gave it to you.

4. Nowadays, a bone-crushing handshake is seen as admirable in the United States and UK, but in much of the East, particularly the Philippines, it is seen as a sign of aggression—just as if you gave any other part of a person's body a hard squeeze!

5. Orthodox Jews will not shake hands with someone of the opposite sex, while a strict Muslim woman will not shake hands with a man, although, to confuse matters, a Muslim man will shake hands with a non-Muslim woman. People in these cultures generally avoid touching people of the opposite sex who are not family members.

6. When dining in China, never force yourself to clear your plate out of politeness—it would be very bad manners for your host not to

keep refilling it. Instead, you should leave some food on your plate at each course as an acknowledgment of your host's generosity.

7. In Japan and Korea, a tip is considered an insult, rather than a compliment, and, for them, accepting tips is akin to begging. However, this tradition is beginning to change as more Westerners bring their customs with them to these countries.

8. The "okay" sign (thumb and forefinger touching to make a circle) is very far from okay in much of the world. In Germany and most of South America, it is an insult, similar to giving someone the finger in the United States, while in Turkey it is a derogatory gesture used to imply that someone is homosexual.

9. Similarly, in the UK, when the two-fingered "V for victory" or "peace" salute is given with the hand turned so that the palm faces inward, it is considered extremely rude, having a meaning similar to raising the middle finger to someone in the United States.

10. In Greece, any signal that involves showing your open palm is extremely offensive. Such gestures include waving, as well as making a "stop" sign. If you do wish to wave goodbye to someone in Greece, you need to do so with your palm facing in, like a beauty pageant contestant or a member of the royal family.

11. In many countries, particularly in Asia and South America, it is essential to remove your shoes when entering someone's home, while in most of Europe it is polite to ask your host whether they would prefer you to do so. The reason, as anyone who's ever owned white carpet will attest, is simple hygiene and cleanliness.

12. Chewing gum might be good for dental hygiene, but in many parts of the world, particularly Luxembourg, Switzerland, and France, public gum-chewing is considered vulgar, while in Singapore most types of gum have been illegal since 1992 when residents grew tired of scraping the sticky stuff off their sidewalks.

13. In most Arab countries, the left hand is considered unclean, and it is extremely rude to offer it for a handshake or to wave a greeting. Similarly, it is impolite to pass food or eat with the left hand. If you must know why, let's just say that, historically, people living in deserts didn't have access to toilet paper, so the left hand was used for "hygienic functions," then cleaned by rubbing it in the sand.

6 Peculiar Museums in the United States

✳ ✳ ✳ ✳

1. Circus World Museum, Baraboo, Wisconsin

This national historic landmark is located on the banks of the Baraboo River where the Ringling Bros. Circus spent the winter months from 1884 to 1918. Circus World Museum is a not-for-profit educational facility that includes a museum, library, and research center to showcase the historic role of the circus in American life. Other exhibits include a miniature circus, a clown exhibit, and the world's largest collection of antique circus wagons. Live circus performances take place from May through September.

2. Liberace Museum and Foundation, Las Vegas, Nevada

The Liberace Museum, located in Las Vegas, houses Liberace's world-famous collection of 18 rare and antique pianos, including a rhinestone-covered Baldwin grand and a mirror-encrusted concert grand. Also on display are the showman's bejeweled, sequined, and rhinestone-encrusted costumes; jewelry; and cars, including a rhinestone-laden roadster and a mirror-tiled Rolls-Royce. In addition, Liberace's lavish bedroom from his Palms Springs estate is recreated in all its glittering splendor. The Liberace Foundation, located in the museum, offers scholarships to talented students pursuing careers in the performing and creative arts.

3. The World's Largest Collection of the World's Smallest Versions of the World's Largest Things, Various Locations

Artist Erika Nelson is the owner of this mobile attraction. She drives a van around the country visiting the world's largest roadside attractions—ball of twine, kachina doll, Paul Bunyan and Babe—

adding data to her archive of information. Then, she crafts and displays miniature renderings of the world's largest things.

4. Sing Sing Prison Museum, Ossining, New York

The 2,000-plus inmates that call Sing Sing Prison home may not think it's worth celebrating, but a museum down the street does just that. Sing Sing Prison Museum houses a variety of artifacts from the town of Ossining and Sing Sing itself. A re-creation of two cell blocks and a replica electric chair are among the highlights, along with a display of confiscated prison weapons.

5. Lizzie Borden Museum, Fall River, Massachusetts

The Fall River Historical Society has a collection of all things related to Lizzie's infamous slaying of her parents—gruesome crime scene photos, bloodstained linen and clothing, and a hatchet purported to be the murder weapon itself. If that's not enough, tourists can spend the night at the scene of the crime when they stay at the Lizzie Borden Bed and Breakfast, which has been faithfully restored to its appearance at the time of the murders.

6. National Museum of Health and Medicine, Washington, D.C.

In a city of stellar museums, this one often gets overlooked. But for those interested in the effects of injuries and disease on the human body, this is one you won't want to miss. The National Museum of Health and Medicine was established in 1862 to research and document the effects of war wounds and disease on the human body. Exhibits include more than 5,000 skeletons, 10,000 preserved organs, and 12,000 historical objects, such as the bullet that killed Abraham Lincoln and bone fragments and hair from his skull. Visitors can compare a smoker's lung to a coal miner's lung, touch the inside of a stomach, and view kidney stones and a brain still attached to the spinal cord.

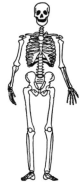

THE WEIRD WIDE WORLD OF SPORTS
9 Odd Sporting Events from Around the World

✳ ✳ ✳ ✳

When it comes to sports, if it involves a ball or a club, men will play it, and if it's on TV, men will watch it. Here are some of the most unusual sports from around the world.

1. Cheese Rolling

If you're a whiz at cheese rolling, you may want to head to Brockworth in Gloucestershire, England, at the annual Cooper's Hill Cheese Roll held each May. The ancient festival dates back hundreds of years and involves pushing and shoving a large, mellow, seven- to eight-pound wheel of ripe Gloucestershire cheese downhill in a race to the bottom. With the wheels of cheese reaching up to 70 miles per hour, runners chase, tumble, and slide down the hill after their cheese but don't usually catch up until the end. The winner gets to take home his or her cheese, while the runners-up get cash prizes.

2. Toe Wrestling

This little piggy went to the World Toe Wrestling Championship held annually in July in Derbyshire, England. Contestants sit facing each other at a "toedium"—a stadium for toes—and try to push each other's bare foot off a small stand called a "toesrack." Three-time champion Paul Beech calls himself the "Toeminator." Toe wrestling began in the town of Wetton in 1970, and the international sport is governed by the World Toe Wrestling Organization, which once applied for Olympic status but was rejected.

3. Tuna Throwing

Popular in Australia, tuna throwing requires contestants to whirl a frozen tuna around their heads with a rope and then fling it like an Olympic hammer thrower. Since 1998, the record holder has been former Olympic hammer thrower Sean Carlin, with a tuna toss of 122 feet. With $7,000 in prize money overall, the event is part of

Tunarama, an annual festival held in late January in Port Lincoln, South Australia. Animal rights activists will be pleased to know that the tuna are spoiled fish that stores refused to sell.

4. Pooh Sticks

Christopher Robin knows that pooh sticks is not a hygiene problem but rather a game played with Winnie the Pooh. The game consists of finding a stick, dropping it into a river, and then seeing how long it takes to get to the finish line. There is even an annual World Pooh Sticks Championship held in mid-March in Oxfordshire, England. Individual event winners receive gold, silver, and bronze medals, and a team event has attracted competitors from Japan, Latvia, and the Czech Republic.

5. Man Versus Horse Marathon

The Man Versus Horse Marathon is an annual race between humans and horse-and-rider teams held in early June in the Welsh town of Llanwrtyd Wells. The event started in 1980 when a pub keeper overheard two men debating which was faster in a long race—man or horse. Slightly shorter than a traditional marathon, the 22-mile course is filled with many natural obstacles, and horses win nearly every year. But in 2004, Huw Lobb made history as the first runner to win the race (in 2 hours, 5 minutes, and 19 seconds), taking the £25,000 (about $47,500) prize, which was the accumulation of 25 yearly £1,000 prizes that had not been claimed. Apparently, the horse doesn't get to keep its winnings.

6. Bull Running

While bullfighting is popular in many countries, the sport of bull running—which should really be called bull outrunning—is pretty much owned by Pamplona, Spain. The event dates back to the 13th and 14th centuries as a combination of festivals honoring St. Fermin and bullfighting. Every morning for a week in July, the half-mile race is on between six bulls and hundreds of people. Most of the participants try to get as close to the bulls as possible, and many think it's good luck to touch one.

7. Tomato Tossing

Tomatoes aren't just for salads and sauce anymore. La Tomatina is a festival held in late August in the small town of Buñol, Spain, where approximately 30,000 people come from all over the world to pelt one another with nearly 140 tons of overripe tomatoes. The fruit fight dates back to the mid-1940s but was banned under Francisco Franco, then returned in the 1970s after his death. After two hours of tomato-tossing at La Tomatina, there are no winners or losers, only stains and sauce, and the cleanup begins.

8. Human Tower Building

If you enjoy watching cheerleaders form human pyramids, you'll love the castellers, people who compete to form giant human towers at festivals around Catalonia, Spain. Castellers form a solid foundation of packed bodies, linking arms and hands together in an intricate way that holds several tons and softens the fall in case the tower collapses, which is not uncommon. Up to eight more levels of people are built, each layer standing on the shoulders of the people below. The top levels are made up of children and when complete, the castell resembles a human Leaning Tower of Pisa.

9. Wife Carrying Championship

During the Wife Carrying Championship, held annually in Sonkajärvi, Finland, contestants carry a woman—it needn't be their wife—over an 832-foot course with various obstacles en route. Dropping the woman incurs a 15-second penalty, and the first team to reach the finish line receives the grand prize—the weight of the "wife" in beer! This bizarre event traces its origins to the 19th century when a local gang of bandits commonly stole women from neighboring villages.

✳ ✳ ✳

"Not every age is fit for childish sports."

—Titus Maccius Plautus, Ancient Roman playwright

Chapter 17
ANIMALS
* * * *
11 Animals that Use Camouflage

The animal kingdom is a wild, wacky place where animals have to be clever in order to survive. One of the most amazing techniques for survival is animal camouflage. Animals have the ability to mimic plants, ground cover, or even other animals in order to hide or hunt. The following is a list of some animals that are particularly gifted in the art of invisibility.

1. Chameleons

Contrary to popular belief, chameleons only change color when in imminent danger. Their everyday skin color, a light khaki, keeps them hidden from enemies during those not-so-dangerous times. Nearly half the world's chameleon species live in Madagascar, but they're also found in Africa, the Middle East, and southern Europe.

2. Leopards

Whether their coats are spotted (useful for hiding in sun-dappled areas in the African outback) or black (perfect for nighttime stalking or lurking in shadows), these elegant and deadly cats are born with fashionable camouflage. Rabbits, young buffalo, and monkeys don't stand a chance when a hidden leopard makes a surprise attack.

3. Polar Bears

Other bears and human poachers are the biggest threats to the majestic polar bear, but by blending into the blindingly white snow of the Arctic with equally white fur coats, some danger can be avoided. Only a polar bear's nose and foot pads are without fur.

4. Turtles

If you're a fish, you better look twice before resting near that big rock…it could be an snapping turtle. There are hundreds of species of turtles and tortoises that use camouflage to blindside their prey and hide from large predators like alligators. Sadly, camouflage can't protect turtles from the poacher's fishnet.

5. Arctic Owls

Ah, the Arctic tundra: cold, barren, and totally white. Arctic owls have a coat of snow-white feathers to keep them warm and safe from predators, such as foxes and wolves.

6. Bark Bugs

For most bugs, birds are the bad guys. For bark bugs, which hang out on trees around the world, this is especially true. In order to hide in the middle of nature's birdhouses, bark bugs appear to be part of the tree itself.

7. Ornate Wobbegongs

If you're ever swimming in the shallow waters off Australia or New Guinea, look for the ornate wobbegong—though you probably won't be able to see it! This shark's body flattens out on the seafloor where its spots and blotchy lines resemble rock and coral. Wobbegongs take camouflage a step further with a little "beard" under their chins that looks like seaweed. Prey that swim in front of their mouths are gobbled up without knowing what hit them.

8. Gaboon Vipers

In order to hide from their prey, gaboon vipers—among the most venomous snakes on Earth—make the most of their brownish-gray, mottled scales. These big snakes hide in the layer of dead leaves that carpets the African rain forest floors. They also like to snuggle into forest floor peat and sneak up on unsuspecting prey.

9. Leaf Butterflies

Complete with fake leaf stalk, fake leaf veins, and perfect dead-leaf coloring, leaf butterflies have the whole camouflage thing down pat. Birds pass them by without a second glance since these insects from southeast Asia look more like dead leaves than butterflies.

10. Dragon Lizards

Spiders, snakes, birds, and even other lizards all want a piece of the dragon lizard, so they have some of the most effective camouflage around. Not only do dragon lizards look nearly invisible when hanging out on a tree branch, they keep extraordinarily still, knowing that their predators react to the smallest movements. It doesn't make for an exciting life, but at least they live to tell about it.

11. Flower Mantises

Careful—that flower you're thinking about smelling might have a flower mantis hiding inside. The flower mantis of western Africa uses colorful, pistil-and-stamen-like camouflage to trick smaller insects into smelling the roses, then snap—lunch is served.

13 Incredible Bat Facts

✻ ✻ ✻ ✻

It isn't easy being a bat. With Dracula, a few cases of rabies, their pointy teeth, and the fact that they hang upside down to sleep, bats inspire fear in many people. But as you'll see, bats are amazing creatures, even though they eat bugs . . . and sometimes blood.

1. Bats are the only mammals able to fly.

And you thought it was the winged marmoset! Bats are exceptional in the air. Their wings are thin, giving them what is called, in flight terms, "airfoil." The power bats have to push forward is called "propulsion."

2. A single brown bat can catch around 1,200 mosquito-size insects in one hour.
In Bracken Cave, Texas, it's estimated that the 20 million Mexican free-tailed bats that live there eat about 200 tons of insects . . . each night.

3. Vampire bats don't suck blood. They lap it up. Calm down. There are only three species of vampire bats in the whole world. If you are traveling in Central or South America, however, you might see a vampire bat bite a cow and then lick blood from the wound—no sucking involved.

4. Bats don't have "fat days." The metabolism of a bat is enviable—they can digest bananas, mangoes, and berries in about 20 minutes.

5. Fewer than 10 people in the last 50 years have contracted rabies from North American bats. Due to movies and television, bats are thought to be germ machines, bringing disease and toxins to innocent victims. Not true. Bats *avoid* people. If you are bitten by a bat, go to the doctor, but don't start making funeral arrangements—you'll probably be fine.

6. Bats use echolocation to get around in the dark. Bats don't see very well and do a  lot of living at night, so they have to rely on navigational methods other than sight. Bats send out beeps and listen for variations in the echoes that bounce back at them and that's how they get around. Bats are nocturnal, mostly because it's easier to hunt bugs and stay out of the way of predators when it's dark. Bats do use their eyesight to see things in the daytime, but most bat business is done under the blanket of night for convenience.

7. Bats make up a quarter of all mammals. Yep, you read that right. A quarter of all mammals are bats. There are more than 1,100 species of bats in the world. That's a lot of bats!

8. More than 50 percent of bat species in the United States are either in severe decline or are listed as endangered. You don't know what you've got until it's gone. Industry, deforestation, pollution, and good old-fashioned killing have wiped out many bats and their habitats. For information on how to help keep bats around, contact your local conservation society.

9. **Cold night? Curl up next to a bat!** Inside those drafty caves they like so much, bats keep warm by folding their wings around them, trapping air against their bodies for instant insulation.

10. **An anticoagulant found in vampire bat saliva may soon be used to treat human cardiac patients.** The same stuff that keeps blood flowing from vampire bats' prey seems to keep blood flowing in human beings, too. Scientists in several countries are trying to copy the enzymes found in vampire bat saliva to treat heart conditions and stop the effects of strokes in humans.

11. **Bats have only one pup a year.** Most mammals of smallish size have way more offspring than that. Think cats, rabbits, and rats.

12. **The average bat will probably outlive your pet dog.** The average lifespan of a bat varies, but some species of brown bat can live to be 30 years old. Considering that other small mammals live only two years or so, that's impressive.

13. **Bats wash behind their ears.** Bats spend more time grooming themselves than even the most image-obsessed teenager. They clean themselves and each other meticulously by licking and scratching for hours.

ROVER-ACHIEVERS
8 Top Dogs

✳ ✳ ✳ ✳

Everyone who has ever loved a dog feels that their dog is the best dog ever. We're not about to get between a man (or woman) and their best friend, but here are a few dogs that truly stand out in a crowd of canines.

1. Coolest Dog on the Playground: Olive Oyl
In 1998, Russian wolfhound Olive Oyl of Grayslake, Illinois, made the *Guinness Book of World Records* when she skipped rope 63 times in one minute.

2. Smallest Dog: Tiny Tim

Measuring three inches tall at the shoulder and four inches long from wet nose to wagging tail, Chihuahua and shih tzu mix Tiny Tim of London holds the record (as of 2004) for being the tiniest dog ever. The little guy weighs just over a pound.

3. The Quietest Dog: The Basenji

A yip or a yap, a whine or a woof—if you don't want a barking dog, consider a basenji. The favorite dog of ancient Egyptians, this breed is incapable of barking, instead uttering a sound called a yodel, which makes them perfect for those living in an apartment with thin walls or touchy neighbors.

4. The Heaviest (and Longest) Dog: Zorba

In Kazantzakis' famous novel, Zorba the Greek tackled spiritual and metaphysical quandaries; Zorba the dog apparently tackled his dinner. Zorba, an Old English mastiff, was the world's heaviest and longest dog ever recorded. Zorba weighed 343 pounds and, from nose to tail, was eight feet three inches long.

5. The Oldest Dog: Bluey

The oldest dog reliably documented was an Australian cattle dog named Bluey. After 29 years and 5 months of faithful service, Bluey was put to rest in 1939. We can only hope that now Bluey is chasing cows in the big cattle ranch in the sky.

6. Most Courageous Dogs: September 11 Search and Rescue Dogs (SAR Dogs)

Okay, so any dog serving its country as a SAR dog gets the "Most Courageous Dog" distinction, but the SAR dogs that waded into the rubble in the wake of the terrorist attacks on September 11, 2001, get an extra gold star. Hundreds of SAR dogs scoured the debris and braved the chaos in the days following the attack. While German shepherds are often trained for SAR duties, any working, herding, or sporting breed can be trained to be a hero.

7. The Dog that Might Score Low on an IQ Test: A Hound

We couldn't bring ourselves to say *dumbest,* but it looks like the hound group is given this reputation most often. Hounds weren't bred for taking IQ tests, or doing much of anything except hunting and following scents, so expecting them to quickly learn how to sit or stay is a big mistake. It's just not in their nature, so have patience with your hound—they're not dumb, they're different.

8. Dog Most Likely to Help You with Your Algebra Homework: The Border Collie

Border collies are widely regarded as the smartest of dogs, since they have been bred to work closely with humans for centuries. Again, different dogs are better at certain tasks and are more apt to thrive in different environments. However, collies can appear hyper and less-than-brilliant if they're not given enough stimulation.

22 Peculiar Names for Groups of Animals

✳ ✳ ✳ ✳

1. A *shrewdness* of apes
2. A *battery* of barracudas
3. A *kaleidoscope* of butterflies
4. A *quiver* of cobras
5. A *murder* of crows
6. A *convocation* of eagles
7. A *charm* of finches
8. A *skulk* of foxes
9. A *troubling* of goldfish
10. A *smack* of jellyfish
11. A *mob* of kangaroos
12. An *exaltation* of larks
13. A *troop* of monkeys
14. A *parliament* of owls
15. An *ostentation* of peacocks
16. A *rookery* of penguins

17. A *prickle* of porcupines
18. An *unkindness* of ravens
19. A *shiver* of sharks
20. A *pod* of whales
21. A *descent* of woodpeckers
22. A *zeal* of zebras

FABULOUS FELINES
9 Top Cats

✳ ✳ ✳ ✳

*Some people are cat people. They take pictures of their cats,
tell stories about their cats, and feed their cats designer food.
For a cat lover, even the most unremarkable cat is special,
but the following cats have been singled out
for extra-noteworthy achievements or distinctions.*

1. Cat Most in Need of a Babysitter: Bluebell

Bluebell, a Persian cat from South Africa, gave birth to 14 kittens in one litter. She holds the record for having the most kittens at once, with all of her offspring surviving—rare for a litter so large.

2. Most Aloof Cat: Big Boy

When Hurricane George hit Gulfport, Mississippi, in 1998, Big Boy was blown up into a big oak tree. In 2001, Big Boy's owner claimed the cat never left the tree. The feline eats, sleeps, and eliminates in the tree and climbs from branch to branch for exercise.

3. Big Mama: Dusty

In 1952, a seemingly ordinary tabby cat gave new meaning to the term "maternal instinct." Texas-born Dusty set the record for birthing more kittens than any other cat in history. Dusty had more than 420 kittens before her last litter at age 18.

4. Oldest Cat: Cream Puff

More than 37 years old at the time of her death, Cream Puff, another Texan, is recognized as the oldest cat to have ever lived. In human years, she was about 165 years old when she died.

5. Best-dressed Cat: The Birman

The Birman cat breed originally came from Burma (now Myanmar) where these longhairs were bred as companions for priests. A Birman cat can be identified by its white "gloves." All Birmans have four white paws, which give them that oh-so-aristocratic look.

6. Most Ruthless Killer: Towser

In Scotland, a tortoiseshell tabby named Towser was reported to have slain 28,899 mice throughout her 21 years—an average of about four mice per day. Her bloodlust finally satiated, Towser died in 1987. (The mice of Scotland are rumored to celebrate her passing as a national holiday.)

7. Most Itty-Bitty Kitty in the Whole World: Tinker Toy

Though this Blue Point Himalayan died in 1997, this cat still holds the record for being the smallest cat ever. Tinker Toy was just 2.75 inches tall and 7.5 inches long and weighed about one pound eight ounces.

8. Cat Most in Need of a Diet: Himmy

According to the *Guinness Book of World Records,* the heaviest cat in recorded history was an Australian kitty named Himmy that reportedly weighed more than 46 pounds in 1986. If the data is accurate, Himmy's waistline measured about 33 inches. Guinness has removed this category from their record roster, so as not to encourage people to overfeed their animals.

9. First Cat: The Eocene Kitty

Fossils from the Eocene period show that cats roamed the earth more than 50 million years ago. Sure, they looked a little different, but these remains show that today's domestic cats have a family tree that goes way, way back.

15 Tips for Surviving a Bear Encounter

✳ ✳ ✳ ✳

*In North America, there are two species of bear—
black and brown (which includes subspecies grizzly
and Kodiak bears)—but it is often difficult to distinguish
between the two. Both types are known to attack humans,
and, in the past century, approximately 100 people have died
in North America due to bear attacks. In the interest of not
becoming part of that "grizzly" statistic, the following list
offers a few tips to avoid or survive a bear attack.*

1. Why Are You Here?

Avoid investigating dark, unknown caves or hollow logs, where
bears make their dens, and avoid areas identified by scavengers,
such as raccoons, as there may be a feeding bear nearby.

2. You're Kidding with the Camera, Right?

Leave pictures of bears to professional wildlife photographers.
Many attacks have occurred because someone decided to try to
snap a photo in bear territory. Bears don't like you, and they don't
want their picture taken.

3. Whoa, Mama!

If you see a bear with a cub, leave quickly. A mother bear with her
cubs is not open to negotiation. She will attack if she thinks she or
her cubs are in danger.

4. Leave No Trace

If you're camping, pick up all garbage, cooking supplies, and other
materials. Clean up thoroughly after meals, and secure food overnight high above the ground (by hanging it from a tree branch) to
prevent it from attracting bears. Not only do sloppy campers damage the area's ecosystem, they're also more likely to come face-to-
face with a bear that has followed their gravy train.

5. Keep a Lookout

As you hike through bear country, keep an eye out for claw marks or droppings, and note any scratched up trees or fresh kills, such as deer.

6. Raise a Ruckus, Ring a Bell

Some experts recommend tying a bell to your foot or backpack to make noise as you travel. You can also sing or holler at your hiking buddies. Just don't be a ninja. Bears don't like to be surprised.

7. Freeze! Stick 'Em Up!

Okay, so you've spotted a bear, and the bear has spotted you. Stop right there, and don't move. Speak to the bear in a low, calm voice, and slowly raise your arms up above your head. This makes you appear larger.

8. Back Off

Clearly, you should try to leave now. Do it slowly and go back from whence you came. Don't cross the path of the bear (or any cubs, if present). Just rewind, slowly, and don't come back.

9. Don't Run!

The worst thing you could do at this point would be to get out your camera or try to feed the bear a snack. The second worst thing you could do would be to run. Bears run faster than humans, and they think chasing prey is fun.

10. Hello, Tree

"But bears can climb trees," you say. You're right: some bears, like black bears, can climb trees. But others, like grizzly bears, cannot. Either way, if you can get more than 12 feet up into a tree, you should be okay. That's pretty far up, so this is not your best option.

11. Grizzly Bear? Play Dead!

If a bear is charging you, you've got a couple of less-than-desirable options. The first thing you might try is going into the fetal position and playing dead. This might make you seem vulnerable to the grizzly bear and he or she will sniff you, growl at you, and hopefully leave you alone. Being in the fetal position will also protect your vital organs. *IMPORTANT: If you're dealing with a black bear, do NOT play dead. They'll be thrilled that the work's been done for them and will commence lunch. If you can't tell what kind of bear you're dealing with, don't try it!*

12. Go Undercover

While you're in the fetal position, try to put your backpack up on top of you to give you an extra layer of protection.

13. Bang, Bang

If a bear is charging you and you've got a gun, now might be the time to use it. Make sure you've got a clean shot because it usually takes more than one bullet to kill a bear and bad aim will only make it angrier. This should only be used as a last resort—wrongful killing of a bear in the United States incurs a hefty fine up to $20,000.

14. Spray, Spray

Many camping and national park areas don't allow firearms, so some recommend bear spray or pepper spray. But beware: If you spray halfheartedly, it will only make the bear angrier.

15. The Fight of Your Life

Your last option is to fight back with everything you've got. There's really no need to tell you that, at this point, you're in big trouble. Kick, scream, flail your arms, go for the eyes—do whatever you can because you're in for the fight of your life.

✳ ✳ ✳

"Bears are made of the same dust as we, and breathe the same winds and drink of the same waters. A bear's days are warmed by the same sun, his dwellings are overdomed by the same blue sky, and his life turns and ebbs with heart-pulsings like ours and was poured from the same fountain."

—John Muir, American author and environmentalist

7 Animals that Can Be Heard for Long Distances

❋ ❋ ❋ ❋

Animals send out messages for very specific reasons,
such as to signal danger or for mating rituals. Some of these calls,
like the ones that follow, are so loud they can travel through water
or bounce off trees for miles to get to their recipient.

1. Blue Whale

The call of the mighty blue whale is the loudest on Earth, regis-
tering a whopping 188 decibels. (The average rock concert only
reaches about 100 decibels.) Male blue whales use their deafening,
rumbling call to attract mates hundreds of miles away.

2. Howler Monkey

Found in the rain forests of the Americas, this monkey grows
to about four feet tall and has a howl that can travel more than
two miles.

3. Elephant

When an elephant stomps its feet, the vibrations created can travel 20 miles through
the ground. They receive messages through
their feet, too. Research on African and
Indian elephants has identified a message
for warning, another for greeting, and
another for announcing, "Let's go." These sounds register from
80 to 90 decibels, which is louder than most humans can yell.

4. North American Bullfrog

The name comes from the loud, deep bellow that male frogs emit.
This call can be heard up to a half mile away, making them seem
bigger and more ferocious than they really are. To create this reso-
nating sound used for his mating call, the male frog pumps air back
and forth between his lungs and mouth, and across his vocal cords.

5. Hyena

If you happen to hear the call of a "laughing" or spotted hyena, we recommend you leave the building. Hyenas make the staccato, high-pitched series of hee-hee-hee sounds (called "giggles" by zoologists) when they're being threatened, chased, or attacked. This disturbing "laugh" can be heard up to eight miles away.

6. African Lion

Perhaps the most recognizable animal call, the roar of a lion is used by males to chase off rivals and exhibit dominance. Female lions roar to protect their cubs and attract the attention of males. Lions have reportedly been heard roaring a whopping five miles away.

7. Northern Elephant Seal Bull

Along the coastline of California live strange-looking elephant seals, with huge snouts and big, floppy bodies. When it's time to mate, the males, or "bulls," let out a call similar to an elephant's trumpet. This call, which can be heard for several miles, lets other males—and all the females nearby—know who's in control of the area.

10 Things to Do if You've Been Skunked

❈ ❈ ❈ ❈

Skunks have it pretty rough. Their small size makes them prey for scores of large predators. They're scavengers, which means lunch is literally garbage, and many of them end up as roadkill. Read on to learn about how to avoid the path of a disgruntled skunk and what to do if you do tangle with one.

1. Stay Away

The best way to avoid getting skunked is to stay away from them. Skunks only spray when they're threatened, so don't threaten them and you shouldn't have a problem.

2. Speak Softly and Walk with a Big Stomp

If you must approach a skunk, do so with caution. Speak in a low voice and stomp your feet. Skunks have poor vision and often spray in defense because they simply don't know what's going on.

3. Freeze!

Another tactic for avoiding a skunking is to stand perfectly still and wait for the skunk to go away. Passive, but effective.

4. Run . . . or Shut Your Eyes and Hang on Tight

Right before a skunk lets loose its spray of stinkiness, it stomps its feet and turns around, as the spray glands are located near the anus. If you see a skunk doing this little dance, run away or hang on tight, because you're about to get skunked.

5. Flush It Out

If you get sprayed in the face, immediately flush your face and eyes with water. The sulfur-alcohol compound that skunks emit can cause temporary blindness, which could lead to bigger problems.

6. Take It Outside

Now that you've been skunked, anything you come into contact with is going to smell like you do. You smell like skunk, if you hadn't already noticed. So try to stay outside, if at all possible.

7. Skip the V8, Air Freshener, and Lemon Juice

No matter what Grandma said, tomato juice does *not* take the smell of skunk off of you, your dog, or your clothes. And unless you like "fresh morning dew" skunk, vanilla skunk, or lemony skunk, don't even bother with air fresheners or lemon juice. These products don't eliminate skunk smell, they only make it worse by coating it with another cloying scent.

8. Mix Up a Peroxide Bath

To get rid of the skunk smell, you must neutralize the chemicals in the spray. This home remedy seems to work well on animals or humans: Mix one quart of 3 percent hydrogen peroxide, one teaspoon mild dishwashing detergent, and ¼ cup baking soda in a bucket. Lather, rinse, repeat.

9. Buy Deodorizing Spray

These special sprays are available at pet stores and some home and garden stores, too. They work well because they're specially formulated to neutralize the intense odor of skunk.

10. Call the Public Health Department or Your Doctor...

...if you've been bitten. Skunks have been known to carry rabies, even though they rarely resort to biting. The same goes for your pet—get it to the vet quickly if the skunk did more than spray. Also, notify the public health department within 24 hours.

11 Celebrity Canines

❋ ❋ ❋ ❋

If you're a dog owner, you're probably convinced that you've got the greatest dog in the world. But can your dog bring home a paycheck? Whether they've stolen our hearts, made us laugh, or scared us silly, no one can deny that the dogs listed below are one of a kind.

1. Benji

In the 1970s and 1980s, several feature films centered around the adventures and loving personality of Benji, a terrier with an uncanny ability to sniff out trouble just in the nick of time. Created by Joe Camp, the films were produced in Texas starting in 1974. The dog that played Benji in the original film was actually named Higgins. Other Benjis have come and gone over the course of nine feature-length films, the most recent released in 2004.

2. Lassie

Author Eric Knight's original short story entitled "Lassie Come Home" tells the story of a young boy and his loyal collie. After being separated under dire circumstances, Lassie crosses hundreds of miles to find her master. The story first appeared in *The Satur-*

day Evening Post in 1940, and, in 1954, *Lassie* the TV show made its debut. The show ran for 20 years, using nine different dogs to portray the faithful pooch.

3. Toto

In L. Frank Baum's famous story *The Wonderful Wizard of Oz,* a little terrier named Toto accompanies Dorothy on her adventures and eventually saves the day. The legendary movie, starring Judy Garland, helped make the story—and the dog—pop culture favorites. The dog that played Toto in the classic movie reportedly received $125 per week—more than twice as much as the people playing the Munchkins.

4. Rin Tin Tin

Rin Tin Tin was one of America's first doggie stars. American serviceman Lee Duncan found Rin in a bombed-out dog kennel in France during World War I. Duncan took the German shepherd home with him to California and taught him how to do tricks and perform in dog shows. More show-biz opportunities followed, including a role as a wolf in a 1922 motion picture. For the next decade, Rin had parts in 26 films, making him as big a star as any of his human counterparts. Rin Tin Tin was honored with a star on the Hollywood Walk of Fame, and, during the 1950s, his offspring portrayed him on the television show, *The Adventures of Rin Tin Tin.*

5. Rowlf the Dog

Muppets come in every shape, color, and size, but the biggest stars are the basic characters: the frog, the pig, and the dog. Originally created by Jim Henson and Don Sahlin for a Purina Dog Chow commercial, Rowlf quickly became an in-demand dog. Rowlf was a perfect sidekick for Jimmy on the popular *Jimmy Dean Show,* making him the first Muppet to have a regular gig on a network TV show. In 1976, Rowlf made a career change—he joined the cast of *The Muppet Show* as the in-house pianist. Rowlf favored Beethoven and standards, but he was so amiable and friendly, we're guessing he was okay with taking requests, too.

6. Blue

In 1994, Nickelodeon's parent company, Viacom, decided to commit more than $60 million to new programming, and *Blue's Clues* was born. The formula for the show, marketed toward preschoolers, was simple: A blue puppy places clues around her world for the kids watching. Through these clues, the kids can figure out what Blue wants to do. As it turned out, kids wanted to do whatever Blue wanted to, and computer games, live tours, books, DVDs, apparel, and food products prove that Blue is still one popular puppy.

7. Cujo

No human fear has been left untouched by horror writer Stephen King, so when he turned his attention to dogs in the 1981 book *Cujo,* the results were terrifying. The story, which was later made into a movie, tells of a friendly St. Bernard that contracts a nasty case of rabies. Disaster, death, and mayhem ensue, and the main characters—a mother and her asthmatic son—are held hostage by the drooling, psychotic dog.

8. Goofy

Disney's lovably stupid dog first appeared in a 1932 cartoon short as an audience member watching Mickey onstage. Goofy was originally known by the even less dignified moniker Dippy Dawg. The tall mutt in overalls had an incredibly dopey laugh, supplied by Disney writer, musician, and former circus clown Pinto Colvig. When Disney heard Colvig's laugh, he decided that Goofy should get a little more face time. Soon, Goofy was appearing in his own cartoons and has been a favorite ever since.

9. Buck

The main character in Jack London's *The Call of the Wild,* Buck is a St. Bernard–Scots shepherd mix that lives a comfortable, somewhat pampered life in northern California, in the late 19th century. But his life is turned upside down when he is kidnapped, sold as a sled dog, and shipped off to the Yukon Territory in the upper reaches of northwestern Canada. Buck quickly learns to survive on his own and discovers basic instincts he didn't know he had.

10. Eddie

In 1993, the world was introduced to Eddie on the hit sitcom *Frasier*. The rascally Jack Russell terrier was intelligent, adorable, and more than a little prone to taunting Kelsey Grammer's character, Dr. Frasier Crane. Eddie was played by a father and son team—Moose was the original Eddie, then when he retired, his son Enzo stepped in to play the role. Eddie rounded out the cast of the popular *Cheers* spin-off, which ran for 11 seasons.

11. Snoopy

Once upon a time, on a sunny day at the Daisy Hill Puppy farm, a litter of seven adorable beagles was born, including a particularly mischievous puppy named Snoopy. *Peanuts,* the classic cartoon strip created by Charles M. Schulz in 1950, still runs in newspapers around the world despite Schulz's passing in 2000. Snoopy, Charlie Brown's faithful dog, is one of the most recognized dogs in history. Heavy on personality but light on words, the feisty beagle was a foil or friend to every character in the *Peanuts* pantheon. The popular pooch even has his own attraction—Camp Snoopy—at several major theme parks across the country.

10 Most Dangerous Dogs

✳ ✳ ✳ ✳

1. Pit bull
2. Rottweiler
3. German shepherd
4. Huskie
5. Alaskan malamute
6. Doberman pinscher
7. Chow chow
8. Great Dane
9. St. Bernard
10. Akita

Source: Centers for Disease Control and Prevention (CDC)

8 Famous Felines

✳ ✳ ✳ ✳

They say, "Dogs have masters, cats have staff." That certainly rings true for these famous felines. Some are real, some are fictional, but either way, they don't answer to anyone.

1. Garfield

A cat that eats lasagna? That would be Garfield, the star of the most widely syndicated comic strip in the world. Created by Jim Davis in 1978, *Garfield* now appears in more than 2,500 newspapers, as well as movies, TV specials, and video games. The pudgy orange and black feline is best known for his love of Italian food, his disdain for Mondays, and his constant tormenting of canine pal Odie.

2. Morris

Rescued from a Hinsdale, Illinois, shelter in 1968, Morris, the 15-pound, orange-striped tabby went on to earn fame and fortune as the "spokescat" for 9Lives cat food. He also starred opposite Burt Reynolds in 1973's *Shamus* and even ran for president in 1988 and 1992 on the Finicky Party platform.

3. The Cheshire Cat

The Cheshire cat first appeared—and disappeared—in Lewis Carroll's children's story, *Alice's Adventures in Wonderland.* The cat pops in and out of Alice's adventure, often turning her innocent queries into philosophical discussions. But the scene that forever seals the Cheshire cat's place in history is when he makes the rest of his body gradually disappear, leaving only his smile behind, hence the phrase "grinning like a Cheshire cat" to describe someone with a mischievous grin.

4. Socks: The First Cat

Socks knew a good thing when he saw it. The eventual First Cat joined the Clinton family in 1991 when he jumped into Chelsea's arms at her piano teacher's house in Little Rock, Arkansas. Socks, a black-and-white kitty, spent eight years in the White House and became a star in his own right, appearing on an episode of *Murphy Brown* and inspiring two books: *Socks Goes to Washington: The Diary of America's First Cat* and *Dear Socks, Dear Buddy: Kids' Letters to the First Pets*. When the Clintons left the White House in 2001, Socks was given to Clinton's secretary, Betty Currie. Socks still lives with the Curries in Maryland.

5. The Cat in the Hat

The Cat in the Hat is a troublemaker of the most lovable sort. A creation of whimsical children's author Dr. Seuss, the cat attempts to entertain two children who are stuck inside on a rainy day. He wreaks a bit of havoc and upsets the family goldfish to no end, but all is well by the time Mother returns home. The black-and-white cat, with his signature red-and-white striped top hat and red bow tie, first appeared in the classic tale in 1957. He has since appeared in numerous books, TV specials, and in the 2003 live-action movie of the same name, which starred Mike Myers.

6. Catwoman

Don't mess with Catwoman, as Halle Berry will attest. The Oscar-winning actress portrayed the infamous comic book character in 2004's *Catwoman* and, in the process, earned herself critical pans and a Razzie Award for worst actress. Catwoman first appeared in the *Batman* comic book series in 1940 as an expert burglar with above-average agility. She's been portrayed by actresses such as Julie Newmar, Eartha Kitt, and Michelle Pfieffer, all of whom remained fairly true to the original character's signature traits. But when Berry's character departed from the *Batman* story line, the claws came out.

7. Orangey

Audrey Hepburn won an Emmy, a Grammy, an Oscar, and a Tony. But did she ever win a Patsy? Nope, that honor belongs to her *Breakfast at Tiffany's* costar, Orangey. The orange and black tabby that portrayed Holly Golightly's lazy cat in the 1961 classic actually broke onto the Hollywood scene in 1951's *Rhubarb,* a movie about an eccentric millionaire who adopts a feral cat. Orangey won his first Patsy (Picture Animal Top Star of the Year) for the *Rhubarb* role, so awards were old hat by the time he shared a screen with Hepburn. Orangey also appeared in *Gigot* (1962) alongside Jackie Gleason and in the 1950s sitcom *Our Miss Brooks.*

8. Puss in Boots

Puss in Boots began life as a boot-wearing hero that used his feline wiles to gain wealth for his impoverished master in a collection of Mother Goose fairy tales published in 1697. He went on to become the star of a 1913 opera by Cesar Cui and made numerous film appearances, including a 1922 animated short by Walt Disney, a 1969 Japanese anime feature, and Antonio Banderas's character in the *Shrek* sequels.

15 Tips for Surviving a Shark Attack

✳ ✳ ✳ ✳

In 2005, there were 58 unprovoked shark attacks reported. Less than ten of those attacks, which occurred off the coasts of California, Hawaii, and Brazil, proved fatal. The numbers may seem low, but still, that's 58 people who came face-to-face with a shark. Below are some tips for staying out of the way of a hungry shark and what to do if you happen to cross paths with one.

1. Check with the Locals

If you don't want to tangle with a shark, don't go where sharks hang out. If you plan to vacation near the ocean, contact local tourism offices and ask for shark stats in the area.

2. Skip the Bling

Sharks see contrast well, so wearing bright colors like yellow and orange is not a great idea. Also avoid shiny jewelry as sharks may mistake it for fish scales.

3. Know Your Sharks

Three species of shark are responsible for most human attacks: great white, tiger, and bull sharks. A hammerhead might freak you out, but it probably won't bite you.

4. Be Adventurous, But Don't Be Ridiculous

Who knows why you might want to swim in murky waters, around harbor entrances or steep drop-offs, or among rocky, underwater cliffs, but if you do choose to swim in these dangerous places, don't be surprised if you come face-to-face with a shark.

5. Swim Smart

Always swim with a buddy, and don't swim at dusk or at night. Sharks don't have the best vision, so when it's dark, you look like dinner to them.

6. Check with the Turtles

Creatures of the sea know much more about the waters than you ever will. So, if turtles and fish start freaking out, there's probably a reason. If you witness erratic behavior from other animals, there might be a very large, toothy beast approaching. Take a cue from those who have seen it before and take off.

7. For the Ladies...

If you're menstruating, stick to the sand. Blood attracts sharks. Think of it as a great excuse to stay out of the water and work on your tan! Female or male, if you cut yourself on a reef or a rock while swimming, it's best to get out right away—the smell of blood to a shark is like the smell of fresh doughnuts to humans.

8. Keep Fido on the Beach

Allowing dogs to swim in the ocean can be dangerous if you're in shark territory. Animals swim erratically, attracting the attention of sharks. Don't let pets stay in the water for long periods of time.

9. See a Shark? Shout!

If there's a dorsal fin on the horizon, letting people know is a good idea. The more people know what's going on, the better off you are if the situation worsens. Then quickly swim toward shore as if your life depends on it...because it just might.

10. Shark Approaching: Stay Silent and Immobile
If you aren't able to get to shore and a shark approaches you, try to stay still and be quiet to avoid an attack.

11. Shark Zigzagging: Find Something Solid
The zigzagging shark is looking for angles, so if you can back up against a reef, a piling, or some other kind of outcropping, do so. This reduces the number of angles the shark has to come at you. If you're in open water, get back-to-back with your swimming buddy. You *do* have a swimming buddy, right?

12. Shark Circling: Uh-Oh
This is not good. If a shark is circling you, that means it's about to strike. Time to fight back!

13. Shark Attacking: The Eyes Have It
It might sound ridiculous, but try to stay calm. If you're being attacked by a shark, go for the eyes and gills, the most vulnerable parts of the shark. If you can wound the eyes, you've got a chance.

14. Go for the Nose (Or Not...)
Although opinions differ, the general consensus seems to be that if you can get a clear shot, hitting the shark on the nose can be highly effective at ending the attack. Trouble is, when you're being attacked, hitting a specific target becomes challenging at best.

15. What Not to Do
Don't play dead. This does nothing but make the shark think it has won. The shark will then commence chomping. Clearly, this is not what you want it to do. Also, if you've been attacked, get away as fast as you possibly can. Sharks smell blood. You didn't fare too well with the first one and there are probably more on the way.

6 Pets that Traveled Long Distances to Get Home

✳ ✳ ✳ ✳

Salmon follow the smell of their home waters.
Birds and bees appear to navigate by the sun, stars, and moon.
We can't really explain how so many lost dogs and cats magically
seem to find their way back to their owners over great distances,
so we'll just tell you about them instead.

1. Emily the cat went across the pond. Lesley and Donny McElhiney's home in Appleton, Wisconsin, wasn't the same after their one-year-old tabby Emily disappeared. But she didn't just disappear, she went on a 4,500-mile adventure! It seems Emily was on her evening prowl when she found herself on a truck to Chicago inside a container of paper bales. From there she was shipped to Belgium, finally arriving in France where employees at a laminating company found her thin and thirsty. Since she was wearing tags, it didn't take long for Emily to be reunited with her family, compliments of Continental Airlines.

2. Howie the Persian cat crossed the Australian outback. The Hicks family wanted their cat to be lovingly cared for while they went on an extended vacation overseas. So, they took him to stay with relatives who lived more than 1,000 miles away. Months later, when they returned to retrieve Howie, they were told that he had run away. The Hicks were distraught, assuming that because Howie was an indoor cat, he wouldn't have the survival skills to make it on his own. A year later, their daughter returned home from school one day and saw a mangy, unkempt, and starving cat. Yep, it was Howie. It had taken him 12 months to cross 1,000 miles of Australian outback, but Howie had come home.

3. Tony the mutt finds his family. When the Doolen family of Aurora, Illinois, moved to East Lansing, Michigan, nearly 260 miles away, they gave away their mixed-breed dog Tony. Six weeks later, who came trotting down the street in East Lansing and made himself known to Mr. Doolen? That's right—Tony. Doolen recognized a notch on Tony's collar that he'd cut while still living in Illinois.

4. **Madonna heads to the massage parlor.** Now here's a finicky cat! This seven-year-old tabby moved from Kitchener, Ontario, with her owner Nina in order to start a new branch of the family massage parlor business. Their new home base was Windsor, but within weeks, Madonna was nowhere to be found. She eventually showed up at her original massage parlor, where Nina's sister was the new proprietor. Total walking distance? About 150 miles.

5. **Troubles finds his way through ten miles of jungle.** Troubles, a scout dog, and his handler William Richardson were taken via helicopter deep into the war zone in South Vietnam in the late 1960s. When Richardson was wounded by enemy fire and taken to a hospital, Troubles was abandoned by the rest of the unit. Three weeks later, Troubles showed up at his home at the First Air Cavalry Division Headquarters in An Khe, South Vietnam. But he wouldn't let anyone near him—he was on a mission! Troubles searched the tents and eventually curled up for a nap after he found a pile of Richardson's clothes to use for a bed.

6. **Misele the farm cat goes to the hospital.** When 82-year-old Alfonse Mondry was taken to a hospital in France, his cat Misele missed him greatly. So she took off and walked across cattle fields, rock quarries, forests, and busy highways. She entered the hospital—where she had never been before—and found her owner's room. The nurses called the doctor right away when they found Mondry resting comfortably with his cat purring on his lap.

✳ ✳ ✳

"A dog is the only thing on earth that loves you more than he loves himself."
—Josh Billings, American humorist

Chapter 18
THIS & THAT

✳ ✳ ✳ ✳
9 Youngest in Their Fields

*The people on this list made a name for themselves early
in life and probably don't intend to fade away any time soon.
The good news—maybe your kid will be on the list one day!
The bad news—if you're over 20 and you're not on a list like
this, we recommend shooting for the "Oldest" list.*

1. Youngest Person to Climb Mount Everest

Temba Tsheri, a Nepalese boy traveling with a French hiking
group, reached the summit of Mount Everest in 2001 at age 16. It's
no easy task—Everest is approximately 29,035 feet high and claims
more than a few lives each year.

2. Youngest Person to Sail Solo Across the Atlantic Ocean

Michael Perham, a 14-year-old chap from Hertfordshire, England,
completed the 3,500-mile trek across the Atlantic Ocean in his
yacht, the *Cheeky Monkey,* in January 2007, after six weeks at sea.

3. Youngest Bill Gates Employee

Arfa Karim Randhawa of Pakistan has become a good pal of Bill
Gates since she passed her Microsoft Certified Professional examinations at age ten. She asked for a job, but Gates told her she ought
to stay in school a while longer, offering her an internship instead.

4. Youngest College Student at Oxford

At 11 years old, child prodigy Ruth Elke Lawrence passed the
Oxford entrance exam in mathematics and, in 1981, became the
youngest person ever to attend the prestigious university. Her
father accompanied her to classes, and she graduated with a bachelor's degree in two years instead of the usual three. Now in her
thirties, Lawrence teaches at Hebrew University in Jerusalem.

5. Youngest Tibetan Buddhist Monarch

In southern Asia, there's a tiny, mountainous country called Bhutan. In 1972, Jigme Singye Wangchuck became the "Druk Gyalpo," or "Dragon King," of the tiny country at age 17, making him the youngest monarch in the world. He remained in power until December 2006, when he handed the throne to his eldest son.

6. Youngest Person with a Stethoscope

Born in 1977, Balamurali Ambati was the youngest person to become a doctor, according to the *Guinness Book of World Records*. After graduating from NYU at age 13 and Mount Sinai's School of Medicine at 17, Ambati became the youngest doctor in the world in 1995. His list of awards and honors is lengthy, and he currently teaches and does research in ophthalmology.

7. Youngest Golf Champ

American Michelle Wie is a professional golfer known for long drives and USGA wins. In 2003, Wie won the Women's Amateur Public Links tournament at the tender age of 14, making her the world's youngest golf champion.

8. Youngest Person to Win an Oscar

In 1974, at age ten, actor Tatum O'Neal became the youngest person to win an Academy Award for her role in *Paper Moon,* costarring her father Ryan O'Neal. Her career didn't exactly take off after that, but she has recently returned to acting with several TV roles.

9. Youngest Billionaire

The Thurn und Taxis family of Germany created Europe's first mail service back in the 16th century and has scads of profitable business ventures to this day. When Prince Albert von Thurn und Taxis turned 18 in 2001, he inherited a fortune.  According to a 2007 report by *Forbes* magazine, he's worth a cool $2 billion, making him the world's youngest billionaire.

10 Countries with the Most Cell Phones

❉ ❉ ❉ ❉

Country	Number of Cell Phones (millions)
1. China	437
2. United States	219
3. Russia	120
4. Japan	94
5. Brazil	86
6. Germany	79
7. Italy	72
8. India	69
9. United Kingdom	61
10. France	49

Source: CIA World Factbook

TYPHOID MARY HAD NOTHING ON THE REST OF THE YEAR
11 Highlights of 1907

❉ ❉ ❉ ❉

In 1907, Americans had a life expectancy of just 45.6 years for men and 49.9 for women. Even worse, this was the year that typhoid, an abdominal disease spread through water and food supplies, ravaged the nation. But alas! Public health officials discovered that 47 people stricken with the disease were all from families that employed a cook named Mary. With "Typhoid Mary" safely quarantined, these were the highlights of that year.

1. The Creation of Mother's Day

After her mother died, Anna Jarvis started a letter-writing campaign in support of the celebration of mothers everywhere. A minister in

Grafton, West Virginia, obliged and dedicated the second Sunday in May specifically to the late Mrs. Jarvis. Ironically, the woman who is credited with creating what we now know as Mother's Day never became a mother herself. Her entire life was dedicated to caring for others: first her elderly mother and then her blind sister. Jarvis never married and, in 1948, died a pauper.

2. The Invention of the Paper Towel

The paper towel was created by a crafty teacher in Philadelphia who found a way to keep her students from perpetuating a cold epidemic. Instead of sharing the same cloth towel, she put her scissors to use and cut some paper into individual squares. The Scott Paper Company, which was already making toilet paper, got wind of the story. As luck would have it, the company had an entire railroad car full of paper that was rolled too thick to be used in the bathroom. Arthur Scott came up with a way to copy the teacher's design on a bigger scale. It didn't take long before he was selling them as a product called the Sani-Towel.

3. The Beginnings of UPS

Seattle entrepreneur James E. Casey was only 19 in 1907 when he borrowed $100 to create a delivery service he called the American Messenger Company. He and his friends ran errands and delivered packages and trays of food. Most deliveries were done on foot, with longer trips made via bicycle. A Model T Ford was added six years later and the name was changed to Merchants Parcel Delivery. By 1919, the company had expanded beyond Seattle and was renamed United Parcel Service.

4. The First Electric Washing Machine

By 1907, U.S. power companies were growing in technology and scale. As a result, life became a little easier for housewives, especially when the Thor washing machine was introduced by Hurley Machine Company of Chicago. To go with the Thor, a company in Düsseldorf, Germany, came up with the first household detergent in the same year. It was called Persil.

5. Swimming Without a Skirt is a Police Matter

When Australian long-distance swimmer Annette Kellerman decided to swim at Boston's Revere Beach in a one-piece bathing suit—*without* a skirt—she was arrested. The charge? Indecent exposure, of course! The 22-year-old wasn't the only one under scrutiny. Even infants were required to wear complete bathing costumes in the land of the free until a quarter of a century later.

6. The "Monobosom" and Other Fashionable Styles

Ladies of the early 20th century certainly didn't show much skin. However, they were very creative in enhancing their fully clothed silhouettes. The hourglass figure was highly coveted, but if you weren't a full-bodied woman by nature, you simply had to work harder. Corset strings were pulled so tightly that the hips were forced back and the chest thrust forward creating a "monobosom." But things loosened up a tad after dark. To show off their fine jewelry, women of 1907 wore low sweetheart necklines often accented with feathered boas.

7. And Now for the Tresses

In 1907, America was at war against tuberculosis, which killed hundreds of people from the 1880s to the 1950s. To complement their pale complexions, survivors opted for masses of ringlets, thanks to the invention of the waving iron in the 1870s. Hair coloring was frowned upon, but the brave went for it anyway, using herbs, rust, and other concoctions. To promote hair growth, petroleum jelly, castor oil, and gallic acid were also part of the beauty arsenal.

8. No One Wanted Their MTV

A lucky few enjoyed phonographs in 1907, but the most common way to hear a new song was by piano. People would trade, borrow, and collect the sheet music to their favorite songs. A popular choice was George M. Cohan's "You're a Grand Old Rag" from his hit Broadway musical *George Washington, Jr.* The song quickly spread beyond New York City and became a staple in piano benches across the country. Eventually, Cohan changed the title to "You're a Grand Old Flag," and the song remains a national treasure.

9. A Movie for a Nickel

Way before the TV network and even before the Ryan and Tatum O'Neal film, the word *nickelodeon* meant a small neighborhood theater where people would gather to see a movie. The cost? A nickel, of course! These theaters held about 200 chairs and featured live piano music before each show. Movies were comedic sketches, animal acts, or vaudeville acts that lasted around 15 minutes each.

10. An Economic Boom

Industrial capitalism was on the rise in 1907 and with it came lots of jobs. New businesses created a need for more clerical help and a new "white collar" mentality was born. More and more workers received a salary instead of an hourly wage. Retail jobs also flourished and women were working more than ever before.

11. The Chicago Cubs Win the World Series!

The World Series was only four years old in 1907. What's more, Ty Cobb was merely 20. But youth was on the side of the Chicago Cubs as they won the World Series, beating Cobb and his Detroit Tigers four games to none. The Series wasn't without its share of drama—the first game was called because of darkness.

8 of the Oldest...

❋ ❋ ❋ ❋

Western culture has become so age-obsessed that people in their thirties are trying to recapture that youthful glow. Well, outta the way, kiddies! There's something to be said for withstanding the tests of time, so this list pays homage to the old!

1. Oldest Tavern in America

Established in 1795, Boston's Bell in Hand Tavern is the longest continuously running tavern in America. Founded by town crier Jimmy Wilson, the Bell in Hand still serves frosty mugs and food to an often full house. Famous customers have included Paul Revere and President McKinley.

2. Oldest Male Stripper

The next time you're in Miami Beach, check out Bernie Baker at Club LeBare. In 2000, after a bout with prostate cancer, Baker reinvented himself as an erotic dancer at the tender age of 60. Still gyrating, Baker has plenty of loyal fans and has won many awards.

3. Oldest City

In 2001, archaeologists found signs of an ancient city in the Gulf of Cambay in western India. In the 5.6-mile stretch of submerged city, carbon dating found evidence dating back to 7500 B.C., about 4,500 years older than what were believed to be the first cities, located in the Sumer Valley of Mesopotamia.

4. Oldest Company

Headquartered in Osaka, Japan, Kongo Gumi Co., Ltd., has been continuously operating for more than 1,400 years. Their business? Construction. Since A.D. 578, when the company built the still standing Shitennoji Temple, Kongo Gumi has had a hand in building Osaka Castle (16th century) and other famous Japanese buildings and temples. In 2006, the company had financial trouble and liquidated its assets, but it still maintains its identity and continues to function in Japan as a wholly owned subsidiary of the Takamatsu Corporation.

5. Oldest Professional Chorus Line

When the Tivoli Lovelies of Melbourne, Australia, entered *Guinness World Records* in 2004, the ten dancers had a combined age of 746 years and some change. The geriatric ladies still kick as high and wear the sequins of younger chorus girls, and they certainly have more experience.

6. Oldest Nut Collection

In 2003, scientists at the University of Bonn uncovered a burrow containing 1,800 fossilized nuts. They were digging in a mine near Garzweiler, Germany, and came across the nuts, probably winter food supplies stashed away by a large hamster or squirrel more than 17 million years ago.

7. Oldest Person to View Earth from Space

John Glenn was a U.S. pilot during World War II and, in 1967, became a national hero as the first American and third person to orbit Earth when he rode in the *Friendship 7*, a NASA space capsule that successfully circled the globe three times. In 1998, Glenn went back into the great beyond at age 77, making him the oldest person to travel into space. The reason? To test the effects of space travel on the elderly, of course.

8. Oldest Person

Some come close, but so far, no one's been older than Jeanne Louise Calment, who died at age 122 in Arles, France. Calment was born in February 1875, a year before Alexander Graham Bell invented the telephone. She met Vincent Van Gogh at age 13 and was famous for her wit until her death, famously saying, "I've only ever had one wrinkle and I'm sitting on it."

10 Countries with the Most Televisions

❋ ❋ ❋ ❋

Country	Number of Televisions per 1,000 People
1. Bermuda	1,010
2. Monaco	771
3. United States	741
4. Malta	703
5. Japan	679
6. Canada	655
7. Guam	629
8. Virgin Islands	626
9. Germany	624
10. Finland	613

Source: CIA World Factbook

9 Bits of Irony

Throughout history, people have made bold proclamations that were not only incorrect but many times contradicted their own actions. Here are a few examples.

1. The Beatles

On January 1, 1962, Paul McCartney, John Lennon, George Harrison, and Pete Best auditioned at Decca Records, performing 15 songs in just under an hour. The songs included Lennon-McCartney originals and covers of other songs, but their performance was mediocre. In fact, producer Mike Smith flatly rejected them saying, "We don't like their sound. Groups of guitars are on their way out." The Beatles went on to sign with producer George Martin at EMI Records and proved Smith extraordinarily wrong.

2. Take Me Out to the Ball Game

Next to the national anthem, the song most associated with the game of baseball is "Take Me Out to the Ball Game," an early-20th-century song usually played during the seventh-inning stretch. Ironically, it was written by two men who had never attended a baseball game. Jack Norworth wrote the words in 1908, after seeing a sign that said, "Baseball Today—Polo Grounds." Albert Von Tilzer added the music. The song gained popularity in vaudeville acts, and now it's played at nearly every baseball game in the country.

3. James Dean

In 1955, actor James Dean advised teens about the dangers of speeding and drag racing in a two-minute televised public service announcement. Dean talked about how he used to "fly around quite a bit" on the highways, but then he took up track racing, and after that he became "extra cautious" on the highways. He also warned, "The life you save may be *mine.*" On September 30, 1955, Dean was pulled over for speeding in his Porsche 550 Spyder on his way to a race in Palm Springs, California. Later that afternoon, an oncoming vehicle crossed into Dean's lane and the two cars collided almost head-on. Dean was pronounced dead at the hospital.

4. Clark Gable

William Clark Gable was a high school dropout with big ears who eventually became known as the "King of Hollywood." In 1924, Gable's friendship with Lionel Barrymore helped him land a screen test at MGM. Producer Irving Thalberg thought Gable's screen test was awful and referred to his ears as "bat-like." In spite of that, he was signed to a contract and went on to make a number of hit movies for the studio. When MGM head Louis B. Mayer decided that Gable was getting difficult to work with, he loaned the actor to the Columbia studio. Ironically, Gable won an Academy Award for his 1934 performance in the Columbia film *It Happened One Night*.

5. Tom Seaver

In 1966, baseball pitcher Tom Seaver signed with the New York Mets and was assigned to a minor league team in Jacksonville, Florida. After seeing Seaver pitch, Chicago Cubs scout Gordon Goldsberry said, "He won't make it." On the contrary—when Seaver was called up by the Mets in 1967, he had 18 complete games with 16 wins, including two shutouts. Seaver was named the National League Rookie of the Year and went on to a 20-year career with 311 wins, 3,640 strikeouts, and a 2.86 ERA. Nicknamed "Tom Terrific," Seaver was elected to the Baseball Hall of Fame in 1992.

6. Ludwig van Beethoven

German composer Ludwig van Beethoven is generally regarded as one of the greatest composers in history and was a dominant figure in the transitional period between the Classical and Romantic eras in Western music. Around age 28, Beethoven developed a severe case of tinnitus and began to lose his hearing. His hearing loss did not affect his ability to compose music, but it made concerts increasingly difficult. According to one story, at the premiere of his Ninth Symphony, he had to be turned around to see the applause of the audience because he could not hear it. In 1811, after a failed attempt to play his own Piano Concerto No. 5, *Emperor,* he never performed in public again.

7. Gus Grissom

Virgil "Gus" Grissom was America's second astronaut in space aboard the capsule *Liberty Bell 7.* After landing in the Atlantic, a hatch on the capsule opened prematurely, and Grissom nearly drowned before being rescued by helicopter. To prevent this from happening again, Grissom recommended to NASA designers that the hatch on the three-man *Apollo* capsule be made more difficult to open. Ironically, while testing the *Apollo* capsule before its first flight, Grissom was killed in a fire along with fellow astronauts Ed White and Roger B. Chaffee when the new hatch proved too difficult to open.

8. Television

Darryl F. Zanuck was an actor, writer, producer, and director who helped develop the Hollywood studio system in the 1920s. He also cofounded Twentieth Century Pictures in 1933. In 1946, television was in its infancy, but the movie industry was worried. When asked his thoughts, Zanuck said, "Television won't be able to hold on to any market it captures after the first six months. People will soon get tired of staring at a plywood box every night." Of course, television thrived, but it did not bring an end to movies.

9. Charles Justice

In 1900, Charles Justice was serving time at the Ohio State Penitentiary in Columbus. While performing cleaning duties in the death chamber, he thought of a way to improve the restraints on the electric chair. Justice suggested that metal clamps replace the leather straps, allowing the inmate to be secured more firmly and minimizing the problem of burnt flesh. These changes were made, and Justice was later paroled from prison. In an ironic twist of fate, after his release, he was convicted of murder and sentenced to death. On November 9, 1911, justice was served and the inmate found out firsthand how well those metal clamps worked on the same electric chair he had improved.

FINS, HULA HOOPS, AND A BOY NAMED BEAVER
17 Bits of Nostalgia from 1957

❊ ❊ ❊ ❊

Life in America in 1957 was much simpler. Everybody loved Lucy and Father always knew best. Make yourself a root beer float, sit on the davenport, and take a look at life in 1957.

1. You know what they say about the size of a man's fin.
General Motors and Ford were duking it out with their "Olds vs. Edsel" wars. Ford's Edsel included such forward-thinking features as lights that reminded drivers that it was time to service the engine. Chevrolet opted to put their money into advertising. This is the year that had Dinah Shore singing "See the USA in your Chevrolet" on radio and TV spots. Whatever people chose to drive, the average cost of a car was only $2,749. Brace yourself—gasoline was only 24 cents a gallon!

2. "Welcome to Babyville."
After World War II, people were settling down and getting back to the business of creating the American dream. Record numbers of babies were born between 1946 and 1964, and, even today, this generation is referred to as the "Baby Boomers." By 1957, everybody on the fast track was moving out to the suburbs. Doctors, lawyers, teachers, and cops created a mass exodus to the land of lawn mowers and charcoal grills. With all the new babies being born, it's no wonder that suburbia became known as "Babyville."

3. All eyes toward the sky.
In July 1957, American John Glenn set a new transcontinental speed record. The navy test pilot flew a supersonic jet from California to New York in just 3 hours, 23 minutes, and 8.4 seconds.

4. What's with all the hips?

Music lovers had plenty of choices in the year when rock 'n' roll took over the charts. Songs like Sam Cooke's, "You Send Me" and Jimmie Rodgers's "Honeycomb" were popular, but the true sensation of the year was Elvis Presley. He rocked teens across the country with hits like "All Shook Up" and "Jailhouse Rock." You could buy a 45-rpm record (that's the little one) for 79 cents or an album (the big one) for about three bucks. The only problem was that a hi-fi record player cost $79.95.

5. And the Oscar goes to...

...*The Bridge on the River Kwai,* for Best Picture. Alec Guinness also won the Oscar for Best Actor for his role in the movie. Joanne Woodward claimed her statue for Best Actress in *The Three Faces of Eve.* Other favorites were *An Affair to Remember, 12 Angry Men,* and that kid who swivels his hips in a movie called *Jailhouse Rock.* With the average price of a movie ticket at just 50 cents, you could afford to see them all!

6. The Braves win the World Series!

They weren't from Atlanta, however. In 1957, they were the Milwaukee Braves (just four years earlier they were the Boston Braves). In the 1957 World Series, the Braves, led by Hank Aaron, beat Mickey Mantle and the New York Yankees, but it wasn't easy; it took all seven games.

7. Does this price include the white picket fence?

The American dream was a whole lot cheaper in 1957. You could buy your very own house for about $12,200. A custom built, split-level cost a little more—around $19,000. For those who weren't quite ready to buy, rent was only about $90 a month!

8. It's all relative.

Those house prices look pretty good, but what was the average household income in 1957? On average, people made around $4,500 a year. If you sold cars, you made $7,000 to $10,000 a year. A secretary made about $3,900 a year. So, could you afford to own?

9. It was a small world, after all.

In 1957, the Census Bureau reported that there were 171,984,130 people in the United States, and 2,889,768,830 in the entire world. Today, there are 6.6 billion people in the world, including more than 300 million Americans.

10. Rabbit ears were popping up all over the place.

In 1957, there were 47,200,000 TV sets in America; the RCA Victor model cost $78. What was everybody watching? Top shows included *Gunsmoke, The Danny Thomas Show, I Love Lucy,* and *The Ed Sullivan Show.*

11. What's a Sputnik?

Before astronauts, space missions flew without a crew. The first of these, *Sputnik,* came from the Soviet Union. *Sputnik* technically wasn't a satellite, it was a 184-pound basketball-size bundle of radio transmitters that took only 98 minutes to orbit Earth. When it was launched on October 4, 1957, during the height of the Cold War, the United States was caught completely by surprise and the "Space Race" was on!

12. This black and white had nothing to do with TV.

In the interest of school desegregation, President Eisenhower sent army troops to keep the peace at Central High School in Little Rock, Arkansas, so that nine black students could attend the formerly all-white school. These kids are forever stamped in history as the Little Rock Nine.

13. Who's Dick Clark?

People started bopping in the middle of the family room in 1957 when ABC began airing *American Bandstand,* hosted by Dick Clark. Teens danced to the hits of the day and each week a different band performed. After each song, Clark would interview the teens and have them rate the song for its "danceability." The first nationwide audience poll ranked Patti Page as *American Bandstand*'s favorite female vocalist of the year. The show went off the air in 1989.

14. Teen idols were "dreamy."

Teenage girls had plenty of swooning to do thanks to the many teen idols of the late 1950s. Ricky Nelson rocked and rolled on his family's hit TV show, *Ozzie and Harriet,* and people tuned in every week just to see if he'd sing. And Pat Boone cut such a wholesome image in his white patent leather shoes that even parents couldn't object. In 1957, he topped the charts with "Love Letters in the Sand."

15. "Fashion Forward" had nothing to do with Paris.

In 1957, American women had houses to clean, children to rear, and parties to plan. With cardigans, pearls, knee-length skirts, and heels, a lady always looked good. Teenage girls opted for bobby socks, saddle shoes, and poodle skirts. Females young and old even wore pants from time to time, especially pedal pushers or Capri pants. For guys, a leather jacket or a letterman sweater was a must.

16. Lennon and McCartney meet for the first time.

In 1957, a chance meeting at a church in Liverpool would forever change the face of rock music. On July 6, The Quarrymen, a skiffle group led by singer and guitarist John Lennon, performed a gig at the Woolton Parish Church. Among those in attendance was a young musician named Paul McCartney. The two future Beatles were introduced by a mutual friend, and McCartney helped Lennon set up for the gig. Lennon was so impressed with McCartney's musical abilities that he invited him to join the group. The Quarrymen eventually became The Beatles, and the rest is music history.

17. Baseball moves to California.

Due to aging stadiums and slumping ticket sales, the archrival Brooklyn Dodgers and New York Giants moved west following the 1957 season. The Dodgers played one final game at Ebbets Field on September 24, 1957, before moving to Los Angeles. The stadium remained without a team until it was torn down in 1960. The Giants played one last game at the Polo Grounds on September 29, 1957, before heading to San Francisco. The stadium was vacant until the Mets moved in for the 1962 and 1963 seasons. It was demolished in 1964.

18 Odd Items for Sale in Japanese Vending Machines

※ ※ ※ ※

Japan seems to have a yen for selling unusual products via vending machine—they sell more than any other country. Aside from the usual candy, gum, and cigarettes, here are some of the more obscure items available for purchase in Japanese vending machines.

1. Fresh eggs
2. Bags of rice in various sizes
3. Fishing line, fish hooks, and fish bait
4. Toilet paper in small packets—most public restrooms in Japan charge a fee for toilet paper
5. Fresh flowers
6. Frequent flyer miles—Japan Air Lines (JAL) has a machine that reads a credit card and boarding pass and issues frequent flyer miles
7. Beer in cans or two-liter jugs
8. Film and disposable cameras
9. Pornographic magazines
10. Designer condoms
11. Batteries
12. Live rhinoceros beetles—a popular pet for Japanese children
13. Kerosene—for home space heaters
14. Dry ice—sold at supermarkets for keeping frozen food cold until the customer gets home
15. Sake in preheated containers
16. Cups of hot noodles
17. Fortunes—found at shrines and temples
18. Umbrellas—for both rain and shade

7 Famous Curses

✳ ✳ ✳ ✳

*No one really knows for sure if there's any truth to these curses,
but if you want to take James Dean's car for a spin, or dig up an
ancient mummy, don't expect us to help!*

1. James Dean and "Little Bastard"

On September 30, 1955, James Dean was killed when the silver
Porsche 550 Spyder he called "Little Bastard" was struck by an
oncoming vehicle. Within a year or so of Dean's crash, the car was
involved in two more fatal accidents and caused injury to at least six
other people. After the accident, the car was purchased by hot-rod
designer George Barris. While getting a tune up, Little Bastard
fell on the mechanic's legs and crushed them. Barris later sold
the engine and transmission to two doctors who raced cars. While
racing against each other, one driver was killed, the other seriously
injured. Someone else had purchased the tires, which blew simultaneously, sending the driver to the hospital. Little Bastard was
set to appear in a car show, but a fire broke out in the building the
night before the show, destroying every car except Little Bastard,
which survived without so much as a smudge. The car was then
loaded onto a truck to go back to Salinas, California. The driver lost
control en route, was thrown from the cab, and was crushed by the
car when it fell off the trailer. In 1960, after being exhibited by the
California Highway Patrol, Little Bastard disappeared and hasn't
been seen since.

2. The Curse of Tutankhamen's Tomb

In 1922, English explorer Howard Carter, leading an expedition
funded by George Herbert, Fifth Earl of Carnarvon, discovered
the ancient Egyptian king's tomb and the riches inside. After opening the tomb, however, strange and unpleasant events began to
take place in the lives of those involved in the expedition. Lord
Carnarvon's story is the most bizarre. The adventurer apparently

died from pneumonia and blood poisoning following complications from a mosquito bite. Allegedly, at the exact moment Carnarvon passed away in Cairo, all the lights in the city mysteriously went out. Carnarvon's dog dropped dead that morning, too. Some point to the foreboding inscription, "Death comes on wings to he who enters the tomb of a pharaoh" as proof that King Tut put a curse on anyone who disturbed his final resting place.

3. "The Club"

If you're a rock star and you're about to turn 27, you might want to consider taking a year off to avoid membership in "The Club." Robert Johnson, an African-American musician, who Eric Clapton called "the most important blues musician who ever lived," played the guitar so well that some said he must have made a deal with the devil. So when he died at 27, folks said it must have been time to pay up. Since Johnson, a host of musical geniuses have gone to an early grave at age 27. Brian Jones, founding member of the Rolling Stones, died at age 27 in 1969. Then it was both Jimi Hendrix and Janis Joplin in 1970 and Jim Morrison the following year. Kurt Cobain joined "The Club" in 1994. All 27 years old. Coincidence? Or were these musical geniuses paying debts, too?

4. "Da Billy Goat" Curse

In 1945, William "Billy Goat" Sianis brought his pet goat, Murphy, to Wrigley Field to see the fourth game of the 1945 World Series between the Chicago Cubs and the Detroit Tigers. Sianis and his goat were later ejected from the game, and Sianis reportedly put a curse on the team that day. Ever since, the Cubs have had legendarily bad luck. Over the years, Cubs fans have experienced agony in repeated late-season collapses when victory seemed imminent. In 1969, 1984, 1989, and 2003, the Cubs were painfully close to advancing to the World Series but couldn't hold the lead. Even those who don't consider themselves Cubs fans blame the hex for the weird and almost comical losses year after year. The Cubs have not won a World Series since 1908—no other team in the history of the game has gone as long without a championship.

5. Rasputin and the Romanovs

Rasputin, the self-proclaimed magician and cult leader, wormed his way into the palace of the Romanovs, Russia's ruling family, around the turn of the last century. After getting a little too big for his britches, a few of the Romanovs allegedly decided to have him killed. But he was exceptionally resilient. Reportedly it took poison, falling down a staircase, and repeated gunshots before Rasputin was finally dead. It's said that Rasputin mumbled a curse from his deathbed, assuring Russia's ruling monarchs that they would all be dead within a year. That did come to pass, as the Romanov family was brutally murdered in a mass execution less than a year later.

6. Tecumseh and the American Presidents

The curse of Tippecanoe, or "Tecumseh's Curse," is a widely held explanation of the fact that from 1840 to 1960, every U.S. president elected (or reelected) every twentieth year has died in office. Popular belief is that Tecumseh administered the curse when William Henry Harrison's troops defeated the Native American leader and his forces at the Battle of Tippecanoe. Check it out:

- William Henry Harrison was elected president in 1840. He caught a cold during his inauguration, which quickly turned into pneumonia. He died April 4, 1841, after only one month in office.

- Abraham Lincoln was elected president in 1860 and reelected four years later. Lincoln was assassinated and died April 15, 1865.

- James Garfield was elected president in 1880. Charles Guiteau shot him in July 1881. Garfield died several months later, from complications following the gunshot wound.

- William McKinley was elected president in 1896 and reelected in 1900. On September 6, 1901, McKinley was shot by Leon F. Czolgosz, who considered the president an "enemy of the people." McKinley died eight days later.

- Three years after Warren G. Harding was elected president in 1920, he died suddenly of either a heart attack or stroke while traveling in San Francisco.

- Franklin D. Roosevelt was elected president in 1932 and reelected in 1936, 1940, and 1944. His health wasn't great, but he died rather suddenly in 1945, of a cerebral hemorrhage or stroke.

- John F. Kennedy was elected president in 1960 and assassinated in Dallas three years later.

- Ronald Reagan was elected president in 1980, and though he was shot by an assassin in 1981, he did survive. Some say this broke the curse, which should make George W. Bush happy. At the time of this writing, Bush, who was elected in 2000, is serving his second term in office.

7. The Curse of the Kennedy Family

Okay, so maybe if this family had stayed out of politics and off airplanes, their fate might be different. Regardless, the number of Kennedy family tragedies have led some to believe there must be a curse on the whole bunch. You decide:

- JFK's brother Joseph, Jr., and sister Kathleen both died in separate plane crashes in 1944 and 1948, respectively.

- JFK's other sister, Rosemary, was institutionalized in a mental hospital for years.

- John F. Kennedy himself, America's 35th president, was assassinated in 1963 at age 46.

- Robert Kennedy, JFK's younger brother, was assassinated in 1968.

- Senator Ted Kennedy, JFK's youngest brother, survived a plane crash in 1964. In 1969, he was driving a car that went off a bridge, causing the death of his companion, Mary Jo Kopechne. His presidential goals were pretty much squashed after that.

- In 1984, Robert Kennedy's son David died of a drug overdose. Another son, Michael, died in a skiing accident in 1997.

- In 1999, JFK, Jr., his wife, and his sister-in-law died when the small plane he was piloting crashed into the Atlantic Ocean.

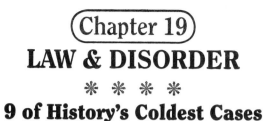

Chapter 19
LAW & DISORDER
✳ ✳ ✳ ✳
9 of History's Coldest Cases

They were gruesome crimes that shocked us with their brutality. But as time passed, we heard less and less about them until we forgot about the crime, not even realizing that the perpetrator remained among us. Yet the files remain open, and the families of the victims live on in a state of semi-paralysis. Here are some of the world's most famous cold cases.

1. Elizabeth Short

Elizabeth Short, also known as the Black Dahlia, was murdered in 1947. Like thousands of others, Elizabeth wanted to be a star. Unlike the bevy of blondes who trekked to Hollywood, this 22-year-old beauty from Massachusetts was dark and mysterious. She was last seen alive outside the Biltmore Hotel in Los Angeles on the evening of January 9, 1947.

Short's body was found on a vacant lot in Los Angeles. It had been cut in half at the waist and both parts had been drained of blood and then cleaned. Her body parts appeared to be surgically dissected, and her remains were suggestively posed. Despite receiving a number of false confessions and taunting letters that admonished police to "catch me if you can," the crime remains unsolved.

2. The Zodiac Killer

The Zodiac Killer was responsible for several murders in the San Francisco area in the 1960s and 1970s. His victims were shot, stabbed, and bludgeoned to death. After the first few kills, he began sending letters to the local press in which he taunted police and made public threats, such as planning to blow up a school bus. In a letter sent to the *San Francisco Chronicle* two days after the murder of cabbie Paul Stine in October 1969, the killer, who called himself "The Zodiac," included in the package pieces of Stine's blood-soaked shirt. In the letters, which continued until 1978, he claimed a cumulative tally of 37 murders.

3. Swedish Prime Minister Olof Palme

On February 28, 1986, Swedish Prime Minister Olof Palme was gunned down on a Stockholm street as he and his wife strolled home from the movies unprotected around midnight. The prime minister was fatally shot in the back. His wife was seriously wounded but survived.

In 1988, a petty thief and drug addict named Christer Petterson was convicted of the murder because he was picked out of a lineup by Palme's widow. The conviction was later overturned on appeal when doubts were raised as to the reliability of Mrs. Palme's evidence. Despite many theories, the assassin remains at large.

4. The Torso Killer

In Cleveland, Ohio, during the 1930s, more than a dozen limbless torsos were found. Despite the efforts of famed crime fighter Eliot Ness, the torso killer was never found. The first two bodies, found in September 1935, were missing heads and had been horribly mutilated. Similar murders occurred during the next three years. Desperate to stop the killings, Ness ordered a raid on a run-down area known as Kingsbury's Run, where most of the victims were from. The place was torched, and hundreds of vagrants were taken into custody. After that, there were no more killings.

The key suspect in the murders was Frank Dolezal, a vagrant who lived in the area. He was a known bully with a fiery temper. Dolezal was arrested and subsequently confessed, but his confession was full of inaccuracies. He died shortly thereafter under suspicious circumstances.

5. Bob Crane

In 1978, Bob Crane, star of TV's *Hogan's Heroes*, was clubbed to death in his apartment. Crane shared a close friendship with John Carpenter, a pioneer in the development of video technology. The two shared an affinity for debauchery and sexual excesses, which were recorded on videotape. But by late 1978, Crane was tiring of Carpenter's dependence on him and had let him know that the friendship was over.

The following day, June 29, 1978, Crane was bludgeoned to death with a camera tripod in his Scottsdale, Arizona, apartment. Suspicion immediately fell on Carpenter, and a small spattering of blood was found in Carpenter's rental car, but police were unable to connect it to the crime. Examiners also found a tiny piece of human tissue in the car. Sixteen years after the killing, Carpenter finally went to trial, but he was acquitted due to lack of evidence.

6. Tupac Shakur

On September 7, 1996, successful rap artist Tupac Shakur was shot four times in a drive-by shooting in Las Vegas. He died six days later. Two years prior to that, Shakur had been shot five times in the lobby of a Manhattan recording studio the day before he was found guilty of sexual assault. He survived that attack, only to spend the next 11 months in jail. The 1994 shooting was a major catalyst for an East Coast–West Coast feud that would envelop the hip-hop industry and culminate in the deaths of both Shakur and Notorious B.I.G. (Christopher Wallace).

On the night of the fatal shooting, Shakur attended the Mike Tyson–Bruce Seldon fight at the MGM Grand in Las Vegas. After the fight, Shakur and his entourage got into a scuffle with a gang member. Shakur then headed for a nightclub, but he never made it. No one was ever arrested for the killing.

7. Jack the Ripper

In London in the late 1880s, a brutal killer known as Jack the Ripper preyed on local prostitutes. His first victim was 43-year-old Mary Ann Nichols, who was nearly decapitated during a savage knife attack. Days later, 47-year-old Annie Chapman had her organs removed from her abdomen before being left for dead. The press stirred up a wave of panic reporting that a serial killer was at large. Three weeks later, the killer was interrupted as he tore apart Swedish prostitute Elizabeth Stride. He managed to get away, only to strike again later that same night. This time the victim was Kate Eddowes. The killer, by now dubbed Jack the Ripper, removed a kidney in the process of hacking up Eddowes's body. His final kill was the most gruesome. On the night of November 9, 1888, Mary Kelly was methodically cut into pieces in an onslaught that must have lasted for several hours.

Dozens of potential Jacks have been implicated in the killings, including failed lawyer Montague John Druitt, whose body was fished out of the Thames River days after the last murder was committed. The nature of the bodily dissections has led many to conclude that Jack was a skilled physician with an advanced knowledge of anatomy. But more than a century after the savage attacks, the identity of Jack the Ripper remains a mystery.

8. Jimmy Hoffa

In 1975, labor leader Jimmy Hoffa disappeared on his way to a Detroit-area restaurant. Hoffa was the president of the Teamsters Union during the 1950s and 1960s. In 1964, he went to jail for bribing a grand juror investigating corruption in the union. In 1971, he was released on the condition that he not participate in any further union activity. Hoffa was preparing a legal challenge to that injunction when he disappeared on July 30, 1975. He was last seen in the parking lot of the Machus Red Fox Restaurant.

Hoffa had strong connections to the Mafia, and several mobsters have claimed that he met a grisly end on their say so. Although his body has never been found, authorities officially declared him dead on July 30, 1982. As recently as November 2006, the FBI dug up farmland in Michigan hoping to turn up a corpse. So far, no luck.

9. JonBenét Ramsey

In the early hours of December 26, 1996, Patsy Ramsey reported that her six-year-old daughter, JonBenét, had been abducted from her Boulder, Colorado, home. Police rushed to the Ramsey home where, hours later, John Ramsey found his little girl dead in the basement. She had been battered, sexually assaulted, and strangled.

Police found several tantalizing bits of evidence—a number of footprints, a rope that did not belong on the premises, marks on the body that suggested the use of a stun gun, and DNA samples on the girl's body. The ransom note was also suspicious. Police found that it was written with a pen and pad of paper belonging to the Ramseys. The amount demanded, $118,000, was a surprisingly small amount, considering that John Ramsey was worth more than $6 million. It is also interesting to note that Mr. Ramsey had just received a year-end bonus of $118,117.50.

A number of suspects were considered, but one by one they were cleared. Finally, the police zeroed in on the parents. For years, the Ramseys were put under intense pressure by authorities and the public alike to confess to the murder. However, a grand jury investigation ended with no indictments. In 2003, a judge ruled that an intruder had killed JonBenét. Then, in August 2006, John Mark Karr confessed, claiming that he was with the girl when she died. However, Karr's DNA did not match that found on JonBenét. He was not charged, and the case remains unsolved.

13 Outrageous Mafia Nicknames

✳ ✳ ✳ ✳

1. Crooked Nose
2. The Teflon Don
3. Bugsy
4. Lefty Guns
5. The Turk
6. Stevie Beef
7. Flat Nose
8. Balloon Head
9. Jimmy Legs
10. Sally Fruits
11. Ice Pick
12. Big Tuna
13. Cut Nose

20 Silly and Unusual U.S. Laws

✳ ✳ ✳ ✳

1. In Fairbanks, Alaska, it is illegal to serve alcohol to a moose.

2. In Glendale, Arizona, it is illegal to drive a car in reverse, so virtually everyone in a mall parking lot is breaking the law.

3. In San Francisco, California, it is illegal to wipe your car with used underwear. So, is it okay to use clean underwear?

4. In Quitman, Georgia, it's illegal to change the clothes on a storefront mannequin unless the shades are down.

5. In South Bend, Indiana, it's illegal for monkeys to smoke cigarettes. Apparently cigars are okay, but only if the monkey goes outside.

6. In New Orleans, Louisiana, it's against the law to gargle in public.

7. In Boston, Massachusetts, it's illegal to take a bath unless one has been ordered by a physician to do so.

8. In Minnesota, women may face 30 days in jail for impersonating Santa Claus.

9. In Hornytown, North Carolina, it's illegal to open a massage parlor.

10. In Fargo, North Dakota, it's illegal to lie down and fall asleep with your shoes on.

11. In Oxford, Ohio, it is illegal for a woman to disrobe in front of a man's picture. Is it legal if his eyes are closed in the photo?

12. In Oklahoma, people who make ugly faces at dogs can be fined or jailed. Apparently, it's okay for bulldogs to make ugly faces at people because they can't help it.

13. In Marion, Oregon, ministers are forbidden from eating garlic or onions before delivering a sermon.

14. In Morrisville, Pennsylvania, women need a permit to wear makeup.

15. In South Dakota, it's illegal to lie down and fall asleep in a cheese factory.

16. At restaurants in Memphis, Tennessee, all pie must be eaten on the premises, as it is illegal to take unfinished pie home.

17. In Utah, birds have the right-of-way on all highways.

18. In Seattle, Washington, women who sit on men's laps on buses or trains without placing a pillow between them face an automatic six-month jail term.

19. In Nicholas County, West Virginia, no clergy member may tell jokes or humorous stories from the pulpit during church services.

20. In St. Croix, Wisconsin, women are not allowed to wear anything red in public.

GREAT ART: SOMETIMES, IT'S A STEAL!
7 Notorious Art Thefts

✳ ✳ ✳ ✳

Some people just can't keep their hands off other people's things—even the world's greatest art. Art thieves take their loot from museums, places of worship, and private residences. Because they would have trouble selling the fruits of their labor on the open market—auction houses and galleries tend to avoid stolen works—art burglars often either keep the art for themselves or try to ransom the hot property back to the original owner. Among the major robberies in the past hundred years are these daring thefts of very expensive art (values estimated at the time of the theft).

1. Boston, March 1990: $300 million
Two men dressed as police officers visited the Isabella Stewart Gardner Museum in the wee hours of the morning. After overpowering two guards and grabbing the security system's surveillance tape, they collected Rembrandt's only seascape, *Storm on the Sea*

of Galilee, as well as Vermeer's *The Concert*, Manet's *Chez Tortoni*, and several other works. Authorities have yet to find the criminals despite investigating everyone from the Irish Republican Army to a Boston mob boss!

2. Oslo, August 2004: $120 million

Two armed and masked thieves threatened workers at the Munch Museum during a daring daylight theft. They stole a pair of Edvard Munch paintings, *The Scream* and *The Madonna*, estimated at a combined value of 100 million euros. In May 2006, authorities convicted three men who received between four and eight years in jail. The paintings were recovered three months later.

3. Paris, August 1911: $100 million

In the world's most notorious art theft to date, Vincenzo Peruggia, an employee of the Louvre, stole Leonardo da Vinci's *Mona Lisa* from the storied museum in the heart of Paris. Peruggia simply hid in a closet, grabbed the painting once alone in the room, hid it under his long smock, and walked out of the famed museum after it had closed. The theft turned the moderately popular *Mona Lisa* into the best-known painting in the world. Police questioned Pablo Picasso and French poet Guillaume Apollinaire about the crime, but they found the real thief—and the *Mona Lisa*—two years later when Peruggia tried to sell it to an art dealer in Florence.

4. Oslo, February 1994: $60–75 million

The Scream has been a popular target for thieves in Norway. On the day the 1994 Winter Olympics began in Lillehammer, a different version of Munch's famous work—he painted four—was taken from Oslo's National Art Museum. In less than one minute, the crooks came in through a window, cut the wires holding up the painting, and left through the same window. They attempted to ransom the painting to the Norwegian government, but they had left a piece of the frame at a bus stop—a clue that helped authorities recover the painting within a few months. Four men were convicted of the crime in January 1996.

5. Scotland, August 2003: $65 million

Blending in apparently has its advantages for art thieves. Two men joined a tour of Scotland's Drumlanrig Castle, subdued a guard, and made off with Leonardo da Vinci's *Madonna with the Yarnwinder.* Alarms around the art were not set during the day, and the thieves dissuaded tourists from intervening, reportedly telling them: "Don't worry...we're the police. This is just practice." Escaping in a white Volkswagen Golf, the perpetrators have never been identified—and the painting remains missing.

6. Stockholm, December 2000: $30 million+

Caught! Eight criminals each got up to six and half years behind bars for conspiring to take a Rembrandt and two Renoirs—all of them eventually recovered—from Stockholm's National Museum. You have to give the three masked men who actually grabbed the paintings credit for a dramatic exit. In a scene reminiscent of an action movie, they fled the scene by motorboat. Police unraveled the plot after recovering one of the paintings during an unrelated drug investigation four months after the theft.

7. Amsterdam, December 2002: $30 million

Robbers used a ladder to get onto the roof of the Van Gogh Museum, then broke in and stole two of the Dutch master's paintings, *View of the Sea at Scheveningen* and *Congregation Leaving the Reformed Church in Nuenen,* together worth $30 million. Police told the press that the thieves worked so quickly that, despite setting off the museum's alarms, they had disappeared before police could get there. Authorities in the Netherlands arrested two men in 2003, based on DNA from hair inside two hats left at the scene, but they have been unable to recover the paintings, which the men deny taking.

✳ ✳ ✳

"Indeed, history is nothing more than a tableau
of crimes and misfortunes."
—Voltaire

11 Stupid Legal Warnings

✳ ✳ ✳ ✳

Our lawsuit-obsessed society has forced product manufacturers to cover their "you-know-whats" by writing warning labels to protect us from ourselves. Some are funny, some are absolutely ridiculous, but all are guaranteed to stand up in court.

1. Child-size Superman and Batman costumes come with this warning label: "Wearing of this garment does not enable you to fly."

2. A clothes iron comes with this caution: "Warning: Never iron clothes on the body." Ouch!

3. The instructions for a medical thermometer advise: "Do not use orally after using rectally."

4. The side of a Slush Puppy cup warns: "This ice may be cold." The only thing dumber than this would be a disclaimer stating: "No puppies were harmed in the making of this product."

5. The box of a 500-piece puzzle reads: "Some assembly required."

6. A Power Puff Girls costume discourages: "You cannot save the world!"

7. A box of PMS relief tablets has this advice: "Warning: Do not use if you have prostate problems."

8. Cans of Easy Cheese contain this instruction: "For best results, remove cap."

9. A warning label on a nighttime sleep-aid reads: "Warning: May cause drowsiness."

10. Cans of self-defense pepper spray caution: "May irritate eyes."

11. Both boys and girls should read the label on the Harry Potter toy broom: "This broom does not actually fly."

12 Countries with the Highest Prison Population

❋ ❋ ❋ ❋

Country	Prisoners per 100,000 People
1. United States	737
2. Russia	613
3. U.S. Virgin Islands	549
4. St. Kitts and Nevis	547
5. Belize	505
6. Turkmenistan	489
7. Cuba	487
8. Palau	478
9. Bermuda (UK) (tied)	464
10. British Virgin Islands (tied)	464
11. Bahamas	462
12. Cayman Islands (UK)	453

Source: King's College of London: International Centre for Prison Studies

SO SUE ME!
8 Outrageous Lawsuits

❋ ❋ ❋ ❋

*One of the benefits of living in a democratic country with
a well-established judicial system is the opportunity to use
the courts to achieve justice and set wrongs right.
But there is a drawback—some folks go to court about things
that make most of us shake our heads. Take a look at
these odd cases and judge for yourself.*

1. All Toys Are Not Equal
Jodee Berry, a Hooter's waitress in Florida, won the restaurant's
sales contest and thought she'd just won the new Toyota that her

bosses said the champion would get. The prize was actually a toy Yoda, not a Toyota, so she left her job and sued the franchisee for breach of contract and fraudulent misrepresentation. The force was with Berry—the out-of-court settlement in May 2002 allowed her to pick out any Toyota car she wanted.

2. Fingered as a Scam

In March 2005, Ann Ayala filed a claim against a Wendy's franchise owner, asserting that she had found a fingertip in a bowl of chili. But authorities found no evidence of missing fingers at the accused restaurant. Suspicion turned on Ayala, who dropped the suit when reporters discovered that she had previously accused several other companies of wrongdoing.

3. No Good Deed Goes Unpunished

In July 2004, two teenage girls in Colorado baked cookies and delivered them to their neighbors. But the door-knocking apparently scared Wanita Young, who had an anxiety attack, went to the hospital, and sued the girls' families. A local judge awarded Young almost $900 for medical expenses but denied her half-baked demand for nearly $3,000 in itemized expenses, including lost wages and new motion-sensor lights for her porch.

4. Bubbles Aren't Always Fun

Early on the morning of July 7, 2001, a prankster dumped detergent into a public park fountain in Duluth, Minnesota, creating a mountain of bubbles. A few hours later, passerby Kathy Kelly fell down and suffered several injuries. She sued the city because it had not cleaned up the suds (on Saturday morning) or posted warnings to citizens urging them not to walk through the slippery wall of bubbles. A jury in March 2004 found the city 70 percent responsible for Kelly's injuries—leaving her with only 30 percent of the blame—and thus awarded her $125,000.

5. School Responsible for Bad Break-Up

In February 2004, a New York court ordered a school district to pay a former student $375,000 when his two-year affair with a school secretary ended. The young basketball star claimed that the break-up brought "emotional and psychological trauma," ruining any prospects for a professional hard-court career. The jury determined that the school was culpable for failing to supervise the secretary properly. It also ordered the secretary to pay the student another $375,000—even though she had not been named in the lawsuit.

6. Trespass at the Owner's Risk

Let's say you're illegally sneaking onto a railroad's property so you can get a view from the top of a boxcar—and then an electrical wire above the car electrocutes you. What do you do? Obviously, you sue the railroad! In October 2006, a jury awarded more than $24 million to two young men who were severely burned while atop a parked railroad car in Lancaster, Pennsylvania, in 2002. The jury said that, although they were trespassing, the 17-year-old boys bore no responsibility. Instead the blame fell entirely on Amtrak and Norfolk Southern for failing to post signs warning of the danger from the electrified wires that power locomotives. For medical costs, pain and suffering, and "loss of life pleasures," one boy received $17.3 million and the other $6.8 million.

7. Sue the Pants Off Them

In 2005, in one of the most outrageous lawsuits of recent times, Roy Pearson, a Washington, D.C. judge, sued a small mom-and-pop dry cleaner for $54 million for misplacing his pants. The shop's owners, Jin and Soo Chung, returned the pants a week later, but Pearson refused them, saying they were not his $800 trousers but a cheap imitation. He also sued the Chungs and their son $1,500 each, per day for more than a year, claiming that the store's signs, which read "Satisfaction Guaranteed" and "Same Day Service," were fraudulent. In 2007, a judge ruled in favor of the Chungs and ordered Pearson to pay the couple's court costs, and possibly their attorney fees as well.

8. Spilling the (Coffee) Beans

This list can only end with the most notorious of lawsuits: Stella Liebeck, of Albuquerque, sued McDonald's in 1992 after spilling a cup of the restaurant's coffee, which burned her lap severely and hospitalized her for a week. Two years later, a jury awarded her $160,000 in direct damages and $2.7 million in punitive damages, which a court later reduced to $480,000. Both parties appealed, and they eventually settled out of court for an undisclosed amount—surely enough for her to buy McDonald's coffee for the rest of her life. Liebeck inspired the creation of the Stella Awards, which highlight particularly "wild, outrageous, or ridiculous lawsuits."

9 of the Grisliest Crimes of the 20th Century

❊ ❊ ❊ ❊

Our TV screens are saturated with crime. Every night we witness more bizarre slayings and mayhem than the night before. Makes you wonder how far-fetched those scriptwriters will get. After all, real people don't commit those types of crimes, right? Wrong. In fact, the annals of history are crammed with crimes even more gruesome than anything seen on television. Here are some of the 20th century's wildest crimes.

1. Ed Kemper

Ed Kemper had a genius IQ, but his appetite for murder took over at age 15 when he shot his grandparents because he wanted to see what it felt like. Nine years later, he'd done his time for that crime, and during 1972 and 1973, Kemper hit the California highways, picking up pretty students and killing them before taking the corpses back to his apartment, having sex with them, then dissecting them. He killed six women in that manner and then took an ax to his own mother, decapitating and raping her, then using her body as a dartboard. Still not satisfied, he killed one of his mother's friends as well.

Upset that his crimes didn't garner the media attention he thought they warranted, Kemper confessed to police. He gleefully went into detail about his penchant for necrophilia and decapitation. He asked to be executed, but because capital punishment was suspended at the time, he got life imprisonment and remains incarcerated in California.

2. Andrei Chikatilo

Andrei Chikatilo was Russia's most notorious serial killer. Known as the Rostov Ripper, his rampage began in 1978 in the city of Shakhty where he began abducting teenagers, subjecting them to unspeakable torture before raping and murdering them, and, often, cannibalizing their bodies. Authorities gave the crimes little attention, but as the body count grew, police were forced to face the facts—Russia had a serial killer.

Chikatilo was actually brought in for questioning when the police found a rope and butcher knife in his bag during a routine search, but he was released and allowed to continue his killing spree. In the end, he got careless and was arrested near the scene of his latest murder. Under interrogation, he confessed to 56 murders. During the trial, he was kept in a cage in the middle of the court, playing up the image of the deranged lunatic. It didn't help his cause, though. He was found guilty and executed with a shot to the back of the head on February 14, 1994.

3. Cameron Hooker

With the assistance of his wife Janice, Cameron Hooker snatched a 20-year-old woman, who was hitchhiking to a friend's house in northern California in May 1977. He locked her in a wooden box that was kept under the bed he shared with Janice, who was well aware of what lay beneath. During the next seven years, the young woman was repeatedly tortured, beaten, and sexually assaulted. Eventually, she was allowed out of the box to do household chores, but she was forced to wear a slave collar. As time went by, Hooker allowed his prisoner more and more freedom, even letting her get a part-time job. Janice's conscience finally got the best of her, and she helped the young woman escape. After seven years of hell, she simply got on a bus and left. Hooker was convicted and sentenced to 104 years in a box of his own.

4. Andras Pandy

Andras Pandy was a Belgian pastor who had eight children by two different wives. Between 1986 and 1989, his former wives and four of the children disappeared. Pandy tried to appease investigators by faking papers to show that they were living in Hungary. He even coerced other children into impersonating the missing ones. Then, under intense questioning, Pandy's daughter Agnes broke down. She told authorities that she had been held by her father as a teenage sex slave and then was forced to join him in killing her family members, including her mother, brothers, stepmother, and stepsister. The bodies were chopped up, dissolved in drain cleaner, and flushed down the drain. Pandy was sentenced to life in prison, while Agnes received 21 years as an accomplice. To this day he still claims that all of the missing family members are alive and well in Hungary.

5. Harold Shipman

The most prolific serial killer in modern history was British doctor Harold Shipman, who murdered up to 400 of his patients between 1970 and 1998. Shipman was a respected member of the community, but in March 1998, a colleague became alarmed at the high death rate among his patients. She went to the local coroner, who in turn went to the police. They investigated, but found nothing out of the ordinary. But when Kathleen Grundy died a few months later, it was revealed that she had cut her daughter Angela out of her will and, instead, bequeathed £386,000 to Shipman. Angela became suspicious, so she went to the police who began another investigation. Kathleen Grundy's body was exhumed and examined, and traces of diamorphine (heroin) were found in her system. Shipman was arrested and charged with murder. When police examined his patient files more closely, they realized that Shipman was overdosing patients with diamorphine, then forging their medical records to state that they were in poor health.

Shipman was found guilty and sentenced to 15 consecutive life sentences, but he hung himself in his cell in January 2004.

6. Fred and Rose West

In the early 1970s, a pattern developed in which young women were lured to the home of Fred and Rose West in Gloucester, England, subjected to sexual depravities, and then ritually slaughtered in the soundproof basement. The bodies were dismembered and disposed of under the cellar floor. As the number of victims increased, the garden became a secondary burial plot. This became the final resting place of their own daughter, 16-year-old Heather, who was butchered in June 1983.

Police became increasingly concerned about the whereabouts of Heather. One day they decided to take the family joke that she was "buried under the patio" seriously. When they began excavating the property in June 1994, the number of body parts uncovered shocked the world. With overwhelming evidence stacked against him, Fred West committed suicide while in custody in 1995. Rose received life imprisonment.

7. John Wayne Gacy

In the mid-1960s, John Wayne Gacy was, by all outward appearances, a happily married Chicago-area businessman who doted on his two young children. But when Gacy was convicted of sodomy in 1968, he got ten years in jail, and his wife divorced him.

Eighteen months later, Gacy was out on parole. He started a construction company, and in his spare time, he volunteered as a clown to entertain sick children. He also began picking up homeless male prostitutes. After taking them home, Gacy would beat, rape, and slaughter his victims before depositing the bodies in the crawl space underneath his house.

In 1978, an investigation into the disappearance of 15-year-old Robert Piest led police to Gacy, following reports that the two had been seen together on the night the boy disappeared. Suspicions were heightened when detectives uncovered Gacy's sodomy conviction, and a warrant was issued to search his home. Detectives found a piece of jewelry belonging to a boy who had disappeared a year before. They returned to the house with excavating equipment and they made a gruesome discovery.

Gacy tried to escape the death penalty with a tale of multiple personalities, but it didn't impress the jury. It took them only two hours to convict him of 33 murders. On May 10, 1994, he was put to death by lethal injection.

8. Ed Gein

Ed Gein was the son of an overbearing mother who taught him that sex was sinful. When she died in 1945, he was a 39-year-old bachelor living alone in a rundown farmhouse in Plainfield, Wisconsin. After his mother's death, he developed a morbid fascination with the medical atrocities performed by the Nazis during World War II. This fascination led him to dig up female corpses from cemeteries, take them home, and perform his own experiments on them, such as removing the skin from the body and draping it over a tailor's dummy. He was also fascinated with female genitalia, which he would fondle and, on occasion, stuff into women's panties and wear around the house.

He soon tired of decomposing corpses and set out in search of fresher bodies. Most of his victims were women around his mother's age. He went a step too far, however, when he abducted the mother of local sheriff's deputy Frank Worden. Learning that his missing mother had been seen with Gein on the day of her disappearance, Worden went to the Gein house to question the recluse. What he found there belied belief. Human heads sat as prize trophies in the living room along with a belt made from human nipples and a chair completely upholstered in human skin. But for Worden, the worst sight was in the woodshed. Strung up by the feet was the headless body of his mother. Her front had been slit open and her heart was found on a plate in the dining room.

Gein confessed but couldn't recall how many people he'd killed. He told detectives that he liked to dress up in the carved out torsos of his victims and pretend to be his mother. He spent ten years in an insane asylum before he was judged fit to stand trial. He was found guilty, but criminally insane, and died of heart failure in 1984, at age 77.

9. Jeffrey Dahmer

Jeffrey Dahmer looked like an all-American boy, but as a child, he performed autopsies on small animals, including neighborhood dogs. At age 18, he graduated to humans, picking up a 19-year-old boy and taking him home to drink beer. Dahmer attacked him with a barbell, dismembered his body, and buried it in the backyard. More abductions and murders followed, and Dahmer also began to eat his victims.

In 1989, Dahmer was sentenced to eight years in jail for child molestation but only served ten months. After his release, he immediately resumed the slaughter. In May 1991, Dahmer picked up a 14-year-old boy, gave him money to pose for suggestive photos, and then plied him with alcohol and sleeping pills. While the boy slept, Dahmer went to the store. Waking up alone, the boy fled but ran straight into Dahmer. When they were approached by police, Dahmer convinced the officers that the two were lovers. Upon returning to the apartment, Dahmer slaughtered the boy and then had sex with his corpse.

Two months later this scenario was virtually reenacted when a 31-year-old man escaped from the apartment. With handcuffs dangling from one arm, he approached a nearby police officer. This time the officer decided to check out the apartment. What the officer and his partner saw horrified them. Dismembered bodies, skulls, and internal organs littered the place, and a skeleton hung in the shower. When they opened the refrigerator, they were confronted with a human head. Three more heads were wrapped up in the freezer, and a pan on the stove contained human brains.

During the ensuing trial, another gruesome fact emerged—Dahmer had drilled holes into the skulls of some of his victims and poured in acid in an attempt to keep them alive as zombielike sex slaves. He was given 15 life terms, but in November 1994, he was beaten to death in prison.

Chapter 20

WORDS

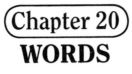

DUDE—WHERE'S MY SLANG DICTIONARY?

53 Slang Terms by Decade

Every generation has its slang—new words and phrases that allow kids to communicate without their parents understanding. Read on to learn some of the most popular slang terms through the decades.

1920s

1. 23 skiddoo—to get going; move along; leave; or scram
2. The cat's pajamas—the best; the height of excellence
3. Gams—legs
4. The real McCoy—sincere; genuine; the real thing
5. Hotsy-totsy—perfect
6. Moll—a female companion of a gangster
7. Speakeasy—a place where alcohol was illegally sold and drunk during Prohibition
8. The bee's knees—excellent; outstanding

1930s

9. I'll be a monkey's uncle—sign of disbelief; I don't believe it!
10. Gig—a job
11. Girl Friday—a secretary or female assistant
12. Juke joint—a casual and inexpensive establishment with drinking, dancing, and blues music, typically in the southeastern United States
13. Skivvies—men's underwear

1940s

14. Blockbuster—a huge success
15. Keeping up with the Joneses—competing to have a lifestyle or socioeconomic status comparable to one's neighbors

16. Cool—excellent; clever; sophisticated; fashionable; or enjoyable
17. Sitting in the hot seat—in a highly uncomfortable or embarrassing situation
18. Smooch—kiss

1950s

19. Big brother is watching you—someone of authority is monitoring your actions
20. Boo-boo—a mistake; a wound
21. Hi-fi—high fidelity; a record player or turntable
22. Hipster—an innovative and trendy person

1960s

23. Daddy-o—a man; used to address a hipster or beatnik
24. Groovy—cool; hip; excellent
25. Hippie—derived from hipster; a young adult who rebelled against established institutions, criticized middle-class values, opposed the Vietnam War, and promoted sexual freedom
26. The Man—a person of authority; a group in power

1970s

27. Catch you on the flip side—see you later
28. Dig it—to like or understand something
29. Get down/Boogie—dance
30. Mind-blowing—unbelievable; originally an expression for the effects of hallucinogenic drugs
31. Pump iron—lift weights
32. Workaholic—a person who works too much or is addicted to his or her job

1980s

33. Bodacious—beautiful
34. Chillin'—relaxing
35. Dweeb—a nerd; someone who is not cool
36. Fly—cool; very hip
37. Gag me with a spoon—disgusting
38. Gnarly—exceptional; very cool

39. Preppy—one who dresses in designer clothing and has a neat, clean-cut appearance
40. Wicked—excellent; great
41. Yuppie—Young Urban Professional; a college-educated person with a well-paying job who lives near a big city; often associated with a materialistic and superficial personality

1990s
42. Diss—show disrespect
43. Get jiggy—dance; flirt
44. Homey/Homeboy—a friend or buddy
45. My bad—my mistake
46. Phat—cool or hip; highly attractive; hot
47. Wassup?—What's up?; How are you?
48. Word—yes; I agree

2000s
49. Barney Bag—a gigantic purse
50. Newbie—a newcomer; someone who is inexperienced
51. Peeps—friends; people
52. Rents—parents
53. Sweet—beyond cool

14 Pangrams

✳ ✳ ✳ ✳

A pangram, or holoalphabetic sentence, includes every letter of the alphabet at least once. The most challenging pangrams are the ones with the fewest letters. Here are a few of the best.

1. Waltz, bad nymph, for quick jigs vex. (28 letters)
2. Quick zephyrs blow, vexing daft Jim. (29 letters)
3. Sphinx of black quartz, judge my vow. (29 letters)
4. Two driven jocks help fax my big quiz. (30 letters)
5. Five quacking zephyrs jolt my wax bed. (31 letters)
6. The five boxing wizards jump quickly. (31 letters)

7. Pack my box with five dozen liquor jugs. (32 letters)
8. The quick brown fox jumps over the lazy dog. (35 letters)
9. Jinxed wizards pluck ivy from the big quilt. (36 letters)
10. Crazy Fredrick bought many very exquisite opal jewels. (46 letters)
11. We promptly judged antique ivory buckles for the next prize. (50 letters)
12. A mad boxer shot a quick, gloved jab to the jaw of his dizzy opponent. (54 letters)
13. Jaded zombies acted quaintly but kept driving their oxen forward. (55 letters)
14. The job requires extra pluck and zeal from every young wage earner. (55 letters)

15 Terms Popularized by Walter Winchell

※ ※ ※ ※

Walter Winchell was not only the forefather of gossip columnists, he also dished the dirt with such style and wit that even the libel attorneys couldn't touch him. He did so by making up his own words and by delivering his scoops at an average of 197 words per minute! Here are just a few terms from the American vernacular created by Winchell.

1. Scram

This means to make a quick getaway. Here's an example of how underworld mobster speak was brought to the mainstream, thanks to Winchell's column.

2. G-Man

This is slang for an FBI agent. The *G* stands for government.

3. Pushover

Mobster Dutch Schultz wasn't too pleased when Winchell wrote about his personal liaisons with blonde women, describing Schultz as a "pushover" for fair-haired beauties.

4. Uh-Huh; Pashing It; Garboing It; Trouser Crease Eraser

Do you give up? This is how Winchell referred to people who were falling in love!

5. Cupiding; Making Whoopee

Not to be confused with falling in love, these were Winchell's code words for making love. Although "Making Whoopee" was a 1928 song written by Gus Kahn, it is believed that Winchell used the term first.

6. Middle Aisle It; Altar It; Sealed; Handcuffed

It stands to reason, at least in some cases, that those who have "Garboed it" or have been "making whoopee" for a while would likely get married. These are the interesting terms that Winchell had for that sacred event.

7. Blessed Event; Infanticipate; Get Storked

This is how Winchell described couples who were about to have a baby. He had three children, so he "infanticipated" a few times, too.

8. Reno-vated; Tell It to a Judge; Curdled

In 1929, a divorce was granted in America every two minutes. So it's only natural that Winchell would eventually coin a phrase for that phase in life as well.

9. Keptive

Maybe there were so many divorces because husbands had mistresses! This is what Winchell called the women who waited for their married lovers to call.

10. Orange Juice Gulch

The next time you watch the ball drop in Times Square on New Year's Eve ponder this: Winchell used to call this famous block "Orange Juice Gulch." Vendors such as Orange Julius and Nedick's (a hot dog and orange drink joint) populated the area in Winchell's day. Had he been in the biz a generation later when strip clubs littered the Square, surely he would've coined a more colorful phrase!

11. A New York Heartbeat

You've heard the phrase "a New York minute" used to imply a very short period of time. Winchell edited the phrase to include the beat of New York, implying a more frenzied pace.

12. Giggle Water

Booze!

13. Flicker

A horse? A ballpoint pen? A lighter? Nope, it's a movie!

14. Swaticooties; Pink Stinkos; Chicagorillas

Stay away from this crowd. These are the bad guys.

15. Ratzis

These are the worst "pink stinkos" of all. This was Winchell's term for the Nazis. Much to the dismay of his network and sponsors, Winchell would not allow censorship! He simply coined his own phrases in order to discuss Hitler and his "swastinkas."

WE GARUNTEE YOUR GOING TOO LEARN ALOT!
48 Commonly Misspelled Words

❋ ❋ ❋ ❋

1. accommodate
2. a lot
3. arctic
4. calendar
5. cemetery
6. conscience
7. conscious
8. definitely
9. embarrass
10. existence
11. foreign
12. gauge
13. grammar

14. guarantee
15. harass
16. height
17. independent
18. inoculate
19. its/it's
20. liaison
21. license
22. maintenance
23. millennium
24. minuscule
25. mischievous
26. misspell
27. noticeable
28. occurrence
29. perseverance
30. playwright
31. possession
32. preceding
33. prejudice
34. principle/principal
35. privilege
36. pronunciation
37. questionnaire
38. receipt
39. recommend
40. rhythm
41. separate
42. sergeant
43. stationary/stationery
44. supersede
45. their/there/they're
46. twelfth
47. until
48. vague

17 Favorite Quotes on Creativity

✳ ✳ ✳ ✳

Take a look at what some famous folks throughout history have said about creativity.

1. "The chief enemy of creativity is good taste."
—Pablo Picasso, painter

2. "The secret to creativity is knowing how to hide your sources."
—Albert Einstein, physicist

3. "Creativity is allowing yourself to make mistakes. Art is knowing which ones to keep."
—Scott Adams, cartoonist

4. "Creativity is the sudden cessation of stupidity."
—Edwin H. Land, scientist and inventor

5. "Necessity is the mother of invention, it is true, but its father is creativity, and knowledge is the midwife."
—Jonathan Schattke, scientist

6. "The whole difference between construction and creation is this: that a thing constructed can only be loved after it is constructed; but a thing created is loved before it exists."
—Charles Dickens, author

7. "Creativity is a drug I can't do without."
—Cecil B. DeMille, film producer

8. "It is wise to learn; it is God-like to create."
—John Saxe, poet

9. "Our current obsession with creativity is the result of our continued striving for immortality in an era when most people no longer believe in an afterlife."
—Arianna Huffington, author and pundit

10. "True creativity often starts where language ends."
—Arthur Koestler, novelist and essayist

11. "The art of creation is older than the art of killing."
—Andrei Voznesensky, poet

12. "Human salvation lies in the hands of the creatively maladjusted."
—Martin Luther King, Jr., civil rights activist

13. "The life of the creative man is led, directed and controlled by boredom. Avoiding boredom is one of our most important purposes."
—Saul Steinberg, artist

14. "No matter how old you get, if you can keep the desire to be creative, you're keeping the man-child alive."
—John Cassavetes, actor

15. "A hunch is creativity trying to tell you something."
—Frank Capra, American film director

16. "There is a correlation between the creative and the screwball. So we must suffer the screwball gladly."
—Kingman Brewster, American diplomat, former president of Yale University

17. "Creative minds always have been known to survive any kind of bad training."
—Anna Freud, founder of child psychoanalysis

15 Oxymorons

An oxymoron is a combination of words that contradict each other. Here are some of our favorites.

1. virtual reality
2. original copy
3. old news

4. act naturally
5. pretty ugly
6. living dead
7. jumbo shrimp
8. rolling stop
9. constant variable
10. exact estimate
11. paid volunteers
12. civil war
13. sound of silence
14. clever fool
15. only choice

14 Spoonerisms

❋ ❋ ❋ ❋

*Spoonerisms are slips of the tongue created by transposing
the sounds of words, usually by accident. The term* spoonerism
*is derived from W. A. Spooner (1844–1930), an English
clergyman noted for such slips.*

1. Tips of the slung .... Slips of the tongue
2. Pleating and humming .... Heating and plumbing
3. A lack of pies... A pack of lies
4. Fighting a liar .... Lighting a fire
5. I hit my bunny phone. .... I hit my funny bone.
6. Chilled grease.. Grilled cheese
7. The Wince of Prales .... The Prince of Wales
8. Chewing the doors .... Doing the chores
9. Sparking pace .... Parking space
10. Clappy as a ham..................................... Happy as a clam
11. Tease my ears... Ease my tears
12. It's roaring with pain. .... It's pouring with rain.
13. Wave the sails .... Save the whales
14. Our queer old dean............................... Our dear old Queen

I SPY SOMETHING SECRET
11 Terms Used by Spies

✳ ✳ ✳ ✳

Spies have their own secret language to keep from being discovered. By spying on these spies, we've managed to uncover the meaning of some of their terms.

1. Black Bag Job

A black bag job, or black bag operation, is a covert entry into a building to plant surveillance equipment or find and copy documents, computer data, or cryptographic keys. The name is derived from the black bags spies used to carry the equipment for such operations. In 1972, the Supreme Court declared black bag jobs unconstitutional, but are bags of different colors okay?

2. Brush Contact

A brush contact is a brief and public meeting in which two spies discreetly exchange documents, funds, or information without speaking to each other, except perhaps to utter "Excuse me" or other pleasantries. To the average person, the interaction would seem like an accidental encounter between two strangers.

3. L-Pill

An L-pill is a lethal pill carried by spies to prevent them from revealing secrets if captured and tortured. During World War II, some L-pills contained a lethal dose of cyanide encased in a glass capsule that could be concealed in a fake tooth and released by the agent's tongue. If he bit into the capsule and broke the glass, he would die almost immediately. But if the pill came loose and was swallowed accidentally while the agent was sleeping or chewing gum, it would pass through his system without causing any harm, as long as it didn't break and release the poison.

4. Window Dressing

The best spies are able to blend into any situation. To accomplish this, they use window dressing—the cover story and accessories they use to convince the authorities and casual observers that they are everyday people and not spies. For example, if a spy is disguised as a construction worker to cover the fact that he is planting a listening device, his window dressing might include official-looking work orders, tools, and knowledge of the people who would have authorized his presence.

5. Sheep Dipping

In farming, sheep dipping is a chemical bath given to sheep to rid them of bugs or disease or to clean their wool before shearing. In CIA terminology, sheep dipping means disguising the identity of an agent by placing him within a legitimate organization. This establishes clean credentials that can later be used to penetrate adversary groups or organizations. Similar to the real sheep, the agent is cleaned up so that nobody knows where he's been, kind of like money laundering.

6. Canary Trap

Do you suspect a leak in your organization? Even if the leakers aren't small yellow birds, you might be able to catch them by setting a canary trap—giving different versions of sensitive information to each suspected leaker and seeing which version gets leaked. Although this method has been around for years, the term was popularized by Tom Clancy in the novel *Patriot Games*.

7. Dangle

In spy terminology, a dangle is an agent who pretends to be interested in defecting to or joining another intelligence agency or group. The dangle convinces the new agency that they have changed loyalties by offering to act as a double agent. The dangle then feeds information to their original agency while giving disinformation to the other.

8. Honeypot

A honeypot is a trap that uses sex to lure an enemy agent into disclosing classified information or, in some cases, to capture or kill them. In the classic Hitchcock film *North by Northwest,* Eva Marie

Saint's character was both a honeypot and a double agent. In real life, in 1961, U.S. diplomat Irvin Scarbeck was blackmailed into providing secrets after he was lured by a female Polish agent and photographed in a compromising position.

9. Camp Swampy

Camp Swampy is the nickname of the CIA's secret training base. That's about all that is known about it, except that it was named for the Camp Swampy in the *Beetle Bailey* comic strip.

10. Uncle

Uncle is a slang term referring to the headquarters of any espionage service. One such headquarters is the United Network Command for Law and Enforcement or U.N.C.L.E., the headquarters on the 1960s spy series *The Man from U.N.C.L.E.*, starring Robert Vaughn, David McCallum, and Leo G. Carroll.

11. Starburst Maneuver

How does a spy lose someone who is tailing him? One way is by employing a starburst maneuver—a tactic in which several identical looking vehicles suddenly go in different directions, forcing the surveillance team to quickly decide which one to follow. A classic example of this strategy was utilized in the 2003 film *The Italian Job*. Similar-looking agents can also be used instead of vehicles. Kids, don't try this with your parents.

13 Anagrams

✳ ✳ ✳ ✳

Anagrams are new words or phrases made by rearranging the letters of the original word or phrase. Check out our favorites.

1. Adios, amigos. ....I go so I am sad.
2. Butterfly...Flutter by
3. Camry ....My car
4. Clint Eastwood ....Old West action

5. Computer station meltdown ....We lost important document.
6. Forensic evidence ....Science over fiend
7. President George W. Bush has won. ....Ah! Depressing news brought woe.
8. Snooze alarms..Alas! No more z's.
9. Statue of Liberty...Built to stay free
10. The countryside...No city dust here.
11. The eyes..They see.
12. The famous painter Pablo Ruiz Picasso ......Popularizes cubism into a phase of art
13. The Morse code...Here come dots.

15 Palindromes

✳ ✳ ✳ ✳

Palindromes are words or sentences that read the same backward or forward. Here are some of our favorites.

1. Go hang a salami. I'm a lasagna hog.
2. Do geese see God?
3. Was it Eliot's toilet I saw?
4. Are we not drawn onward, we few, drawn onward to new era?
5. A nut for a jar of tuna.
6. Dennis and Edna sinned.
7. Oozy rat in a sanitary zoo
8. A man, a plan, a canal: Panama!
9. Ana, nab a banana.
10. Borrow or rob?
11. Vanna, wanna V?
12. We panic in a pew.
13. Never odd or even.
14. Madam in Eden, I'm Adam.
15. Murder for a jar of red rum.

OY VEY! WHAT MAVEN HAS THE CHUTZPAH TO EXPLAIN WHAT THIS MEANS?
20 Common Yiddish Terms

❊ ❊ ❊ ❊

Yiddish, a language based on the Hebrew alphabet, was developed in the 10th century by Jews living in central and eastern Europe. Today, about three million people speak it, but millions more use Yiddish words and phrases every day without realizing it. Plop your tush in a comfy chair and check out these favorites.

1. Yenta

A yenta is a talkative or gossipy woman; a blabbermouth. "Don't tell her a secret because she's such a yenta." *Yenta* comes from the female name Yentl.

2. Schlep

To schlep means to drag or haul something that's especially burdensome, or to make a tedious journey. "No one will help me schlep my stuff to my new apartment." A schlep can also refer to someone who is a drag. "He's such a schlep." *Schlep* comes from the Yiddish word *shlepn,* which means "to drag."

3. Schmuck

A schmuck is a despicable or foolish person, a real jerk. "His lazy brother is such a *schmuck.*" This is a pretty derogatory thing to say about someone because *schmuck* comes from *shmok,* the Yiddish word for penis.

4. Oy vey!

Oy vey! is an expression of pain or grief, similar to "woe is me." "My car won't start. Oy vey!" It is derived from the German phrase *Oh weh,* meaning "oh pain."

5. Tush

Your tush is your rear end or posterior. "She has a nice tush." It comes from the Yiddish word *tuchus* meaning "buttocks."

6. Mitzvah

Mitzvah originally referred to any one of the 613 commandments Jews are expected to follow, but since most of them have to do with being kind to others, it has come to mean "a good deed." "Helping that man across the street was a mitzvah." A bar mitzvah is a ceremony held at a synagogue when a Jewish boy turns 13. The term literally means "son of the commandment" and signifies that the boy is now old enough to understand the religious laws. A bat mitzvah is a similar ceremony held for 12-year-old girls.

7. Kvetch

A kvetch is a person who always complains, and that constant, habitual complaining is called kvetching. "Take your kvetching to the complaint department." It comes from the Yiddish word *kvetshn,* which means "to press or squeeze."

8. Klutz

A klutz is a clumsy person. "Abe tripped over his own feet—what a klutz!" The word comes from the Yiddish word *klots,* which means "wooden beam."

9. Bubkes

If a person has bubkes, it means he has nothing. *Bubkes* can also mean "an inadequate reward or compensation," as in "He worked at that place for 40 years for bubkes." It comes from the Yiddish word *kozebubkes,* meaning "goat droppings," which may be derived from the Polish word *bób,* meaning "beans."

10. Putz

Putz comes from the Yiddish *pots,* which means "penis," but it is more commonly used to refer to someone who is a jerk. "I won't go out with him because he's such a putz!"

11. Maven

A maven is an expert. "She's a maven when it comes to cooking." *Maven* comes from the Hebrew word *mevin,* which means "one who understands."

12. Meshuggener

A meshuggener is a crazy person. A meshuggener's actions are called meshugas, meaning "madness, nonsense or irrational idiosyncrasy."

13. Shmear

If you order a bagel with a shmear, it will come with cream cheese on top. *Shmear* means "spread," and it comes from Yiddish word *shmir* meaning "to smear."

14. Schlock

If you buy something that's schlock, it means it's cheap, shoddy, or inferior. The person who sold it to you is a schlockmeister. "This cardboard chainsaw is schlock." It comes from the Yiddish word *shlak,* which means "nuisance."

15. Schnook

A schlockmeister likes to sell his schlock to a schnook—a gullible person. "Anyone who buys a cardboard chainsaw is a schnook."

16. Schmooze

When you schmooze, you're chatting, gossiping, or attempting to win favor with someone. "Sam tried to schmooze his boss into giving him the promotion." The word comes from the Yiddish *schmues,* meaning "to talk."

17. Spiel

To convince a schnook to buy his schlock, a schlockmeister gives him a spiel, which is a sales pitch or persuasive speech. "I had to buy the car because the salesman had such a great spiel." *Spiel* comes from the Yiddish word *shpil,* which means "play."

18. Shtick

A person's—usually a comedian's—routine is called his shtick, which can also mean "a special trait or distinguishing feature." Saying "You're fired!" is Donald Trump's shtick. *Shtick* comes from the Yiddish word *shtik,* which means "piece."

19. Mazel tov!

Mazel tov!, which literally means "good luck," has become a popular toast of congratulations. *Mazel* comes from the Hebrew word *mazzāl* meaning "planet or luck" and *tōbh* is Hebrew for "good."

20. Chutzpah

A schlockmeister who tries to sell junk to schnooks needs chutzpah, which means "guts, audacity, or nerve."

21 Ways to Say Goodbye

❋ ❋ ❋ ❋

1. Afrikaans .... Totsiens
2. Chinese (Cantonese) .... Joi gin
3. Chinese (Mandarin) .... Zai jian
4. Danish............................ Farvel
5. Dutch............................ Vaarwel
6. English .... Goodbye
7. French .... Au revoir
8. German............................ Auf Wiedersehen
9. Greek .... Adio
10. Hawaiian............................ Aloha
11. Hungarian............................ Viszontlátásra
12. Irish Gaelic .... Slán
13. Italian............................ Arrivederci/ciao
14. Japanese .... Sayonara
15. Polish .... Do widzenia
16. Portuguese............................ Adeus
17. Russian............................ Do svidaniya
18. Scottish Gaelic............................ Beannachd leibh
19. Spanish............................ Adiós
20. Swedish .... Adjö
21. Welsh .... Ffarwél